This book provides a much-needed thematic and historical introduction to Hinduism, the religion of the majority of people in India. Beginning with the question 'What is Hinduism?', Dr Flood traces the development of Hindu traditions from their ancient origins, through the major deities of Viṣṇu, Śiva and the Goddess, to the modern world. Hinduism as both a global religion and a form of nationalism are discussed. Particular emphasis is given to the tantric traditions, which have been so influential; to Hindu ritual, which is more fundamental to the life of the religion than are specific beliefs or doctrines; and to Dravidian influences from south India. *An introduction to Hinduism* examines the ideas of *dharma* (particularly in relation to the ideology of kingship), caste and world renunciation. Dr Flood also introduces some debates within contemporary scholarship about the nature of Hinduism. His book is suitable both for the beginning student and for the general reader, and as such will be an ideal starting point, and an indispensable companion, for anybody interested in learning more about a religious tradition of major and continuing significance.

An introduction to Hinduism

Frontispiece Kṛṣṇa riding through the air on a symbolic elephant made of cowgirls. Rajasthan, Jaipur School *c.* 1800.

An introduction to Hinduism

GAVIN FLOOD

Lecturer in Religious Studies
Department of Theology and Religious Studies
University of Wales, Lampeter

CAMBRIDGE
UNIVERSITY PRESS

Published in South Asia by:

Cambridge University Press India Pvt. Ltd.
Cambridge House
4381/4, Ansari Road,
Daryaganj, New Delhi- 110002

First South Asian edition 2004
Reprinted 2009, 2014

ISBN-13 978-81-7596-028-2

[redacted]

This edition of *Gavin Flood/ An introduction to Hinduism* is published
by arrangement with Cambridge University Press, The Edinburg
Building, Shaftesbury Road, Cambridge CB2 2RU, UK.

Printed in India by Akash Press, New Delhi 110 020

For Leela and Claire

Contents

Illustrations

Plates

Unless otherwise stated, the author is responsible for the plates.
Symbolic elephant (Reproduced by kind permission of the Victoria and Albert Museum.) *frontispiece*

Between pages 304 and 305

Maps

Figures

Acknowledgements

Many sources contribute to the formation of a book and I would like to acknowledge my debt both to people and to other writings. A number of excellent introductions to Hinduism have influenced the present work, particularly those by John Brockington, Chris Fuller, Klaus Klostermaier, Julius Lipner and, from a previous generation, R. C. Zaehner.

I should like to extend thanks to Professor John Clayton of Lancaster University for initially suggesting the project to me, and to Dr David Smith of the same university, who first introduced me to the study of Hinduism. I have been deeply influenced by the work of Dr Rich Freeman of the University of Pennsylvania who introduced me to the traditions of Kerala. I should also like to acknowledge conversations with Dr Sumati Ramaswami of the University of Pennsylvania, Steve Jacobs (a postgraduate student at the University of Wales), Sri A. Thamban of Payannur in Kerala, and an afternoon spent in the hospitality of Sri K. P. C. Anujan Bhattatirippatu, the Tantri of the Peruvanam Temple near Trichur. Many fruitful discussions with Dr Oliver Davies of the University of Wales, Lampeter, have influenced the work, and Professor Paul Morris of Victoria University, New Zealand, and the Cambridge University Press reader offered useful suggestions concerning the text itself. Dr R. Blurton of the British Museum allowed me to reproduce illustrations from the museum collection. I should also like to thank Ms Kim Baxter of Lancaster College of Higher Education for her help with illustrative material, and Mr Alex Wright of Cambridge University Press for his interest and encouragement.

A note on language and transliteration

The languages of Hinduism are Sanskrit and the Indian vernaculars, particularly Tamil. This book follows the standard form of transliteration with the exception of place names and some proper names which are written in their generally acknowledged anglicized forms without diacritical marks. There is a distinction in Sanskrit between the stem form of a word and the nominative or subject case. I generally use the stem form of Sanskrit words with the exception of common terms such as *karma* (which is the nominative singular) and some proper names such as Hanumān (rather than Hanumat) and Bhagavān (rather than Bhagavat). Sanskrit is a phonetic language, so transliteration reflects correct pronunciation. There are short vowels in Sanskrit (*a*, *i*, *u*, *ṛ*, *ḷ*) and long vowels (*ā*, *ī*, *ū*, *ṝ*, *e*, *o*, *ai*, *au*), twice as long as the short. The vowels are approximately pronounced as follows:

a like 'a' in 'woman'

ā like 'a' in 'rather'

i like 'i' in 'sit'

ī like 'ee' in 'meet'

u like 'u' in 'put'

ū like 'u' in 'rule'

ṛ like 'ri' in 'rig'

ṝ like 'ri' in 'reel'

ḷ like 'le' in 'table'

e like 'e' in 'red'
ai like 'ai' in 'aisle'
o like 'o' in 'go'
au like 'ow' in 'vow'

Consonants are unaspirated (such as *ka*, *ga*, *pa*) and aspirated (such as *kha*, *gha*, *pha*). The retroflex sounds *ṭa*, *ṭha*, *ḍa*, *ḍha* and *ṇa* are pronounced with the tip of the tongue bent backwards to touch the palate. The dentals *ta*, *tha*, *da*, *dha* and *na* are pronounced with the tip of the tongue behind the teeth. The gutteral nasal *ṅa*, pronounced 'ng', and the palatal *ña*, pronounced 'nya', are always found in conjunction with other consonants of their class (except in the case of some 'seed' mantras). Thus *liṅga* and *añjali*. The *ṃ* sound or *anusvāra* represents a nasalization of the preceding vowel and the *ḥ* sound or *visarga* represents an aspiration of the preceding vowel: a 'h' sound followed by a slight echo of the vowel (e.g. *devaḥ* is *devah*^{a}). Apart from these sounds, two Tamil consonants which have no English equivalents are *ḻa* and *ṟa* which are retroflex sounds.

Abbreviations and texts

The following are abbreviations for Sanskrit texts referred to. Assuming that the Sanskrit editions of the texts will be of little use to the readers of this book, only bibliographical details of English translations are given, where available.

Ait.Ar.	*Aitareya Āraṇyaka*
Ap.Gr.S.	*Āpasthamba Gṛhya Sūtra*. H. Oldenberg, *The Gṛhya Sūtras*, SBE 29, 30 (Delhi: MLBD, reprint 1964–5)
Ap.S.S.	*Āpasthamba Śrauta Sūtra*
Ar.S.	*Ārtha Śāstra of Kautilya*. L. N. Rangarajan, *The Arthashastra* (Delhi: Penguin, 1992)
As.Gr.S.	*Aśvalāyana Gṛhya Sūtra*. H. Oldenberg, *The Gṛhya Sūtras*, SBE 29, 30 (Delhi: MLBD, reprint 1964–5)
Ast.	*Aṣṭādhyāyī* of Pānini. See G. Cardona, *Pānini, His Work and its Traditions*, vol. 1 (Delhi: MLBD, 1988)
Ath.V.	*Atharva Veda*. M. Bloomfield, *Hymns of the Atharva Veda*, SBE 42 (1897; Delhi: MLBD, reprint 1967)
BAU	*Bṛhadāraṇyaka Upaniṣad*, S. Radhakrishnan, *The Principal Upaniṣads* (London: Unwin Hyman, 1953)
Baud.SS.	*Baudhāyana Śrauta Sūtra*
Bh.G.	*Bhagavad Gītā*. J. van Buitenen, *The Bhagavadgītā in the Mahābhārata* (Chicago and London: University of Chicago Press, 1981)
BSB	*Brahma Sūtra Bhāṣya*. G. Thibaut, *Vedānta Sūtras with*

	Commentary by Śaṅkarācārya, 2 vols., SBE 34, 38 (Delhi: MLBD, reprint 1987)
Ch.U.	*Chāndogya Upanisad*. Radhakrishnan, *The Principal Upanisads*
Dbh.Pur.	*Devībhāgavata Purāṇa*. See C. M. Brown, *The Triumph of the Goddess: The Canonical Models and Theological Visions of the Devī-Bhāgavata-Purāṇa* (Albany: SUNY Press, 1990)
Devma.	*Devīmahātmya*. T. B. Coburn, *Encountering the Goddess, a Translation of the Devīmahātmya and a Study of Its Interpretation* (Albany: SUNY Press, 1991)
Gaut.Dh.	*Gautama Dharma Śāstra*. G. Bühler, *The Sacred Laws of the Āryas*, SBE 2 (Delhi: MLBD, reprint 1987)
Hat.Yog.	*Haṭhayogapradīpikā* of Svātmarāma. T. Tatya, *The Haṭhayogapradīpikā of Svātmarāma* (Madras: Adyar Library, 1972)
Jab.U.	*Jābāla Upaniṣad*. Patricke Olivelle, *The Saṃnyāsa Upaniṣads: Hindu Scriptures on Asceticism and Renunciation* (New York and Oxford: Oxford University Press, 1992)
Jay.Sam.	*Jayākhya Saṃhitā*
Kat.U.	*Kaṭha Upaniṣad*. Radhakrishnan, *The Principal Upaniṣads*
Kau.	*Kaulakjñānanirṇaya*
KBT	*Kubjikāmata Tantra*
Kur.Pur.	*Kūrma Purāṇa*. A Board of Scholars, *The Kūrma Purāṇa*, All India Tradition and Mythology (Delhi: MLBD, 1973)
Mahbhas.	*Mahābhāṣya* of Patañjali
Mahnar.U.	*Mahānārāyaṇa Upaniṣad*
Mait.U.	*Maitrī Upaniṣad*
Manu	*Manu-smṛti*. W. Doniger, *The Laws of Manu* (Harmondsworth: Penguin, 1991)
Mark.Pur.	*Mārkandeya Purāṇa*. F. E. Pargiter, *The Mārkandeya Purāṇa* (Delhi: MLBD, reprint 1969)
Mat.Pur.	*Matsya Purāṇa*. A Board of Scholars, *The Matsya Purāṇa* (Delhi: AITM, 1973)
Mbh.	*Mahābhārata*. J. A. B. van Buitenen, *The Mahābhārata*, 3 vols. (University of Chicago Press, 1973–8). W. Buck, *The Mahābhārata Retold* (Berkeley and Los Angeles: University of California Press, 1973)

MLBD	Motilal Banarsidass
MS.	*Mīmāṃsā Sūtras* of Jaimini. M. C. Sandal, *The Mīmāṃsa Sūtras of Jaimini*, 2 vols. (Delhi: MLBD, reprint 1980)
M.Stav.	*Mahimnastava.* Arthur Avalon, *The Greatness of Śiva, Mahimnastava of Puṣpadanta* (Madras: Ganesh and Co., reprint 1963)
Nar.U.	*Nāradaparivrājaka Upaniṣad.* P. Olivelle, *The Saṃnyāsa Upanisads*
Pas.Su.	*Pāśupata Sūtra.* H. Chakraborti, *Pāśupata-Sūtram with Pañchārtha-Bhāṣya of Kauṇḍinya* (Calcutta: Academic Publishers, 1970)
RV	*Ṛg Veda Samhitā*, A selection of hymns can be found in M. Müller, *Vedic Hymns*, 2 vols., SBE 32, 46 (Delhi: MLBD, reprint 1973); W. D. O'Flaherty, *The Rig Veda* (Harmondsworth: Penguin, 1981)
Sam.Kar.	*Sāṃkhya Kārikā* of Īśvarakṛṣṇa. G. Larson, *Classical Sāṃkhya* (Delhi: MLBD, 1979)
Sat.Br.	*Śatapatha Brāhmaṇa.* J. Eggeling, *The Śatapatha-Brahmana*, 5 vols., SBE 12, 26, 41, 43, 44 (Delhi: MLBD, reprint 1978–82)
SBE	Sacred books of the East
Sp.Nir.	*Spanda-Nirṇaya* of Kṣemarāja. J. Singh, *Spanda Kārikās* (Delhi: MLBD, 1980)
Sribha.	*Śrībhāṣya* of Rāmānuja. G. Thibaut, *The Vedānta-sūtras with Commentary by Rāmānuja*, SBE 48 (Delhi: MLBD, reprint 1976)
Svet.U.	*Śvetāśvatara Upaniṣad.* Radhakrishnan, *The Principal Upaniṣads*
TA	*Tantrāloka* of Abhinavagupta
Tait.Sam.	*Taittirīya Samhitā.* A. B. Keith, in *The Veda of the Black Yajus School Entitled Taittiriya Sanhita*, 2 vols., Harvard Oriental Series 18, 19 (Cambridge: Mass.: Harvard University Press, 1914)
Tait.Up.	*Taittirīya Upaniṣad.* Radhakrishnan, *The Principal Upaniṣads*
Vaj.Sam.	*Vājasaneyi Samhitā*
Vakpad.	*Vākyapādiya* of Bhartṛhari. K. A. Iyer, *The Vākyapadīya* (Poona: Deccan College, 1965)
Vay.Pur.	*Vāyu Purāṇa.* A Board of Scholars, *The Vāyu Purāṇa*, All India Tradition and Mythology (Delhi: MLBD, 1973)

Vis.Pur.	*Viṣṇu Purāṇa.* H. H. Wilson, *The Viṣṇu Purāṇa: A System of Hindu Mythology and Tradition* (Calcutta: Punthi Pustak, reprint 1967)
Vis.Smrt.	*Viṣṇu Smṛti.* J. Jolly, *The Institutes of Viṣṇu*, SBE 7 (Delhi: MLBD, reprint 1965)
Yog.U.	*Yogatattva Upaniṣad.* T. R. S. Ayyangar, *The Yoga Upaniṣads* (Madras: Adyar Library, 1952)
YS	*Yoga Sūtras* of Patañjali. See YS bhaṣya
YS bhaṣya	*Yoga Sūtra-bhāṣya* of Vyāsa. Swami H. Āraṇya, *Yoga Philosophy of Patañjali* (Albany: SUNY Press, 1983)

Introduction

Visiting India during the first half of the eleventh century, the remarkable Islamic scholar Al-Bīrūnī made a distinction between the views of the Hindu philosophers and the ordinary people.[1] In the former he thought he could find analogues for his own monotheistic belief. Al-Bīrūnī may or may not be correct in this, but what is significant is that we have here an early recognition, by an outsider, of both the diversity of Hinduism and its seemingly unifying features. For Al Bīrūnī, underlying the diversity of the popular religion is a philosophical unity to Hindu traditions. In this book I hope to survey the wide diversity of what has become known as 'Hinduism' as well as to indicate some common elements and unifying themes.

Hinduism is the religion of the majority of people in India and Nepal, as well as being an important cultural force in all other continents. Any visitor to south Asia from the West is struck by the colour, sounds, smells and vibrancy of daily ritual observances, and by the centrality of religion in people's lives. There are innumerable wayside shrines to local goddesses or divinized ancestors, majestic temples to the 'great' deities such as Viṣṇu or Śiva, festivals, pilgrimages to rivers and sacred places, and garlanded pictures of deities and saints in buses, shops and homes. Hindus will often say that Hinduism is not so much a religion, but a way of life. Hinduism also contains developed and elaborate traditions of philosophy and theology, which can be very different from those of the West, Al-Bīrūnī's comments notwithstanding.

This book is both a historical and thematic survey of Hinduism. It is an

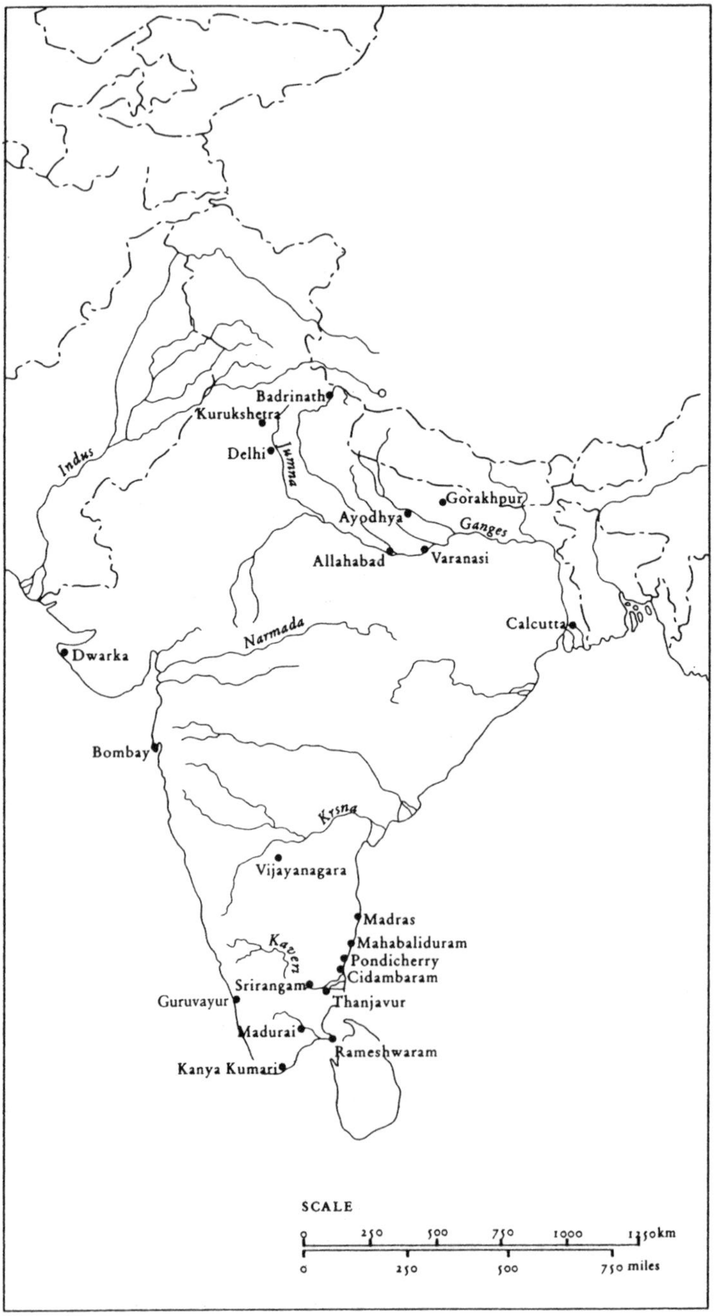

Map 1 India showing some important sacred sites

attempt to make clear the structures of Hinduism and to explain its internal coherence as well as its apparent inconsistencies. While recognizing that it is impossible to include everything in a subject which covers a time-span of 5,000 years and which has existed over a vast geographical area, this book aims at giving comprehensive coverage of the history, traditions, rituals and theologies of Hinduism. Inevitably, in an approach which is both thematic and historical, there is some overlap in the material covered, but it is hoped that this will provide mutual reinforcement of important themes and ideas. The book presents the realms of the householder and the renouncer as distinct, and highlights ritual as a unifying feature of Hindu traditions. It also lays emphasis on the influence of Tantra which has often been underestimated. For the reader wishing to get a general impression of Hinduism, the introductory chapter 1 and chapter 9 on Hindu ritual (which I take to be more important than doctrine in understanding Hinduism) are the most relevant. For the reader mainly interested in theology and philosophy, chapter 10 provides a systematic overview. The book's intended readers are students taking humanities courses in universities and colleges, though it is hoped that others, particularly from Hindu communities themselves, may find something of interest in its pages.

Chapter 1 begins with the question 'what is Hinduism?' This is a complex issue, as the term 'Hindu' has only been in wide circulation for a couple of centuries and reading 'Hinduism' into the past is problematic. This chapter discusses these issues, goes on to develop ideas about Hinduism's general features and relates its study to some contemporary scholarly debates. The second chapter begins the historical survey of Hindu traditions, starting with the vedic religion and examining the relation between the Aryan culture which produced the Veda, Hinduism's revelation, and the Indus valley culture. Chapter 3 develops the historical survey, discussing the idea of *dharma*, truth and duty, and the institutions of caste and kingship. Chapter 4 introduces the idea of world renunciation and examines its ideals of liberation from the cycle of reincarnation through asceticism and yoga. Chapters 5 to 8 describe the great traditions of Vaiṣṇavism, whose focus is the deity of Viṣṇu and his incarnations, Śaivism, whose focus is Śiva, and Śāktism, whose focus is the Goddess, Devī. Chapters 9 and 10 are thematic, examining Hindu ritual and Hindu theology respectively, and chapter 11 traces the development of Hinduism as a world religion and its more recent manifestations in Hindu nationalist politics.

In writing this book, I have assumed that the study of religion is of vital importance in the modern world in which everyone is, in some sense, a 'global citizen', and in which issues of identity and meaning are as important as ever. In Hinduism we see two contemporary cultural forces which are characteristic of modern communities: on the one hand a movement towards globalization and identity formation which locates Hinduism as a trans-national world religion alongside Christianity, Buddhism or Islam; on the other, a fragmentation which identifies Hinduism with a narrowly conceived national identity. Both of these forces, towards globalization and a fragmented nationalism, are strong within Hinduism and it remains to be seen which becomes the more prominent voice.

I hope that Hindus reading this book will recognize their tradition in its pages, and I leave it for the reader to judge the appropriateness of the 'discourses' I have highlighted and those I have thereby occluded.

1 Points of departure

What is Hinduism? A simple answer might be that Hinduism is a term which denotes the religions of the majority of people in India and Nepal, and of some communities in other continents, who refer to themselves as 'Hindus'. The difficulties arise when we try to understand precisely what this means, for the diversity of Hinduism is truly vast and its history long and complex. Some might claim, both from within the tradition and from outside it, that because of this diversity there is 'no such thing as Hinduism', while others might claim that, in spite of its diversity, there is an 'essence' which structures or patterns its manifestations. The truth of the matter probably lies somewhere between these claims. Ask many Hindus and they will be sure of their identity as 'Hindu', in contrast to being Christian, Muslim or Buddhist, yet the kinds of Hindus they are will vary a very great deal and differences between Hindus might be as great as differences between Hindus and Buddhists or Christians.

In India's population of approximately 900 million people,[1] 700 million are Hindus, the remainder are Muslims, Sikhs, Christians, Jains, Buddhists, Parsees, Jews and followers of 'tribal' religions. There are 120 million Muslims and 45 million tribal peoples or *ādivāsīs*, with 14 million Sikhs and an estimated 14 million Christians.[2] This is a wide mix of religions and cultural groups, all of which interact with Hinduism in a number of ways. There are also sizeable Hindu communities beyond the boundaries of south Asia in South Africa, East Africa, South America, the West Indies, the USA, Canada, Europe, Australia, New Zealand, Bali and Java. The 1981 census in the USA estimated the population of Indian communities to be

387,223, most of whom would be Hindu, while in the UK the number of Hindus for the same year is estimated at 300,000.[3] There are also many Westerners from Europe and America who would claim to follow Hinduism or religions deriving from it and Hindu ideas, such as karma, yoga and vegetarianism, are now commonplace in the West.

The actual term 'hindu' first occurs as a Persian geographical term for the people who lived beyond the river Indus (Sanskrit: *sindhu*). In Arabic texts, Al-Hind is a term for the people of modern-day India[4] and 'Hindu', or 'Hindoo', was used towards the end of the eighteenth century by the British to refer to the people of 'Hindustan', the area of northwest India. Eventually 'Hindu' became virtually equivalent to an 'Indian' who was not a Muslim, Sikh, Jain or Christian, thereby encompassing a range of religious beliefs and practices. The '-ism' was added to 'Hindu' in around 1830 to denote the culture and religion of the high-caste Brahmans in contrast to other religions, and the term was soon appropriated by Indians themselves in the context of establishing a national identity opposed to colonialism,[5] though the term 'Hindu' was used in Sanskrit and Bengali hagiographic texts in contrast to 'Yavana' or Muslim, as early as the sixteenth century.[6]

Defining Hinduism

Because of the wide range of traditions and ideas incorporated by the term 'Hindu', it is a problem arriving at a definition. Most Hindu traditions revere a body of sacred literature, the Veda, as revelation, though some do not; some traditions regard certain rituals as essential for salvation, others do not; some Hindu philosophies postulate a theistic reality who creates, maintains and destroys the universe, others reject this claim. Hinduism is often characterized as belief in reincarnation (*saṃsāra*) determined by the law that all actions have effects (*karma*), and that salvation is freedom from this cycle. Yet other religions in south Asia, such as Buddhism and Jainism, also believe in this. Part of the problem of definition is due to the fact that Hinduism does not have a single historical founder, as do so many other world religions; it does not have a unified system of belief encoded in a creed or declaration of faith; it does not have a single system of soteriology; and it does not have a centralized authority and bureaucratic structure. It is therefore a very different kind of religion in these respects from the monotheistic, western traditions of Christianity and Islam, though there are arguably stronger affinities with Judaism.

Jawaharlal Nehru, the first prime minister of independent India, said that Hinduism is 'all things to all men',[7] certainly an inclusive definition, but so inclusive as to be of little use for our purposes. Yet while it might not be possible to arrive at a watertight definition of Hinduism, this does not mean that the term is empty. There are clearly some kinds of practices, texts and beliefs which are central to the concept of being a 'Hindu', and there are others which are on the edges of Hinduism. I take the view that while 'Hinduism' is not a category in the classical sense of an essence defined by certain properties, there are nevertheless prototypical forms of Hindu practice and belief. The beliefs and practices of a high-caste devotee of the Hindu god Viṣṇu, living in Tamilnadu in south India, fall clearly within the category of 'Hindu' and are prototypical of that category. The beliefs and practices of a Radhasaomi devotee in the Punjab, who worships a God without attributes, who does not accept the Veda as revelation and even rejects many Hindu teachings, are not prototypically Hindu, yet are still within the sphere, and category, of Hinduism. The south Indian devotee of Viṣṇu is a more typical member of the category 'Hindu' than the Radhasoami devotee. In other words, 'Hinduism' is not a category in the classical sense – to which something either belongs or it does not – but more in the sense of prototype theory.

Prototype theory, developed by George Lakoff,[8] maintains that categories do not have rigid boundaries, but rather there are degrees of category membership; some members of a category are more prototypical than others. These degrees may be related through family resemblance; the idea that 'members of a category may be related to one another without all members having any properties in common that define the category'.[9] Hinduism can be seen as a category in this sense. It has fuzzy edges. Some forms of religion are central to Hinduism, while others are less clearly central but still within the category.

To say what is or is not central to the category of Hinduism is, of course, to make judgements about the degree of prototypicality. The question of the basis of such judgements arises. Here we must turn, on the one hand, to Hindu self-understandings, for Hinduism has developed categories for its own self-description,[10] as well as, on the other, to the scholar's understandings of common features or structuring principles seen from outside the tradition.

Although I have some sympathy with Jonathan Z. Smith's remark that religion is the creation of the scholar's imagination,[11] in so far as the act of scholarship involves a reduction, a selection, a highlighting of some discourses and texts and a backgrounding of others, there is nevertheless a wide body of ritual practices, forms of behaviour, doctrines, stories, texts, and deeply felt personal experiences and testimonies, to which the term 'Hinduism' refers. The term 'Hindu' certainly does refer in the contemporary world to the dominant religion of south Asia, albeit a religion which embraces a wide variety within it. It is important to bear in mind that the formation of Hinduism, as the world religion we know today, has only occurred since the nineteenth century, when the term was used by Hindu reformers and western orientalists. However, its origins and the 'streams' which feed into it are very ancient, extending back to the Indus valley civilization.[12] I take the view that 'Hinduism' is not purely the construction of western orientalists attempting to make sense of the plurality of religious phenomena within the vast geographical area of south Asia, as some scholars have maintained,[13] but that 'Hinduism' is also a development of Hindu self-understanding; a transformation in the modern world of themes already present. I shall use the term 'Hindu' to refer not only to the contemporary world religion, but, with the necessary qualifications, to the traditions which have led to its present formation.

Religion and the sacred

What we understand by Hinduism as a religion partly depends upon what we mean by 'religion'. Our understanding of Hinduism has been mediated by western notions of what religion is and the projection of Hinduism as an 'other' to the West's Christianity.[14] While this is not the place for an elaborate discussion of the meaning of religion, it is nevertheless important to make some remarks about it, and to indicate some parameters of its use. The category 'religion' has developed out of a Christian, largely Protestant, understanding, which defines it in terms of belief. This is indicated by the frequent use of the term 'faith' as a synonym for 'religion'. If 'religion' is to contribute to our understanding of human views and practices, its characterization purely in terms of belief is clearly inadequate and would need to be modified to include a variety of human practices.

Definitions of religion provoke much debate and disagreement, but to use the term we have to have some idea of what we mean by it. Religion needs to be located squarely within human society and culture; there is no privileged discourse of religion outside of particular cultures and societies. The famous sociologist Emile Durkheim in *The Elementary Forms of the*

Religious Life, first published in 1915, defined religion as 'a unified set of beliefs and practices relative to sacred things' which creates a social bond between people.[15] This unified set of beliefs and practices is a system of symbols which acts, to use Peter Berger's phrase, as a 'sacred canopy', imbuing individual and social life with meaning. The 'sacred' refers to a quality of mysterious power which is believed to dwell within certain objects, persons and places and which is opposed to chaos and death. Religion, following Berger, establishes a 'sacred cosmos' which provides the 'ultimate shield against the terror of anomy'.[16]

This sense of sacred power is of vital importance to the experience of men and women throughout the history of religions. In Hinduism a sense of the sacred might be experienced as the sense of a greater being outside of the self, a 'numinous' experience to use the term coined by the German theologian Rudolf Otto, characterized by a feeling of awe, fascination and mystery;[17] or the sense of the sacred might occur as an inner or contemplative experience within the self, what might be called a 'mystical' experience.[18]

There has been a tendency in recent studies to reduce the 'religious' to the 'political'.[19] While it is important to recognize that the religious exists only within specific cultural contexts, as does the political, the concept of the sacred is distinctive to a religious discourse within cultures. The sacred is regarded as divine power manifested in a variety of contexts: temples, locations, images and people. While this power is not divorced from political power, it can nevertheless exist independently, as is seen in popular religious festivals and personal devotional and ascetic practices which result in states of inner ecstasy.

The sacred exists entirely within culture. The categories of the sacred and the everyday are not substantive, as Jonathan Smith has observed, but relational; they change according to circumstances and situation. There is nothing in Hinduism which is inherently sacred. The sacredness of time, objects or persons depends upon context and the boundaries between the sacred and the everyday are fluid. A ritual dance performer who is possessed by a god one day, mediating between the community and the divine, will the next day be simply human again; or the temple image or icon prior to consecration is merely stone, metal, or wood, but once consecrated is empowered and becomes the focus of mediation: 'it becomes sacred by having our attention directed to it in a special way'.[20] The sacred in Hinduism is mediated through innumerable, changing forms which bear witness to a deeply rich, religious imagination, centred on mediation and transformation.

The understanding of these aspects of human experience is, as Ninian Smart has pointed out, indispensable in the plural cultures of the contemporary world.[21] This study of Hinduism assumes this point and assumes that the academic study of religion, or religious studies, draws on a number of methods within the human sciences: anthropology, history, philosophy and phenomenology. There has been much recent debate concerning the nature of objective studies of other cultures by 'western' social scientists and a questioning of the very possibility, or desirability, of objectivity. The French social thinker Pierre Bourdieu has asked that we clarify the position of the author, and that the researcher be aware of the limitations of his or her perspective on the object of study.[22] While it may be true that we are all personally affected by what draws us, methodologically, the present study is written from a perspective standing outside Hinduism, rather than from inside. We should, however, be wary of regarding these categories as watertight, for there is a dialectical relation between the objective structures of Hinduism, its beliefs and practices, and the dispositions of the method used.[23] The methods of religious studies must mediate between, on the one hand, the objective structure of Hindu traditions and Hindu self-reflection, and, on the other, the community of 'readers' who are external (whether or not they happen to be Hindus).[24] Needless to say, I am not concerned with the truth or falsity of the claims made by the traditions described here. These claims are part of the social and psychological fabric of Hindu communities which have given them life, and which have had profound personal significance for people within them.

General features of Hinduism

Many Hindus believe in a transcendent God, beyond the universe, who is yet within all living beings and who can be approached in a variety of ways. Such a Hindu might say that this supreme being can be worshipped in innumerable forms: as a handsome young man, as a majestic king, as a beautiful young girl, as an old woman, or even as a featureless stone. The transcendent is mediated through icons in temples, through natural phenomena, or through living teachers and saints. Hinduism is often characterized as being polytheistic, and while it is true that innumerable deities are the objects of worship, many Hindus will regard these as an aspect or manifestation of sacred power. Devotion (*bhakti*) to deities mediated through icons and holy persons provides refuge in times of crisis and even final liberation (*mokṣa*) from action (*karma*) and the cycle of reincarnation (*saṃsāra*). The transcendent is also revealed in sacred literature, called the 'Veda', and in codes of ritual, social and ethical behaviour, called *dharma*, which that literature reveals. The two terms *veda* and *dharma* are of central importance in what might be called Hindu self-understanding.

VEDA AND *DHARMA*

The Veda is a large body of literature composed in Sanskrit, a sacred language of Hinduism, revered as revelation (*śruti*) and as the source of *dharma*. The term *veda* means 'knowledge', originally revealed to the ancient sages (*ṛṣi*), conveyed to the community by them, and passed through the generations initially as an oral tradition. There is also a large body of Sanskrit literature, inspired but nevertheless regarded as being of human authorship, comprising rules of conduct (the Dharma literature) and stories about people and gods (the Epics and mythological texts called Purāṇas). These texts might be regarded as a secondary or indirect revelation (*smṛti*).[25] There are also texts in vernacular Indian languages, particularly Tamil, which are revered as being equal to the Veda by some Hindus.

The Veda as revelation is of vital importance in understanding Hinduism, though its acceptance is not universal among Hindus and there are forms of Hinduism which have rejected the Veda and its legitimizing authority in the sanctioning of a hierarchical social order. However, all Hindu traditions make some reference to the Veda, whether in its acceptance or rejection, and some scholars have regarded reference to its legitimizing authority as a criterion of being Hindu.[26] While revelation as an abstract, or even notional entity, is important, the actual content of the Veda has often been neglected by Hindu traditions. It has acted rather as a reference point for the construction of Hindu identity and self-understanding.[27]

Dharma is revealed by the Veda. It is the nearest semantic equivalent in Sanskrit to the English term 'religion', but has a wider connotation than this, incorporating the ideas of 'truth', 'duty', 'ethics', 'law' and even 'natural law'. It is that power which upholds or supports society and the cosmos; that power which constrains phenomena into their particularity, which makes things what they are.[28] The nineteenth-century Hindu reformers speak of Hinduism as the eternal religion or law (*sanātana dharma*), a common idea among modern Hindus today in their self-description. More specifically, *dharma* refers to the duty of high-caste Hindus with regard to social position, one's caste or class (*varṇa*), and the stage of life one is at (*āśrama*). All this is incorporated by the term *varṇāśrama-dharma*.

One striking feature of Hinduism is that practice takes precedence over belief. What a Hindu does is more important than what a Hindu believes. Hinduism is not credal. Adherence to *dharma* is therefore not an acceptance of certain beliefs, but the practice or performance of certain duties, which are defined in accordance with dharmic social stratification. The boundaries of what a Hindu can and cannot do have been largely determined by his or her particular endogamous social group, or caste, stratified in a hierarchical order, and, of course, by gender. This social hierarchy is governed by the distinction between purity and pollution, with the higher, purer castes at the top of the structure, and the lower, polluted and polluting, castes at the bottom. Behaviour, expressing Hindu values and power structures, takes precedence over belief, orthopraxy over orthodoxy. As Frits Staal says, a Hindu 'may be a theist, pantheist, atheist, communist and believe whatever he likes, but what makes him into a Hindu are the ritual practices he performs and the rules to which he adheres, in short, what he *does*'.[29]

This sociological characterization of Hinduism is very compelling. A Hindu is someone born within an Indian social group, a caste, who adheres to its rules with regard to purity and marriage, and who performs its prescribed rituals which usually focus on one of the many Hindu deities such as Śiva or Viṣṇu. One might add that these rituals and social rules are derived from the Hindu primary revelation, the Veda, and from the secondary revelation, the inspired texts of human authorship. The Veda and its ritual reciters, the highest caste or Brahmans, are the closest Hinduism gets to a legitimizing authority, for the Brahman class has been extremely important in the dissemination and maintenance of Hindu culture. It is generally the Brahman class that has attempted to structure coherently the multiple expressions of Hinduism, and whose self-understanding any account of Hinduism needs to take seriously.

RITUAL AND SALVATION

Dharma implies a fundamental distinction between the affirmation of worldly life and social values on the one hand, and the rejection of worldly life or renunciation (*saṃnyāsa*) in order to achieve salvation or liberation (*mokṣa*) on the other. Religion in worldly life is concerned with practical needs; the help of deities in times of crisis such as a child's illness, the ensuring of a better lot in this life and the next, and the regulating of one's passage through time in the social institutions into which one is born. This kind of religion is concerned with birth, marriage and funeral rites; the regular ordering of life through ritual which is generally distinct from religion as leading to personal salvation or liberation (*mokṣa*). Richard Gombrich, who has highlighted this distinction, has called the former 'communal religion' to distinguish it from soteriology, the path of salvation.[30] Religion as soteriology is concerned with the individual and his/her own salvation, howsoever conceptualized, whereas communal religion is concerned with the regulation of communities, the ritual structuring of a person's passage through life, and the successful transition, at death, to another world. The former involves an element of faith and, more importantly, initiation into the particular way or method leading to the practitioner's spiritual goal. The latter is concerned with legitimizing hierarchical social relationships and propitiating deities.

The relationship between soteriology and practical religion is variable. Paths might demand complete celibacy and the renouncing of social life, in which case the Hindu would become a renouncer (*saṃnyāsin*), a wandering ascetic, or they might be adapted to the householder continuing to live in the world, for example by demanding a certain yoga practice. Some spiritual paths might allow women to be initiated, others might not; some might be open to Untouchable castes, while others might not. The aim of a spiritual path is eventual liberation rather than worldly prosperity which is the legitimate goal for the follower of practical religion. Hindus might, and do, participate in both forms of religion.

This distinction between practical religion and religion as soteriology, between appeasement and mysticism, is expressed at the social level in the figures of the householder, who maintains his family and performs his ritual obligations, and the renouncer who abandons social life, performs his own funeral and seeks final release. The purposes of the householder and renouncer, as Louis Dumont has shown,[31] are quite different, even contradictory, yet are both legitimated within Hindu traditions. The high-caste householder is born with three debts (*ṛṇa*) to be paid: the debt of vedic study to the sages (*ṛṣi*) as a celibate student (*brahmacārin*), the debt of ritual to the gods (*deva*) as a householder, and the debt of begetting a son to make funeral offerings to the ancestors (*pitṛ*). Traditionally, only once these debts have been paid can a householder go forth to seek liberation. Sometimes, as in the famous text of secondary revelation, the *Bhagavad Gītā*, the ideals of household obligation and ascetic renunciation are brought together by saying that a person can work towards liberation while still fulfilling his worldly responsibilities.

ONE AND MANY GODS

The term polytheism can be applied to Hinduism in so far as there is a multiplicity of divine forms, from pan-Hindu deities such as Śiva, Viṣṇu and Gaṇeśa to deities in regional temples, such as Lord Jagannāth at Puri, and deities in local village shrines. These deities are distinct and particular to their location; the goddess in a shrine in one village is distinct from the goddess in a different shrine. While most Hindus will regard these deities as distinct, many Hindus will also say that they are aspects or manifestations of a single, transcendent God. Some Hindus will identify this transcendent focus with a specific God, say Kṛṣṇa or Śiva, and maintain that the other deities are lower manifestations of this supreme God. Other Hindus will say that all deities are aspects of an impersonal absolute and that deities of mythology and the icons in temples are windows into this ultimate reality. What is important is that the deities as icons in temples mediate between the human world and a divine or sacred reality and that the icon as deity might be seen as a 'spiritualization' of matter.

MEDIATION AND THE SACRED

Central to any understanding of Hinduism is the role of mediation between the sacred and the everyday or 'profane'. The place of the interaction of the sacred with the human is the place of mediation; the connection between the community or individual and the religious focus. Mediation underlines difference; the difference between humans and deities, and the differences between human groups. These differences are mediated temporarily through ritual and festival cycles, and spatially through temples, icons, holy persons and holy places. In ritual, offering incense to the icon of a deity mediates between, or is thought to open a channel of communication between, the Hindu and the transcendent power embodied in the icon. Similarly, renouncers and gurus mediate between the sacred and the everyday worlds, as do people who become temporarily possessed during certain festivals.

The distinction between the sacred and the everyday overlaps with the important distinctions between the pure and the impure, and the auspicious and the inauspicious: distinctions which have been emphasized in recent studies of Hinduism.[32] The sacred is generally regarded as pure, though may also be manifested in impurity, as in the Aghori ascetic living in the polluting cremation ground. The sacred is also auspicious, yet may on occasion be inauspicious, as when a goddess of smallpox and other diseases visits one's family.

The possessed man or woman recapitulates the temple icon. Both contain sacred power and are identified with the deity. Both icon and possessed person are not merely representations of the deity, but have actually become the deity within the particular, circumscribed, ritual situation. The transformation of the non-empowered icon into empowered icon, or of the low-caste performer into the sacred deity, is a central structure of Hindu religious consciousness. The icon, or person who has become an icon, mediates between the sacred realm and the human community. Should the divine interact with the human outside ritual contexts, such as in an unexpected possession illness, then the unlooked-for mediation might not be welcome and, indeed, could be dangerous.

Not only certain people, but also certain places, mediate between the sacred and the everyday. Places of pilgrimage are called 'crossings' (*tīrṭha*). One such crossing is the sacred city of Varanasi which is so sacred that liberation will occur at death for those lucky enough to die there. Here, the crossing from everyday to the sacred will be permanent. Again, rivers, such as the Ganges in the north or Kaveri in the south, are places where the sacred is manifested and Hindus receive blessings through visiting these sites.

Yet, while difference mediated by innumerable spatial and temporal forms is central, identity rather than hierarchy, and by implication the absence of mediation, is also important. While the deity is worshipped as distinct, the deity and devotee nevertheless share in the same essence and at a deep level they are one.[33] The idea of a boundless identity is at the heart of many Hindu soteriologies which assert the essence of a person, their true self (*ātman*), to be identical with the essence of the cosmos, the absolute (*brahman*). Even traditions which emphasize the distinction between God and the self at some level usually accept the identity or partial identity of worshipper and worshipped, of lover and beloved. This idea of an identity between the worshipper and the deity has even been called, by the anthropologist Chris Fuller, one of Hinduism's 'axiomatic truths'.[34] Yet the coexistence of identity and difference, of immediacy and mediation, is also axiomatic. There is unity, yet there is difference: the god Kṛṣṇa's consort, Rādhā, is united with him, yet she retains her distinct identity; the self and the absolute might be one, yet caste and gender differences matter.

Hindu traditions

The idea of tradition inevitably stresses unity at the cost of difference and divergence. In pre-Islamic India there would have been a number of distinct sects and regional religious identities, perhaps united by common cultural symbols, but no notion of 'Hinduism' as a comprehensive entity. Yet there are nevertheless striking continuities in Hindu traditions. There are essentially two models of tradition: the arboreal model and the river model. The arboreal model claims that various sub-traditions branch off from a central, original tradition, often founded by a specific person. The river model, the exact inverse of the arboreal model, claims that a tradition comprises multiple-streams which merge into a single mainstream.[35] Contemporary Hinduism cannot be traced to a common origin, so the discussion is directed towards whether Hinduism fits the river model or, to extend the metaphor, whether the term 'Hinduism' simply refers to a number of quite distinct rivers. While these models have restricted use in that they suggest a teleological direction or intention, the river model would seem to be more appropriate in that it emphasizes the multiple origins of Hinduism.

The many traditions which feed in to contemporary Hinduism can be subsumed under three broad headings: the traditions of brahmanical orthopraxy, the renouncer traditions and popular or local traditions. The tradition of brahmanical orthopraxy has played the role of 'master narrative', transmitting a body of knowledge and behaviour through time, and defining the conditions of orthopraxy, such as adherence to *varṇāśrama-dharma*.

BRAHMANICAL TRADITIONS

The brahmanical tradition can itself be subdivided into a number of systems or religions which are distinct yet interrelated, and which refer to themselves as 'traditions' (*saṃpradāya*) or systems of teacher–disciple transmission (*paramparā*). These traditions, which developed significantly during the first millennium CE, are focused upon a particular deity or group of deities. Among these broadly brahmanical systems, three are particularly important in Hindu self-representation: Vaiṣṇava traditions, focused on the deity Viṣṇu and his incarnations; Śaiva traditions, focused on Śiva; and Śākta traditions, focused on the Goddess or Devī. There is also an important tradition of Brahmans called Smārtas, those who follow the *smṛti* or secondary revelation, and who worship five deities, Viṣṇu, Śiva, Sūrya, Gaṇeśa and Devī. These traditions have their own sacred texts and rituals, while still being within the general category of Hinduism.[36]

Cutting across these religious traditions is the theology of Vedānta; the unfolding of a sophisticated discourse about the nature and content of sacred scriptures, which explores questions of existence and knowledge. The Vedānta is the theological articulation of the vedic traditions, a discourse which penetrated Vaiṣṇava and, though to a lesser extent, Śaiva and Śākta thinking. The Vedānta tradition became the philosophical basis of the Hindu renaissance during the nineteenth century and is pervasive in the world religion which Hinduism has become.

THE RENOUNCER TRADITIONS

The renouncer traditions, while their value system is distinct from that of the Brahman householders, are nevertheless closely related to the brahmanical religions. Indeed, some brahmanical householder traditions, such as Śaivism, originated among the world-renouncers seeking liberation while living on the edges of society in wild places and in cremation grounds. The renouncer traditions espouse the values of asceticism and world transcendence in contrast to the brahmanical householder values of affirming the goals of worldly responsibility (*dharma*), worldly success and profit (*artha*), and erotic and aesthetic pleasure (*kāma*). The ideal of renunciation is incorporated within the structure of orthoprax Hinduism, though orthoprax renunciation must be seen in the context of general Indian renouncer traditions known as the Śramaṇa traditions. These Śramaṇa traditions, including Buddhism and Jainism, developed during the first millennium BCE and were in conflict with brahmanical, vedic orthopraxy.

POPULAR TRADITIONS

While there are pan-Hindu traditions of Vaiṣṇavism, Śaivism and Śāktism alongside the renouncer traditions, there are also local or popular traditions which exist within a bounded geographical area, even within a particular village. Their languages of transmission are the regional, vernacular languages rather than the Sanskrit of the brahmanical tradition. They are less concerned with asceticism than with ensuring that crops grow, that illness keeps away from the children, and that one is not haunted or possessed by ghosts. Such popular traditions are low-caste and need to appease 'hot' deities, particularly goddesses, who demand offerings of blood and alcohol. While the concerns of popular religion are different from those of the renouncer and brahmanical traditions, they are nevertheless informed by the 'higher' culture.

The process whereby the brahmanical tradition influences popular religion is called Sanskritization. Local deities become identified with the great deities of the brahmanical tradition and local myths become identified with the great, pan-Hindu myths. For example, the Dravidian goddess of pustular diseases, Māriyammaṉ, might be identified as a manifestation of the great pan-Hindu goddess Durgā. Local deities can also become pan-Hindu deities and local narratives become commonly shared myths.[37] The god Kṛṣṇa, for example, may have been a local deity who became pan-Hindu. More recent examples might be the northern Goddess Santoṣī Ma, who has become a pan-Hindu deity through having become the subject of a movie, or the Kerala deity Aiyappan, who is coming to have trans-regional appeal. The influence of south Indian Dravidian culture on the grand narrative of the Sanskritic, brahmanical tradition has been underestimated and, until recently, little investigated.

The relationship between the popular and the brahmanical levels of culture is the focus of much debate among scholars of Hinduism. On the one hand popular tradition can be seen as a residue or consequence of the grand narrative of the brahmanical tradition: an imitation of the higher culture. On the other hand popular tradition can be seen to function independently of the high, brahmanical culture, but interacting with it.[38] Scholars who interpret Hinduism holistically, such as Madeleine Biardeau, tend to favour the importance of brahmanical culture in shaping the tradition.[39] Others, particularly anthropologists who have carried out fieldwork in a specific locality, stress the discontinuities of tradition, emphasizing the importance and independence of regional or popular religion.[40]

Hindu traditions, with their emphasis on continuity and the importance of the teacher or *guru* in the transference of knowledge, are essentially conservative and resistant to change. There is a fine balance between such conservatism, which preserves the tradition, and the necessity to adapt to prevalent historical conditions. If traditions adapt too much then they are no longer the traditions that they were, yet if they do not adapt they are in danger of dying out. Some Hindu traditions have faded and others have arisen. Hinduism has adapted and reacted to political and social upheavals throughout its history, while maintaining many of its ritual traditions and social structures almost unchanged for centuries. The impact of modernity and the development of a middle class in India will inevitably effect Hinduism, and debates about civil rights, nationalism, the rights of the scheduled castes, and the Indian women's movement will inevitably transform it.

Hinduism and contemporary debate

Issues which have arisen in the contemporary study of Hinduism relate to wider cultural problems and general intellectual debates about agency, the relation of religion to politics, and gender issues. Many of these issues have arisen out of what is generally termed 'postmodernism', a movement originating in the West, which manifests in all areas of culture, and a discourse which questions and challenges traditional, rationalist views. Cultural studies, which cuts across traditional divisions in the humanities of sociology, history, philosophy and even theology, has developed within the general postmodernist framework. In 'deconstructing' rationalist discourses, cultural studies has highlighted traditions which have been occluded, both in the West and the East.

One of the most important examples of this with regard to India and Hinduism has been the work of the historian Ranajit Guha and his colleagues, who have worked on the subordinated or subaltern classes of India. One of the themes of this group is that in western, i.e. colonial and post-colonial, historiography of India, the highlighting of some themes and backgrounding of others has demonstrated the exercise of power and a denial of the agency of those who were oppressed. Historical discourse, according to Guha, has tended to write out subaltern classes (the lowest castes) and to see protests by those groups as merely an 'eruption' of discontent akin to natural disasters.[41] This critique of the western scholarship of India, particularly of the discipline of Indology, can also be seen in Ronald Inden's important and influential book, *Imagining India.*[42] Inden critiques the epistemological assumptions and political biases of orientalist 'constructions' of Hinduism, which have seen Hinduism primarily in terms of caste, as a romanticized, idyllic community, or as 'oriental despotism'. He argues that all these views deprive Hindus of agency and sees them governed by external forces outside of their control.

Related to the discussion about the importance of understanding human agency and practice, in contrast to emphasizing impersonal structures which govern people's lives,[43] is the debate about gender issues. The history of Hinduism is the history of a male discourse. Its written texts and narratives have, with the exception of some notable devotional poetry, been composed by men, usually of the highest, brahmanical caste. In a tradition's self-reflection it is generally high-caste, male perceptions of themselves and of women which have come down to us, though some modern scholarship has highlighted women's voices from the past.[44] Because Hinduism has been dominated by men, this book reflects this fact, while being aware that women's self-perceptions and experience have generally been 'written-out' of the tradition. These debates, of course, are not exclusive to Hinduism and some contemporary concerns of the Indian women's movement, about whether Hinduism is inherently androcentric or whether Hinduism can be separated from androcentrism, have echoes in Christianity and other religions. Recent scholarship has begun to uncover these marginalized traditions and I refer the reader to some of that work where appropriate.

The chronology of Hinduism

Before the first millennium CE there is no historiography in the south Asian cultural region and texts are not dated. The chronology of Indian religions has therefore been notoriously difficult to establish. We have to rely on archaeological evidence of coins, pottery and, particularly, inscriptions, and on the internal evidence of texts. The dating of early texts is very problematic. The sequence of texts can sometimes be established in that if one text is quoted by another, the former must be earlier, but precise dating is impossible. Chinese translations of Buddhist texts are dated, which helps establish the chronology of Buddhism, but is less useful with regard to Hindu material. The more accurate dating of the Buddha to almost a century later than the traditional dating of 566, to 486, BCE, discovered by Richard Gombrich and Heinz Bechert,[45] will hopefully lead to reassessment of the dating of all early Indian material.

One of the cliches about Hinduism has been that it is ahistorical and sees time as cyclic rather than linear, which has militated against the keep-

(40)

ing of accurate historical records. While it is true that Hinduism does have a view of time repeating itself over vast periods, it is not the case that Hindus have not been interested in their past. Within India, as elsewhere, the record of the past has reflected the concerns of the present, though any historical awareness has been embedded in myths, biographies of people in authority (the *carita* literature), in genealogies of families (the *vaṃśānucarita* sections of the Purāṇas), and in histories of ruling families in specific locations (the *vaṃśāvalī* literature). The earliest writing of history in the south Asian region occurs in the fourth century CE with the chronicles written by Sri Lankan Buddhist monks.[46] Myths and genealogies have been recorded particularly in the Hindu Epics and texts called Purāṇas, reaching their present form in the mid first millennium CE.[47] A particularly striking text, part of the *vaṃśāvalī* genre, more concerned with historicity than with mythology, is the 'History of the Kings of Kashmir', the *Rājataraṅgiṇī* composed during the twelfth century by Kalhaṇa. This records the genealogies of the kings and brief descriptions of their exploits.[48]

The chronology of south Asia has been divided into ancient, classical, medieval and modern periods. While this scheme does reflect genres of texts, it is important to remember that there are continuities between these periods. The following pages assume the following general chronological scheme:

- the Indus valley civilization (*c.* 2500 to 1500 BCE). Elements of Hinduism may be traced back to this period.
- the vedic period (*c.* 1500 to 500 BCE). The rise of Aryan, in contrast to Dravidian, culture occurs during this period, though there may be more continuity between the Aryan and Indus valley cultures than was previously supposed. During this period the Veda was formulated and texts of Dharma and ritual composed.
- the epic and purāṇic period (*c.* 500 BCE to 500 CE). This period sees the composition of the *Mahābhārata* and *Rāmāyaṇa*, as well as the bulk of the Purāṇas. A number of important kingdoms arise, particularly the Gupta dynasty (*c.* 320 CE to 500 CE), and the great traditions of Vaiṣṇavism, Śaivism and Śāktism begin to develop.
- the medieval period (*c.* 500 CE to 1500 CE) sees the development of devotion (*bhakti*) to the major Hindu deities, particularly Viṣṇu, Śiva and Devī. There are major developments in the theistic traditions of Vaiṣṇavism, Śaivism and Śāktism. This period sees the composition of

devotional and poetic literature in Sanskrit and vernacular languages, as well as the composition of tantric literature.

- the modern period (*c.* 1500 CE to the present) sees the rise and fall of two great empires, the Mughal and the British, and the origin of India as a nation state. The traditions continue, but without significant royal patronage. The nineteenth century sees the rise of Renaissance Hinduism and the twentieth century the development of Hinduism as a major world religion.

2 Ancient origins

The origins of Hinduism lie in two ancient cultural complexes, the Indus valley civilization which flourished from 2500 BCE to about 1500 BCE, though its roots are much earlier, and the Aryan culture which developed during the second millennium BCE. There is some controversy regarding the relationship between these two cultures. The traditional view, still supported by some scholars, is that the Indus valley civilization declined, to be replaced by the culture of the Aryans, an Indo-European people originating in the Caucasus region who migrated into south Asia and spread across the fertile, northern plains, which, throughout India's long history, have offered no obstacle to invaders or migrants. The alternative view is that Aryan culture is a development from the Indus valley civilization and was not introduced by outside invaders or migrants; that there is no cultural disjunction in ancient south Asian history, but rather a continuity from an early period. Yet, whether the Aryans came from outside the subcontinent or not, Hinduism might be regarded as the development over the next 2,000 years of Aryan culture, interacting with non-Aryan or Dravidian and tribal cultures, though it is Aryan culture which has provided the 'master narrative', absorbing and controlling other discourses.

The views and arguments regarding the origins of Hinduism have not been free from ideological interests and the quest for origins itself has been a factor in the development of Hinduism over the last two centuries. Hindu revivalists in the nineteenth century, such as Dayānanda Sarasvatī, looked to Hinduism's Aryan past to imbue it with new moral impetus and the search for origins has been important for Indology as a scholarly articulation and justification for colonialism. The quest for origins is also relevant in the contemporary politics of Hinduism, which traces continuity between an ancient past and the present, bearing witness to India's past, Hindu, greatness (see p. 262).

In examining the roots of Hinduism we must be aware of the rhetoric of origins, as it might be called. Indeed, the very quest for an 'origin' may suggest an 'essence' which is highly problematic. In searching for an origin we find only 'traces' or signs which constantly point beyond themselves, are constantly deferred.[1] That is, an 'origin' is always the consequence of something which has gone before, and the 'origin' cannot be regarded in a teleological way, with hindsight, as pointing towards that which follows. In examining the 'traces' which constitute a past culture, we should remember that such a culture was complete in itself rather than in some sense preliminary, lived by people who experienced the fullness and contradictions of human life, and that any sketch must necessarily be selective and restrictive.

With these qualifications in mind, this chapter will examine the roots of Hinduism in the Indus valley and Aryan cultures, and discuss the vedic religion of early Indian society.

The Indus valley civilization

In 1921 Sir John Marshall, Director General of the Archaeological Survey of India, directed D. R. Sahni to begin excavations at Harappa. He and R. D. Banerjee, excavating at Mohenjo-Daro in Sind, discovered the Indus valley civilization. As with the great civilizations of Sumer and pharaoic Egypt, this urban civilization was centred on a river and located in the basin of the Indus which flows through present-day Pakistan. This Indus valley or Harappan civilization developed from about 2500 BCE, though its origins reach back to the Neolithic Period (7000 – 6000 BCE), reached its peak around 2300–2000 BCE (trade links with Mesopotamia have been dated to this period), was in decline by 1800 BCE and had faded away by 1500.[2]

This was a developed, urban culture. Mohenjo-Daro and Harappa, separated by some 40 miles, were two of this civilization's most important cities and housed some 40,000 inhabitants who enjoyed a high standard of living. The cities had sophisticated water technologies, most of the houses having drainage systems, wells, and rubbish chutes emptying into waste-pots which were emptied municipally.[3] As in ancient Mesopotamia, grain was the basis of the economy and the large store-houses in the Indus towns may have been for grain collected as tax. There were trade contacts with the Middle East and with the hunter-gatherer tribes of Gujurat, the town of Lothal in Gujarat being one of the most important centres for importing and exporting goods. There remain other cities of the Indus valley civilization yet to be excavated, at Judeiro-Daro, Lurewala Ther and Ganaweriwala Ther on the course of the Hakra, an ancient dried-up river in present day Haryana. The antecedents of this culture can be traced to the site of Mergarh, 150 miles north of Mohenjo-Daro in Baluchistan, where the French archaeologist Jean-Françoise Jarrige has dated the agricultural community to before 6000 BCE and has established an unbroken cultural continuity from that early date to the period of the Indus valley civilzation.[4]

THE DEVELOPMENT AND CONTINUITY OF THE INDUS VALLEY

The development and expansion of the Indus valley culture was probably the consequence of a growth in population, itself due to the development of farming and the availability of food supplies grown on the rich alluvial deposits of the Indus valley. Indeed, the importance of arable farming is demonstrated by the large granaries in Mohenjo-Daro on the west bank of the Indus, and in Harappa on the east bank of the Ravi. Evidence for this civilization has come mainly through the excavations of these two cities and from other, smaller, sites. Apart from Mergarh, the sites at Amri, 100 miles south of Mohenjo-Daro, at Kalibangan in the Punjab, and at Lothal near Ahmadabad in Rajasthan, are notable.

This culture was very extensive and archaeological evidence for the mature Indus valley civilization has been found at over 1,000 sites covering an area of 750,000 square miles, from Rupar in the east in the foothills of the Himalayas near Simla, to Sutkagen Dor in the west near the Iranian border, to Lothal on the Gujarat coast.[5] Judging by the archaeological record, there was a unity of material culture, notably pottery, architecture and writing, in the Indus valley by as early as the fourth millennium BCE, which was preceded by a period of continuous development at different sites from the early Neolithic Period. The Indus valley culture did not develop due to the direct influence of external cultural forces from Sumer or Egypt, but was an indigenous development in the Baluchistan and Indus regions, growing out of earlier, local cultures.

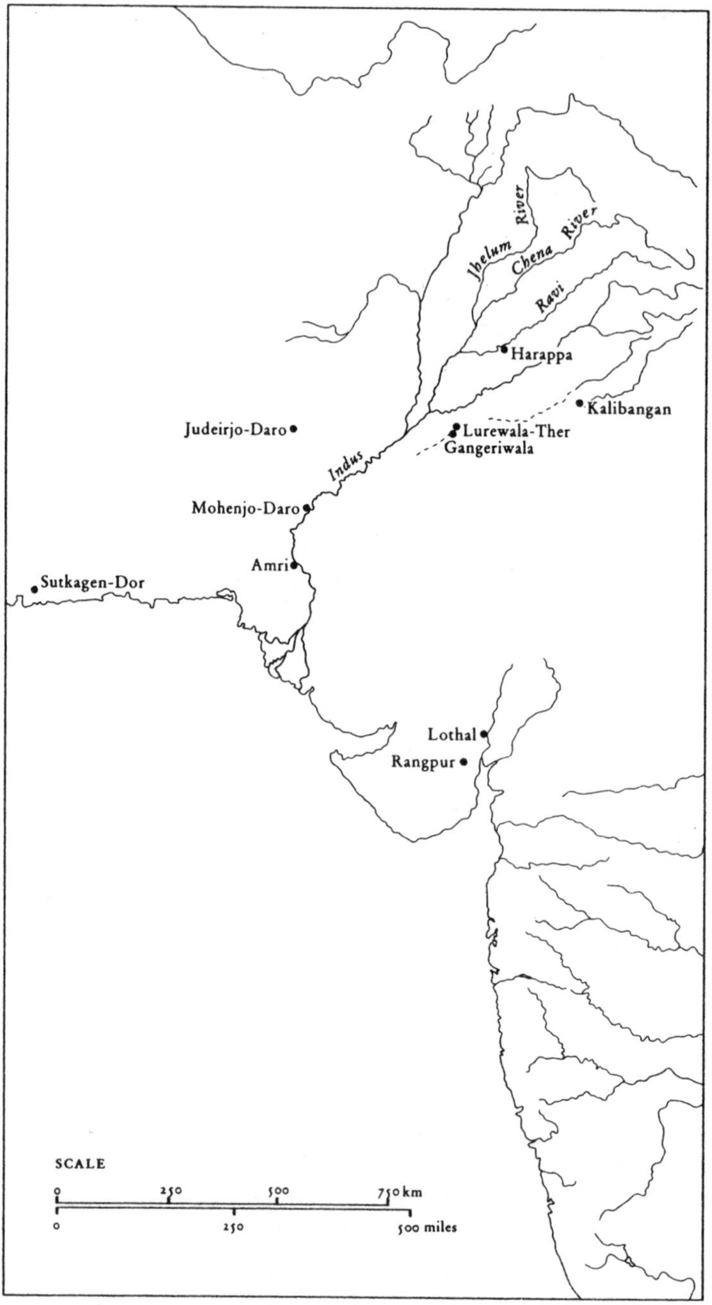

Map 2 Major sites of the Indus valley civilization (adapted from Parpola, *Deciphering the Indus Script*, p. 7)

THE RELIGION OF THE INDUS VALLEY

Needless to say, we know little of the polity or religion of this civilization. There is a system of writing, the Indus valley script, which has been found inscribed on steatite seals and copper plates, but this has not yet been successfully deciphered and, until more samples or a bilingual inscription are found, will probably remain largely obscure. The biggest issue which has bearing on the development of Hindu traditions from the Indus valley, lies in the answer to the questions: what is the language of the steatite seals? And to what group of languages is it related? There have been two predominant views among scholars, one that it represents a language belonging to the Dravidian linguistic family, the other that it is an early form of Indo-European.[6]

The Dravidian languages include the south Indian languages of Tamil, Kannada, Telegu and Malayalam, as well as Brahui, the language of a hill people in Pakistan. The presence of these languages is strong evidence for there being a pan-Indian Dravidian presence, before the predominance of the Indo-Iranian language group, itself a part of the Indo-European family. The Indo-European languages include Greek, Latin, and the Indo-Iranian languages which comprise Avestan (the sacred language of the Zoroastrians), Sanskrit, and the north Indian vernaculars of Gujarati, Urdu, Hindi, Kashmiri, Oriya and Bengali.

Colin Renfrew makes the point that in deciphering the script we need to begin with something known, but there are no bilingual inscriptions, so decipherers assume a solution and then try to demonstrate its plausibility.[7] The successful decipherment of the script would tell us something about the daily transactions of these people and might tell us something of their religion or religions. As it stands we have to infer social and religious contents from the material culture, though Asko Parpola claims to have made significant advances in understanding the Indus script and its relation to Dravidian languages and Dravidian forms of Hinduism.

Perhaps the most striking thing about the Indus civilization is the high degree of uniformity of urban planning and even a conformity in size of building bricks. Many of the houses were built on a similar ground plan around a central courtyard, and many houses had a water supply and drainage system. This suggests a sophisticated administration and a hierarchical structure of authority. In both Harappa and Mohenjo-Daro there was a fortified lower city separated from a fortified citadel or 'acropolis' situated on a raised mound, which contained halls and temples. Such uniformity may suggest more than wide diffusion of a culture, even a polity imposed on a large area through conquest, with the centre of this empire and its administration at Mohenjo-Daro. If so, this would be the earliest imperial formation in South Asia, which may also have involved the imposition of an official religion, perhaps centred on the cult of the king. There is, however, no conclusive evidence without the decipherment of the Indus valley script and ideas about the nature of the state must remain speculative.

The religion of the mature Indus valley culture has to be inferred from the buildings which were most probably temples, stone statues, terracotta figurines and particularly the steatite seals. The state religion seems to have involved temple rituals, perhaps animal sacrifice, and ritual bathing in the 'great bath' found in the citadel at Mohenjo-Daro. This bath is reminiscent of tanks found in later Hindu temples and reflects a concern with ritual purification through water, an important idea in Hinduism. At Kalibangan a ritual area has been found in which animal sacrifice seems to have been practised and seven 'fire altars' have been located. Indeed, the brick platforms by the great bath at Mohenjo-Daro may have served a similar purpose.[8]

The large number of female terracotta figurines unearthed during the excavations, may have been goddess images and the presence of the goddess in later Hinduism may be traced back to this early period. It is, of course, impossible to say whether there is a continuity in the cult of the goddess from this early age, and the fact that the goddesses are the focus of worship in the Indus culture does not necessarily mean that these are the forerunners of the Hindu goddesses. Goddess worship and the central concerns of fertility seem to have been common in the ancient world and the Harappan goddess or goddesses may have more in common with Sumerian than with later Hindu deities.

Perhaps suggestive of the later religions are the images on the remarkable steatite seals, particularly the 'Pasupati' seal, of a seated, perhaps ithyphallic, figure surrounded by animals, either horned or wearing a headdress. Sir John Marshall and others have claimed that this figure is a prototype of the Hindu god Śiva, the yogin and Lord of the animals (*paśupati*), sometimes represented with three faces, and the posture with the knees out and feet joined has been interpreted as evidence of yoga in pre-Aryan culture (see fig. 1).[9] However, it is not clear from the seals that the 'proto-Śiva' figure has three faces, as is claimed, nor is it clear that he is

Figure 1 Indus valley 'proto-Śiva' seal

seated in a yogic posture. Asko Parpola has convincingly suggested that the proto-Śiva is in fact a 'seated' bull, almost identical to figures of seated bulls found on early Elamite seals (*c.* 3000–2750 BCE).[10] While the claim that in the seals we have representations of a proto-Śiva is speculative, it is nevertheless possible that iconographic features are echoed in the iconography of Śiva; the half-moon in Śiva's hair resembling the horns of the bull-god. 'Phallic'-shaped stones have also been found, suggestive of the later aniconic representation of Śiva, the *liṅga*.

However, while these connections may be speculative, Parpola has tried to demonstrate that there are a number of linguistic and iconographic continuities between the Indus valley civilization and south Indian, Dravidian forms of Hinduism. The South Indian god Murugan, the young man identified with the god of war, Skanda, is represented in the Indus valley script, argues Parpola, by two intersecting circles (the word *muruku* in Dravidian languages, suggestively denotes 'bangle'), and a seal depicting a person bowing to a figure standing in the middle of a fig tree echoes in later Indian iconography of fig trees (such as the Buddhist banyan tree which indicates the Buddha in early representations). The fig is furthermore associated with the planet Venus, which is in turn later associated with the goddess Durgā, and with the *tilak*, a red dot worn on the forehead.[11]

It is tempting to speculate that there are continuities of religion from the Indus valley into Hinduism, which would make the roots of the religion go back a very long way, but we must exercise caution. The ritual bath, the fire altars, the female figurines, the horned deities and the '*liṅgas*' are certainly suggestive of later Hindu traditions. However, ritual purity, an emphasis on fertility, sacrifice, and goddess worship are common to other religions of the ancient world as well. Indeed, the steatite image of a figure battling with lions is more reminiscent of the Mesopotamian Gilgamesh myth than anything found in later Hinduism, though again Parpola has argued continuities with the Goddess Durgā battling with the buffalo demon.[12]

The Indus valley civilization seems to have declined rather suddenly between 1800 and 1700 BCE, primarily due to environmental causes such as flooding or a decrease in rainfall. A squatter's period continued for some time after this and smaller Indus valley towns and villages survived the abandonment of the large cities. At Mohenjo-Daro a number of skeletons were found where they had fallen, the victims of a violent death. It has been claimed that these deaths were caused by early Aryan invaders.[13]

The Aryans

The most commonly accepted theory to date has been that Hinduism is the consequence of incursions of groups known as Aryans into the northern plains of India from central Asia, via the mountain passes of Afghanistan, around 1500 BCE. Some of these groups went into Iran and there are close affinities between the Iranian religion of the Avesta (the sacred scripture of Zoroastrianism) and the religion of the Veda. This narrative has maintained that the Aryans were of the same stock as groups which went west into Europe. Their language was an Indo-European tongue which developed into vedic Sanskrit and finally into classical Sanskrit, the sacred language of Hinduism, and they worshipped primarily a fire god, Agni, a hallucinogenic plant, Soma, and a warrior god, Indra. The self-designation of these people was the Sanskrit *ārya*, meaning 'noble' or 'honourable', which referred to the three highest social classes of their society, as distinct from the indigenous people of south Asia whom they encountered and subjugated by means of a superior war technology. They spread over the northern plains and, some time after 1000 BCE, reached the Ganges region which became known as the 'Aryan homeland' (*āryāvarta*). Aryan culture slowly spread to the Deccan and was established in south India by around the sixth century CE. Thus the Indo-European-speaking Aryans are contrasted with the indigenous, Dravidian-speaking descendants of the Indus valley civilization whom they conquered. Knowledge of the Aryans comes mostly from their sacred text the *Ṛg Veda Saṃhitā*, the earliest literature of Hinduism.

The predominance of Aryan culture over Dravidian culture is not disputed, but the origin of the Aryans as coming from outside the subcontinent has recently been questioned. Two theories concerning the origin of the Aryans have emerged: what might be called the Aryan migration thesis and the cultural transformation thesis.

- The Aryan migration thesis. The Indus valley civilization, which speaks a Dravidian language, declines between 2000 and 1800 BCE. The Aryan migrations, or even invasions, occur from about 1500 BCE and the Aryans become the dominant cultural force. This has been the traditional, scholarly picture and is the one roughly sketched above.
- The cultural transformation thesis. Aryan culture is a development of the Indus valley culture whose language belongs to the Indo-European family, possibly spoken in the region as far back as the Neolithic Period, in interaction with Dravidian culture. On this view there were no Aryan incursions into India, but Indus valley culture is an early Aryan or vedic culture.

These positions are stated rather baldly here for the sake of clarity and there may be variations of these.

THE MIGRATION THESIS AND THE ARYAN MYTH

Although there is an undisputed connection between Sanskrit and other Indo-European languages, the picture may be much more complex than the Aryan migration thesis allows. Indeed, the history which has been portrayed of the Aryans in India may reflect to a large extent the European social world in which the theory developed. According to Poliakov, the idea of invading Indo-Aryans developed in the eighteenth century when western scholars were wishing to be free from the confines of Judeo-Christian thought while at the same time becoming aware of Indian culture through colonization.[14] The idea of an Aryan invasion developed with interest in Sanskrit, linguistics and vedic studies and, according to Shaffer, was perpetuated by Indian historians after independence in order to demonstrate the equality of ancient India with Europe.[15]

Laying aside, for the moment, the question concerning the truth or falsity of Aryan migrations into north India, this history, which Poliakov has called the 'Aryan Myth', has constructed Hinduism in a certain way. The Aryans, representing a world-ordering rationality, a 'higher' religion, are contrasted with the irrationality of the Dravidians, the pre-Aryan original inhabitants of India. According to this line of thinking, the Dravidian culture increasingly makes incursions into 'Hinduism' after the vedic period. Inden has shown how the history of Hinduism has been seen by 'the founders of Indological discourse' as an initial phase of pure, intellectual vedic religion, followed by the classical phase which reacted with devotionalism against the 'higher' religion of the earlier period, followed by a third religion of an animistic folk level, 'the religion of the Dravidian or pre-Aryan race'.[16]

Essentially, the argument goes, the intellectual, nature-religion of the Aryans – a religion with Greek and Scandinavian equivalents – became corrupted by the emotional devotionalism of the Dravidians. In other words, western reconstructions of Indian history, particularly the early period of its formation, have been governed by deeper cultural interests. This picture has recently been questioned.

THE CULTURAL TRANSFORMATION THESIS

If there were Aryan migrations, let alone an invasion, into India after the decline of the Indus valley culture, then this would hopefully be corroborated by archaeological evidence. The most convincing evidence to date for the Aryan incursions has been a kind of pottery, painted grey ware, found in the Ganges–Yamuna region, supposedly occupied by the Aryans. Carbon 14 dating places this painted grey ware between 1100 and 300 BCE, precisely the dates of the postulated Aryan migrations. Some of the sites where this pottery has been found, such as Hastinapur, have been associated with the later Sanskrit epic poem the *Mahābhārata*, thereby further establishing the connection between the Indo-Aryans and the painted grey ware.[17]

However, continuities have been found between the painted grey ware and indigenous protohistoric cultures of the region, thereby suggesting a continuity of culture rather than a disjunction as would be implied by

Aryan incursions. Furthermore, Shaffer has argued that iron technology developed within the Indian subcontinent itself,[18] rather than being introduced by an external source such as the Aryan invaders. According to Shaffer, modern archaeological evidence does not support the idea of Aryan migrations into India. Rather, in Shaffer's words, 'it is possible to document archaeologically a series of cultural changes reflecting indigenous cultural development from prehistoric to historic periods'.[19] The idea of Aryan incursions based on the linguistic evidence of the connections between Sanskrit and European languages has been read back into the archaeological record which, upon re-evaluation, is not supportive of that theory. It should be noted here, however, that Parpola thinks that the pattern of distribution of painted grey ware corresponds to the distribution of vedic, Aryan culture.[20]

Even if the Shaffer line of argument is correct – that the painted grey ware is incompatible with Aryan incursions – there is still the linguistic evidence to be considered. On the one hand archaeological evidence supports the idea of a continuity of culture from the earliest times in north India, and, according to some, does not support the Aryan migration thesis. Yet, on the other, the strong links established between Sanskrit and Indo-European languages and between vedic religion and the religions of other Indo-European groups is undeniable.

One argument which brings these ideas together is that the language of the Indus valley does not belong to the Dravidian language family, but, as Colin Renfrew and others suggest, to the Indo-European. This hypothesis 'would carry the history of the Indo-European languages in north India and Iran back to the early Neolithic Period in those areas'.[21] There would then be continuity at all levels from the Indus valley through to the Aryan culture of the first millennium BCE. According to this view, Indus valley religion develops into the religion of the Hindus. Indus valley language develops into vedic Sanskrit and Indus valley agriculture develops into the vedic agrarian lifestyle.

THE ARYAN MIGRATIONS RECONSIDERED

Both the Aryan migration thesis and the cultural transformation thesis have bodies of supporting evidence. Arguably, however, the meticulous, thorough work of Asko Parpola establishes strong evidence for the Indus valley script belonging to the Dravidian language group. His evidence is based on an analysis of language from a wide-ranging cultural sphere, from Anatolia to the Deccan; on iconographic continuities between Indus valley and Dravidian forms of Hinduism, and on discontinuities between vedic or Aryan forms and those of the Indus valley. The Aryan sacred text, the *Ṛg Veda* speaks of the Aryans subduing cities of the Dāsas, which it describes as comprising circular, multiple concentric walls. While this seems not to refer to the cities of the Indus valley, which are square, it does, Parpola argues, correspond to the hundreds of fortified Bronze Age villages in Bactria. The Dāsas, the enemies of the Aryans, are not the inhabitants of the Indus valley, but other groups who spoke an Aryan language, and whose migration preceded those of the Aryans.

One piece of evidence that the Indus valley people could not have been Indo-European speakers, suggests Parpola, is the absence of the horse and the chariot. Wherever Indo-Aryan cultures have been identified, horse remains have been found as well as chariots. The Aryan tribes who entered the north-west of India, argues Parpola, drove in two-wheeled war-chariots drawn by horses, terms which have Indo-European etymology. Nowhere in the Indus valley culture have the remains of horses been found, and nowhere depicted on the seals.[22] The horse is an Aryan animal and the chariot an example of a superior war technology.

A modified Aryan migration theory is therefore supported by Parpola's work. At the beginning of the second millennium BCE, Aryan nomads entered the Indian subcontinent. They were, of course, a minority, and, while the Indus valley culture continues without a break, as the archaeological record shows, the Aryan culture lived and developed alongside it and absorbed elements of it. However, there is little doubt that there are continuities between the Indus valley and vedic cultures. The new groups, who possessed *ārya*, 'nobility', formed a dominating elite speaking the Aryan language, though Sanskrit has absorbed proto-Dravidian features, such as the retroflex sound which does not exist in other Indo-European languages, as well as agricultural terms. Dravidian languages, as one would expect, have also absorbed elements of Sanskrit.[23] Over a number of centuries bilingualism would have developed until the majority of the population adopted the Aryan language, a form of vedic Sanskrit, as Modern French developed from vulgar Latin.[24]

The idea of bilingualism is perhaps problematic – there would need to be strong social pressures to adopt a new language – but Parpola's arguments are well supported. The vital evidence must come from the Indus valley script, and only when that is successfully deciphered can the question of the relation between Aryan and Indus valley culture be adequately addressed. Yet, wherever the Aryans originated, whether their culture was a development of indigenous cultures or whether they migrated from elsewhere, our knowledge of their social structure, their mythologies and, above all, their ritual comes from their self-representation in their Sanskrit texts, the Veda.

The Veda

The Veda is regarded by some Hindus as a timeless revelation which is not of human authorship (*apauruṣya*), is eternal, and contains all knowledge, while others regard it to be the revelation of God. It was received or 'seen' by the ancient seers (*ṛṣi*) who communicated it to other men and was put together in its present form by the sage Vyāsa. Indeed, a popular definition of a Hindu is somebody who accepts the Veda as revelation. This idea is not without problems and exceptions, but indicates the undoubted importance of the Veda in Hindu self-perception and self-representation.

From the perspective of the believer the Veda is timeless revelation, yet from the text-critical perspective of the western-trained scholar, it was compiled over a long period of time and reflects different periods of social and religious development. The two perspectives are not, of course, incompatible: revelation could be gradual and there have been, and are, many scholars who have also been believers.

The term 'text' or 'canon' in the Indian context implies an oral tradition passed down with meticulous care and accuracy through the generations from, according to tradition, the vedic Aryan seers of *ṛṣis*. The priestly class of the vedic Aryans, the Brahmans, were – and continue to be – the preservers of this tradition, who preserve the oral recitation of the texts. Indeed the Veda was not written down until some thousand years after its composition and the very act of writing was itself regarded as a polluting activity.[25] Although the main body of the Veda is clearly delineated, the category of 'revelation' sometimes incorporates more recent material. For example, texts calling themselves 'Upaniṣad' were composed into the seventeenth century CE and even the writings of modern holy men and women might be regarded as revelation. It is this Sanskrit, vedic tradition which has maintained a continuity into modern times and which has provided the most important resource and inspiration for Hindu traditions and individuals. The Veda is the foundation for most later developments in what is known as Hinduism.

The Veda is intimately connected with vedic ritual and its primary function is a ritual one. The categorization of the Veda is not only the way in which Hinduism has organized its scriptures, but is also connected with ritual. One of the primary vedic distinctions for its own literature is between *mantra*, verses used in liturgy which make up the collection of texts called Saṃhitā, and *brāhmaṇa*, texts of ritual exegesis. The Brāhmaṇas are texts describing rules for ritual and explanations about it concerning its meaning and purpose. They contain aeteological myths, posit elaborate correspondences (*bandhu*) between the rite and the cosmos, and even maintain that the sacrifice ensures the continuity of the cosmos. The Āraṇyakas, texts composed in the forest, form the concluding parts of several Brāhmaṇas. They are concerned with ritual and its interpretation and form a transitional link between the Brāhmaṇas and the Upaniṣads. The Upaniṣads develop the concerns of the Āraṇyakas, explaining the true nature and meaning of ritual.

THE STRUCTURE OF THE VEDA

The term *veda* is used in two senses. It is a synonym for 'revelation' (*śruti*), which is 'heard' by the sages, and so can denote the whole body of revealed texts, and is also used in a restricted sense to refer to the earliest layers of vedic literature. The Veda in the former, general sense comprises four traditions, the Ṛg, Yajur, Sāma and Atharva, which are divided into three or four categories of texts: the Saṃhitās, Brāhmaṇas, Āraṇyakas and Upaniṣads (these last two are sometimes classified together). In the latter, more restricted sense, the term *veda* refers to the Saṃhitā portion of this literature; itself comprising four groups of text identified by the four traditions, the *Ṛg Veda Saṃhitā*, *Sāma Veda Saṃhitā*, *Yajur Veda Saṃhitā* and the *Atharva Veda Saṃhitā*. Each of these would have its own Brāhmaṇa, Āraṇyaka ('forest treatise') and/or Upaniṣad ('Secret Scripture'). A further group, the *sūtra* literature is sometimes added to this scheme, but this group is not part of the primary revelation (*śruti*) but part of secondary revelation (*smṛti*), the texts composed by human beings. This sequence is roughly in chronological order, the earliest text being the *Ṛg Veda Saṃhitā*, the latest being the Upaniṣads. As we shall see, this pattern reflects an interest in ritual which becomes overlaid with an interest in the understanding and interpretation of ritual, an important move in the development of Hindu ideas. The structure is therefore as follows:

Saṃhitā:	Ṛg	Yajur	Sāma	Atharva
Brāhmaṇa:				
Āraṇyaka:				
Upaniṣad:				

The *Ṛg Veda* is a collection (*saṃhitā*) in ten books (*maṇḍala*) of 1028 hymns to various deities, composed in vedic Sanskrit from as early as 1200 BCE over a period of several hundred years.[26] Each of its ten books was composed by sages of different families, the oldest being books two to seven. These texts are our earliest and most important sources of knowledge about vedic religion and society. The *Sāma Veda* is a book of songs (*sāman*) based on the *Ṛg Veda* with instructions on their recitation (*gaṇa*). The *Yajur Veda* is a collection of short prose formulae used in ritual, of which there are two recensions, the 'black' and the 'white' – the former being a mixture of prose and verses, the latter being composed entirely of verses or *mantras*. The white Yajur Veda contains one book, the *Vājasaneyi-Saṃhitā*, the black Yajur Veda comprises three books, the *Taittirīya Saṃhitā*, the *Maitrāyanī Saṃhitā* and the *Kāṭhaka-Saṃhitā*. Lastly the *Atharva Veda* is a collection of hymns and magical formulae compiled around 900 BCE, though some of its material may go back to the time of the *Ṛg Veda*. The *Atharva Veda* has less connection with sacrifice and has been considered somewhat inferior to the other three Saṃhitās. Most of this truly vast literature has yet to be translated into any modern European language.

THE DATING OF THE VEDA

Although difficult to date, the earliest text and the most important for our understanding of the early Indo-Aryans is the *Ṛg Veda Saṃhitā* composed probably around 1200 BCE, though some, such as Kak and Frawley, would date it very much earlier to the Indus valley culture, assuming that the Indus valley language was Indo-European.[27] The more sober chronology proposed by Max Müller suggests a date of 1500 to 1200 BCE. Assuming the birth of the Buddha to be around 500 BCE (which scholars now think is later), Müller suggested that the Upaniṣads were composed from 800 to 600 BCE. However, this dating may be rather early. Given the re-dating of the Buddha to the fourth or fifth rather than the fifth or sixth centuries BCE, the Upaniṣads were probably composed between 600 and 300 BCE, as some texts are post-Buddhist. The earlier Brāhmana literature

Saṃhitā	Brāhmaṇa	Āraṇyaka	Upaniṣad	Śrauta-Sūtra	Gṛhya-Sūtra
Ṛg	Aitareya	Aitareya	Aitareya	Āśvalāyana	Āśvalāyana
	Kauṣītaki	Kauṣītaki	Kauṣītaki	Śāṅkhāyana	Śāṅkhāyana
Taittirīya	Taittirīya	Taittirīya	Taittirīya	Baudhāyana	Baudhāyana
				Bharadvāja	Bharadvāja
				Āpastamba	Āpastamba
				Hiranyakeśin	Hiranyakeśin
Kāṭhaka	Kaṭha	Kaṭha	Kaṭha	Kāṭhaka	Kāṭhaka
Maitrāyaṇī			Maitrī	Mānava	Mānava
Vājasaneyi	Śathapatha	Śathapatha	Bṛhadāraṇyaka	Kātyāyana	Pāraskara

Figure 2 The traditions of the *Ṛg* and Yajur Vedas

Müller dates between 1000 to 800 and the Saṃhitā literature around 1200 to 1000, allowing about 200 years for the formulation of each class of texts, though even Müller admits that the *Ṛg Veda* could be earlier.[28] The Brāhmaṇa literature, however, may be later than the dates proposed by Müller, given the probable later date of the Upaniṣads.

THE VEDIC SCHOOLS

The classification scheme of the Veda is further complicated by theological schools or branches (*śākhā*) which specialized in learning certain texts. A Veda might have a number of theological schools associated with it. For example, Brahmans of the Taittirīya branch would learn the *Taittirīya Saṃhitā* of the black Yajur Veda, its Brāhmaṇa, Āraṇyaka, Upaniṣad and Śrauta Sūtras. The school of the *Sāma Veda* would learn its Brāhmaṇa, the *Jaiminīya Brāhmaṇa*, and the *Lāṭyāyana Śrauta Sūtra*. The Brahmans of the *Ṛg Veda* would learn the *Aitareya* and *Kauṣītakī Brāhmaṇas*, which include the Āraṇyakas of the same name, the *Aitareya* and *Kauṣītakī Upaniṣads* and the *Āśvalāyana* and *Śāṅkhāyana Śrauta Sūtras*, and so on (see fig. 2). These schools ensured the accurate transmission of the Veda through the generations with the help of rules for recitation, even though the meaning of the early texts may have been lost to most reciters as the language moved away from its vedic origins. An example of this structure can be seen in fig. 2 which shows the branches of the *Ṛg* and Yajur Vedas.

Perhaps the most remarkable thing about vedic literature is that it has been orally transmitted with little change to its contents for up to 3,000 years. This accuracy has been enabled by a system of double checking. The texts were learned at least twice: as a continuous recitation, called the *saṃhitāpāṭha*, in which the Sanskrit rules for combining words (*sandhi*) operated, and as the recitation of words without the rules of euphonic combination, called the *padapāṭha*. Frits Staal gives an illustrative example from the vedic Saṃhitās, the verse 'the immortal goddess has pervaded the wide space, the depths and the heights' is remembered in two versions, as the continuous flow of the *saṃhitāpāṭha* ('orv apra amartya nivato devy udvataḥ') and word for word in the *padapāṭha* ('a/ uru/ apraḥ/ amartya/ nivataḥ/ devi/ udvataḥ//').[29]

However, not only has the Veda been preserved through oral traditions of recitation, but also through the transmission of ritual. The Veda is primarily a liturgical text and its use in ritual has been its primary and invariant function. Interpretations of the ritual enter Hinduism at a later date with the Upaniṣads.

The Upaniṣads

The Upaniṣads are a development of the Āraṇyakas and there is no clear break between the two genres. The *Aitareya Āraṇyaka*, attached to the *Ṛg Veda*, calls itself an *upaniṣad*,[30] and one of the earliest, if not the earliest, of the Upaniṣads, the *Bṛhadāraṇyaka* ('Great Forest') of the white *Yajur Veda*, calls itself an *āraṇyaka* (as does the last book of the *Śatapatha Brāhmaṇa* belonging to the same *śākhā*). The oldest Upaniṣads (the *Bṛhadāraṇyaka*, *Chāndogya* and *Taittirīya*) are in prose, while the later Upaniṣads, moving away from the Āraṇyakas, are in verse.

The Upaniṣads are not a homogeneous group of texts. Even the older texts were composed over a wide expanse of time from about 600 to 300 BCE, given that some early texts are post-Buddhist, and texts with the title *upaniṣad* continue to be composed throughout the middle ages into the modern period. Because of this some scholars have begun to re-evaluate the category of 'revelation' (*śruti*), which, Thomas Coburn argues, must be seen as an 'ongoing and experientially based feature of the Hindu religious tradition'.[31] Yet it is nevertheless the case that the older group of Upaniṣads, rather than later ones, have been taken to be authoritative and been commented upon by Hindu theologians.[32]

Vedic ritual

The central religious practice of the vedic Aryans was sacrifice and sharing of the sacrificial meal with each other and with the many supernatural beings or *devas*. In sacrifice the gods could be propitiated, material benefits such as sons or cattle received from them, and the social standing, power, or purity of the sacrificer (*yajamāna*), the person who had instigated it, enhanced. Such religious practice would not require elaborate buildings or icons, but merely the presence of the qualified priests who knew the necessary procedures and recitations. Jamison has observed that vedic religion is 'the ideally portable religion' with no fixed places of worship and no images or sacred texts to be carried around,[33] perhaps suggestive of a nomadic lifestyle. The term 'sacrifice' (*homa*, *yajña*) is not confined to the immolation of animals, but refers more widely to any offering into the sacred fire, notably of milk, clarified butter or ghee, curds, grains such as rice and barley, and the *soma* plant, as well as domestic animals (goats, cattle, sheep and horses). Indeed the offering of milk into the fire was more common than animal offerings. These ritual substances would be transported through the fire to the *deva* or *devas* which had been invoked. Fire is the central focus of vedic ritual and is both a substance or element and a *deva*: the transformative link between the worldly and divine realms.

THE SOLEMN AND DOMESTIC RITES

Two kinds of ritual were developed, the *śrauta* or solemn, public rites and the *gṛhya*, domestic and life-cycle rites. The *śrauta* rites are the older and the two types can be formally distinguished from each other by the number of fires used. The *śrauta* rites required the burning of three sacred fires, while the domestic observances required only one. The principal deities which were the focus of the *ṣrauta* observances were the fire god Agni and the plant god Soma, to whom milk, clarified butter, curds, vegetable cakes, animals or the stalks of the *soma* plant itself would be offered into the fire. Vedic religion was closely associated with the rhythms of the day and the seasons and *śrauta* rites would involve offerings at various junctures (*parvan*) between night and day, at the new and full moons and at the junctures of the three seasons (rainy, autumn, hot).

Our information concerning the *śrauta* rituals comes mainly from the Śrauta Sūtras associated with the various branches of vedic knowledge and formulated between the eighth and fourth centuries BCE. Although this is about half a millennium after the composition of the *Ṛg Veda*, we can assume that some form of the *śrauta* rites was already established at that early period. The *Ṛg Veda* refers to the various, numerous kinds of priests involved in the rituals, refers extensively to *soma* and its preparation, and describes the horse sacrifice (*aśvamedha*).[34] There was also a human sacrifice (*puruṣamedha*) modelled on the horse sacrifice, though the human victims were set free after their consecration.[35]

Among some Brahmans, notably some Nambudri families in Kerala studied by Frits Staal, the *śrauta* rituals have remained intact to the present day, since at least the time of the Śrauta Sūtras.[36] The pre Ṛg-vedic origin of ritual is, of course, inaccessible, unless it lies in the fragmentary suggestions of the Indus valley.

This continuity of ritual traditions in south Asia needs to be stressed. On the whole they have, surprisingly, survived even radical political changes and a variety of different interpretations. This ritual continuity, which may be linked to a continuity of social relations, is the most important factor in linking modern forms with ancient traditions, though admittedly the elaborate *śrauta* rites are only performed among a minority of Brahmans in Kerala.

Although the central act of all vedic ritual, both solemn and domestic, is simple – the offering of substances into the fire – the preparatory and closing rites can be very complex due to the embedding of one type of ritual and its accompanying verses into another. In the *śrauta* rites, the complexity is compounded by the need for a number of specialists. These specialists, and their assistants, were required for specific parts of the rituals and would know the appropriate recitations from the Veda. In the most elaborate rituals, such as the sacrifice of the *soma* plant, four priests would be present, each of whom would be a specialist in one of the four Saṃhitās, though only two priests would be necessary in most rites. The chief priest or *hotṛ* would recite verses from the *Ṛg Veda*, a second priest, the *udgatṛ*, would chant or sing songs (*stotra*) comprising verses set to the melodies of the *Sāma Veda*, and the *adhvaryu* priest would chant verses from the *Yajur Veda* and perform many of the necessary ritual actions. In later times all this would be overseen by a priest associated with the *Atharva Veda*, the *brahman*, whose function was to watch out for omissions or incorrect procedures. There were originally only three priests associated with the first three Saṃhitās, for the Brahman as overseer of the rites does not appear in the *Ṛg Veda* and is only incorporated later, thereby showing the acceptance of the *Atharva Veda*, which had been somewhat distinct from the other Saṃhitās and identified with lower social strata, as being of equal standing with the other texts.

Śrauta rites would minimally involve the establishing of the three fires: the householder's fire (*gārhapatya*) in the west, the fire to be offered into (*āhavaniya*) to the east and a third southern fire (*dakṣiṇāgni*). The altar or *vedi*, which was a shallow pit, narrow in the centre and strewn with grass, or, for specific rites, a more elaborate brick structure, was placed between the eastern and western fires. The ritual implements needed for the sacrifice were placed there and the sacrificers and gods invited to sit there. For animal sacrifice a post (*yupa*) would be required, to which the victim was tied.

A number of śrauta rituals, ranging in complexity, are recorded in vedic texts. The *agniṣṭoma* was a fairly simple one-day *soma* sacrifice, though preceded by various preparations, and the *agnicayana*, the 'piling up of

Agni', a complex proceeding lasting several days. The *agnicayana* rite as a living tradition among Nambudri Brahmans in Kerala, has been clearly documented and analyzed by Staal.[37] This rite involved the building of an altar from over 2,000 bricks, in the shape of a large bird, to the west of the standard ritual enclosure of three fires. Near to this altar are two areas for chanting the texts and for preparing *soma*. This altar is built in five layers with the appropriate recitation of mantras. Over a period of twelve days a number of ritual sequences are performed, which involve singing verses (*stotra*) from the *Sāma Veda*, reciting from the *Ṛg Veda*, offering *soma* to the deities and the drinking of *soma* by the sacrificer and some priests. The sacrificer or patron (*yajamāna*), who has paid a fee of cattle or money for the rites, reaps the benefits, though throughout the proceedings he remains fairly passive. Before the ritual the *yajamāna*, accompanied by his wife, undergoes an initiation (*dīkṣā*), which might involve some degree of asceticism (*tapas*) such as fasting, to achieve purification.

SOMA

The *soma* drink, requiring an elaborate preparation during the Soma sacrifice, was probably originally a hallucinogenic or intoxicating substance prepared from the *soma* plant. It was almost certainly not a fermented drink which the vedic Aryans also possessed and called *sūrā*. This 'plant', Gordon Wasson has argued, may have been the fly agaric mushroom (*Amanita muscaria*) whose use in inducing mystical states of consciousness is attested in Shamanism.[38] Alternatively many scholars now think that it was *ephedra*, the 'sea grape'; a jointed but leafless desert plant. Traces of this plant have been found in jars from sites in Iran, where *soma* was called *haoma*.[39] *Ephedra* is a stimulant rather than a hallucinogen, but if *soma* was *ephedra*, then this circumvents the problem of the fly agaric mushroom not growing in northern India.

Whatever its identity, the important point is that *soma* induced exalted states and possibly visions in its takers.[40] The original *soma* was eventually lost by the vedic Aryans and replaced by *soma* substitutes; plants without intoxicating properties. We can see in the vedic material that ritual was the primary religious concern of the Indo-Aryans, but also that mystical experience induced by the *soma* plant was, at an early date in the development of the tradition, important. These two concerns, ritual and mysticism, are found throughout the later traditions of India.

The *soma* sacrifice was embedded within other rituals as well, most notably within animal sacrifices, the most important of which was the horse sacrifice (*aśvamedha*), and the consecration of a king (*rājasūya*). The horse sacrifice[41] described in the *Ṛg Veda* and in the Brāhmaṇas[42] could only be carried out by a king. The sacrifice involved allowing a stallion to wander free for a year before it was ritually suffocated. Before the horse was dismembered and the various parts of its body offered to different deities, the king's wife would symbolically copulate with the dead stallion: divine power from the horse – who is also identified with the deity Prajāpati – entering the queen and thereby entering the king and the people.[43]

The meaning and functions of ritual in Indo-Aryan culture cannot be reduced to any one factor. Sacrifice could have had a cathartic function, expressing a society's aggression in a controlled and socially acceptable way, as Girard has argued.[44] Whether or not the sacrifice had a cathartic effect, it certainly functioned to establish the patron's status and power within the community and may, in a Durkheimian sense, have served to reinforce social values and legitimate power relations within a society, not only in allowing only higher classes of society to perform the rituals, but also in excluding others. The ritual was important not only for those it included, but for those it excluded as well, drawing a line between higher and lower social groupings.[45]

Vedic mythology and theology

The vedic universe is populated with benevolent and malevolent supernatural beings of various kinds. In one sense every tree and river has a divine being associated with it, yet undoubtedly some deities are more important than others. In the *Bṛhadāraṇyaka Upaniṣad*[46] the sage Yājñavalkya is asked how many gods there are, and he gives an ambiguous reply. Firstly he says there are 303, then that there are 3,003, when pressed further that there are 33, 6, 3, 2, 1½, and finally 1. In the next verse he settles on 33. Although this must be seen in the light of the later monistic philosophy of the Upaniṣads – that all deities are manifestations of a single power – the text is certainly echoing the early vedic identification of the various gods with each other; the Moon is identified with Soma, Soma is identified with Agni, Agni with the Sun and so on.

THE *DEVAS*

The *Ṛg Veda* is filled with hymns of praise to the various deities (*deva*) invoked in ritual. There are, however, few straight narrative accounts of the gods, either in the *Ṛg Veda* or in the Brāhmaṇas, and the texts assume a common knowledge of their stories. The great nineteenth-century Sanskritist, Max Müller, thought that all the deities of the Veda were 'the agents postulated behind the great phenomena of nature', such as fire, water, rain, the sun and storms etc.[47] While it is certainly true that many deities of the Veda are related to natural phenomena, some gods do not fit into this model and vedic scholarship no longer accepts this as an explanation of the pantheon. The gods also have human qualities. The majority of deities are male, though there are a few goddesses (*devī*) such as Aditi, the mother of the universe, Uṣas, the dawn, Nirṛti, destruction, and Vāc, speech. They can be addressed in hymns, they share in human emotions, they have desire, they can be invited to the sacrifice and can share in the ritual meal.

Indeed in the later texts, the Brāhmaṇas, their connection with the sacrifice is what distinguishes them from other supernatural beings such as the 'demons' or 'anti-gods', the *asuras*. According to the *Śatapatha Brāhmaṇa*[48] both the *devas* and the *asuras* are said to have been born from Prajāpati, the 'lord of creatures', a deity who becomes the creator god. The *asuras* made sacrificial offerings to themselves, whereas the *devas* made offerings to each other. Because of this, Prajāpati gave himself to the latter as their nourishment and so the *devas* accept ritual offerings, whereas the *asuras* do not. The *devas* are beings intimately connected with, and, indeed, defined by, the sacrifice as the class of supernatural beings who accept offerings and, in return, give help or, in the case of more wrathful deities such as Rudra, simply stay away from the human world. It is possible that the *devas* represent the original deities of the Aryans and the *asuras* the deities of their enemies the Dāsas.

The *devas* inhabit a hierarchical cosmos. In one scheme, encapsulated in the three utterances pronounced each day by orthodox Brahmans, this cosmos is divided into the three worlds of sky or heaven (*svar*), atmosphere (*bhuvas*), and earth (*bhūr*), each realm populated by different deities. The three realms and the principal deities they contain are:

- heaven (*svar*), contains the sky god Dyaus; the lord of righteousness (*ṛta*) and of night, Varuṇa; the companion of Varuṇa and god of night, Mitra; the nourisher Pūṣan; and the pervader Viṣṇu.
- atmosphere (*bhuvas*) contains the warrior Indra; the wind Vāyu; the storm gods, the Maruts; and the terrible Rudra.
- earth (*bhūr*) contains the plant god Soma; the fire Agni; and the priestly god of creative power, Bṛhaspati.

Another classification places a group of gods called Ādityas, the sons of the Goddess Aditi (namely Mitra, Aryaman, Bhaga, Varuṇa, Dakṣa, and Aṃśa), within the category of heaven; the Maruts or Rudras, the sons of Rudra, within the atmosphere; and the Vasus, the attendants of Indra, personifications of natural phenomena, namely Āpa (water), Dhruva (the pole star), Soma (the moon), Dhara (the earth), Anila (wind), Anala (fire), Prabhāsa (dawn), and Pratyūṣa (light), at the level of the earth.

There is no supreme deity in the *Ṛg Veda*, though some are undoubtedly more important than others. The two most significant *devas*, placed at the level of the earth, are Agni and Soma. Agni mysteriously pervades the world as heat and is identified with the earth as the sacred cow Pṛśni, with the sun, with the dawn and with fire hidden in its stomach.[49] While being simply fire, Agni is particularly the sacrificial fire. He transports the dead to the realm of Yama, the lord of death, and transports, and purifies, all offerings to the realm of the gods. The mythology of Agni plays on the idea of fire being hidden within the world and awakened by the fuel-sticks which kindle him.

Like Agni, Soma is a deity who intercedes between men and gods and is regarded as a link between the human and divine, the pillar of the sky and bringer of ecstasy and understanding of the divine realms.[50] Indeed Soma is identified with Agni and with the moon which contains the ambrosia of immortality (*amṛta*) and there are parallels between the mythology of Soma and that of Agni. Agni, hiding within the waters from where he was originally born, is discovered by the gods and agrees to convey the sacrifice to them.[51] Similarly Soma, like Agni, was hidden from the gods upon a mountain and captured by Indra riding an eagle.[52] There are parallels here with the Greek myth of Prometheus and both Agni and Soma can be seen as bringers of culture, as things which distinguish the human world from the natural world.

Other deities in the *Ṛg Veda* are important, though none have such transforming power in the world as Agni and Soma. Indra is the warrior king, empowered by *soma*, who destroys obstacles with his thunderbolt club. His most famous myth is the destruction of the snake Vṛtra (whose name means 'obstacle'), symbolizing cosmic chaos, thus freeing the waters of the sky.[53] The storm gods, the Maruts, accompany Indra on his adventures which seem to reflect the warrior ethos of vedic society: Indra captures the cows as the Aryan warriors would have gone on cattle raids to neighbouring groups.

Although Indra stands out in clear profile, many of the gods in the Veda are opaque. The Ādityas, the sons of the goddess Aditi, include Varuṇa, the distant, majestic sky god who protects the cosmic and social order (*ṛta*); Mitra, the god of social responsibilities or contracts, who accompanies Varuṇa; Aryaman, the god of custom such as marriage, and, though very inferior to these other three, Pūṣan, presider over journeys.[54] Of these, Varuṇa, the lord of the ethical order, is the most important, and is asked for forgiveness and mercy for any moral transgression or for 'going against the current'.[55]

The young Aśvin twins are deities of good fortune and health. Apart from these, the elements and natural phenomena are deified, such as the sun (Sūrya), the sun at dawn and sunset (Savitṛ), the wind (Vāyu), the waters (Apas), the goddess earth (Pṛthivī) and her consort, father sky (Dyaus Pitar). There are other deities in the pantheon such as Viṣṇu and Rudra (i.e. Śiva) who become the central focuses of later traditions.

EARLY THEOLOGY

In the vedic worldview ritual has supreme importance and the vedic Saṃhitās primarily serve as liturgical texts. Although their use is primarily liturgical, the contents of the vedic songs or hymns reflect and presuppose narrative traditions about the gods, and the origins of the world and of human society. There are also philosophical speculations concerning the origins of life. The most famous of these hymns[56] asks unanswerable questions about what existed at the beginning of time when there was neither existence (*sat*) nor non-existence (*asat*), neither death nor immortality, neither light nor dark. The final verse conveys the hymn's sense of cosmic mystery and we can read into it both the beginnings of a theistic tradition and also the beginnings of Indian scepticism. It reads: 'Whence this creation has arisen – perhaps it formed itself, or perhaps it did not – the one who looks down on it, in the highest heaven, only he knows – or perhaps he does not know.'[57]

However, it is with the Brāhmaṇas, later developed in the Upaniṣads, that more systematic speculation begins, particularly on the nature of sacrifice. The Brāhmaṇas are a discourse by the Brahmans on the *śrauta* rituals, which attempt to explain ritual action and relate it to wider cosmic and mythological phenomena; one Indian commentator on the *Taittirīya Saṃhitā* clearly and succinctly defined a Brāhmaṇa as 'an explanation of a ritual act and of the *mantras* belonging to it'.[58] The sociologist Emile

Durkheim once wrote that 'the moment when men have an idea that there are internal connections between things, science and philosophy become possible'.[59] One of the Brāhmaṇas' central concerns was the establishing of such hidden or inner connections (*bandhu*, *nidāna*) between the *śrauta* rituals and their purposes, and between ritual and mythology. For example, the *Śatapatha Brāhmaṇa* clarifies the connection between the upper and lower fire-sticks used to kindle the sacred fires and the divine beings Urvaśī and her husband Purūravas, whose names are invoked during the fire-kindling ceremony. The redactor of the text is aware of the sexual symbolism of the fire sticks and identifies the ghee in the ghee pan, touched by the *adjvaryu* priest, with Āyu, the child of the divine couple, which is placed on the lower (female) fire stick. Ghee is also identified with semen (*retas*), and *retas* in turn is identified with an embryo and also with rain.[60] These kinds of identifications and analogies are found throughout the texts and express a cosmology in which the hierarchical structure of the wider cosmos is recapitulated in the structure of society, in the individual's body and in the ritual. The ritual is a microcosm reflecting the wider macrocosm of the cosmos and the mesocosm of society.

COSMICAL HOMOLOGY

Identification, or 'cosmical homology', as the historian of religions Mircea Eliade has called it,[61] along with hierarchy, might be said to be a principle of Indian religion. It is present in the vedic tradition from the *Ṛg Veda* and is found in all later Indian traditions, including Buddhism and Jainism. One of the fundamental vedic identifications or homologies, which becomes central in later esoteric traditions, is between the body, the universe and the sacrifice. A key text here, occurring late in the *Ṛg Veda*, which is quoted and reiterated throughout the Hindu tradition, is the famous hymn of the cosmic man, the *Puruṣa Sūkta*.[62] This hymn occurs in a late book of the *Ṛg Veda* and probably does not accurately reflect vedic society in the earlier period which may have had less clearly delineated boundaries between social groups.

This hymn describes the creation of the world by the gods, who sacrifice and dismember a cosmic giant, the 'male person' (*puruṣa*), from the different parts of whose body the cosmos and society are formed and even the verses, songs and formulae of the Veda itself. The highest sacerdotal class, the Brahmans, came from his mouth as society's voice; the warrior class (*rājanya*, or later *kṣatriya*), as society's strength, came from his arms;

the common people (*vaiśya*) came from his thighs as society's support, and the serfs (*śūdra*), those on whom society stands, came from his feet.[63] In many ways this is an idealized picture; the Brahmans as the priests sustaining the community with spiritual sustenance, that is, performing vedic ritual; the rulers or warriors protecting and ruling the community; the common folk practising, primarily, animal husbandry and agriculture; and the serfs serving the other classes. Yet this important hymn shows that the hierarchical, hereditary social groups were part of the structure of the cosmos. If the cosmos was in some sense sacred, then so was society which manifested its hierarchical order. Moreover, this order is reflected in sacrifice and in the hierarchical structure of the body. The scale of this order was the degree of purity or pollution associated with the body: the head, as the highest part of the body, was the purest and the feet, the lowest part, the most polluted. The social and individual bodies were reflections of each other, and both were part of the larger structure or body of the cosmos. This integration of society and cosmos, of body and society, is the sacred order or law (*ṛta*) of the universe, which is eternal and unchanging, brought to life in vedic ritual, expressed in the songs of the vedic seers, and elucidated in the Brāhmaṇas.

Vedic society

Of the four classes (*varṇa*) of Aryan society, the highest three are known as the 'twice-born' (*dvija*) because their male members have undergone an initiation (*upanayana*), a rite of passage, which gives them access to being full members of society, who can marry and perpetuate the ritual traditions. This rite separates the twice-born from the fourth estate, the 'serfs' (*śūdra*), and clearly marks the boundary between those who have access to the vedic tradition and those who do not. Georges Dumézil, a scholar of Indo-European studies, has argued that Indo-European ideology is characterized by a social structure of three classes or functions: the function of the priest, the warrior or ruler and the farmer.[64] The sacerdotal class would serve the ruling, military aristocracy. This structure has been present throughout Indo-European communities.

In vedic India, Dumézil's three functions correspond to the twice-born classes of priests (*brāhmaṇa*), warriors or rulers (*kṣatriya*, *rājanya*) and commoners (*vaiśya*). The argument has been that upon entering the subcontinent the Aryans with their tripartite social structure placed the local population on the bottom, which is the serf class (*śūdra*) composed of non-Aryan Dravidians. However, the process of class formation in early Indian society is more complex and may go back to an indigenous structure in the ancient past, perhaps present in the Indus valley civilization. Indeed, the priestly and ruling classes of the Indus valley cities probably lived separately in or near the citadels of their towns.

Whatever the origins of the system, it must be remembered that the fourfold class structure is a theoretical model and ideological justification based on sacred revelation. The reality of social classes in vedic society seems to have been more complex. Rather than a priestly class serving a ruling aristocracy, at least at the time of the *Ṛg Veda*, there seems to have been two ruling elites, the Sūris and the Aris, each of which were served by their own priesthoods. Aguilar i Matas has argued that Ṛg-vedic religion was patronized by the Sūris and so the *Ṛg Veda* favours them at the expense of the Aris who have a negative reputation in the text. This is reflected at cultic and theological levels when Indra, the favourite god of the Sūris, triumphs over and becomes more important than Varuṇa, the supreme god of the Aris. Furthermore the two liturgical deities Agni and Soma, pass from the side of Varuṇa to Indra, thereby ensuring the Sūris' ritual power.[65]

Summary

We have seen how the origins of Hinduism lay in the ancient cultures of the Indus valley civilization and Aryan culture. Although the issue is contentious, there is strong supporting evidence to show that the language of the Indus valley civilization was Dravidian, which contrasts with the Indo-European language of the vedic Aryans. These two cultures, the Dravidian Indus valley culture and the Aryan vedic, contribute to the formation of Hindu traditions, and Hindu civilization can be seen as a product of the complex interaction between the Dravidian and Aryan cultural spheres. While the Aryan culture of the Brahmans provides the 'master narrative' for later traditions, the importance of the Dravidian cultural sphere should not be underestimated and Aryan culture itself, including the Sanskrit language, has absorbed Dravidian elements.

3 *Dharma*

During the late vedic period by the time of the composition of the *Śatapatha Brāhmaṇa* and the early Upaniṣads, Aryan culture had become established in the Ganges plain; we know that the *Śatapatha Brāhmaṇa* and *Bṛhadāraṇyaka Upaniṣad* were composed in the Videha region.[1] Larger kingdoms replaced smaller ones and a process of urbanization began. This was a formative period in the history of Indian religions, which saw the rise of the renouncer traditions, particularly Buddhism, and the establishing of brahmanical ideology. Between the Mauryan dynasty (*c.* 320–185 BCE) and the Gupta empire (320–500 CE), there was a politically unsettled period prompted by incursions from the north-west. The last Mauryan king, Bṛhadratha, was assassinated by his Brahman general Puśyamitra Śuṅga in 185 BCE. The Śuṅga dynasty (*c.* 185–73 BCE) lost much of its empire to Greek invaders from Bactria under King Demetrios who founded an extensive empire, the most important king of which was Menander (*c.* 166–150 BCE). After Menander's death the kingdom broke up to be eventually replaced by the Śāka empire, established by Sai-Wang tribes from central Asia (*c.* 140 BCE – 78 CE). With a slight decline in Śāka power, the Kuṣāṇas (Kuei-shang) invaded, and established an empire which extended along the Ganges plain to beyond Varanasi, culminating in the rule of Kaniśka (between 78 and 144 CE). Finally the Gupta empire was founded by Candragupta I (*c.* 320 CE) and spread across all of northern, and much of central, India.

Political support for religions varied with different dynasties and with different kings. Aśoka (268–233 BCE) was favourable to Buddhism, as was

Kaniśka (first century CE), though both kings seem to have been tolerant of other religions within their realms. Candragupta Maurya may have been a Jain. With the death of the last Mauryan, his assassin Puśyamitra favoured a return to vedic sacrificial religion and performed the horse sacrifice and seems to have performed a human sacrifice at the city of Kausambi, perhaps in celebration of a victory over the Greeks. Although official patronage of religions varied, brahmanical ideology grew in importance and established itself as the centre of a sociopolitical religion, intimately allied to the status of the king, an ideology central to the Guptas (320–600 CE) and to later dynasties. This brahmanical religion was concerned with the ritual status of the king, the maintaining of boundaries between social groups, and the regulation of individual behaviour in accordance with the overarching principle of *dharma*. With the rise of the kingdoms culminating with the Guptas, *dharma* becomes an ideal operating in the domestic realm of the high-caste householder and in the political realm of the Hindu state.

The brahmanical ideology of *dharma* was articulated by the vedic traditions or schools (*śākhā*) in texts concerned with the performance of vedic ritual and social ethics, and expressed in the domestic realm by the figure of the ideal Brahman and in the political realm by the figure of the ideal king. These two figures, the Brahman and the king, were intimately connected. It was the king who legitimized the Brahman's power through his patronage, yet it was the Brahmans who performed the ritual consecration of the king. The ideology of *dharma* was articulated at the level of the court, embodied in the figure of the king, and manifested in the social world in rules of interpersonal interaction and ritual injunction. In this chapter we shall examine the institutions of *dharma* as they are developed in the Dharma literature and as they became expressed in Hindu history.

The idea of *dharma*

The term '*dharma*' is untranslatable in that it has no direct semantic equivalents in any western languages which convey the resonance of associations expressed by the term. It has been variously translated as 'duty', 'religion', 'justice', 'law', 'ethics', 'religious merit', 'principle' and 'right'.[2] More particularly *dharma* is the performance of vedic ritual by the Brahmans. It is 'the ritualistic order of Vedic sacrifice',[3] which refers especially to the performance of the 'solemn' rites (*śrauta*) enjoined on all Brahmans, to the domestic rituals (*gṛhya*), and to obligations appropriate to one's family and social group. *Dharma* is an all-encompassing ideology which embraces both ritual and moral behaviour, whose neglect would have bad social and personal consequences. The philosopher of the Mīmāṃsā school (see p. 236), Jaimini, defines *dharma* as that of which the characteristic is an injunction (*vidhi*).[4] This means that *dharma* is an obligation, declared by the Veda, to perform ritual action (*karma*), which brings of itself no reward other than that its non-performance would be 'that which is not dharma' (*adharma*) and result in retribution or 'sin' (*pāpa*). The rituals, particularly the solemn rites, are for their own realization: it is ritual for ritual's sake, though it does create reward in heaven for the ritual patron. A Brahman can also perform supererogatory rituals for gaining wealth and happiness in this world and the next, but these are not obligatory. *Dharma* is identified with vedic obligation, which is eternal, and with action which is particular: the transcendent *dharma* is expressed or manifested at a human level in ritual action in order to produce that which is good.

The sources of *dharma*

While the source of *dharma* is ultimately the Veda, oral texts were formulated between the eighth and fourth centuries BCE, within the vedic traditions (*śākhā*), concerned with ritual and law. These texts, the Kalpa Sūtras, form part of a body of knowledge, the auxiliary sciences, known as the 'limbs of the Veda' (*vedāṅga*). The Vedāṅgas are:

śīkṣa, correct pronunciation of vedic texts;

kalpa, the correct performance of ritual;

vyākaraṇa, the study of grammar;

nirukta, etymology of vedic words;

chaṇḍas, prosody;

jyotiṣa, astrology.

The *Gautama Dharma Sūtra* says that the Veda is the source of *dharma* and also of the traditions which flow from it.[5] There are three sources of *dharma* according to the Dharma Sūtras: revelation (i.e. the Veda), tradition (*smṛti*), and the customs or 'good custom' of the virtuous or those learned in the Veda. The *Manu Smṛti* or *Mānava Dharma Śāstra* adds to these three 'what is pleasing to oneself' which might be rendered as 'conscience'.[6]

The Kalpa Sūtras, the second source of *dharma*, are categorized into three groups:

- the Śrauta Sūtras, texts dealing with the correct performance of the solemn or public rites;
- the Gṛhya Sūtras, dealing with domestic rites;
- the Dharma Sūtras, dealing with law and social ethics.

While the Veda is revelation, the Kalpa Sūtras are tradition or secondary revelation, 'remembered' texts (*smṛti*) composed by human sages within the various vedic schools, though regarded as inspired and extraordinary humans. Each sage is thought to have composed a text in all three classes, though in fact only three sages, Āpastamba, Hiranyakeśin and Baudhāyana, have Śrauta, Dharma, and Gṛhya Sūtras attributed to them. In all of these texts we see how *dharma* was seen very much in terms of ritual; to perform *dharma* correctly is to fulfil one's ritual obligations.

THE ŚRAUTA SŪTRAS

These texts, called *śrauta* because they follow from *śruti*, lay down the rules, in a highly technical form, for the performance of public, vedic ritual. The actual *śrauta* rites are primarily focused upon Agni and Soma to whom vegetarian and non-vegetarian offerings are made into three or five fires established upon altars. These public rituals are older and more complex than the simpler, domestic rites, and surprisingly have survived political upheavals and social changes throughout India's long history. During the Gupta period they underwent a revival and are preserved in present times among the Nambudri Brahmans of Kerala. The Śrauta Sūtras are ritual manuals which lay out the rules for the performance of *śrauta* rites. The earliest is by Baudhāyana (sixth century BCE or earlier) whose text is the first example of the sūtra style. A *sūtra*, literally 'thread', is a pithy aphorism which states a principle or rule. These rules are cumulative, the later rules assuming the earlier. Thus, in an injunction to make an oblation, an oblation made with ghee is understood.[7] The Śrauta Sūtras are technical manuals comprising rules and metarules for what Frits Staal has called a 'science of ritual'. This science of ritual has close parallels to the science of language which developed a little later, but which uses the same sūtra style. This science is furthermore distinct from the Brāhmaṇa literature which preceded it, in not speculating about the hidden meanings of ritual, but rather concentrating on the rules by which it should be performed. These texts, as Staal has shown, are also distinct from the later Mīmāṃsā philosophy which is concerned with arguing a viewpoint, particularly against the Buddhists.[8]

THE GṚHYA SŪTRAS

The Gṛhya Sūtras describe different kinds of ritual (*yajña*) to be performed in the home. These domestic rituals may have been permitted for all twice-born classes in the earlier vedic period, but came to be restricted to the Brahman class. A Brahman could perform them for himself or for the other twice-born classes. These texts contain instructions on kindling the domestic fire which it is incumbent upon the Brahman to keep; rules for ritual purity; and rites of passage, particularly birth, initiation, marriage and death. Indeed, a household might employ a Brahman to perform domestic rituals only for rites of passage, classified as 'occasional rites' (*naimittika-karma*) rather than 'daily rites' (*nitya-karma*). Concern for ritual became supplemented in the Dharma Sūtras with a concern for regulating and defining social relationships within and between groups. It is interesting to note that at the level of self-representation, ritual procedures took precedence over social considerations, though the two spheres became intimately connected: to perform one's ritual obligations was to act in accordance with one's social status which was to act ethically. That is, from the perspective of *dharma* there is no gap between ritual performance and social or ethical obligation, an idea which the renouncer traditions, particularly Buddhism, were to reject.

THE DHARMA SŪTRAS

These texts develop material found in the Gṛhya Sūtras and are concerned with customs and correct human conduct. In contrast to the Śrauta Sūtras, the Gṛhya Sūtras demonstrate the domestic concerns of the Brahman householder, laying emphasis on domestic rituals and codes of acceptable behaviour. The most important of the Dharma Sūtras are ascribed to the sages Gautama, Baudhāyana, Vasiṣṭha and Āpastamba, whose texts contain rules for performing domestic rites, jurisprudence, and rules pertaining to the four stages of life (*āśrama*). The significance of these texts is that they lay down rules for the performance of *dharma* for the Aryan householder, and lay the foundations for the important traditions of the Dharma Śāstra.

THE DHARMA ŚĀSTRAS

The Dharma Śāstras are a slightly later group of texts, though they contain older material, which elaborates upon the topics of the Sūtra literature. While other texts of human authorship were regarded as *smṛti*, particularly the Epics (*itihāsa*) and narrative traditions (*purāṇa*), it is the Dharma Śāstras which are particularly associated with *smṛti* and are, indeed, sometimes simply referred to by that name. The Dharma Śāstras differ from the earlier Sūtras in that they are composed in verse in contrast to the prose or mixture of prose and verse of the Sūtras. The subject matter is the same, though the Śāstras give more explication where the Sūtras are silent, and contain more material of a juridical nature, particularly pertaining to the role of the king.[9] It is these texts which are particularly important as sources of *dharma* and which provide clear indications for the high-caste householder as to what duties he should perform, what was expected of him, what was prohibited, and how these rules relate to a wider, cosmic sense of law and duty. The Brahmans who followed the teachings of these texts were known as Smārtas, those who followed the *smṛtis*, and were particularly concerned with *dharma* in respect to caste and stage of life, the *varṇāśrama-dharma*.

The rules of *dharma* in the Dharma Śāstras merge into jurisprudence and they become important texts in Hindu legislation and litigation, even during the period of British rule in India. Indeed, one of the first Sanskrit texts 'discovered' by the British was the *Manu Smṛti* or *Mānava Dharma Śāstra*, first translated into English by the founder of Indology, Sir William Jones, and published in 1794. While the *Manu Smṛti* is the oldest and most important text of this genre, composed between the second century BCE and third century CE, other Dharma Śāstras are important for their legal material, particularly the *Yājñavalkya Smṛti* and the *Nārada Smṛti*, probably composed during the Gupta period (320–500 CE). The Sanskrit commentaries are also important, particularly Medhātithi's commentary on the *Manu Smṛti*. These texts contain a doctrine of *dharma* as a universal, all-encompassing law, which is yet flexible and adaptable to different circumstances and a variety of situations. They were used particularly by assemblies of Brahmans throughout the history of Hinduism to help decide legal matters. We know something of their use from twelfth-century epigraphic evidence. In one inscription, the caste of Wheelwrights, the *rathakāras* (lit. 'cart-makers'), are disputing their position in the vedic social hierarchy. With quotations from a number of Sanskrit sources, including the *Nārada* and *Yājñavalkya Smṛtis*, the stone records the decision that there are two types of wheelwrights, one group born from 'respectable' or hypergamous marriages of the twice-born classes, and another, menial group, born from the marriages of high-caste women with low-caste men.[10]

Such inscriptions show that the Dharma Śāstras were important and were used in an advisory capacity to help settle ambiguous legal matters. In quoting from a wide range of textual sources, not only from the Dharma Śāstras, the inscriptions suggest an awareness of a scholarly Hindu tradition and a high degree of assertiveness and self-awareness among lower social groups. These inscriptions also show us that texts were open to a continuous process of interpretation in the light of contemporary social events. The Śāstras reflect the dominant brahmanical ideology and a vision of social order in which the Brahmans, the class with the highest status, had an important place as the upholders of ritual and moral purity and the conveyors of the sacred traditions.

The context-sensitivity of *dharma*

While *dharma* has been an important concept associated with kingship and has pervaded all classes of Hindu society, the law books have been mainly concerned with the obligations of Brahmans. To fulfil his *dharma* a Brahman's ritual action must be pure (*śuddhi*). Although there is some debate concerning the importance of purity in Hinduism, whether the status of purity is subordinate to political power or superior to it, purity is undoubtedly a very important concept. The body, which is polluted every day by its effluents, should be in as pure a state as possible through ritual purification, principally by water. There is, however, a deeper level of pollution which is a property of the body and differentiates one social group from another. The polarity of purity and pollution organizes Hindu social space, a principle recognized in the Dharma Śāstras which view social ethics as the maintenance of order and the boundaries between groups and genders as governed by degrees of purity and pollution. The Brahman, by virtue of being the highest class of person, is excluded from certain kinds of interaction with other classes; rules of commensality and strict marriage regulations ensure the clear maintenance of boundaries.

At a universal level *dharma* refers to a cosmic, eternal principle, yet it must also relate to the world of human transaction. At a particular level, *dharma* applies to specific laws and the contexts to which they are applied. One of the sources of *dharma* according to *Manu*, is 'custom'. This means that *dharma* can be adapted to particular situations and particular applications of it were decided by a local assembly of a number of learned men;[11] as Wendy Doniger has observed, *dharma* is 'context sensitive'.[12] The Dharma Śāstras provide us with examples of this. The religious obligations of men differ at different ages and vary according to caste (*jāti*), family (*kula*), and country (*deśa*).[13] A king, for instance, must judge according to the customs and particular duties (*svadharma*) of each region. This idea of *svadharma* is important in understanding that *dharma* is relative to different contexts: what is correct action for a warrior would be incorrect for a Brahman, what is correct for a man may be incorrect for a woman, and so on. *Manu* says: 'one's own duty, [even] without any good qualities, is better than someone else's duty well-done'.[14]

Varṇāśrama-dharma

Two concerns in particular dominate the Dharma Sūtras and Śāstras, one's obligation (*dharma*) with regard to one's position in society, that is, class (*varṇa*), and obligation with regard to one's stage of life (*āśrama*). These two concerns together became known as *varṇāśrama-dharma* whose fulfilment was a sign of brahmanical orthopraxy and, indeed, part of an essentialist definition of a Hindu. While it should be remembered that some Hindu traditions have rejected this model, its influence has been substantial in terms of Hindu self-perception and self-representation, and in terms of the West's perception of Hinduism. It has been integral to brahmanical ideology and many Hindu traditions, such as tantric traditions, have defined themselves against this brahmanical norm.

CLASS (*VARṆA*) AND CASTE (*JĀTI*)

Vedic society, as we have seen, was divided into four classes, the Brahmans, the Nobles or Warriors (*rājanya*, *kṣatriya*), the Commoners (*vaiśya*) and the Serfs (*śūdra*), the top three classes being called the 'twice-born' (*dvija*) because boys underwent an initiation (*upanayana*). This system was part of a larger 'chain of being', fitting into a cosmical hierarchy in which various categories (*jāti*) were arranged in varying degrees of subtlety and purity and associated with each other.[15] Only the twice-born classes were allowed to hear the Veda and, while in an earlier period all twice-born were eligible to learn it, only the Brahmans came to be its guardians, learning it and reciting it during rituals. The *Viṣṇu Smṛti* states clearly that the Brahmans' duties are to teach the Veda and to sacrifice for others, the Kṣatriya's is to practise with arms and protect the people, the Vaiśya should tend cattle, practise agriculture and money-lending, and the Śūdra should serve the other classes and practise art.[16] The term translated as 'class' is *varṇa*, 'colour', which refers not to any supposed racial characteristics, but to a system of colour symbolism reflecting the social hierarchy as well as the qualities (*guṇa*) which are present in varying degrees in all things. The Brahmans were associated with white, the colour of purity and lightness, the Kṣatriyas with red, the colour of passion and energy, the Vaiśyas with yellow, the colour of the earth, and the Śūdras with black, the colour of darkness and inertia.

While the term *varṇa* refers to the four classes of vedic society, the term *jāti* ('birth') refers to those endogamous sections of Hindu society which we know as 'castes'. Castes are characterized by the following features:

- castes are arranged in a hierarchical structure in any region, with the Brahmans at the top, the Untouchables (*harijans*, as Gandhi called them; *dalits* as they call themselves) at the bottom. Between these are a wide array of other castes.
- the caste hierarchy is based on the polarity between purity and pollution, the Brahmans being the most pure, the Untouchables the most impure.
- the caste of any individual is inalienable; it is a property of the body and cannot be removed (except according to some traditions by initiation).
- there are strict rules of caste endogamy and commensality.

The term *jāti* refers not only to social classes, but to all categories of beings. Insects, plants, domestic animals, wild animals and celestial beings are all *jātis*, which shows that differences between human castes might be regarded as being as great as differences between different species. Members of a *jāti* share the same bodily substance, substances which are ranked hierarchically.[17] This 'substance' has been regarded by some anthropologists as something which is exchanged in transactions: social actors constantly emit and absorb each other's substances and so are not autonomous individuals.[18] The human *jātis* are a highly complex social reality which incorporate within them many sub-divisions. Indeed the Brahman and Kṣatriya *varṇas* are also taken to be *jātis*. The caste system, while having changed through time, as do all human social institutions, has nevertheless retained a continuity. It is probable that the caste system was complex even at the time of *Manu*, and fluid in the sense that different castes can change their rank relative to each other in any region over a period of time by, for example, creating a pure, legendary origin. The *varṇas* on the other hand, provide a stable model for a stratified social order in which each group is clearly defined and functions as part of an organic whole: as part of the body of society which is also the body of the primal person or being, sacrificed at the beginning of time, as the *Ṛg Veda* states.

The exact historical relationship between *varṇa* and *jāti* is unclear. It is not certain that the 'castes' or *jātis* developed from the *varṇa* system. Indeed philosophical texts do not consistently distinguish between the two terms and, according to Halbfass, *jāti* is used in the sense of *varṇa* in the Dharma Śāstra literature.[19] The traditional view is that the *jātis* represent a proliferation of social groups from the *varṇa* system. *Manu* could be attempting to make sense of a pre-given social stratification in terms of the clear ideology of the vedic classes, when he attempts to explain the proliferation of *jātis* in terms of miscegenation amongst the *varṇas*, against the dangers of which he warns the twice-born.[20] Indeed *Manu* prescribes some severe penalties for 'sexual misconduct'. A Brahman who sleeps with a Śūdra woman goes to hell and loses brahmanical status upon the birth of a son; homosexuality is punished by loss of caste, and adultery by the woman being 'eaten by dogs in a place frequented by many' and the man 'burnt on a red hot iron bed'.[21]

It is not certain whether such severe punishments were ever actually carried out, but these examples certainly have rhetorical impact and Manu clearly makes the point that sex outside the boundaries of marriage prescribed by *dharma* is not to be tolerated by an ordered society. Yet while *Manu* presents a clear vision of social ethics based on caste hierarchy, there are nevertheless subtleties in *dharma* which accommodate various human situations. For example, sex outside caste-restricted marriage is wrong, yet there is the institution of the temporary *gāndharva* marriage for the satisfaction of desire, and while killing is wrong, there are circumstances in which it is permitted. *Dharma*, the universal moral law, must be adapted to human situations and to the everyday reality of the householder.

Although cross-caste marriages are condemned in *Manu*, if they are to occur, then those in which the man is of higher caste than the woman, marriages 'with the grain' (*anuloma*), are better than marriages of low-caste men with high-caste women, marriages 'against the grain' (*pratiloma*). The *jātis*, according to *Manu*, are the consequences of such mixed marriages. For example, three of the lowest or outcast groups – the castes of carpenters, carvers, and the 'fierce' Untouchables (*caṇḍāla*) – are born from the union of Śūdra women with Commoners, Warriors and Brahmans respectively.[22] The 'fierce' caste, the *caṇḍālas*, whom *Manu* classifies as a group whom he contemptuously calls 'dog-cookers', are taken as exemplifying the lowest social groups, highly polluting to the higher castes, and so becoming known as 'untouchables' in the West, though the actual term *asprṣṭa*, 'untouched', is not much used in Sanskrit sources. There was never a literal caste of 'dog-cookers', this is merely *Manu*'s rhetoric for groups identified with the most impure of creatures, cocks, dogs and pigs. If a Brahman is touched by a member of one of these groups, amongst others such as one fallen from caste or a menstruating woman, he should purify himself with a bath.[23]

Although untouchability is now legally prohibited in India, Untouchable castes constitute about a fifth of India's population. They were totally excluded from vedic society and high-caste ritual traditions, 'outcaste' beyond the system of the four classes (*avarṇa*). Even the Śūdras were within the class system, though forbidden to hear the Veda and outside the twice-born designation, but the Untouchables had no place within the higher social orders, living on the outside of villages, as *Manu* directs,[24] and living by performing menial and polluting tasks such as working with leather and sweeping excrement from the village. The fifth-century Chinese Buddhist pilgrim, Fa-hsien, mentions the Untouchables as having to strike a piece of wood before entering a town as a warning for people to avoid them.[25] The untouchable classes almost certainly go back into the first millennium BCE. The dating of *Manu* is unsure, though it is earlier than the third century CE and probably far older. There is evidence, cited by Dumont, of untouchable castes several centuries before the common era, from the Buddhist Jātakas, stories of the previous lives of the Buddha, and Dumont not implausibly suggests that both Brahmans and Untouchables were established at the same time, for the impurity of the Untouchable is inseparable from the purity of the Brahman; they are at opposite ends of the status hierarchy.[26]

THE *ĀŚRAMA* SYSTEM

The second concept in the ideology of *dharma* is that of life's stages or the *āśramas*. These are codifications of different elements present in vedic society and an attempt to integrate them into a coherent system. The four stages are: that of the celibate student (*brahmacārya*), householder (*gṛhastha*), hermit or forest dweller (*vanaprastha*), and renouncer (*samnyāsa*). Patrick Olivelle has shown that the *āśrama* system, as a theological construct within the Hindu hermeneutical tradition, should be distinguished from the socio-religious institutions comprehended by the system.[27] The *āśramas* are a theological entity whose object of reflection is the social institution, or institutions, which the system reflects upon.

The *āśrama* system arose during the fifth century BCE as a result of changes within the brahmanical tradition. Initially the term referred to a 'hermitage' (*āśrama*, the source of the anglicized 'ashram') and came to be applied to the style of life of those Brahmans who lived there. The brahmanical 'hermits' who lived in an *āśrama* were householders within the vedic fold, performing the domestic sacrifice, who pursued a religious life, probably in areas removed from towns and villages. The term, as Olivelle has shown, referred to this special category of brahmanical householder.[28] The meaning of the term came to be extended, referring not only to the place where the brahmanical householder-hermits dwelled, but to the style of life they led, and eventually came to refer to other brahmanical styles of life as well. In the Dharma Sūtras the *āśramas* are not regarded as successive stages through which a man must pass, but as permanent possibilities – or lifestyle choices – open to the twice-born male after completing his studies. The twice-born boy would be separated from childhood by the vedic initiation. He would then become a 'student' in the house of a teacher, during which time he would learn about the duties and responsibilities of each of the four *āśramas*. At the end of this period of study he would choose one of the *āśramas* that he would wish to follow for the rest of his adult life.[29] Thus, he could choose a life of study and continue as a 'student' or *brahmacārin*. By the time of the Dharma Śāstras, the *āśramas* have solidified into successive stages through which the twice-born should pass, and much space in the Śāstras is devoted to describing the demands of each stage. As with the *varṇa* system, the *āśramas* are a model, this time concerned not with the ordering of society but with the diachronic ordering of the individual's life: they are a paradigm of how the high-caste man should live.

The celibate student stage of life (*brahmacārya*) refers to the traditional period after the high-caste initiation (*upanayana*) when a boy would go to the home of his teacher (*ācārya, guru*) to learn the Veda. The student of the

Veda or *brahmacārin*, 'one who moves with or applies himself to *brahman*', is known as early as the *Atharva Veda*,[30] where he has all the characteristics of the student portrayed in the Dharma Śāstras: he begs for food, practises penances, wears an antelope skin, collects fuel, and practises heat-generating austerity (*tapas*).[31] Yet, unlike the contemporary idea of the student, the *brahmacārin* is in a holy condition in which he is identified with Prajāpati, the creator deity in the Brāhmaṇas, and is under a strict rule of celibacy. Indeed the term *brahmacārin* can mean 'one who is celibate', the idea behind this, common to all Indian religions, being that to remain celibate is to be unpolluted by sex and to control sexual energy which, usually understood as the retention of semen, can be sublimated for a religious purpose. According to *Manu*, this state would last between nine and as many as thirty-six years, during which time the student would learn all, or a number of, the Vedas. After this the student would undergo a home-coming ritual and would soon be married and entered upon the householder's life.[32]

When a householder is wrinkled and grey and sees his grandchildren, then, says *Manu*, he should retire and become a hermit or forest-dweller (*vanaprastha*). In this stage a man, along with his wife if he so wishes, retires from householder's duties to live an ascetic life in the forest and to devote himself to ritual. Here, in the words of *Manu*, 'constantly devoting himself to the recitation of the Veda, he should be controlled, friendly, and mentally composed; he should always be a giver and a non-taker, compassionate to all living beings'.[33] He is not a complete renunciate and has not given up fire for cooking and, more importantly, for making the daily offerings into the three sacrificial fires. Nevertheless, from the descriptions of this stage in the Dharma Śāstras, we can see that *vanaprastha* practised severe bodily asceticism, eating only certain kinds of food such as vegetables, flowers, roots and fruits and even practising extreme austerity such as sitting surrounded by five fires in the summer or wearing wet clothes in winter, in order to generate spiritual energy or 'inner heat' (*tapas*).[34] The significant difference between this stage and that of the total world renouncer is the use of fire. The renouncer has gone beyond the vedic injunctions of maintaining his sacred fires; living entirely by begging he does not cook his own food. If fire and cooked food are symbols of culture and raw food of nature, as Lévi-Strauss has suggested, then the renouncer in relinquishing fire has, in a sense, relinquished culture; he is attempting to transcend culture for a pure, trans-human realm of spiritual liberation.

If a Brahman follows through the stages of life, says *Manu*, and has paid his three debts (*ṛṇa*) of vedic study to the seers (*ṛṣi*), of ritual to the gods (*deva*), and of begetting sons to make funeral offerings to the ancestors (*pitṛ*), then he may aim at attaining liberation (*mokṣa*). However, if he has not fulfilled his social obligations then he goes to hell, making it clear that while renunciation and the goal of liberation are valid, they must be deferred until social obligations have been met: here, *dharma*, in the sense of social obligation, is clearly superior to *mokṣa*.

Of the *āśramas* the householder and renouncer stages are clearly the most important both ideologically and in terms of concrete historical developments. These two stages, or rather the figures of the householder and the renouncer who pass through them, reflect the distinction between sociopolitical religion and soteriology. While throughout the history of Hinduism there are attempts to reconcile the householder and the renouncer ideals, the two images, and two institutions, remain in tension.

The Dharma Śāstras favour the householder's life. *Manu* explicitly states that, of the four stages, the householder's is the best because the householder supports the others and his activity is the supreme good.[35] The text presents a picture of the Brahman as a learned man, a model of rational self-control who restrains his senses 'as a charioteer his race-horses',[36] and who performs the correct ritual activity. He abides by the ritual injunctions (*vidhi*) of the Veda, namely the performance of obligatory daily rituals (*nitya-karma*), occasional rituals (*naimittika-karma*) – such as the life-cycle rituals (*saṃskāra*) of birth, high-caste initiation, and death rites – and rites performed for a desired result (*kāmya-karma*) such as going to heaven. This is in contrast to the renouncer, who has given up home, the use of fire for ritual and cooking, and who cultivates total detachment, treating everything with equanimity and going beyond attachment to the material world.[37]

The image of the renouncer might be contrasted not only with the Brahman but also with the image of the king, the ideal householder, who, unlike the renouncer, possesses political power, and, unlike the Brahman, does not possess brahmanical purity, being lower in the *varṇa* hierarchy and having corpse-pollution due to war and punishment. The relation between the images of the renouncer, the Brahman householder and the king, has been contentious. Some scholars, such as Louis Dumont, have regarded the renouncer and the householder to be the central contrast with Hinduism, while others, notably Jan Heesterman, have argued for the similarity between the renouncer and the Brahman and have emphasized the contrast between the Brahman and the king[38] (see p. 72).

Gender roles

All these stages are characterized by different regimens of the body, particularly the control of diet and sexuality. The first and last *āśramas* are explicitly celibate; celibacy is a defining characteristic of *brahmacārya*, the central ascetic idea being that sexual power contained in semen can be redirected to a spiritual end and, indeed, be stored in the head. The forest-dweller and the renouncer, like the *brahmacārin*, are seeking to transcend and transform sexual power for the purposes of the higher goal of liberation. Only the householder can express and explore his sexuality as a legitimate goal of life (*kāmārtha*), concerning which there is an extensive literature, the Kāma Śāstras, and the most notable text, Vatsyāyana's *Kāma Sūtra*, a text to which, exceptionally, women had access. Sexual enjoyment was regarded as the foremost of pleasures and a man of wealth, particularly a king, would experience *kāma* with courtesans trained in the arts of love. Yet even the Brahman's sexuality stands within his rational control; a control which orders his world according to the principles of maintaining ritual purity and of controlling elements within it which threaten to disrupt that purity, particularly his own desire and its focus, namely his wife and other women of his household.

That physical love (*kāma*) is a legitimate purpose of life is significant in demonstrating a strand in brahmanical ideology which was generally positive towards the body and sexuality. Sex is not inherently sinful but can be legitimately explored and expressed within the correct caste-specific boundaries, especially by men with wealth and power. Even Manu, a text which in the light of contemporary western sensibilities seems oppressive of women's rights, recognizes the need for the mutual sexual satisfaction of husband and wife.[39] This is also the case in Hindu erotic literature where women are not simply the instruments of male desire. As Biardeau observes, love (*kāma*) was a traditional art which women handed down to one another through the generations; love was a woman's *svadharma*, or more correctly her *strīdharma*, 'woman's duty',[40] and a realm of human experience which is legitimized in the Smṛti literature. However, sexuality beyond rational control, that is, outside of caste restrictions and pollution controls, was anathema to the orthodox Brahman for it threatened his ritual purity and threatened the stability of society and the family.

Manu's attitude to women expresses the ambivalence of the general brahmanical ideal. Women are to be revered and kept happy by the householder in order that the family may thrive, yet women are also polluting to the Brahman male during menstruation. According to *Manu*, women are to be subject to male control throughout their lives. A high-caste woman must do nothing independently (*svatantra*), but must be subject to male authority – as a child to her father, as a married woman to her husband, and as a widow to her sons.[41] By leading a life subject to male authority, a woman's virtuous behaviour will be rewarded by heaven upon her death.[42] In later brahmanical tradition, a 'good woman' (*satī*) is one who dies on her husband's funeral pyre if he predeceases her, a practice which had developed by the fourteenth century though it was not known to *Manu*, and although now illegal, still sometimes occurs in contemporary India.[43]

An eighteenth-century dharmic text, Tryambaka's *Strīdharma Paddhati*, gives details of the wife's duties towards her husband, who is treated by her as a *deva*, and his expectations of her. Above all, obedient service to her husband is her primary religious duty, even beyond regard for her own life.[44] However, probably the text which best portrays the ideal high-caste woman is not a technical law book, but the Hindu epic poem composed perhaps as early as the fifth century BCE, the *Rāmāyaṇa*. In this narrative the god-king Rāma is banished to the forest with his brother Balarāma and his wife Sītā. Sītā is demure, modest, beautiful and dedicated to her Lord Rāma, yet she is also strong in herself, endures great hardship and displays great devotion to her husband. She is the ideal high-caste wife.

In examining Hindu literature on *dharma* we are dealing with brahmanical self-representations and idealized images of gender roles. In *Manu* we have the brahmanical view of how things should be, a clear picture of brahmanical ideology, but the degree to which this reflected social reality is unclear. Women probably wielded power within the home, within the realm of domesticity, but wielded little power in the realms of public office, administration and politics, a situation which, in India as elsewhere, has only begun to change in the twentieth century.

Purity and auspiciousness

Two distinctions have been important in the history of Hindu society: on the one hand the distinction between purity (*śauca*, *śuddhi*) and pollution (*aśauca*, *aśuddhi*) and on the other the distinction between auspiciousness (*śubha*, *maṅgala*) and inauspiciousness (*aśubha*, *amaṅgala*). The scale of purity and pollution is a scale of status hierarchy which corresponds to the caste hierarchy with the Brahmans at the top and the *dalits* at the bottom. Hindu society is arranged around this scale. Auspiciousness and inauspiciousness, on the other hand, is a scale of the degree to which events, times and relationships are conducive to the well-being of the society or individual. Astrology is particularly important here in determining the degree of auspiciousness for a particular event such as a marriage.

The degree of purity and pollution is concerned with status, the degree of auspiciousness and inauspiciousness concerned with power, particularly political power. While purity has been the predominant concern of the Brahman, auspiciousness has been the predominant concern of the king and the local dominant caste. While the Brahman creates a ritually pure environment, so the king must create an auspicious kingdom; one in which there is good fortune and prosperity. The ability to create auspiciousness in the kingdom is a function of the king's divinity. The king, like the icon in a temple, might be regarded as a channel for divine power and the level of prosperity in the kingdom related to the degree to which he lives up to this responsibility.

The political theology of kingship

One of the most important aspects of *dharma* is its applicability to kingship. Kingship has been very important in Hinduism, both as an ideal and as a sociopolitical reality, intimately linked to the idea of the sacred. As the icon of a deity is thought to mediate between the divine and human realms, similarly the king was thought to do so. Whereas the Gṛhya Sūtras are concerned only with domestic ritual, the Dharma texts have wider interests in the four stages of life, social or caste obligation, jurisprudence and, particularly, the rites and duties of kings. From these texts we see that, while *dharma* is timeless and transcendent, it was also the province of domestic affairs and public, social relationships, and had a political dimension in governing the status and behaviour of the king. Regardless of the actions of any particular king, the ideal of kingship was upheld throughout Hindu history from the vedic period onwards, an ideal in which the king was the centre of the Hindu universe. This ideal of kingship plays an important role even in contemporary Hinduism and rituals of kingship persist into the present.[45]

Although in one sense the king is the ideal householder, able to fulfil the goals of *dharma*, of wealth, and of sexual love with innumerable courtesans, he is also divine. Worldly power in the history of Hindu kingship is legitimated in terms of a religious symbolism in which the qualities of deities are attributed to kings. The king was regarded as a divine being – a divinity which is attested in one of the names for king, *deva* – particularly identified in the medieval period with the god Viṣṇu. The beginnings of this ideology are found in the *Ṛg Veda Saṃhitā* where Indra is the king 'of that which moves and that which rests, of the tame and of the horned. He rules the people as their king, encircling all this as a rim encircles spokes.'[46] Similarly the human king is lord of his kingdom or sphere and as such should protect his realm and wage war against his enemies.[47] The king ideally aspires to be a 'ruler of the universe' or *cakravārtin* ('one who is at the centre of the wheel').

The kings of the early vedic period were constrained by the power of tribal councils, but this changed in the later vedic period when the power of the king became more absolute. While the king is not endowed with divine origin in the Dharma Sūtras, later texts clearly identify the king with a deity or deities. It is from the Dharma Śāstras, Kauṭilya's *Artha Śāstra* and the great epic poem the *Mahābhārata*, that we can build a clearer picture of the ideology of sacral kingship in early Indian politics. This model of sacral kingship was later embellished by the tantric identification of the king with the deity, particularly the Goddess, and by the ideology of the deity's energy (*śakti*) flowing through him.[48]

Once consecrated, generally even if not a Kṣatriya, the king is no mere human being but a god. According to *Manu*, the king is emitted by the Lord of the Cosmos. He is a great deity in the form of a man, or rather a composite deity, being formed from fragments of the different vedic gods Indra, Vāyu, Yama, Sūrya, Agni, Varuṇa, Soma and Kubera and in some sense might be said to contain all gods. *Manu* writes:

> Because a king is made from particles of these lords of the gods, therefore he surpasses all living beings in brilliant energy, and, like the Sun, he burns eyes and hearts, and no one on earth is able even to look at him. Through his special power he becomes Fire and Wind; he is the Sun and the Moon, and he is (Yama) the King of Justice, he is Kubera [Lord of wealth] and he is Varuna, and he is great Indra.[49]

This passage shows the king as the highest point of the kingdom or polity. Even a child king is no mere mortal but a great deity in human form.

It was not so much the charisma of any particular king which maintained power, but the tradition and legitimation of the institution of kingship through the idea of the descent of power from above during the king's anointing. From the king, power descends to the court and to the rest of the realm.

While there is much rhetoric in the Dharma literature concerning the need for the king to administer justice, the Hindu king was more important as a ritual figure in close proximity to the divine than as a ruler involved with the bureaucracy and running of the kingdom. The ruler of a large kingdom, a *dharmarāja*, was more important as a moral and ritual source, than in the practical concerns of the day-to-day running of a region or regions. The politically segmentary nature of the Hindu kingdom was ritually united in the figure of the king. We cannot simply regard the Hindu king as a despot or the institution of divine kingship as a peculiar consequence of caste society. Rather, the king was an integral part of a whole structure in which he and those below him, down to common people in the villages, functioned in an integrated way. The Hindu polity was a complex structure, an 'imperial formation', to use Ronald Inden's term, in which each part played a role in its maintenance. Inden writes that within this world 'the kingship equated with the sun, its officialdom with the lesser gods of the sky, the queen with the earth, were, together with the commoners, all parts'.[50]

THE SEGMENTARY HINDU STATE

The Hindu kingdom, as historian Burton Stein has shown, was segmentary, comprising a number of embedded elements or socio-political groupings which formed a pyramidal structure. These elements were embedded within each other; the village within the locality, the locality within the supralocality, and the supralocality within the kingdom.[51] Lesser kings gave ritual and symbolic loyalty to more powerful kings and chieftains paid homage to lesser kings. For most of the history of south Asia from the advent of kingship to domination by foreign powers, each region would have been ruled by a chief or petty-king who acknowledged and paid allegiance to a sacred centre. The Hindu king would have been the ritual focus of the sacred centre, a ritual figure who held together his kingdom not so much as a united administrative entity, but as a segmented political structure within a common moral frame of reference. This model is found in Kauṭilya's *Artha Śāstra* which presents the king as the centre of a state formation held together by alliances and wars.

Furthermore, the kingdom was embedded within a hierarchical cosmos. In vedic and later Hindu cosmologies, the universe is regarded as a hierarchical structure in which purer, more refined worlds are located 'above', yet at the same time they incorporate, lower, impure worlds which, as in the segmentary Hindu kingdom, have some autonomy. In this hierarchical cosmology the various worlds or realms are governed by an overlord or god who also embodies the principles controlling or governing that world. The various worlds which comprise the cosmos are controlled by forces which are also 'persons'. Inden has observed that the 'natural world of ancient and medieval India was person-based, constructed by a cosmic overlord out of himself'.[52] The human realm must be located within the context of this wider cosmology of which it was thought to be a part. There is a 'chain of being' within the Hindu universe which is reflected in the sociopolitical realm of the Hindu segmentary state. As a god might rule a sphere of the cosmos, so the king rules his kingdom.

THE BODY OF THE KINGDOM

The famous study by Kantorowicz shows how in medieval Europe the king had two bodies, a natural body subject to disease and death and an immutable political body in which resided his sovereignty.[53] This model can be applied to kingship in south Asia. While the physical body of the king was subject to death, as are all human bodies, the political body of the king as a manifestation of the gods, contained splendour and great power. The physical body of the king could be killed, but the political body, the body of the kingdom[54] lived on in the form of the new king, regenerated by the act of royal consecration.

The king is the pivotal point of the body politic: the 'body of the kingdom' is recapitulated in his own body. If he acts in accordance with *dharma* the kingdom prospers, but if he acts against *dharma*, the body of the kingdom – which means the people – suffers. The king's body, which expressed the social body, was the worldly counterpart of the cosmic man's immolated body which comprised the cosmos. The king could be seen, therefore, as the intermediary between the eternal, cosmic law of *dharma* and its worldly manifestations in justice administered through the courts of a segmented hierarchical structure. Whatever happens to him as the pinnacle of the social body affects the domain for good or bad. As the king is a manifestation of the gods, so society is a recapitulation of the cosmic body of the primal man.

THE KING'S FUNCTIONS

According to the Dharma literature, the central functions of the king, the *rājadharma*, are:

- the protection of the people;
- the maintaining of social order through the control of caste boundaries;
- the administration of justice (*daṇḍa*).

Manu says that the king is created 'as the protector of the classes and stages of life'.[55] He is the supreme upholder of justice in the social world who ensures the prosperity and protection of the communities which he governs so that his subjects live with a sense of security. The king is the absolute dispenser of justice, the term for which, *daṇḍa* (literally 'the stick'), also meant punishment.

Daṇḍa is the way in which *dharma* is manifested upon the earth. It creates fear in all beings so that they do not wander from their own, caste-specific duties and ensures the obedience of the castes to the dharmic ideal. It keeps the whole world in order, governs all created beings, protects them while they sleep and without it there would be no order in society; castes would be mixed and the whole world would be in a state of rage.[56] Through the legal processes of the state, the king should see that justice is done and so maintain social order and harmony. A bad king, one who neglects the protection of the people and neglects the administration of justice, would bring about social disharmony and chaos.

With British colonialism the power of kings in India diminished but was not wholly eradicated. As Fuller notes, there were still 565 kingdoms or princely states not under direct British rule in 1947, and even up until the 1930s the Maharaj of Mysore, a kingdom which had developed out of the ruins of Vijayanagara, celebrated the *navarātri* festival, a direct legacy from the festival of the Vijayanagara kings. The ritual importance of the king should not be underestimated, and even at an ideological level, the king as upholder of cosmic order or *dharma* is central to the contemporary Hindu politics (see p. 262). The king was the centre of the Hindu universe in the material world, and the ideal state was the ideal kingdom ruled by a king who was the analogue of the deity; an ideal established in ritual.

The jajmānī system

While the king of kings ruled over a number of kingdoms, themselves ruled by kings, those kings in turn ruled over a number of regions controlled by a dominant caste or coalition of castes. These controlling castes are usually not Brahmans, but other castes, often Śūdras. The *jajmān* is a local, powerful landowner who employs Brahmans to perform rituals for him in return for a fee. He also gives a portion of grain to other castes who provide him with services. The term is derived from the vedic *yajamāna*, the 'sacrificer' or ritual patron for whom sacrifices were performed by the Brahmans. The jajmānī system is not a purely economic arrangement, but is rooted in the socio-ritual structure of caste hierarchy which itself is regarded as sacred.

Dumont has observed that castes can be divided into those who own land and those who do not. The caste in a village or region which owns the land is the caste with political power and control over other castes, because it controls the means of subsistence. The other castes gain access to the means of subsistence through personal relationships with the dominant caste. There is a reciprocal relationship here. The dominant caste employs Brahmans for its ritual needs, barbers, carpenters, and untouchable labourers who in turn receive 'gifts' for their services.[57] At the level of the kingdom, the king might be regarded as a jajmān, receiving the services of others, including worship, and giving in turn gifts and, above all, protection.

Royal power and transcendence

The worldly power of the king, a Kṣatriya, has been contrasted with the purity of the Brahman. Heesterman contrasts the Brahman, who embodies an ideal of world transcendence in performing the ritual, with the king, who is necessarily embroiled in the worldly concerns of power and violence. According to Heesterman, the king aspires to participate in the transcendent realm of the Brahman, but necessarily fails because of his involvement and entanglement in the world of politics, desire and interests. There is a rift between the king's order of conflict and the Brahman's and renouncer's order of transcendence.[58] By employing Brahmans in his court to perform the necessary sacrifices, the king hopes to participate in their sacred level, yet in becoming entangled in the world, the Brahman moves away from that transcendence. There is thus an insoluble problem here and a gap between the power of the king operating in the 'turbulent order of conflict' and the authority or status of the Brahman, operating in the 'static order of transcendence'.[59] The Brahman, according to Heesterman, turns towards transcendence, while the king, lacking the Brahman's purity and authority, remains within the world of strife and violence.

This contrast is related to a contrast between two senses of *dharma*. On the one hand it refers to an eternal, timeless principle, and, on the other, it refers to worldly or human transactions. The Brahman faces both ways, towards transcendence through ritual, while yet being in the world, while the king is embroiled in the realm of worldly, temporal *dharma*. This is what Heesterman calls the 'inner conflict of tradition'; the need to assert *dharma* as the eternal, timeless principle, in contrast to the need to accommodate to worldly, temporal interests, a contrast which poses an insoluble dilemma. This model has been criticized from the perspective of history and anthropology, particularly by Ronald Inden and Nicholas Dirks. Inden argues, against Heesterman, that there was no such distinction between the pure Brahman and the powerful, but impure, king.[60] Rather there was an intimate relationship between king and Brahmans who lived by the king's patronage. The king would donate wealth, land and other valuables to the Brahmans, and, while they were clearly distinct from the king, there was not the rift between worldly life and transcendence which Heesterman suggests. The Brahman perceived a continuity between his inner life and its outer expression.

Nicholas Dirks has argued against Dumont that caste cannot be understood outside of the ideas of kingship and the structure of the Hindu state. Dirks argues that caste is embedded in kingship and that the dominant ideology has not been one of purity but one of royal authority and social relations based on power and dominance. Caste, and particularly the role of the Brahmans, is based on power related to kingship and the Hindu state. With the general demise of the Hindu state, caste became separated from kingship and survived it, a process which led to the ascendancy of the Brahmans. Until recently, however, kings still ruled the small state of Pudokkottai in the middle of Tamilnadu, where the Brahmans performed rituals for the king and became emblems of the king's sovereignty. The king in return gave the Brahmans land. Their importance was always, argues Dirks, mediated through the king, 'whose kingship was in turn made all the more powerful because of the presence of the Brahmans'.[61] Pudokkottai provides an example in which the power of the Brahmans is directly related to the power of the king and in which the Brahman's purity is subordinated to his dependence on the king's patronage.

Summary

Dharma is the central ideology of orthoprax Hinduism, believed to be eternal and deriving from the revelation of the Veda and from the secondary revelation of the Dharma literature. It is particularly concerned with caste hierarchy expressed in the *varṇāśrama* system and with the nature and behaviour of the Hindu king. The king expresses *dharma* through just rule and so ensures the prosperity of the kingdom. The relation of the Brahman to the king is ambiguous. On the one hand the Brahman is the highest being on the status hierarchy of purity and pollution, yet the Brahman is dependent upon the power of the king for patronage. Heesterman has described the tension between the world-transcending tendencies of the Brahman and his worldly concerns as the inner conflict of tradition. Studies by Inden and Dirks, in contrast, have argued for the closer proximity of the Brahman to the king and Dirks has argued that the status of the Brahman cannot be separated from the power of the king; the religious realm of the Brahman cannot be understood outside the political realm of the king.

Whether there is an opposition between the Brahman and the king, or whether the two figures are closer than has been thought, is a matter of continuing debate. However, one contrast which is made by the Hindu tradition is that between the renouncer and the householder. Hinduism contains a sociopolitical ideology of a chain of being which endorses the social hierarchy, caste, and gender roles, alongside an ideology of renunciation which negates those roles at doctrinal and practical levels. In order to come to a fuller understanding of orthoprax Hinduism and the contrasts within it, we need to turn our attention to renunciation, the institution for leaving the sociopolitical world of suffering.

4 Yoga and renunciation

By the sixth century BCE the brahmanical schools are well established and the ritual traditions passed through the generations from teacher to student. Probably the heyday of vedic ritual performance was between 1000 and 500 BCE, though the traditions are never completely attenuated and have survived into the present. Alongside the performances of ritual, speculation about its nature and purpose developed, initially in the Brāhmaṇas and later in the Āraṇyakas and Upaniṣads. In speculating about the ritual patron and the renewing effects of the ritual upon him, the Brahmaṇas begin to represent the ritual as the sustainer of life and posit elaborate correspondences (*bandhu*) between ritual and the wider cosmos. These speculations are developed in the Āraṇyakas and Upaniṣads which completely re-evaluate the nature of ritual, seeing its internalization within the individual as its highest meaning, and subordinating ritual action to knowledge. This spiritual knowledge could be attained by asceticism or world-renunciation and disciplines which came to be known as *yoga*. The Upaniṣads attest to the existence of ascetic traditions and, by the sixth or fifth century BCE, traditions of asceticism and world-renunciation for the purpose of spiritual knowledge and liberation had developed both within the bounds of vedic tradition and outside those boundaries, most notably in the Jain and Buddhist traditions.

General observations

Two ideas of great significance developed between the ninth and sixth centuries BCE, namely that beings are reincarnated into the world (*saṃsāra*) over and over again and that the results of action (*karma*) are reaped in future lives. This process of endless rebirth is one of suffering (*duḥkha*), escape from which can be achieved through the minimizing of action and through spiritual knowledge. Patañjali (second century BCE), a systematizer of yoga practice and philosophy, states that all is suffering to the spiritually discriminating person (*vivekin*).[1] This doctrine that all life is suffering is common to renouncer traditions and is the first noble truth of the Buddha. To be free of suffering one needs to be free from action and its effects. The renunciation of action at first meant ritual action, but comes to refer to all action in the social world. This renunciation of action could be achieved through asceticism (*tapas*) and meditation, which means techniques of altering consciousness or withdrawing consciousness from the world of the senses in order to experience total world transcendence.

The groups of ascetics which grew up during this period are known as, among other names, *śramaṇas* (Pali *samaṇa*), 'strivers', who seek liberation through the efforts of their austerity. They are homeless, depend for food on alms (*bhikṣā*), and minimize, in varying degrees, their ownership of possessions. Buddhism, the first world religion, originated in these groups, as did Jainism. Both Buddhism and Jainism reject the Veda as revelation and emphasize the practice of austerity, in the case of Jainism, and meditation, in the case of Buddhism. Indeed these early renouncer traditions cannot be understood in isolation from each other as there is mutual cross-fertilization of terminologies and ideas: Buddhism influences the brahmanical renouncer religion and brahmanical religion influences Buddhism.[2] The higher states of consciousness or meditative absorptions spoken of in the Buddhist scriptures, the *jhānas* (Pali) or *dhyānas* (Sanskrit), which are certainly pre-Buddhist, are reminiscent of the later Hindu stages of yogic concentration of *samādhi*.

These renouncer traditions offered a new vision of the human condition which became incorporated, to some degree, into the worldview of the Brahman householder. The ideology of asceticism and renunciation seems, at first, discontinuous with the brahmanical ideology of the affirmation of social obligations and the performance of public and domestic rituals. Indeed, there has been some debate as to whether asceticism and its ideas of retributive action, reincarnation and spiritual liberation, might not have originated outside the orthodox vedic sphere, or even outside Aryan culture: that a divergent historical origin might account for the apparent contradiction within 'Hinduism' between the world affirmation of the householder and the world negation of the renouncer. However, this dichotomization is too simplistic, for continuities can undoubtedly be found between renunciation and vedic Brahmanism, while elements from non-brahmanical, Śramaṇa traditions also played an important part in the formation of the renunciate ideal. Indeed there are continuities between vedic Brahmanism and Buddhism, and it has been argued that the Buddha sought to return to the ideals of a vedic society which he saw as being eroded in his own day.[3]

General ideological features of world renunciation common to different renouncer traditions can be summarized as follows:

- action leads to rebirth and suffering.
- detachment from action, or even non-action, leads to spiritual emancipation.
- complete detachment, and therefore spiritual emancipation can be achieved through asceticism and methods of making consciousness focused and concentrated.

Ascetics in the Veda

In the *Ṛg Veda Saṃhitā* the important religious figures are the priests who officiate at the ritual and the inspired seers (*ṛṣi*) who receive the Veda. There are, however, some references in the vedic corpus to figures who do not have a ritual function and seem to be outside the brahmanical, vedic community. Two groups are of particular note, the Keśins and the Vrātyas.

THE KEŚINS

One famous hymn in the *Ṛg Veda Saṃhitā* describes long-haired ascetics (*keśin*) or silent ones (*muni*), who strongly resemble later Hindu ascetics. The text describes them as either naked ('swathed in wind') or clothed in red tatters. They have ecstatic experiences, being 'possessed by the gods', and they fly outside the body, perhaps suggestive of what have become known as 'out-of-the-body experiences'. The text also indicates that they possess the ability to read minds, a power attributed to accomplished yogins in later yoga traditions. Such experiences are seemingly induced by an unidentified 'drug' (*viṣa*) which the ascetic drinks with the god Rudra, and which is prepared by a (possibly hunch-backed) goddess Kunaṃnamā.[4]

Whether the hymn describes a drug-induced visionary experience depends upon the interpretation of the term *viṣa*, which is usually taken to mean 'poison'. Some scholars have argued that *viṣa* here refers to a hallucinogenic drug, though distinct from *soma*,[5] while others have argued that to see the hymn in terms of a chemically induced ecstasy is to disregard the symbolic nature of the vedic texts, and that drinking poison is akin to the myth of Śiva's drinking the poison churned up from the world ocean. On this view the Keśin attained his mystical state through a yoga practice, and the poison he drinks refers to his ability to remain in the poisonous material world, while being unaffected by it.[6] It is, of course, possible to view the hymn as describing a hallucinogen-induced ecstasy and being symbolic at the same time.

The description of the Keśin is reminiscent of later ascetics who undergo extraordinary inner experiences. Regardless of the cause or facilitator, whether through a drug or through ascetic practices, this hymn provides us with one of the earliest recorded descriptions of an ecstatic religious experience. Other features of the hymn, such as the Keśin's association with Rudra, are significant in establishing a connection with later yogic traditions. Rudra, who later becomes Śiva, the archetypal ascetic, himself associated with the hallucinogenic plant *datura*, is a terrible deity with long, braided hair, on the edges of vedic society, who is entreated not to harm the communities by taking away their cattle and children.[7] Rudra is peripheral to the vedic pantheon, there are only three hymns to him in the *Ṛg Veda*, and the Keśin's association with him suggests that he too would have been on the edges of the vedic community. The goddess Kunaṃnamā is only mentioned in the Veda in this hymn, again suggestive of the Keśin's location outside of the vedic community.

While it might not be legitimate to argue that the Keśin represents a non-Aryan tradition – after all the composer of the hymn is sympathetic to the Keśin – it would be reasonable to assume that the Keśin represents a strand of asceticism existing outside mainstream, vedic ritual culture and was probably an influence on later renouncer traditions; indeed the Buddha himself, like the Keśin, is described as a *muni*. However, it would be a gross oversimplification to suggest that the renouncer tradition simply developed from this Muni culture. The development of renunciation in the Upaniṣads is intimately connected to the vedic ritual tradition, yet one must also recognize the force of the argument that the Upaniṣads contain a discontinuity of ideas with the vedic ritual tradition; a discontinuity which indicates non-vedic influences, such as are represented by the 'Keśin Hymn'.

THE VRĀTYAS

Apart from the Keśins, Book 15 of the *Atharva Veda Saṃhitā* attests to the existence of a community of aggressive warriors moving about in bands, the *Vrātyas*, who lived on the edges of Aryan society and may have been connected with the Keśins. These Vrātyas comprised itinerant groups, concentrated in the north-east of India, who spoke the same language as the vedic Aryans, but who were regarded with disdain by them. Indeed, there is a special purification ritual, the *vrātyaṣṭoma*, in which they could be assimilated into vedic society and assume the Aryan status which they forfeited by not undertaking the brahmanical rites of passage. While evidence is lacking to say precisely who the Vrātyas were, they certainly seem to have been on the boundary of groups who were acceptable to the vedic Aryans, though Heesterman has suggested that the vedic, sacrificial initiate (*dīkṣita*) derives from the Vrātya.[8] The *Atharva Veda* describes them as wearing turbans, dressed in black, with two ram skins over their shoulders.[9]

The Vrātyas practised their own ceremonies. The precise nature and structure of these rites is unclear, but they were probably concerned with fertility and the magical renewal of life with the seasons. During the summer solstice 'great vow' (*mahāvrata*) ritual, the priest (*hotṛ*) muttered chants which included reference to the three breaths animating the body. These breaths are inhalation, the breath which is retained, and exhalation, and suggest an early kind of breath control which becomes developed as *prāṇāyāma* in later yogic traditions. This rite is accompanied by obscene dialogues and also involves ritual sexual intercourse between a 'bard', who may have otherwise remained celibate, and a 'prostitute'; a rite which has echoes in later tantric ritual (see pp. 189–91).

The Vrātyas demonstrate a close connection, found in later traditions, between asceticism and martialism. Warrior brotherhoods, skilled in physical techniques and the technologies of war, became associated with ascetic, renunciatory practices: the outer war, as it were, becomes an inner war to subdue the body and the passions. This connection between ascetic and martial fraternities is further borne out in that ascetic ideologies and practices emerged within the ruling of warrior classes of Indian society. The Buddha, for example, came from a martial background and the secret teachings of the Upaniṣads are associated with rulers.

While renunciation and asceticism are prefigured in vedic religion, a developed ideology of renunciation comes with a change in social and economic conditions in India from the sixth century BCE. These changes allowed for the development of ideas from outside the strictly brahmanical, ritual frame of reference. To these conditions we now turn.

Individualism and urbanization

Vedic ritualism developed in an agrarian society: the Aryans were pastoralists and later agriculturalists living in rural communities. By the fifth century BCE, however, an urban culture is developing along the Ganges plain and major kingdoms have arisen associated with the growth of urban centres. Of particular note are the kingdoms of Māgadha and Kosala, with the tribal 'republics' of the Vrijis and the Śakyas to the north. Some of these towns, such as Pataliputra (Patna), the capital of the Māgadha empire, were well-fortified centres which rapidly expanded with an increase in population, a food surplus, and the development of trade. With the development of kingdoms, trade routes were secured and roads constructed. Such improved communication in turn meant that new ideas could be more easily disseminated, particularly by wandering ascetics. It is in the context of this urbanization that renouncer traditions developed. Richard Gombrich has outlined this process, showing how the rise of towns under royal protection allowed for trade, for the movement of people, and for greater personal freedom and mobility. Along with this development came a bureaucracy and institutions of control which eroded the traditional, rural social order.[10]

Not only do we need to take these material and political concerns into consideration, but ideological concerns as well. Paul Wheatley has convincingly argued that the earliest towns and cities are not only commercial centres, but primarily ritual complexes, and that the size and complexity of the city's walls might be seen not only in terms of defence, but also in terms of status and prestige which reflect the king's glory.[11] Such a picture clearly fits into the Hindu theology of sacral kingship. The early cities of the Ganges valley are centres of early polities which reflect or symbolize the ritual status of the king. The urban centre as symbol of the king's power is a phenomenon which occurs in the later history of south Asia, for example at Vijayanagara, and attests to a continuity of the ideology of kingship from ancient times to the medieval period.

With urbanization a traditional agrarian lifestyle was eroded and emphasis placed on trade initiatives and enterprise; values which highlight the individual above the wider social group. The move from an agrarian to an urban situation provided a context in which individualism could develop in some segment of the community. With the weakening of traditional, ritualized behaviour patterns, the individual rather than the group, as Gombrich shows, became the important agent in the socioeconomic functioning of towns, as the trader, the shopkeeper, the skilled worker, and the government official.[12] This is not to say that at this time there was an articulate ideology of individualism which stressed autonomy and personal rights – there was not – or that the urban individual was not subject to law and a hierarchical social structure, but merely that socioeconomic functioning was placed more in the hands of innovators than would have been possible in a rural context. The form of individualism that developed in the Protestant West, with its emphasis on autonomy and responsibility, was not present in the ancient world, but a form of individuality which emphasized or particularized the distinct self, did develop in urban centres. Indeed, the separation or distinction of persons is necessary for them to be objects of social control by an abstract social structure, law and bureaucracy.[13]

The earliest ascetic traditions which are well documented, Jainism and Buddhism, grew up in urban contexts, where emerging commercial classes were interested in new ideas. The Buddha visited numerous towns, mentioned in the Buddhist scriptures, and was supported by the urban laity, some of whom were wealthy town-dwellers. Moreover, the majority of his community of monks and nuns seem to have been drawn from the towns rather than the country.[14]

The śramaṇa traditions

From about 800 to 400 BCE Sanskrit and Prakrit texts bear witness to the emergence of the new ideology of renunciation, in which knowledge (*jñāna*) is given precedence over action (*karma*), and detachment from the material and social world is cultivated through ascetic practices (*tapas*), celibacy, poverty and methods of mental training (*yoga*). The purpose of such training is the cultivation of altered or higher states of consciousness which will culminate in the blissful mystical experience of final liberation from the bonds of action and rebirth. While the renouncer of śramaṇa traditions differ on points of doctrine and method, they generally agree that life is characterized by suffering (*duḥkha*) and adhere to a teaching in which liberation (*mokṣa*, *nirvāna*) from suffering is a form of spiritual knowledge or gnosis (*jñāna*, *vidyā*). The spread of disease among the new urban population may well have contributed to the growth of ascetic movements and added poignancy to the doctrine of life as suffering.[15] In these new ascetic ideologies, spiritual salvation cannot be attained simply due to a high-caste birth, but only by liberating insight or understanding the nature of existence. The true Brahman, according to the Buddha, is not someone born to a particular mother, but a person whose conduct is pure and moral.[16] Personal experience in this way is placed above the received knowledge of the vedic revelation. At an early period, during the formation of the Upaniṣads and the rise of Buddhism and Jainism, we must envisage a common heritage of meditation and mental discipline practised by renouncers with varying affiliations to non-orthodox (Veda-rejecting) and orthodox (Veda-accepting) traditions.

The institution of world-renunciation or 'going forth' offers the renouncer (*śramaṇa*, *bhikṣu*, *parivrājaka*) an escape route from worldly suffering, as well as from worldly responsibilities, and a life dedicated to finding understanding and spiritual knowledge; a knowledge which is expressed and conceptualized in various ways according to different systems. While there are elements of doctrine and practice shared by the śramaṇa movements, there are nevertheless wide differences between them. The materialists (*lokāyata*, *cārvāka*), for example, rejected the idea of reincarnation and spiritual insight, while the Ājīvikas rejected free will. While the Buddhists emphasized a middle way between extremes of austerity and indulgence, the Jains emphasized extreme mortification in order to become detached from action.[17] Yet, while there are divergencies within Śramaṇism, all śramaṇa groups shared a common value system and framework of discourse, and all rejected the Veda as revelation and so radically turned against orthodox, brahmanical teaching or reinterpreted those teachings. These schools are understandably regarded as heterodox (*nāstika*) by orthodox (*āstika*) Brahmanism. Their mutual hostility has been pointed out by Romila Thapar who notes that the grammarian Patañjali refers to their attitude towards each other as being like that between a snake and a mongoose.[18]

Yet while Brahmanism rejects the authority and teachings of the śramaṇa schools, teachings akin to those of the Śramaṇas, concerning rebirth, retributive action, and liberation, come to dwell in the heart of the brahmanical tradition and find expression in the Upaniṣads, the fourth layer of the Veda, and in later literature.

Renunciation in the Upaniṣads

The śramaṇa traditions developed a clear identity, defining themselves against what they regard as an empty vedic ritualism which does not lead to liberation. By contrast the Upaniṣads – the Vedānta or 'end of the Veda' – define themselves centrally within the vedic tradition as a reinterpretation of the ritual process and an elucidation of its inner meanings. Indeed the Upaniṣads indicate no explicit awareness of non-vedic, ascetic traditions, though practices found in the Upaniṣads seem to be directly akin to Jain and Buddhist meditation methods.[19] The emphasis on a more personal religious experience is indicated not only in internalized meditation but also in the idea of a direct transmission of teachings from teacher to disciple.[20] The word *upaniṣad* is perhaps derived from the student or disciple sitting at the feet of a teacher to receive his teachings (*upa* = 'near to'; *niṣad* = 'to sit down') and the term *upaniṣad* takes on the general sense of 'esoteric teaching'.

THE INTERNALIZATION OF THE RITUAL

The Upaniṣads continue the work of the Brāhmaṇas and Āraṇyakas in interpreting the meaning of the śrauta ritual. With these texts we see the increasing importance of knowledge of esoteric correspondences as compared to ritual action; the sections on knowledge (*jñānakāṇḍa*) take precedence over sections on ritual (*karmakāṇḍa*). The earlier Upaniṣads continue the magical speculations of the Brāhmaṇas, which maintained that knowledge of the correspondences between ritual and cosmos is a kind of power. The opening verses of the *Bṛhadāraṇyaka Upaniṣad*, for example, begin by identifying the horse sacrifice (*aśvamedha*) with the natural world; the horse's head is the dawn, its eye the sun, its breath the wind and so on.[21] Again, the *Chāndogya Upaniṣad* illustrates this kind of speculation, though combined with the idea that knowledge gives rise to power or energy. Having identified the *udgītha*, the verses of the *Sāma Veda* chanted by the *udgātṛ* priest during the *śrauta* ritual, with the sacred syllable *aum*, the text makes the distinction between knowledge and ignorance:

> Saying *aum* one recites: saying *aum*, one orders: saying *aum*, one sings aloud in honour of that syllable, with its greatness and its essence.

> He who knows this thus, and he who knows not, both perform with it. Knowledge and ignorance, however, are different. What, indeed, one performs with knowledge, faith and meditation, that, indeed, becomes more powerful.[22]

The text then goes on in the next group of verses to internalize the ritual: the sound *aum* is to be contemplated as being identified with various parts of the body: with the breath, speech, eye, ear and mind.

Whereas the Brāhmaṇas are concerned with establishing the hidden connections between the *śrauta* ritual and the cosmos, connections which appear to be fairly arbitrary,[23] the Upaniṣads are concerned with contemplating the deeper significance of these correspondences. The emphasis moves from external performance to internal meditation; the true sacrifice becomes the fire oblation on the breath (*prāṇāgnihotra*), a sacrifice to the self within the self. The internalization of the ritual means that the real purpose of the rite is not its external performance, but knowledge of its deeper meaning, a meaning which points to an underlying foundation or being, supporting the ritual and even the cosmos itself. This being or essence of the ritual, the cosmos, and the self, is termed *brahman* and is identified with the sacred sound *aum* or *oṃ* (called the *pranava*).

BRAHMAN

In the Brāhmaṇas, the term *brahman* means the power of the ritual, apart from which there is nothing more ancient or brighter.[24] *Brahman* is a neuter noun and it should not be confused with the masculine noun Brahmā, the creator god, nor with Brāhmaṇa, the group of texts, nor Brahman (*brāhmaṇa*) the highest caste, though the term is related to these other meanings. In time, a process of abstraction occurred whereby *brahman* became a principle referring not only to the power of the ritual, but also to the essence of the universe; the very being at the heart of all appearances. In the *Bṛhadāraṇyaka Upaniṣad* there is a dialogue between one of the earliest Hindu theologians, Yājñavalkya, and Janaka, the king of Videha, which illustrates the early Upaniṣads' questing spirit for the essence of the universe. King Janaka tells Yājñavalkya the teachings of other sages he has heard concerning *brahman*, that it is speech (*vāc*), vital breath (*prāṇa*), the eye, the mind, and the heart (*hṛdaya*). Yājñavalkya replies that these answers are half-true and that *brahman* is in fact the deeper support of all these phenomena.[25]

This *brahman* is not only the essence of the ritual and of the world, but is also the essence of the self (*ātman*), the truth of a person beyond apparent differences. Uddālaka Āruṇi, who along with Yājñavalkya can be regarded as one of the earliest Hindu theologians, in dialogue with his son Śvetaketu, illustrates how *brahman* is the essence, the smallest particle of the cosmos. In an early example of theological empiricism, he splits a fruit and then the fruit's seed to show how *brahman* cannot be seen. Similarly, as salt placed in water by Śvetaketu completely dissolves and cannot be seen, though it can be tasted, so *brahman* is the essence of all things, which cannot be seen but can be experienced.[26] This essence is the self, and the passage explicating this concludes with the famous lines: 'that which is minute, the totality is that self. That is truth. That is the self. That you are, Śvetaketu.'

This impersonalist monism is central to the earlier Upaniṣads and becomes a theology of great importance, particularly in the later Vedānta tradition and in modern Neo-Hinduism (see ch. 11). The essence of the self is the absolute, realized within the self, through the knowledge of the ritual's inner meaning and the withdrawal of the senses from the sensory world. The emphasis in the Upaniṣads is on the internalization of ritual and the texts are even critical of their external performance. The true meaning of the ritual is not to be found in outer action, but in the realization of its symbolism and its esoteric meaning revealed by the Upaniṣads.[27]

The Upaniṣads represent the culmination of a process which comes to regard the individual self as having great inner depths, and, indeed, as containing the universe within. The truth (*satya*) is the absolute (*brahman*) which is also the self (*ātman*). This is the single reality underlying the diversity of appearances, knowledge of which is the purpose of the ritual's internalization. This knowledge is not simply information to be understood, but a direct and immediate intuition experienced as joy or bliss. To quote the *Taittirīya Upaniṣad*: 'He knew that *brahman* is bliss (*ānanda*). For truly, beings here are born from bliss, when born, they live by bliss and into bliss, when departing, they enter'.[28] This is no ordinary bliss, but is at the top of the hierarchy of blissful experiences, far beyond any ordinary human joy.

KARMA AND REINCARNATION

Such spiritual fulfilment and the blissful experience of realizing one's essence to be *brahman* is the cessation of action and its consequences, namely rebirth. The idea that every action has an effect which must be accounted for in this or future lifetimes, and that the experiences of the present lifetime are the consequences of past actions, is of central importance for Hindu soteriology. Salvation or liberation (*mokṣa, mukti, apavarga*) in most Hindu traditions is freedom from the cycle of reincarnation (*saṃsāra*), which is also to be freed from the store of action (*karma*) built up over innumerable lifetimes. This basic soteriological structure, developed with variations by most later traditions, begins to be articulated in the Upaniṣads.

The origin of the doctrines of karma and *saṃsāra* are obscure. These concepts were certainly circulating among the Śramaṇas, and Jainism and Buddhism developed specific and sophisticated ideas about the process of transmigration. It is very possible that karma and reincarnation entered mainstream brahmanical thought from the śramaṇa or renouncer traditions. Yet on the other hand, although there is no clear doctrine of transmigration in the vedic hymns, there is the idea of 'redeath': that a person, having died in this world, might die yet again in the next. Ritual procedures are meant to prevent this eventuality. From the notion of redeath the idea of a return to this world could have developed. We also have in the *Ṛg Veda* the idea that different parts of a person go to different places upon death: the eyes go to the sun, the breath (*ātman*) to the wind, and the essential 'person' to the ancestors.[29] Rebirth into this world could have developed from this partite view of a person. A third alternative is that the origin of transmigration theory lies outside of vedic or śramaṇa traditions in the tribal religions of the Ganges valley, or even in Dravidian traditions of south India.[30]

In the *Bṛhadāraṇyaka Upaniṣad* retributive action first appears to be a secret and little-known doctrine. Ārtabhāga questions Yājñavalkya about the fate of a person after death. Echoing the *Ṛg Veda*, he asks what becomes of the person after different parts have been dissipated – the eyes to the sun, the breath (*ātman*) to space, the mind to the moon and so on? Yajñavalkya leads him away to a private place and, warning him not to divulge this doctrine, tells him about karma: that meritorious action leads to merit (*puṇya*), while evil action leads to further evil (*pāpa*).[31] Later the text spells out the theory more clearly – that the self (*ātman*) moves from body to body, as a caterpillar or leech moves from one blade of grass to another.[32] By the later Upaniṣads the doctrine is firmly established. The *Śvetāśvatara Upaniṣad* (400–200 BCE), for example, clearly states that the subject, the 'performer of action which bears fruit', wanders in the cycle of transmigration according to his actions (*karma*).[33]

The origins of renunciation

Both brahmanical and śramaṇa asceticism share a number of common features, which presents a problem in understanding the origins of renunciation. On the one hand, the ideology of renunciation can be seen as a natural development from vedic ritual traditions; on the other, it can be argued that renunciation comes from outside the vedic tradition. It may, of course, be the case that both theories are accurate in some respects while lacking in others.

THE ORTHOGENETIC THEORY

What has been called the 'orthogenetic theory' of renunciation maintains that there is a development from the vedic, householder ideology of the śrauta ritual, to the ideology of renunciation. The term 'orthogenetic' is used by Heesterman to refer to this gradual, internal development within vedic thought.[34] In other words, renunciation is not an idea coming from outside the vedic community, perhaps from the pre-Aryan Dravidians, but is a development within vedic culture. Ultimately there is little difference between the ideal Brahman and the ideal renouncer, save one of emphasis. The gap or conflict in brahmanical society is not between the Brahman householder and the renouncer, but rather between the Brahman and the king (see above pp. 72–3).

On this account, renunciation, developed in the Upaniṣads and later codified in the Dharma Śāstras, has its origin in the vedic śrauta rituals as presented in the Brāhmaṇas and Śrauta Sūtras. Here the ritual patron (*yajamāna*) undergoes initiation (*dīkṣā*), becoming 'one who is initiated' (*dīkṣitā*), and performs ascetic practices in preparation for the ritual itself. The ritual symbolically acts out the regeneration or renewal of the patron and also symbolizes the regeneration of the cosmos. The patron is at the centre of the ritual which he has instigated, thereby emphasizing that 'man depends only on his own (ritual) work'.[35] The idea of the ritual as a private process develops, on Heesterman's account, into the upanisadic ideal that the true ritual is its internalization or transcendence, and renunciation develops as a consequence of this internalization.

RENOUNCER AND BRAHMAN

Furthermore, there is a strong parallelism between the ideal code of the Brahman householder and the renouncer; their difference is one of degree rather than kind. Like the renouncer, the Brahman should restrain his senses, be truthful, practise non-violence to all beings, and act with detachment and equanimity[36] – the difference between the two figures being that the Brahman is fulfilling his householder's obligations, whereas the renouncer is in the last stage of life (*āśrama*), exempt from ritual obligations. Whereas the renouncer has turned his back on society, the Brahman has not, or rather has only turned his back on the social world during the śrauta ritual, but returns to it after the rite's conclusion.

Complementing Heesterman's argument, Madeleine Biardeau and Charles Malamoud have also argued for the continuity of vedic tradition. For Biardeau the various traditions within the Hindu universe are united at a deeper level: the diverse, though interrelated, parts are integrated into a complete Hindu culture. This integration is not an institutionalized unity, which is nowhere found in Hinduism, but rather a structural unity – all the fragmented movements within Hinduism, including renunciation, stemming from the vedic revelation.[37] This structural unity can be perceived in the two most important elements within Hindu culture, sacrifice and renunciation, which are two sides of the same coin, the difference being that the householder is concerned with external sacrifice, whereas the renouncer has internalized the sacrifice. The continuity is further stressed in that both the ritual patron and the renouncer undergo purificatory rites and so are structurally related to each other.

NON-VEDIC ORIGINS OF RENUNCIATION

Undoubtedly, as Biardeau and Heesterman have shown, there are elements in the renouncer tradition which are also present in the householder's ritual tradition, and the full documentation of the renouncer traditions is later than texts describing the śrauta rituals. Yet it might be the case that the renouncer traditions develop outside the vedic ritualist circles, and gradually become incorporated and assimilated by the vedic tradition.

Patrick Olivelle has argued in a number of publications that renunciation represents a new ideology which emerges within the context of vedic ritualism and uses the terminology of that tradition, but whose ethos and aims are quite distinct. More than mere difference, there is a conflict between the two traditions. The 'conflict of tradition' is not therefore, as Heesterman argues, between the Brahman ritualist and the king, but rather between the Brahman ritualist and the renouncer. The fault line runs in a different direction, separating the world of the Brahman householder from the world of the renouncer.

This distinction between householder and renouncer has been a focus of Louis Dumont's work, on whose ideas Olivelle builds. Dumont argues that Hinduism can be seen in terms of a dialogue between the 'world-renouncer' and the 'man-in-the-world', namely the Brahman, male, householder. Unlike the renouncer, the man-in-the-world is defined by his social existence, and functions within the restrictions and boundaries of his social context, namely the caste system. The caste system, based on the distinction between purity and impurity, determines the Brahman householder's status. Because of the social restrictions of caste, the man-in-the-world is not an individual, but exists purely in a network of social relationships, unlike the renouncer who has stepped outside this network.[38] According to this view, the renouncer is outside society and so has established an individuality. The renouncer is an individual devoted to his own salvation, from whom the seminal ideas and influences on the householder religion are derived. The renouncer, as an individual outside society, is the true agent of development in Indian religion and the creator of values which enter the brahmanical householder tradition from outside.

While many criticisms can be levelled against Dumont's thesis, particularly that it takes away agency from Indian social actors,[39] the idea that renunciation introduces a 'new' element into Indian religions and presents a challenge to vedic orthodox ritual tradition needs to be taken seriously. Olivelle has developed the distinction between the renouncer ideal and the householder ideal, arguing that the 'profound conflict' between the two cannot be explained if Heesterman is correct in thinking that renunciation is a development of vedic thought. Statements in the later Dharma literature which praise the Brahman as the ideal renouncer, rather than reflecting the close proximity of renouncer and Brahman, show that renouncer values are incorporated into vedic ideology, and statements lauding the Brahman as the ideal renouncer are often 'mere rhetoric'.[40]

To summarize this discussion so far: there are essentially two positions with regard to the origins of renunciation in India: on the one hand it may have developed from vedic ritualism (the view of Heesterman and Biardeau), on the other it may have developed from outside the vedic world, though not necessarily outside the brahmanical world (the view of Olivelle drawing on the work of Dumont). The former position highlights the continuities between the vedic tradition and renouncer traditions, between the individualism of the ritualist and renouncer, and between the purificatory practices of the ritualist and renouncer. The latter position highlights the discontinuities, arguing that the world-negating values of renunciation are quite distinct from the world-affirming values of the ritualist householder. It seems clear that the origins of renunciation cannot be understood simply in terms of either a vedic or a non-vedic tradition. Rather, there is a complex process of assimilation from outside the vedic sphere as well as a transformation of elements within the vedic tradition.

Orthodox renunciation

The early renouncers wandered alone, in small itinerant groups, or, with the advent of Buddhism, joined a monastic community. While there have been women renouncers, most have been men. Renouncers are homeless except for four months of the year during the rainy season, they obtain food by begging and dress in an ochre robe or go naked. It is significant that early Brahmanism does not contain institutions of renunciation akin to those of Buddhism or Jainism. There are certainly lineages of teachers going back many generations, but these are not monastic institutions. No monastic institution develops in Hinduism until the medieval period, though, nevertheless, in the Upaniṣads we do find the idea of giving up worldly life and retiring to the forest to perform religious observances. For example, in the *Bṛhadāraṇyaka Upaniṣad* the sage Yājñavalkya decides to leave his two wives, his status as a householder, and retire to the forest.[41]

While there is no monasticism in early brahmanical tradition, the fourfold system of the āśramas or stages of life develops, in which renunciation (*saṃnyāsa*) is the final, liberating institution. Orthoprax renunciation is open only to the twice-born, and is meant only for those who have fulfilled their worldly, social obligations as householders or for those celibate students who have never become householders. Orthoprax renunciation is only for those who have fulfilled vedic obligations and who correctly perform rules laid down in the Dharma Śāstras. This contrasts with the heteroprax renouncer traditions of Buddhism and Jainism, which accept people from a wider social spectrum and of all ages, though there are some restrictions on people entering the early Buddhist monastic order, including a ban on soldiers and slaves.[42]

The central emphasis of brahmanical religion is on the householder and the performance of the appropriate ritual, though by the time of the

Dharma Śāstras (*c.* 500 BCE–500 CE) renunciation (*saṃnyāsa*) is incorporated into the brahmanical system as the last stage of life (*āśrama*). The actual term *saṃnyāsa* is purely brahmanical, not occurring before the second century BCE, and does not occur in the literatures of Buddhism and Jainism. Later texts develop the idea of renunciation, particularly the Saṃnyāsa Upaniṣads, composed during the first few centuries of the common era. These texts describe the act of renunciation, the behaviour expected of the renouncer, and types of renouncers. Like his heterodox counterpart, the orthodox renouncer seeks liberation from the cycle of birth and death by fostering detachment from worldly concerns and desires through asceticism and yoga practices.

The rite of renunciation is a ritual to end ritual and the shift, at least symbolically, from a ritual to a non-ritual state; from action to non-action. The rite of renunciation will be the last time the renouncer kindles his sacred fire. Renunciation means the abandoning of the religion of vedic ritual and the abandoning of fire, a symbol of the Brahman's status. In giving up fire, the renouncer has given up brahmanical rites, he has given up cooking and must henceforward beg for food, and he has given up life in the home for the homeless life of wandering. The Law Books, such as the *Viṣṇu Smṛti*, state that a renouncer must not stay for more than one night in a village,[43] though he can remain in the same place during the rainy season. Symbolically breathing in the flames during his last rite, the renouncer internalizes the fire of the vedic solemn ritual and so abandons its external use.[44] Taking the fire into himself, the renouncer also gives up his old clothes, becomes naked and so resembles his condition at birth. He offers his sacred thread, a symbol of his high-caste status worn over the shoulder, into the fire and takes on a waistband, loincloth and ochre robe, while bearing a staff, water pot and begging bowl. Some renouncers, the Nagas, remain naked.

There are a number of variations on the ritual of renunciation. Sometimes a renouncer will symbolically perform his own funeral before the fire, which consumes his old, social self. Sometimes the rite will involve the burning of the ritual implements, but, whatever the variations, the important point is that this is the last time the renouncer will kindle fire and thenceforth he will not be allowed to attend further rituals.[45] There are exceptions to this and some renouncers do maintain fires, practising austerity through the 'five fire sacrifice', which involves meditating surrounded by five fires in the heat of the day. Nevertheless, these exceptions aside, generally the renouncer has abandoned fire and will not even be cremated at death, but rather his body placed in a sacred river or buried upright in a special tomb or *samādh*.

Later renunciate orders

When they are not wandering, many renouncers, also known as 'good men' (*sādhus*) and 'good women' (*sādhvīs*), have chosen to live a life alone on the edges of society, by the banks of sacred rivers, or in wild places such as mountainous regions or cremation grounds. Wearing ochre robes, or naked, covered with sacred ash, with shaven heads or long, matted hair, these renouncers develop their own spiritual practice (*sādhana*) for the purpose of liberation while living (*jīvanmukti*). Others have joined communities of renouncers and live in 'hermitages' (*āśramas*) or 'monasteries' (*maṭhas*). Such communities are associated with larger Hindu traditions, particularly the Śaiva and Vaiṣṇava traditions, focused on the great Hindu deities Śiva and Viṣṇu respectively. Some renunciate orders are centrally placed within the vedic tradition, while others, such as cremation ground ascetics associated with the worship of Śiva and the Goddess, are on the edges of vedic orthodoxy and orthopraxy (see p. 161).

While monasticism developed in Buddhism from its inception, similar institutions only appear later in Hinduism. According to tradition, the great Vedānta theologian Śaṅkara (*c.* 788–820 CE) founded monastic centres in the four corners of India, namely at Śringeri in Kerala, Dwarka in the far west, Badrinath in the Himalayas and Puri on the east coast. Another important centre at Kanchi in Tamilnadu may have been founded by Śaṅkara or his disciple Sureśvara. Along with these monastic centres, Śaṅkara founded the renunciate order of the 'ten named ones', the Daśanāmis, namely *giri* ('mountain'), *puri* ('city'), *bhārati* ('learning'), *vana* ('forest'), *āraṇya* ('forest'), *parvata* ('mountain'), *sāgara* ('ocean'), *tīrṭha* ('ford'), *āśrama* ('hermitage') and *sarasvatī* ('eloquence'). These orders are associated with the different monastic centres: the Bhāratis, Puris, and Sarasvatīs at Śringeri; the Tīrṭhas and Āśramas at Dwarka; the Giri, Sāgara and Parvata at Badrinath; and the Āraṇyas and Vanas at Puri. The hierarch of the monastery at Puri is regarded as the head of the entire Daśanāmi order and is referred to as the *jagadguru*, the teacher of the universe. At initiation, the renouncer into these orders is given a new name, often ending in Ānanda, and the name of the order he or she is joining.

The orders founded by Śaṅkara were partly instrumental in eradicating

Jainism and Buddhism from south India and also in giving coherence and a sense of pan-Indian identity to orthodox, vedic traditions. Indeed, renouncers have provided an important sense of coherence within Hinduism, as they wander around the villages teaching and conveying religious ideas to ordinary people. Also of importance in giving a sense of cohesion to vedic tradition is the renouncer's pilgrimage of circumambulating India by visiting the 'four corners' of Badrinath in the north, Puri in the east, Rameshwaram in the south, and Dwarka in the west.

The Daśanāmis are among the most orthodox and learned of Hindu renouncers. Clad in ochre robes they can be contrasted with the naked renouncers, the Nāgas, who, since the seventh century CE have been warrior–Ascetics, protectors of the Daśanāmi tradition. These armed ascetics, like the Daśanāmis, philosophically adhere to a monistic metaphysics (see pp. 241–2) and their tutelary diety is Śiva, the lord of ascetics and yogins. These warrior–ascetic orders develop from the ninth to eighteenth centuries as a response to Muslim invasions and organize themselves into six 'regiments' or *ākhāras* (called Ānanda, Nirañjanī, Junā, Āvāhan, Atal and Nirvāṇī).[46] During the seventeenth century Vaiṣṇava warrior sects arise, the *bairāgīs*, who, unlike the Nāgas, do not go naked. There are also traditions of fighting ascetics who have developed elaborate fighting systems, particularly in Kerala.

Having abandoned the world, the renouncer can practise asceticism or the development of 'inner heat' (*tapas*) in order to attain liberation. Asceticism might take the form of a severe penance, such as vowing not to lie down or sit for twelve years but only rest leaning on a frame, or to hold aloft an arm until the muscles become atrophied. However, an ascetic is particularly encouraged to practise yoga in order to achieve a state of non-action: to still the body, still the breath, and, finally, to still the mind.

Yoga

Alongside concepts of world renunciation, transmigration, karma, and liberation are ideas about the ways or paths to liberation – the methods or technologies which can lead out of the world of suffering. There are a number of responses to the question of how liberation can be attained in Hindu traditions. On the one hand, theistic traditions maintain that liberation occurs through the grace of a benign deity to whom one is devoted, on the other, non-theistic traditions maintain that liberation occurs through the sustained effort of detaching the self from the sensory world through asceticism and meditation, which leads to a state of gnosis (*jñāna*). Both responses can be combined when devotion is seen as a form of knowledge and grace as a complement to effort.

The term *yoga*, derived from the Sanskrit root *yuj*, 'to control', 'to yoke' or 'to unite', refers to these technologies or disciplines of asceticism and meditation which are thought to lead to spiritual experience and profound understanding or insight into the nature of existence. Yoga is the means whereby the mind and senses can be restrained, the limited, empirical self or ego (*ahaṃkāra*) can be transcended and the self's true identity eventually experienced. It is this aspect of Hinduism which is not necessarily confined to any particular Hindu worldview and has, indeed, been exported beyond the boundaries of Hinduism to the contemporary West. While the development of yoga, and the idea of spiritual salvation (*mokṣa*) to which it leads, must be understood historically in the context of traditions of renunciation, which, as we have seen, form an ideological and social complex developing in the new urban centres of ancient India, yoga becomes detached from the institution of renunciation and becomes adapted to the householder's life.

The concept of yoga as a spiritual discipline not confined to any particular sectarian affiliation or social form, contains the following important features:

- consciousness can be transformed through focusing attention on a single point;
- the transformation of consciousness eradicates limiting, mental constraints or impurities such as greed and hate;
- yoga is a discipline, or range of disciplines, constructed to facilitate the transformation of consciousness.

Yoga in Hindu traditions

The history of yoga is long and ancient. The earliest vedic texts, the Brāhmaṇas, bear witness to the existence of ascetic practices (*tapas*) and the vedic Saṃhitās contain some references, as we have seen, to ascetics, namely the Munis or Keśins and the Vrātyas. In the śramaṇa traditions and in the Upaniṣads technologies for controlling the self and experiencing higher states of consciousness in meditation are developed, and the literature of yoga traditions on this subject is extensive. In the Upaniṣads one of the earliest references to meditation is in the *Bṛhadāraṇyaka Upaniṣad*, the earliest Upaniṣad, which states that, having become calm and concentrated, one perceives the self (*ātman*) within oneself.[47] The actual term *yoga* first occurs in the *Kaṭha Upaniṣad* where it is defined as the steady control of the senses, which, along with the cessation of mental activity, leads to the supreme state.[48]

Yoga's appearance in the *Kaṭha Upaniṣad* is in the context of the story of Naciketas and Death. Naciketas, who is banished to the realm of death when he irritates his father, is kept waiting while the god of death, Yama, is out. Upon his return Yama grants Naciketas three boons in recompense for so rudely keeping him waiting. Naciketas' first request is to be returned to his father, for the second he asks about the sacrificial fire which leads to heaven, and for the third he asks how to conquer re-death (*punarmṛtyu*). Yama tries to dissuade him from asking this third question with the promise of long life and riches, but in the face of death, Naciketas replies, 'all life is short'. No matter how long life lasts, death takes it in the end. Yama eventually responds to the question, saying that the wise man realizes God through the practice of self-contemplation. The text goes on to liken a person to a chariot: the self (*ātman*) is the controller of the chariot, the body the chariot itself, and the senses are the horses. As a charioteer controls the horses of the chariot, so the self should control the senses through keeping them restrained.[49]

The *Śvetāśvatara Upaniṣad* similarly says that a yogin should hold the body erect, repress the breathing and restrain the mind as he would 'a chariot yoked with vicious horses'. This yoking of the mind leads to inner visions and, more importantly, 'a body made in the fire of yoga' which ensures that the wise man is healthy, freed from sorrow, his purpose completed.[50] The last of the classical Upaniṣads to deal with yoga to any extent is the *Maitrāyaṇīya* or *Maitrī Upaniṣad*, belonging to the branch of the black Yajur Veda. This text describes a retired king, Bṛhadratha, who practises austerity (*tapas*) by staring at the sun with his arms raised high for 1,000 days. He is then visited by an enlightened ascetic, who tells the old king about the difference between the phenomenal self subject to karma, and the pure self unaffected by action. The seer, Śākāyanya, then teaches the king a six-faceted yoga involving breath-control (*prāṇāyāma*), withdrawal of the senses (*pratyahāra*), meditation (*dhyāna*), concentration (*dhāraṇā*), inquiry (*tarka*) and absorption (*samādhi*), a classification which predates the similar system of Patañjali's classical yoga (see below).[51]

There are several centuries between the composition of the *Kaṭha* and the *Śvetāśvatara Upaniṣads* and we must assume that the yoga tradition developed during this time within the orbit of Hindu thought. Parts of the famous epic poem the *Mahābhārata* (*c* 400 BCE–300 CE) contain passages describing the practice of yoga as does the *Bhagavad Gītā*, including a complete chapter (ch. 6) devoted to traditional yoga practice. The Gītā also introduces the famous three kinds of yoga, 'knowledge' (*jñāna*), 'action' (*karma*), and 'love' (*bhakti*). Upaniṣads continue to be composed into the common era and tend to become sectarian in orientation. One group of about twenty texts, the Yoga Upaniṣads, probably dating from around 100 BCE to 300 CE, contain interesting details about the practice of yoga, such as postures, breath control, inner visions, the yoga of inner sound (*nāda*, *śabda*), and descriptions of esoteric or subtle anatomy.

The most famous of the Yoga Upaniṣads, the *Yogatattva*, mentions four kinds of yoga: *mantra-yoga*, which involves the repetition of mantras; *laya-yoga*, the symbolic dissolution of the cosmos within the body and the raising of a corporeal energy known as Kuṇḍalinī; *haṭha-yoga*, the yoga of 'force' focusing on various postures, breath control, visions of light, and inner sound; and *rāja-yoga* ('royal', or simply 'the best', yoga), which is the classical system of Patañjali. The text also mentions the magical powers (*siddhi*) gained by the yogin. *Haṭha-yoga* itself develops an extensive literature, particularly Svātmarāma's *Haṭhayoga-pradīpikā* (fifteenth century CE), which has links with Indian alchemy, Tantrism and the Siddha tradition.

RĀJA-YOGA

The text which is most significant in the yoga tradition is Patañjali's *Yoga Sūtra*. This text, composed sometime between 100 BCE and 500 CE, contains pithy aphorisms on classical yoga, called the 'eight-limbed' (*aṣṭāṅga*) or 'the best' (*rāja*) yoga. The *Yoga Sūtra* represents a codification of yoga ideas and practices which had been developing for many centuries. Patañjali gives a succinct definition of yoga in the second sūtra: 'yoga is the cessation of mental fluctuations'.[52] That is, yoga is a state of concentration in which the wandering mind, fed by sense impressions and memories, is controlled and made to be one-pointed (*ekāgratā*). This mental control occurs through developing eight aspects or limbs of the yogic path. These are:

1 ethics or restraint (*yama*), comprising non-violence (*ahiṃsā*), telling the truth, not stealing, celibacy and not being greedy;
2 discipline (*niyama*), comprising cleanliness, serenity, asceticism, study, devotion to the Lord;
3 posture (*āsana*);
4 breath-control (*prāṇāyāma*);
5 sense-withdrawal (*pratyahāra*);
6 concentration (*dhāraṇā*);
7 meditation (*dhyāna*);
8 absorbed concentration (*samādhi*), comprising: (i) concentration with the support of objects of consciousness (*samprajñāta samādhi*) sustained on four levels – initial thought (*vitarka*), sustained thought (*vicāra*), joy (*ānanda*), and the sense of 'I' (*asmitā*); (ii) concentration without the support of objects of consciousness (*asamprajñāta samādhi*).

Having developed ethical behaviour and discipline the yogin stills the body and the breath and withdraws attention from the external world, as a tortoise pulls its limbs and head into its shell, in order to control the mind through various degrees of concentration or meditation. There is a clear connection here between consciousness, breath and body; the body is stilled through posture, the breath through *prāṇāyāma* and the mind through concentration. In the state of concentrated absorption or *samādhi* the yogin is no longer conscious of the body or physical environment, but his consciousness is absorbed in a higher state, free from greed, anger and delusion. The states of *samādhi* are classified by Patañjali into various degrees of subtlety and refinement until the transcendent state of 'isolation' is finally achieved. These degrees of absorption represent levels of consciousness purified of limiting constraints.

While the experience of *samādhi* leading up to liberation (*kaivalya*) is ineffable, *kaivalya* is nevertheless conceptualized within a framework of dualist metaphysics, namely the metaphysics of the Sāṃkhya school of philosophy. In this school there is a complete distinction between the self or the passive, conscious observer (*puruṣa*) and matter (*prakṛti*). In his exposition, Patañjali assumes this system as the philosophical backdrop to his thinking. *Kaivalya*, in Patañjali's system, is liberation from the wheel of transmigration. However, unlike the monistic Upaniṣads, liberation is here not the realization of the self's identity with the absolute, but rather the realization of the self's solitude and complete transcendence. This is a condition of pure awareness in which the self has become completely detached from its entanglement with matter. It is a state beyond worldly or sensory experience, in which consciousness is absorbed in itself without an object, or is reflexive, having itself as its own object.

HAṬHA-YOGA

While Patañjali's yoga is primarily concerned with developing mental concentration in order to experience *samādhi*, *haṭha-yoga*, or the 'yoga of force', develops a system of elaborate and difficult postures (*āsana*) accompanied by breathing techniques (*prāṇāyāma*). Although aspects of these practices are much older, *haṭha-yoga* as a complete system was developed from about the ninth century CE by the Nāth or Kānphaṭa sect, which traces its origins to a saint, Matsyendranāth, revered also in Buddhism, and his disciple Gorakhnāth (between the ninth and thirteenth centuries CE). The purpose of *haṭha-yoga* is the realization of liberation during life, in which the self awakens to its innate identity with the absolute (*sahaja*), a realization made possible through cultivating a body made perfect or divine in the 'fire' of yoga.

One of the main texts of the tradition is the *Haṭhayoga-pradīpikā* by Svātmarāma (fifteenth century) which describes the various complex postures (*āsana*), breath control, and 'locks' (*bandha*), which are the muscular constrictions of breath and energy which flow through the body.[53] Other texts of note are the *Gheraṇḍa Saṃhitā*, the *Śiva Saṃhitā* and, probably the oldest Nāth text, the *Siddhasiddhānta Paddhati*. While these texts are concerned with the more subtle levels of meditation, the emphasis is undoubtedly upon disciplines of the body: cleansing the stomach by swallowing a cloth, drawing water into the rectum, cleaning the nose with threads and taking water through the nose and expelling it through the mouth. Such practices are highly regarded as purifications which make the body fit for the more difficult practices of postures and breath control.

ESOTERIC ANATOMY

These texts also describe the existence of a subtle body with centres or 'wheels' (*cakra*) located along its central axis, connected by channels (*nāḍī*) along which flows the energy (*prāṇa*), or the life-force, which animates the body. Of these channels, three are of particular importance: the central channel (*suṣumnā nāḍī*) which connects the base of the trunk to the

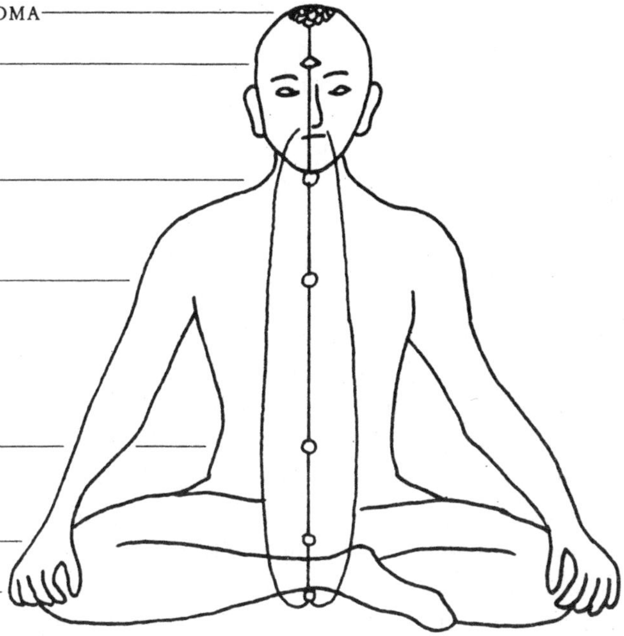

Figure 3 The esoteric anatomy of yoga

crown of the head, forming a vertical axis through the body, and two channels to its right and left, flowing from the nostrils and joining the central channel at its base. Through *haṭha-yoga* the energy lying dormant at the base of the central channel in the 'root centre' (*mūlādhāra*) is awakened. This energy is envisaged as the goddess Kuṇḍalinī, the 'serpent power', which flows up the central channel to the 'thousand petalled lotus' (*sahasrāra padma*) at the crown of the head, where the bliss of liberation is experienced.[54]

While in earlier texts there are various systems of *cakras* and *nāḍīs*, one system of six or seven *cakras* along the body's axis becomes the dominant, pan-Hindu model, adopted by most yoga schools. This system originates in the cult of the tantric goddess Kubjikā in about the eleventh century CE, but rapidly becomes a popular and standardized model of esoteric anatomy. These centres are said to be located in the regions of the perineum, the genitals, the solar plexus, the heart, the throat, between the eyes and at the crown of the head (see fig. 3). The power of Kuṇḍalinī, awakened by *haṭha-yoga* rises up the central channel, piercing these centres until the bliss of union with the god Śiva residing at the crown of the head is achieved. Each centre or lotus is described as being associated with a particular sound and having a specific number of petals, upon which are inscribed the letters of the Sanskrit alphabet. It is not clear that such systems of esoteric anatomy were meant to be understood in a literal or ontological sense; they were rather systems of visualization in meditation for the purpose of achieving *samādhi*.

One important 'centre' for the Nāth yogis, not incorporated into the six-centre scheme, is the 'palate centre' (*talu-cakra*) or uvula, known as the 'royal tooth', from which is said to drip the nectar of immortality (*amṛta*). This part of the body as an important locus for spiritual realization is attested from as early as the *Taittirīya Upaniṣad* which describes this point as the 'birthplace of Indra' where the head is 'split' a hair's width.[55] One of the Nāth practices, known as the *khecarī mudrā*, is to stop the nectar of immortality dripping away through this 'tooth' by turning the tongue back inside the palate and entering the cavity leading into the skull. The *Haṭhayogapradīpikā* details how this is to be achieved by cutting the membrane which connects the tongue with the lower part of the mouth and gradually stretching the tongue.[56] The dripping of the nectar of immortality from the crown of the head through the *talu-cakra* is not only regarded as a metaphor for the attention flowing out into the world, but at one level is taken literally, and the *khecarī mudrā* is meant to stop this flow. A yogin who has performed this technique is said to be not afflicted by disease, not tainted by karma and unaffected by time. He does not need to sleep and can control desire, even if 'embraced by a passionate woman'.[57]

THE YOGA OF INNER SOUND

The practice of Kuṇḍalinī yoga, the raising of energy in the body, and the doctrine of an esoteric anatomy, is accompanied in *haṭha-yoga* by a further practice, the yoga of inner or 'unstruck' sound (*anāhata nāda* or *śabda*). The absolute manifests in the form of sound in *haṭha* and other yoga doctrines. This subtle sound resounds in the central channel and can be heard by the yogin by blocking the ears, nose and eyes and controlling the breath. Through concentrating on this inner sound, which, according to the *Haṭhayogapradīpikā* initially resembles a tinkling sound, then a rumbling sound like a kettledrum, a flute, and then a lute, the yogin becomes absorbed in the supreme reality which is, ultimately, his true self. Through the yoga of inner sound the mind is controlled and becomes absorbed, like a serpent which, on hearing the sound of a flute, 'becomes oblivious of all else, and, absorbed in the one thing, does not move away elsewhere'.[58]

This doctrine of inner sound is well attested in the Yoga Upaniṣads, mostly composed between the fourteenth and fifteenth centuries, though it has precursors in the earlier vedic idea of the syllable *oṃ*, the sound of the universe identified with *brahman*. Indeed mantras might be regarded as expressions of the inner sound and *mantra-yoga*, the repetition (*japa*) of mantras, as a means of accessing the inner sound which is their source. The yoga of inner sound is important for many contemporary Hindu yoga schools, particularly those within the Radhasoami tradition whose central teaching is that of inner sound manifested in the form of the guru.[59]

As in many yoga traditions there is a correlation between psychological experience and cosmology. The inner experiences of yoga, the appreciation of sound and light, are regarded not only as states of individual psychology, but also as subtle levels of a hierarchical cosmos. Like an onion, the yogic cosmos is divided into a number of layers – the lower, grosser levels corresponding to the usual, fluctuating states of human consciousness, the higher levels corresponding to more refined, purer states identified with various levels of *samādhi*. The practice of Kuṇḍalinī yoga and the yoga of inner sound are not only regarded as psychological experiences, but as a journey through the layers of the cosmos back to its source.

MAGICAL POWERS

While the ultimate aim of yoga practice is liberation in life, along the way yoga traditions claim that magical powers are attained, almost incidentally. While generally the cultivation of these powers for worldly ends is frowned upon, they nevertheless hold an important position as indicators of progress along the path. The third section of Patañjali's *Yoga Sūtra* is devoted to magical powers or wonders. Patañjali says that upon attaining concentration, or the mental penetration of the objects of consciousness, various powers begin to arise. These powers include knowledge of past and future, knowledge of past lives, telepathy, the ability to disappear, foreknowledge of one's own death, great strength, supernormal senses, levitation, and omniscience, including knowledge of the cosmic regions.[60] While such powers may be advantageous from the perspective of waking consciousness, they are a hindrance to higher consciousness, for they create attachment.

The commentary on the *Yoga Sūtra* by Vyāsa lists eight magical powers or accomplishments (*siddhi*): the ability to become as small as an atom, levitation, the ability to expand, all-pervasiveness, the power of irresistible will, control over the natural elements, the power to create and the fulfilment of desires.[61] This is a standard list of magical powers found in other texts, though there are variants. These powers are included in the Buddhist system as the first of the five higher knowledges (*abhijñā*) attained by meditation, which shows that the association of meditation or yoga with supernormal powers has been within Indian meditation traditions from an early date. We are dealing here with oral traditions of teachings in which the list of powers, as well as of other states, has been standardized and the original meaning of some of this terminology has become obscure.

Summary

This chapter has surveyed a complex set of concepts, practices and social forms which are at the heart of Hinduism and which have developed over thousands of years. Renunciation, while being incorporated within mainstream vedic tradition, may have originated outside that tradition in the śramaṇa movements of which Buddhism and Jainism are a part. Yet whatever its origin, whether from within the vedic tradition or from outside it, renunciation is a vital institution within Hinduism and central to Hindu soteriology. Along with renunciation go ideas of karma – that a person reaps the consequences of their action – reincarnation, and liberation or salvation from the cycle of rebirth. Yoga is the method of attaining liberation, for both renouncers and laity, and we have in this chapter surveyed the origins of yoga and some of the central developments in its vast history. Yoga has been adapted to different doctrinal systems and has been used in the service of different traditions within Hinduism, most notably of the traditions of Śiva and Viṣṇu. To the latter tradition we now turn.

5 Narrative traditions and early Vaiṣṇavism

The first millennium BCE saw the development of the brahmanical traditions of ritual, adherence to *varṇāśrama-dharma* and the ideology of renunciation. These developments occurred within the context of the growth of kingdoms, such as Māgadha in the fourth century BCE, and an ideology of sacral kingship. From about 500 BCE through the first millennium CE, there was a growth of sectarian worship of particular deities, and vedic sacrifice, though never dying out, gave way to devotional worship (*pūjā*). Performing *pūjā* is a way of expressing love or devotion (*bhakti*) to a deity in some form, and became the central religious practice of Hinduism. Bhakti to a personal God (*Bhagavān*) or Goddess (*Bhagavatī*), became a central, all-pervasive movement. This growth of Hindu theism and devotionalism is reflected in the Sanskrit narrative traditions of the Epics (*itihāsa*), in mythological and ritual treatises known as the Purāṇas, and in devotional poetry in vernacular languages, particularly Tamil. This chapter will trace some of these developments, focusing on the rise of the gods Viṣṇu and Kṛṣṇa and the traditions associated with them, which came to be characterized as 'Vaiṣṇava'.

Hindu narrative traditions

There is no historiography in south Asia, with a few exceptions, of the kind which developed in the Greek, Arabic and European traditions. This lack of historiography has made the dating of Sanskrit texts difficult and has reinforced a tendency to construct India as ahistorical, mythical and irrational, in contrast to the West – seen as historical, scientific and rational. The construction of India as the West's irrational 'other' has tended to hide the strongly 'rationalist' element in Hindu culture (the science of ritual, grammar, architecture, mathematics, logic and philosophy) and to underplay the mythical dimension in western thought. Nevertheless, Hinduism did produce elaborate mythical narratives in which there is no clear distinction between 'history', 'hagiography' and 'mythology'. Indeed, the Sanskrit term *itihāsa* embraces the western categories of 'history' and 'myth'. We have texts written in Sanskrit, and vernacular languages, which are clearly presenting what were regarded as important ideas, stories and presentations of normative and non-normative behaviour, and the historicity of particular events is either assumed, or is simply not an issue. Rather, what seems to be important with these mythological narratives is the story being told, the sense of truth that it conveys, and the sense of communal or traditional values and identity being communicated.

The two most important groups of Hindu narrative traditions embodied in oral and written texts are the two Epics, the *Mahābhārata* and *Rāmāyaṇa*, and the Purāṇas. The *Itihāsa Purāṇa* is even known as the 'fifth Veda', although it is classified as *smṛti*, texts of human authorship, and not *śruti*, revelation, and all castes have access to it, not only the twice-born. In these texts we see reflected the concerns of political life at the court, the concerns of Brahmans, the concerns of ordinary people, and descriptions of ritual, pilgrimage and mythology. These texts also document the rise of the great theistic traditions of Hinduism focused on the gods, particularly Viṣṇu, Śiva and Devī, the Goddess. Hindu traditions have been communicated through the generations in these narrative genres, which still play a vital role in contemporary Hindu life, though sometimes now mediated through the television and cinema screen. The *Itihāsa Purāṇa* has had, and continues to have, immense impact upon Hinduism at all levels.

Although the Epics contain a wealth of material which cannot be neatly categorized as belonging to any particular tradition, there is nevertheless a case for saying that the Epics are primarily Vaiṣṇava in orientation, as, indeed, are many of the Purāṇas. Even the *Mahābhārata* which is sometimes compared to an encyclopaedia of Hindu deities, stories, yoga, rituals and theologies, is orientated towards the traditions of Viṣṇu. Some review of this vast literature is necessary in order to understand the unfolding of Hindu theistic traditions in general and the religions of Viṣṇu in particular.

The Mahābhārata

The *Mahābhārata* is an epic of universal proportions with appeal across centuries and across cultures, as the popularity of Peter Brook's nine-hour English stage production has attested. It is the longest epic poem in the world, comprising over 100,000 verses. According to tradition, the author of the text was the sage Vyāsa whose name means 'an arranger', though scholarship has shown that it was in fact compiled over several centuries from the first half of the first millennium BCE, reaching its established form by the first century CE, though still being formulated by the fourth century. There were probably two major stages in its composition. The first, a version of about 7,000 verses or *ślokas*, attributed to Vyāsa, the second, an elaboration by Vaiśampāyana. By the medieval period the Epic existed in two major recensions, one northern and one southern, and was retold in a Tamil version. The critical edition of the Sanskrit version was produced by scholars at the Bhandarkar Oriental Research Institute at Poona, in India, who compared many different manuscripts.[1] Their version is the one formulated by the Brahman family of Bhārgava, descended from the ancient sage Bhṛgu, who rewrote the epic incorporating into it much material on *dharma*. Indeed, the central hero of the Epic, Yudhiṣṭhira, is the son of Dharma personified as a deity. The text itself is divided into eighteen parts of varying length, the longest comprising over 14,000 verses, the shortest having only 120 verses. The text is further subdivided into 98 sub-portions. There is also a supplement to the Epic, the *Harivaṃśa*, a text about the life of Kṛṣṇa.

Apart from the northern and southern recensions, there are regional variations of the text and it is important to emphasize that the *Mahābhārata* exists not only as a 'critical edition' or as the object of scholarly study, but also as a vital and fluid part of contemporary Hinduism, still in the process of being recast in different modes. The Sanskrit narrative traditions of the *Mahābhārata* are also acted out and recited orally in vernacular languages throughout the villages of India at popular festivals. The *Mahābhārata* lives in these presentations and recitations, not to mention in a television series which presented the story to rapt audiences throughout India in the 1980s.

The origins of the *Mahābhārata* lay in non-brahmanical social groups of the 'Aryan homeland' (*āryāvarta*), namely the Kṣatriya aristocracy, and it gives us some understanding of the life of those groups, though the story was quickly appropriated by orthodox, Sanskritic Brahmans and overlaid by the Bhārgava family with a brahmanical ideology which emphasized the performance of social duty (*dharma*). While the text is enjoyed simply as a story, it is also understood to have different levels of meaning and to be a metaphor for the ethical battle on the human plane, and for the battle between the lower and higher self on a world-transcending plane.

The story is as follows. A king of the lunar dynasty, Vicitravīrya, had two sons, Pāṇḍu and Dhṛtarāṣṭra. Dhṛtarāṣṭra, the elder prince, should have succeeded his father on the throne, but as he was born blind, a particularly inauspicious karma, he could not. Pāṇḍu reigns and has five sons, the Pāṇḍavas or 'sons of Pāṇḍu'. When Pāṇḍu dies, his blind brother Dhṛtarāṣṭra takes over the throne and the Pāṇḍavas (namely Yudhiṣṭhira, Bhīma, Arjuna, Nakula and Sahadeva) grow up with their 100 cousins, the sons of Dhṛtarāṣṭra: the Kauravas. The eldest of the Kauravas, Duryodhana, claims to be the rightful successor to the throne and has the Pāṇḍavas, and their common wife Draupadī, exiled. Duryodhana becomes king and his father abdicates. The Pāṇḍavas, however, challenge his right to the throne, so, to avoid conflict, the blind old ex-king divides the kingdom in two, with Duryodhana ruling in the north from Hastinapur, and Yudhiṣṭhira, the eldest Pāṇḍava, ruling in the south from Indraprasta (modern Delhi). Duryodhana pays a visit to Indraprasta, but while he is there he falls into a lake which provokes laughter from Yudhiṣṭhira. Duryodhana cannot abide this insult and challenges Yudhiṣṭhira to a game of dice at Hastinapur for the entire kingdom. Yudhiṣṭhira who has a passion for gambling, loses everything to Duryodhana, including his wife Draupadī. She is publicly humiliated by the Kauravas who try to tear off her clothing, but it miraculously never unfolds due to the power of Kṛṣṇa's grace. They play one further game of dice, the loser having to go into exile in the forest for twelve years and spend a further year incognito. Once again Yudhiṣṭhira loses and so begins the Pāṇḍavas' thirteen-year exile with Draupadī.

In the forest many adventures befall them, all recorded in the *Mahābhārata*, and there are stories within stories told by different characters. They spend the thirteenth year in disguise in the court of a king and emerge from exile in the fourteenth year to reclaim their kingdom. By now, however, Duryodhana is no longer willing to give up his kingdom and so the stage is set for war. The war lasts eighteen days. On the field of Kurukṣetra the two armies are lined up and the eve of the battle sets the scene for the *Bhagavad Gītā*, the famous dialogue between Kṛṣṇa and Arjuna. The battle is fierce and all the Kauravas are killed. Although the Pāṇḍavas win, they are filled with sorrow at the loss of so many allies and relatives, even though they were their enemies. Yudhiṣṭhira abdicates, leaving the kingdom under the sovereignty of a younger relation, and with his brothers and Draupadī leaves for the realm of Indra's heaven in the Himalayas. Draupadī and four of the brothers die along the way. Only Yudhiṣṭhira, accompanied by a devoted dog which had attached itself to him, continues the journey. Indra in his chariot meets Yudhiṣṭhira and invites him into heaven, but Yudhiṣṭhira will not go without the dog who has been devoted (*bhakta*). The dog, however, turns out to be the god Dharma himself, who then leads Yudhiṣṭhira into heaven where he is astonished to see Duryodhana, the cause of so much suffering, enjoying heaven because he had fulfilled his *dharma* as a warrior. Yudhiṣṭhira, the exemplum of dharmic conduct, has yet to be reborn on earth because of his affection: a last attachment to be purged before liberation can be attained.

Within this basic narrative structure many other stories are embedded which may originally have been independent tales, such as the love story of Nala and Damyantī[2] and the story of the nymph Śakuntalā.[3] The famous *Bhagavad Gītā*, 'the Song of the Lord', dated to not before the second century BCE, may well have been inserted into the *Mahābhārata*, though some scholars think that it was composed as part of the text.[4] This dialogue between Arjuna and Kṛṣṇa, narrated by the sage Sanjaya to the blind king Dhṛtarāṣṭra, became one of the most important texts in Hinduism. As the dialogue unfolds, Kṛṣṇa responds to Arjuna's doubts about the war and gradually reveals himself as a supreme Lord, the creator, maintainer and destroyer of the universe.

The Rāmāyaṇā

The second, slightly shorter, Epic is the *Rāmāyaṇa*, the story of King Rāma, attributed to Vālmīki. This text was certainly in circulation by the first century CE, though on stylistic grounds its origin may be later than the *Mahābhārata*. As with the *Mahābhārata* there are two major recensions, the northern and the southern, the southern being the earlier.[5] There are later Sanskrit versions of the text and versions were composed in vernacular languages, of particular note being Kampaṉ's Tamil rendering (ninth–twelfth centuries) and the famous Hindi *Rāmacaritmānas* ('The

Lake of Rāma'a Deeds') by Tulsīdās (*c.* 1543–1623). Apart from these texts, there are innumerable versions of the text told and retold in different regions.[6] The *Rāmāyaṇa* exists in many versions and in many tellings, from a Hindi television production in 1987 which attracted 80 million viewers to village performances in Tamilnadu or stage productions in the USA.[7] The annual Rām Līlā festivals and performances, particularly at Rāmnagar near Varanasi, attract thousands of pilgrims and express the living, enacted tradition of the *Rāmāyaṇa*.[8]

The story is essentially simple. *Rāma*, a prince of Ayodhyā, son of King Daśaratha, marries Princess Sītā, the daughter of King Janaka of Videha (who first appeared in the *Bṛhadāraṇyaka Upaniṣad*). Because of his father's second wife, Kaikeyī, who makes Daśaratha promise to banish him, Rāma is forced to go into exile into the Daṇḍaka forest, out of filial duty. He is accompanied by his wife and brother Lakṣmaṇa. While the brothers are away hunting, Sītā is abducted by Rāvaṇa, the ten-headed demon-king of Sri Lanka, but with the help of a monkey army sent by the monkey king Sugrīva, Rāma wins her back. Under the leadership of the monkey general Hanumān, who is no ordinary monkey but the son of the wind-god Vāyu, a causeway is built from India to Sri Lanka, which allows Rāma and his army to cross over and defeat the demon-king. Rāvaṇa and his army are killed and Rāma returns with Sītā to Ayodhyā where he reigns as king. The people of the city, however, suspect that Sītā did not remain chaste while held by Rāvaṇa, though Rāma himself has no doubts about her virtue (since she had previously proved this to him by emerging unscathed from a fire ordeal). To fulfil his duty to his subjects, Rāma banishes Sītā to the hermitage of Vālmīki, traditionally the author of the text, where she gives birth to twins. Many years later Rāma discovers the twins and wishes to take back Sītā along with their children, but not wishing to return to Ayodhyā, Sītā calls on the Earth, her mother, who opens and swallows her. The text ends with Rāma and all the inhabitants of Ayodhyā going to the Sarayu river and there entering the body of Viṣṇu.

The *Rāmāyaṇa* is the story of a heroic king who becomes deified. Indeed, by the last books of the text Rāma is referred to as an incarnation (*avatāra*) of Viṣṇu. Above all, however, as with the *Mahābhārata*, it is a tale about *dharma*. Daśaratha is forced to banish his son because he must keep his word, and his word is his power; Rāma must go to the forest to obey his father, as *dharma* dictates; and Rāma must banish Sītā in the end to fulfil his duty to his subjects, even though her virtue is not in question.

The *Rāmāyaṇa* is the story of the triumph of good over evil, of order over chaos, of *dharma* over *adharma*. Rāma and Sītā are ideal examples of dharmic gender roles for Hindu couples. He is honest, brave, the fulfiller of all his ethical responsibilities, and devoted to his wife, while she is modest, demure, virtuous, dedicated to her Lord and husband, yet strong in herself. This strength, and some degree of independence, asserts itself at the end of the narrative when Sītā, whose name means 'furrow' and who perhaps originated as an independent goddess associated with agriculture, returns to her mother the Earth, whence she sprang when her father, Janaka, was ploughing. Sītā is the ideal Hindu woman, fulfilling her 'womanly duty' (*strīsvadharma*) to the letter, yet who retains self-possession and an element of autonomy and identity independent of her husband Rāma.

The story is more straightforward than the *Mahābhārata* and has widespread, popular appeal. The language is beautiful in its detailed descriptions, even down to describing the spiral movements of the hairs on Hanumān's tail, and is a precursor of later Sanskrit poetic literature or *kāvya*. The worship of Rāma became widespread in the medieval period in northern India and the name 'Rām' became a synonym for 'God'.[9] The worship of Rāma has become highly significant today as the focus of politicized Hindu movements in recent years (see pp. 264–5). Yet the *Rāmāyaṇa* is important beyond these considerations and plays a vibrant part in contemporary Hinduism. Like the *Mahābhārata* it is an oral tradition recited and acted out throughout the villages and towns of India.

The Purāṇas

In contrast to the Epics, the Purāṇas, 'stories of the ancient past', are a vast body of complex narratives which contain genealogies of deities and kings up to the Guptas, cosmologies, law codes, and descriptions of ritual and pilgrimages to holy places. With the Purāṇas we are dealing with oral traditions which were written down and which have absorbed influences from the Epics, Upaniṣads, Dharma literature and ritual texts. The Purāṇas would have been recited at gatherings by specialists who were traditionally the sons of Kṣatriya fathers and Brahman mothers, and today the texts are recited by special individuals known by the Hindi term *bhaṭ*.

There are eighteen major Purāṇas and eighteen related subordinate texts known as Upapurāṇas, though there are variations as to which texts are included within the ideal number of eighteen. The Purāṇas have traditionally been classified according to three qualities (*guṇa*) which are inherent in existence, namely the quality of light or purity (*sattva*), passion (*rajas*) and darkness or inertia (*tamas*). Six Purāṇas belong to each category. The *sattva* category contains the Vaiṣṇava Purāṇas (the *Viṣṇu Bhāgavata, Garuḍa, Naradiya, Padma* and *Varāha Purāṇas*), the *rajas* category contains Purāṇas whose central deity is the creator Brahmā (the *Brahma, Brahmāṇḍa, Brahmavaivarta, Mārkaṇḍeya, Bhaviṣya* and *Vāmana Purāṇas*), while the *tamas* category contains the Śaiva Purāṇas, those texts whose central deity is Śiva (the *Śiva, Liṅga, Matsya, Kūrma, Skanda* and *Agni Purāṇas*). This neat classification, although interesting in terms of the tradition's self-understanding, does not really throw light on the nature or contents of these texts, which do not fall easily into this frame of reference for the texts themselves are not exclusively focused upon a single deity. Nevertheless there are tendencies towards sectarian affiliation, and some texts, such as the *Viṣṇu* and *Śiva Purāṇas*, are clearly centred on a particular god. Others such as the *Agni Purāṇa* which contains material about both Viṣṇu and Śiva, are not so clearly sectarian. There are also Purāṇas affiliated with a particular place or temple, the *sthāla* Purāṇas.

We do know that the bulk of the material contained in the Purāṇas was established during the reign of the Guptas (*c.* 320–*c.* 500 CE), though amendments were made to the texts up to later medieval times. Attempts have been made by scholars to establish the original portions and chronologies of individual texts,[10] but this is notoriously difficult. Because these texts developed over a long period of time and had fluid boundaries, it is impossible to precisely date them or to establish an accurate chronology. It is possible to find passages which have parallels across different Purāṇas but it is very difficult to establish the sequence of their composition or inclusion. To understand the Purāṇas it makes more sense to treat them as complete texts in themselves and examine them and their intertextuality synchronically, rather than to try to establish their diachronic or historical sequence.

The Purāṇas contain essential material for understanding the religions of Viṣṇu, Śiva, the Goddess (Devī) and other deities of the Hindu pantheon such as Agni (the god of fire), Skanda (the god of war and son of Śiva), Gaṇeśa (Śiva's elephant-headed son) and Brahmā (the four-headed creator of the universe). They indicate the rise in popularity of Viṣṇu and Śiva and document the brahmanical expression of their cults, showing how popular levels of religion were assimilated by the Brahmans who composed them. Although these texts are related to each other, and material in one is found in another, they nevertheless each present a view of ordering of the world from a particular perspective. They must not be seen as random collections of old tales, but as highly selective and crafted expositions and presentations of worldviews and soteriologies, compiled by particular groups of Brahmans to propagate a particular vision, whether it be focused on Viṣṇu, Śiva or Devī, or, indeed, any number of deities.

The *Viṣṇu Purāṇa* for example (fourth century CE), while generally following the typical puranic style, is centred on Viṣṇu and presents a Vaiṣṇava worldview. Viṣṇu awakens, becomes the creator god Brahmā, creates the universe, sustains it and destroys it as Rudra (a name for Śiva). He then rests on the serpent Śeṣa upon the cosmic ocean. The text thus establishes Viṣṇu as the supreme deity; it is really Viṣṇu, whom the text calls Janārddhana, 'the adored of humanity', who takes the designation Brahmā, Viṣṇu and Śiva.[11] The supremacy of Viṣṇu in this text is also established by narratives such as the story of Prahlāda. Prahlāda is the son of the demon Hiraṇyakaśipu who cannot be killed by day or by night, by man or by beast, within or outside the house. Hiraṇyakaśipu orders the boy to be killed because he is a worshipper of Viṣṇu. Yet despite his efforts the boy cannot be killed and Viṣṇu, to avenge Prahlāda, incarnates as the 'man–lion' Narasiṃha (neither man nor beast), at twilight (neither day nor night), bursting out from a pillar (neither inside nor outside the house) to kill the demon.

PURANIC COSMOLOGY

Although no one text strictly adheres to this pattern, the Purāṇas traditionally cover five topics:

- the creation or manifestation of the universe;
- destruction and re-creation of the universe;
- the genealogies of gods and sages;
- the reigns of the fourteen Manus or mythological progenitors of humanity;
- the history of the solar and lunar dynasties of kings, from which all kings trace their descent.

The most important features of the Purāṇas are the genealogies of various royal lineages, in which history as well as mythology may be embedded, and the elaborate cosmologies occurring over vast expanses of time. The universe is conceptualized as an array of concentric circles spreading out from Mount Meru at the centre, enclosed within the vast 'world egg'. Immediately surrounding Meru is Jambu-dvīpa, the earth or 'island of the rose-apple tree', though itself several thousand miles from Meru. Jambu-dvīpa is surrounded by a salt ocean. Spreading out from here are seven further lands and various kinds of ocean made of sugar-cane juice, wine, ghee, buttermilk, milk and sweet water, until the realm of darkness is reached by the outer shell of the egg. This is very similar to Jain cosmologies which list the oceans as containing salt, black water, clear water, rum, milk, ghee and treacle.[12] Within Jambu-dvīpa are a number of lands, including India (Bhārata) which is subdivided into nine regions ruled by descendants of the culture-hero Pṛthu, who cultivated the earth (*pṛthvī*). Below and above the level of the earth in the cosmic egg are further layers. Below the earth are the seven underworlds and below them at the base of the egg, the hell realms, whose various names, such as 'impaling' and 'red-hot iron', vividly describe their contents. Above the earth (*bhūr*) are the atmosphere (*bhuvas*), sky (*svar*) and various other worlds up Mount Meru to the 'true world' (*satyaloka*) at the top. This entire cosmos is populated by all kinds of beings; humans, animals, plants, gods, snake-beings (*nāga*), nymphs (*apsaras*), heavenly musicians (*gandharva*), domestic beings (*paiśaca*) and many more, and one can be reborn into any of these realms depending upon one's action (*karma*).[13] Life in all of these worlds is, of course, impermanent and one will eventually be reborn elsewhere. Neither hell nor heaven are permanent here.

Alongside a vast conception of the structure of the cosmos, the Purāṇas also have a vast conception of time. The world goes through a cycle of four ages or *yugas*: the perfect *kṛta* or *satya* age which lasts for 1,728,000 human years; the *tretā* age of 1,296,000 years; the *dvāpara* age of 864,000 years; and the dark *kali* age of 432,000 years which began with the Mahābhārata war, traditionally dated to 3102 BCE. This makes a total of 4,320,000 years during which time the world moves from a perfect state to a progressively more morally degenerate state in which *dharma* is forgotten. The *kali-yuga*, the present age of darkness, is characterized by loss of *dharma* which will be renewed by the future incarnation of Viṣṇu, Kalki, who will come to begin a new perfect *kṛta yuga*.[14] The image used is of a cow standing on all four legs in the perfect age, standing on three legs in the *tretā* age, on two legs in the *dvāpara* age, but tottering on only one leg in the *kali* age.

The total period of four *yugas* is called a *manvantara*, the age or life-period of a Manu. After 1,000 manvantaras, which comprise one day for Brahmā, the universe will be destroyed by fire or flood and undergo a night of Brahmā of the same period (i.e. 1,000 manvantaras), until the process begins again for all eternity. A *kalpa* is one such night and day of Brahmā comprising 8,649 million years. There is no end to this process; nor purpose other than the Lord's play (*līlā*).

THE SMĀRTAS

With the composition of the Purāṇas a mainstream form of brahmanical religion developed which expanded and continued into the medieval period. The Brahmans who followed the puranic religion became known as *smārta*, those whose worship was based on the Smṛtis, or *paurāṇika*, those based on the Purāṇas. This form of religion was concerned with the domestic worship of five shrines and their deities, the *pañcāyatana-pūjā*, namely Viṣṇu, Śiva, Gaṇeśa (Śiva's elephant-headed son), Sūrya (the Sun) and the Goddess (Devī). The Smārtas may be seen in contrast to the Śrautas who performed elaborate, public, vedic rituals – the solemn rites – and also in contrast to the Tāntrikas, heterodox followers of non-vedic revelation called the Tantras. Although the authors of the Purāṇas are not Tāntrikas, the texts nevertheless contain a significant amount of tantric material, particularly on ritual. Although the central Smārta practice was the domestic worship of the five deities, while, of course, abiding by vedic social values and purity rules, there also arose worship of particular deities, especially Viṣṇu and Śiva, who were elevated to a supreme position. Thus with the Purāṇas, the normative, mainstream Smārta worship of Viṣṇu and Śiva is established, which absorbs into it external, non-brahamnical and sometimes non-vedic or tantric material.

The development of temple cities

The compiling of the Purāṇas and the development of devotion or *bhakti* to particular deities must be seen firstly in the context of the stability of the Gupta period and secondly, after the collapse of the Guptas, in the context of the rise of regional kingdoms, particularly in the south. During the seventh century these were the kingdoms of the Chalukyas in the central and western Deccan, and the Palavas in the south-east. From about 900 to 1200 these kingdoms are replaced by the dynasties of the Pandeyas in the far south, the Cholas in the Tamil region, and the Rashtrakutas, replacing the

Chalukyas. Each of these kingdoms developed urban centres and these cities became the centres of those kingdoms; cities which were not only centres of commerce and administration, but ritual centres with the temple at the hub of the town and the streets radiating out from there. The ritual sovereignty of the king was established through his brahmanical legitimization in the temple and, from the eleventh to thirteenth centuries, large temple complexes were built as centres of the regional kingdoms. Examples of such cities are the Jagannatha temple at Puri in Orissa, the Naṭarāja temple at Cidambaram in Tamilnadu, and the Rājarājeśvara temple at Tanjavur also in Tamilnadu. Each of these temples would have installed one of the major puranic deities or a manifestation of those deities. Of particular importance are the gods Viṣṇu, Śiva and Devī, all of whom had their own Purāṇas, and all of whom were established in important temples. Viṣṇu in particular is associated with the ideal of the divine king, and it is to his history and tradition we now turn.

Viṣṇu

The late Upaniṣads composed from the eighth to sixth centuries BCE, particularly the *Śvetāśvatara* and the *Mahānārayaṇa*, bear witness to the beginnings of Hindu theism. Theism is the idea that there is a supreme, distinct God (*Bhagavān*) or Goddess (*Bhagavatī*) who generates the cosmos, maintains it, and finally destroys it, and who has the power to save beings through his grace. Two deities begin to become the focus of theistic attention, Śiva, who in the *Ṛg Veda* appeared as Rudra, and Viṣṇu, who both gain in importance and become identified by their devotees as the highest god, the supreme or absolute reality. The devotees of Śiva come to be referred to as Śaivas; those of Viṣṇu and his manifestation, as Vaiṣṇavas.

In the *Ṛg Veda* Viṣṇu is a benevolent, solar deity, often coupled with the warrior god Indra.[15] The name Viṣṇu may be derived from the Sanskrit verbal root *viś* ('to enter'), so Viṣṇu is 'he who enters or pervades the universe'. In one hymn, Viṣṇu takes three strides thereby separating the earth from the sky,[16] a story which forms the basis of the later myth in the Purāṇas where Viṣṇu, incarnated as a dwarf, covers the universe with three strides and destroys the power of the demon Bali.[17]

By the time of the Purāṇas (fourth–sixth century CE), Viṣṇu is iconographically depicted in two ways. Firstly as a dark blue youth, standing upright, possessing four arms and holding in each hand, respectively, a conch, discus, mace and lotus. He wears the jewel called the *kauṣṭubha* and has a curl of hair on his chest, the *śrīvatsa* ('beloved of the goddess Śrī'). The second form is Viṣṇu lying asleep upon the coils of the great cosmic snake, Śeṣa ('remainder') or Ananta ('endless'), floating upon the cosmic ocean. When he awakes, he creates the universe. A lotus emerges from his navel, out of the lotus appears the creator god Brahmā, who then manifests the universe which is maintained by Viṣṇu and then destroyed by Śiva: Brahmā is enfolded by the lotus which withdraws into Viṣṇu's navel who, finally, falls asleep once more. Viṣṇu is married to Lakṣmī and Śrī, who form a single being, though they were initially distinct goddesses. They appear in later Hinduism as other consorts of the god. He is also depicted riding, sometimes with Lakṣmī, upon his mount, the eagle Garuḍa.

For his devotees and in Vaiṣṇava literature, Viṣṇu is the transcendent Lord dwelling in his highest heaven, Vaikuṇṭha, at the top of the cosmic egg, where, with their Lord's grace, his devotees go upon liberation. Yet Vaiṣṇava traditions maintain that the Lord not only dwells in far-off Vaikuṇṭha, but also manifests himself in the world, principally in three ways:

- in his ten incarnations (*avatāra*) upon the earth during times of darkness;
- in his various manifestations or icons (*mūrti*, *arcā*) in temples and shrines;
- within the hearts of all beings as their inner controller (*antaryāmin*).

These ideas are maintained, with varying degrees of emphasis, by all Vaiṣṇava traditions and have been articulated in Sanskrit and in Tamil texts.

The incarnations of Viṣṇu

Viṣṇu is the supreme Lord who manifests himself in the world in times of darkness when *dharma* has disappeared from view. These manifestations are his incarnations or 'descent-forms' (*avatāra*). The classic statement of this doctrine is in the *Bhagavad Gītā*. Here Kṛṣṇa, an incarnation of Viṣṇu, is addressing Arjuna (whom he addresses as Bhārata):

> Although, indeed, I am unborn and imperishable, although I am the lord of the creatures, I do resort to nature, which is mine, and I take on birth by my own wizardry (*māyā*). For whenever the Law (*dharma*) languishes, Bhārata, and lawlessness (*adharma*) flourishes, I

> create myself. I take on existence from aeon to aeon, for the rescue of the good and the destruction of the evil, in order to re-establish the Law (*dharma*).[18]

This is a clear statement of the doctrine. Although particular incarnations are not mentioned here, they do begin to appear in the later epic literature in varying numbers, and by the eighth century CE the standard number of descent-forms in the Vaiṣṇava Purāṇas is ten. These are Matsya ('The Fish'), Kūrma ('The Tortoise'), Varāha ('The Boar'), Narasiṃha ('The Man–Lion'), Vāmana ('The Dwarf'), Paraśurāma ('Rama with the axe'), Rāma or Rāmacandra, Kṛṣṇa, Buddha and Kalkī. Apart from this list, some other figures are mentioned as incarnations in the Purāṇas, such as Balarāma, Kṛṣna's brother; Hayagrīva ('Horse-necked') who recovered the Veda stolen by Titans (*daityas*); and Dattātreya, a rustic, pleasure-seeking figure, later regarded as an incarnation of the three gods, sometimes erroneously referred to as the 'Hindu trinity': Brahmā, Viṣṇu and Śiva. This picture is further complicated by the idea of portions of Viṣṇu (*aṃśa*) manifested in history. These incarnations are represented as appearing during different world ages (*yuga*) which display signs of gradual degeneracy from the first to the fourth or dark age (see above).

The mythology of these incarnations focuses upon the creation, destruction and recreation of the cosmos. The *Matsya Purāṇa* tells how the first man, Manu, is saved from a cosmic deluge by the Fish.[19] The Tortoise places himself at the bottom of the ocean of milk as the support for the mountain Mandara, which is then used as a stick by the gods and demons to churn the cosmic ocean, from which various desired, and undesired, objects emerge, including the nectar of immortality (*amṛta*). The Boar rescues the Earth, personified as a Goddess, from the bottom of the cosmic ocean and brings her to the surface where he spreads her out, piles up mountains and divides her into seven continents.[20] Narasiṃha, the man–lion, destroys the wicked demon Hiraṇyakaśipu, who has tried to destroy his son Prahlāda, a devotee of Viṣṇu (see above). The Dwarf *avatāra* strides across the universe in three steps and destroys the demon Bali (see above). Paraśurāma is incarnated to destroy the arrogant Kṣatriyas who threaten the Brahmans, while Rāmacandra and Kṛṣṇa are the hero kings of the epics. The Buddha is a curious inclusion in this list: an incarnation sent to lead the wicked and the demons astray and so to hasten the end of the current age of darkness (*kali-yuga*). Lastly Kalki, 'The White Horse', will come at the end of the dark age to destroy the wicked and restore purity and righteousness. We see in these incarnations a movement from lower, aquatic life forms to higher life forms living on the land.[21]

Mythological texts are never neutral but always present a particular angle or viewpoint, usually from the perspective of a particular group. The doctrine and mythology of the incarnations is important in Vaiṣṇavism for it emphasizes the supremacy and transcendence of Viṣṇu. The *Viṣṇu Purāṇa* says that all beings, including the gods, worship Viṣṇu's incarnations, for his supreme form is unknowable.[22] This allows for non-Vaiṣṇava deities to be incorporated into the Vaiṣṇava tradition and for other cults to be colonized by Vaiṣṇava ideology. Some, if not all, of the descent-forms may have had an independent life with cults of their own. For example, Balarāma, Kṛṣṇa's brother, was a distinct fertility deity and, indeed, Kṛṣṇa himself was a distinct deity incorporated into the mainstream tradition. The *avatāra* doctrine allows for the universalizing claim of Viṣṇu's total world-transcendence, which is yet expressed in finitude, and allows for Vaiṣṇavism to incorporate other traditions.

Early Vaiṣṇava traditions

The early history of the development of Viṣṇu and his worship is highly complex. In this history Viṣṇu becomes fused with other, originally independent deities, and the traditions which focused upon these deities become merged in the Vaiṣṇava tradition. While there are difficulties in applying the western term 'religion' to Hinduism as a whole before the nineteenth century, the term can be applied with more justification to the great theistic traditions of Vaiṣṇavism and Śaivism. These are religions with revealed, authoritative texts, developed doctrines, rituals and social organizations. In its early stages, Vaiṣṇavism represents the merging of the religions of a number of different social groupings from both north and south India. We shall firstly describe the formation of Vaiṣṇavism in the northern traditions before moving on to the southern. Literature in Sanskrit attests to the existence of a number of originally independent deities – and cults focused upon them – who became fused with Viṣṇu, particularly Vāsudeva, Kṛṣna and Nārāyaṇa. Of these deities Kṛṣṇa is particularly important and Vaiṣṇava traditions tend to cluster around either Viṣṇu or Kṛṣṇa. Indeed, the term 'Kṛṣnaism' has been used to describe the cults of Kṛṣṇa, reserving 'Vaiṣṇavism' for cults focusing on Viṣṇu in which Kṛṣṇa is merely an incarnation, rather than the transcendent being

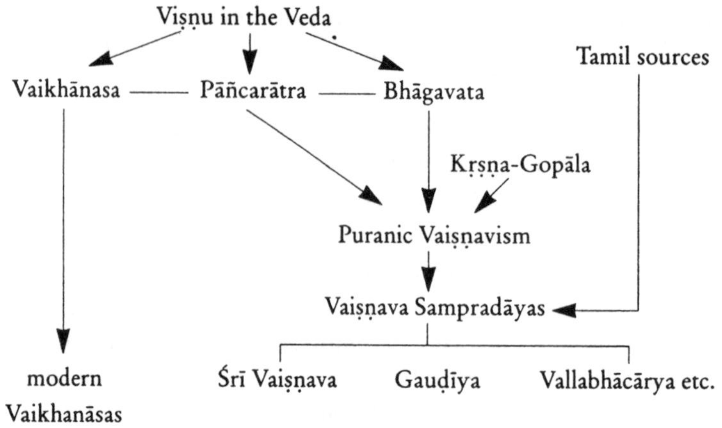

Figure 4 The development of Vaiṣṇava traditions

himself.[23] The independent cults of Vāsudeva-Kṛṣna, Kṛṣṇa-Gopāla, and Nārāyaṇa become merged in Vaiṣṇavism, itself a term used to encompass a number of distinct traditions (*sampradāya*). Yet in spite of the diversity of traditions within the Vaiṣṇava fold, there are certain features which are held in common:

- the Lord is the 'Supreme Person' (*puruṣottama*) with personal qualities (*saguṇa*), rather than an abstract absolute (*nirguṇa*);
- the Lord is the cause of the cosmos, he creates, maintains and destroys it;
- the Lord reveals himself through sacred scriptures, temple icons, in his incarnations (*avatāra*) and in saints.

Early Vaiṣṇava worship focuses on three deities who become fused together, namely Vāsudeva-Kṛṣṇa, Kṛṣṇa-Gopāla and Nārāyaṇa, who in turn all become identified with Viṣṇu. Put simply, Vāsudeva-Kṛṣṇa and Kṛṣṇa-Gopāla were worshipped by groups generally referred to as Bhāgavatas, while Nārāyaṇa was worshipped by the Pāñcarātra sect. The picture is, however, more complex than this, as the traditions intersect over time, with Vāsudeva becoming a term used for the Pañcaratrin's absolute. To help clarify this complex picture, we shall firstly describe the formation of the three deities Vāsudeva-Kṛṣṇa, Kṛṣṇa-Gopāla and Nārāyaṇa, and then move on to describe the traditions associated with them.

THE CULT OF VĀSUDEVA-KṚṢṆA

Vāsudeva, who becomes identified with Kṛṣṇa and Viṣṇu, was the supreme deity of a tribe called the Vṛṣṇis or Satvatas and may have originated as a Vṛṣṇi hero or king, though it is impossible to trace a line back to an original Vāsudeva. The Vṛṣṇis became fused with the Yādavas, the tribe of Kṛṣṇa. The worship of Vāsudeva is recorded as early as the fifth or sixth centuries BCE, being mentioned by the famous grammarian Pāṇini in his book of grammar the *Aṣṭādhyāyi*.[24] Here he explains the term *vāsudevaka* as referring to a devotee (*bhakta*) of the god Vāsudeva. Megasthenes, a Greek ambassador to the court of King Candragupta Maurya (*c.* 320 BCE) at Pataliputra, records that the people of Mathura on the river Yāmuna revered Heracles, thought to be the nearest Greek equivalent of Vāsudeva. Two centuries later another Greek ambassador, Heliodorus, says on an inscription found at Besnagar in Madhya Pradesh, that he erected a column with an image of Garuḍa at the top in honour of Vāsudeva (*c.* 115 BCE). Heliodorus describes himself as a *bhāgavata*, a devotee of Vāsudeva, which shows that the Vāsudeva religion was adopted by (at least some of) the Greeks who ruled Bactria in the far north-west. The scriptures of the Theravāda Buddhists, the Pālī canon written down in the first century BCE, also mention the worshippers of Vāsudeva in a list of various religious sects.[25] Vāsudeva is mentioned in the *Bhagavad Gītā*[26] and in the grammarian Patañjali's *Mahābhāṣya* ('Great Commentary'),[27] a commentary on Pāṇini (*c.* 150 BCE), where he describes Vāsudeva as belonging to the Vṛṣṇi tribe.

Kṛṣṇa was a deity of the Yādava clan, who probably became fused with the deity Vāsudeva. While it is impossible to arrive back at an original Kṛṣṇa – the historical formation of the deity is too complex – it is probably the case that Kṛṣṇa was a deified king or hero. The historicity of Kṛṣṇa is impossible to assess from sources in which hagiography and history are inextricably bound together. However, the historicity of Kṛṣṇa is important for the tradition, and Vaiṣṇavas believe that he was a historical personage.[28] There is a reference to Kṛṣṇa in the *Chāndogya Upaniṣad*,[29] a reference which, for his devotees, places Kṛṣṇa within the vedic frame of reference. In the *Mahābhārata*, Kṛṣṇa appears as the chief of the Yādavas of Dvāraka, present-day Dwarka on the north-west coast, and, indeed, he is one of the central focuses of that text, particularly the *Bhagavad-Gītā*. By the second century BCE Vāsudeva-Kṛṣṇa was worshipped as a distinct deity and finally identified with Viṣṇu in the *Mahābhārata*, appearing, for example, three times in the *Bhagavad Gītā*[30] as synonymous with Viṣṇu.

THE CULT OF KṚṢṆA-GOPĀLA

By the fourth century CE the Bhāgavata tradition, that is, the tradition about Vāsudeva-Kṛṣṇa in the *Mahābhārata*, absorbs another tradition, namely the cult of Kṛṣṇa as a young man in Vṛndāvana: Kṛṣṇa-Gopāla, the protector of cattle. Kṛṣṇa-Gopāla, a tribal god of the Abhīras, along with his brother Balarāma or Saṃkarṣaṇa, were pastoral deities who became assimilated into the Vaiṣṇava tradition. The *Harivaṃśa* (the 'appendix' to the *Mahābhārata*), the *Viṣṇu Purāṇa*, and particularly the *Bhāgavata Purāṇa*, embody narrative traditions about Kṛṣṇa as a boy and young man in Gokula, a settlement of cowherds of the Abhīras clan, on the banks of the Yāmuna. The *Harivaṃśa* directly influenced the *Viṣṇu Purāṇa* which in turn influenced the *Bhāgavata Purāṇa*, though this text was composed in the south under the strong influence of south Indian emotional devotionalism. The *Harivaṃśa* is dated to the first few centuries of the common era and sees itself as supplying information about Kṛṣṇa before the events of the *Mahābhārata* war. These stories, which are so important as the focus of later devotional and folk traditions, describe Kṛṣṇa-Gopāla as an amorous young man, wandering with his brother Balarāma through the forest of Vṛndāvana, destroying demons, dancing and making love with the cowgirls (*gopīs*). The erotic exploits of the young Kṛṣṇa become highlighted in later Vaiṣṇava poetry, such as Jayadeva's *Gītagovinda* (twelfth century) which extols the love between Kṛṣṇa and his favourite *gopī*, Rādhā, and in the poetry of Caṇḍīdās and Vidyāpati (fourteenth century).

THE CULT OF NĀRĀYAṆA

The cult of Nārāyaṇa is another important ingredient in the fusion of traditions which forms Vaiṣṇavism. Nārāyaṇa is a deity found in the *Śatapatha Brāhmaṇa*[31] where he is identified with the cosmic man (*puruṣa*), who possibly originates outside the vedic pantheon as a non-vedic deity from the Hindu Kush mountains. His name, according to *Manu*, means 'resting on the waters',[32] and in the *Nārāyaṇīya* section of the *Mahābhārata* he is the resting place and goal of men,[33] both of which are characteristics of Viṣṇu. Nārāyaṇa appears in the *Mahānārāyaṇa*

Upaniṣad[34] (composed around the fourth century BCE), which praises him as the absolute and highest deity who yet dwells in the heart. In the *Mahābhārata* and in some Purāṇas, he is the supreme deity, lying, like Viṣṇu, on a giant snake in an ocean of milk. According to a later text of the eleventh century, the *Kathāsaritsāgara*, Nārāyaṇa dwells in his heaven of 'white island' where he lies on the body of Śeṣa with Lakṣmī sitting at his feet.[35] Here Nārāyaṇa has clearly become identified with Viṣṇu.

Viṣṇu is therefore a composite figure, a figure who has fused with originally distinct deities and various elements from the mythologies of those deities over the centuries. Yet although these forms become identified with each other, different forms of Viṣṇu still become favoured above others by devotees of particular Vaiṣṇava traditions. This is particularly salient with regard to Kṛṣṇa. For some Vaiṣṇavas, such as the Śrī Vaiṣṇavas, he is an incarnation of Viṣṇu, and therefore subordinated to Viṣṇu, while for others, such as the Gauḍiya Vaiṣṇavas, he is the supreme deity himself.

The Pāñcarātra

The tradition associated with the worship of Nārāyaṇa is the Pāñcarātra.The name '*pāñcarātra*' ('five-night') may well be derived from the 'five night sacrifice' mentioned in the *Śatapatha Brāhmaṇa*,[36] in which Puruṣa-Nārāyaṇa conceives the idea of a sacrifice lasting five nights whereby he would become the highest being. The doctrines of the Pāñcarātra are mentioned in the *Nārāyaṇīya* section of the *Mahābhārata*[37] where Bhagavān Nārāyaṇa, who pervades the universe and is seen in all religious systems, is regarded as the preceptor of the Pāñcarātra tradition. Yet although Nārāyaṇa denotes their supreme deity, the term Vāsudeva is also used. Indeed, the Pāñcarātra is characterized by a doctrine of the manifestation of the absolute through a series of emanations or *vyūhas*. These begin with Vāsuveda who manifests Saṃkarṣaṇa, who in turn manifests Pradyumna, from whom Aniruddha emerges. These are the names of Kṛṣṇa's elder brother, his son, and grandson, respectively, though the familial relation is not particularly significant in the cosmology of the system. This series of *vyūha* emanations comprise the highest level of the universe, the 'pure creation', while below this are intermediate or 'mixed' creation and the 'impure' or 'material' creation. Each *vyūha* has a cosmological function with regard to the lower creation, which manifests through Pradyumna. The cosmos below the *vyūhas* is

The *vyūhas*

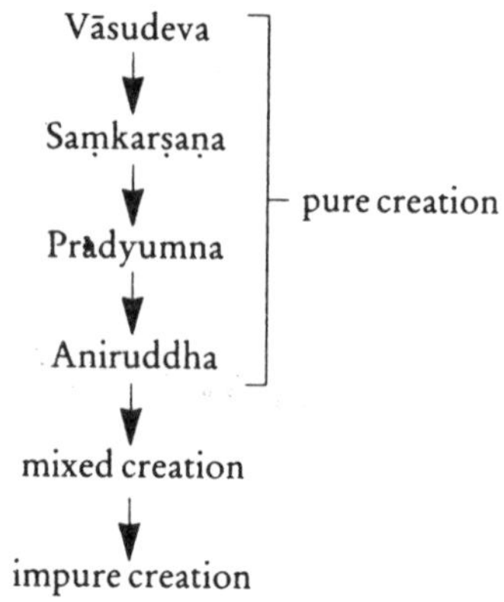

Figure 5 Pāñcarātra cosmology

made up of categories (*tattva*) some of which have their origin in the earlier philosophical system of Sāṃkhya (see p. 232).

Apart from the *Nārāyaṇīya* section of the *Mahābhārata*, which bears witness to the early existence of the tradition, Pāñcarātra literature as a distinct genre develops only from about the seventh or eighth centuries CE. This literature, known as the Pāñcarātra Saṃhitās, is classified as part of a wider group of texts known as Āgamas or Tantras (see pp. 158–61), texts which were rejected by many orthodox Brahmans. The most important of these texts are the 'three gems' of the *Pauṣkara*, *Sāttvata* and *Jakākhya Saṃhitās*, and the *Ahirbudhnya Saṃhitā* and *Lakṣmī Tantra* should also be mentioned as important texts within the tradition.[38] The concerns of this literature are cosmology, initiation (*dīkṣā*), ritual, sacred formulae (*mantra*) and temple building. The texts form the basis of worship in south Indian temples to this day, with vedic mantras replacing tantric mantras and vedic deities replacing tantric deities.

The Pāñcarātra Saṃhitās represent 'tantric' Vaiṣṇavism in contrast to an 'orthodox' vedic Vaiṣṇavism of the Bhāgavatas. While this distinction should not be exaggerated, it is nevertheless an important factor in that many orthodox Brahmans who accepted the authority of the Veda, rejected the authority of the Tantras. Indeed, the status of the Pāñcarātra Saṃhitās within Vaiṣṇavism – whether or not they could be classed as revelation – was an issue which provoked debate, with Yāmuna, one of the teachers of the Śrī Vaiṣṇava tradition, arguing for the status of these texts as revelation.[39] One tradition of Brahmans who are associated with the Pāñcarātra, but who remain distinct from them over this issue of orthodoxy, are the Vaikhānasas.

The Vaikhānasas

The Vaikhānasa sect regards itself as a Vaiṣṇava tradition, wholly orthodox and vedic, being within the Taittirīya school of the black Yajur Veda. The sect has its own *Vaikhānasasmārta Sūtra* (fourth century CE) which describes daily worship of Viṣṇu as a blend of traditional vedic and non-vedic ritual. There is also a collection of Vaikhānasa Saṃhitās, distinct from the Pāñcarātra Saṃhitās, which describe kinds of offerings and the worship of the Lord in his forms as Viṣṇu, Puruṣa, Satya, Acyuta and Aniruddha. There is some connection here with the Pāñcarātra Saṃhitās, for the *Jayākhya* lists Puruṣa, Satya and Acyuta as the *vyūhas* of Vāsudeva.[40] The daily ritual proceeds by making the obligatory vedic offerings into the fire, and making offerings to Viṣṇu in either his essential, indivisible form, installed in the inner sanctum of a temple, or his divisible, movable form. During the worship (*pūjā*), Viṣṇu is welcomed as a royal guest and given food offerings accompanied by the recitation of vedic and non-vedic mantras. With Viṣṇu's grace, the devotee will attain liberation (*mokṣa*), understood as entry into Viṣṇu's heaven (*vaikuṇṭha*).

The Vaikhānasas came to function as chief priests (*ārcaka*) in many south Indian Vaiṣṇava temples, where they remain to this day, particularly at the Tirupati temple, a pilgrimage centre in Andhra Pradesh. In the tradition's self-perception it is clearly distinguished from the 'unorthodox' *tāntrika* tradition of the Pāñcarātra, insisting on its orthodox or *vaidika* status.

The Bhāgavatas

By the second century BCE, if not earlier, the terms Vāsudeva and Kṛṣṇa were used to refer to the same deity. The worshippers of this deity were Bhāgavatas, those who follow Bhagavān, a name which had developed to refer to a personal absolute or theistic God. The term *bhāgavata* might have referred to a general tradition or orientation towards theistic conceptions and modes of worship, particularly of Vāsudeva-Kṛṣṇa, rather than a specific sect in the sense that the Pāñcarātrins or Vaikhānasas were specific sects. The Guptas, who ruled during the fourth to sixth centuries CE, supported the religion of the Bhāgavatas, as well as the Buddhist Yogācāra tradition, though Vaiṣṇavism remained the most important religion in the state. The royal patronage of the Guptas suggests the wide influence and appeal of the Bhāgavata religion – that it was more central to state life and culture than a narrowly defined sect. Indeed, the central text of the Bhāgavatas, the famous and eminent *Bhagavad Gītā*, has had a non-sectarian and universalist appeal in Hinduism, which reflects the non-sect-specific nature of the Bhāgavata tradition. This is not to say that the text does not have a specific theology, but that the theology was established on a broad basis with royal and brahmanical support. The terms Kṛṣṇa, Vāsudeva, Viṣṇu and Bhagavān all refer to the same, supreme, personal deity for the Bhāgavatas, a deity whose qualities are articulated in the *Gītā*.

The *Bhagavad Gītā*

The *Bhagavad Gītā*, the 'Song of the Lord', is perhaps the most famous of the Hindu scriptures, translated into many European and Indian languages and reported to have been Gandhi's favourite book. It has touched the hearts of millions of people both in south Asia and throughout the world. The first English translation was made by Charles Wilkins in 1785, with a preface by Warren Hastings. Numerous renditions have been made since then, and it has even been referred to as the 'Hindu New Testament'. It did not, however, always enjoy popularity and such great interest has only occurred since Hindu revival movements of the nineteenth century, particularly among more educated social groups. Even Gandhi read, and was influenced by the English rendering of the *Gītā* by Sir Edwin Arnold. However, in the villages, rather than the *Gītā*, it is the earthy stories of the *Bhāgavata Purāṇa* which have always had much wider appeal. Although it is important to get the fame of the text into perspective – its mass appeal being a fairly recent phenomenon – we must nevertheless acknowledge the text's theological importance as one which has provoked a number of commentaries upon it by famous Hindu theologians, particularly Śaṅkara, Rāmānuja and Madhva in the Vedānta tradition, and Abhinavagupta in the Śaiva tradition. It was reworked in vernacular languages, notably into a Marathi verse rendering by Jñāneśvara (thirteenth century), and contemporary commentaries have appeared in English, by for example the famous Transcendental Meditation guru Maharishi Mahesh Yogi and the Hare Kṛṣṇa guru Srila Bhaktivedānta Swami Prabhupada.

The Vedānta tradition claims the *Gītā* as its own, as one of three systems which constituted it, along with the Upaniṣads and the *Brahma Sūtra*. However, the text's theology differs considerably from these others and it must be understood on its own terms, as a theology in which devotion to the Lord and action in the world for the sake of social order, performed with detachment, become central. The text puts in narrative form the concerns of Hindu orthodoxy: the importance of *dharma* and of maintaining social stability, the importance of correct and responsible action, and the importance of devotion to the transcendent as a personal Lord (not dissimilar to the ideal king). The *Gītā* displays a number of influences, including the *bhakti* cult of Kṛṣṇa, Sāṃkhya philosophy and even Buddhist ideas and terminology. The main themes of the *Gītā* can be summarized as follows:

- the importance of *dharma*;
- *dharma* and renunciation are compatible: action (*karma*) should be performed with complete detachment;
- the soul is immortal and until liberated is subject to rebirth;
- the Lord is transcendent and immanent;
- the Lord is reached through devotion (*bhakti*) by his grace.

On the eve of the great battle between the Pāṇḍavas and the Kauravas, Arjuna is faced with a moral dilemma: should he fight in the battle and so kill members of his family or would it not be better to renounce and go begging for alms, thereby avoiding, for him, the inevitable bloodshed of the battle? There is a conflict within Arjuna between his duty – as a warrior and son of Pāṇḍu – to fight, and the ideal of non-violence (*ahimsā*), espoused by the renouncer traditions. In response to his deep misgivings, Kṛṣṇa exhorts him to go to battle, for not to do so would be unmanly and dishonourable. Arjuna, however, rejects this argument and refuses to fight, so Kṛṣṇa gives two further reasons for Arjuna's involvement in the battle. Firstly, the soul cannot be killed, it 'is not killed nor does it kill', but rather:

> As a man discards his worn-out clothes
> And puts on different ones that are new,
> So the one in the body discards aged bodies
> And joins with ones that are new.[41]

Regardless of whether Arjuna fights or not, his action will not affect the eternal soul which journeys from body to body in a series of reincarnations. The second, more significant, reason, and the one which convinces

Arjuna to fight, is that it is Arjuna's own-duty (*svadharma*) and responsibility as a warrior to do battle. The war is lawful and should be fought to uphold *dharma*.[42]

A number of themes run through the text: the necessity of doing one's duty which is nevertheless compatible with liberation; the unfolding of Kṛṣṇa's divinity; and the development of the paths to liberation. One of the most important messages that the text conveys is the necessity of performing one's appropriate duty, yet performing these actions with detachment. Kṛṣṇa, as Lord, says to Arjuna that although he is the creator of the four social classes (*varṇa*) he is not bound by action (*karma*) and has no attachment to the results or fruits of his actions. A man who understands the Lord similarly becomes detached from the fruit of his actions. The term 'action' here refers to both everyday action in the world and also to the traditional, vedic ritual action. As the ancient sages who desired liberation were detached from the result of their ritual performances (*karma*), so too Arjuna should become detached and give over the results of his acts to Kṛṣṇa. No action accrues to a person who acts with a controlled mind, without expectation and contented with whatever comes his way. Through non-attachment to action, and knowledge of the Lord, a person will be liberated and be united with the Lord at death.[43]

Kṛṣṇa gradually reveals his divinity to Arjuna, a process which culminates in the theophany of chapter 11. Here Arjuna asks Kṛṣṇa, the Supreme Person (*puruṣottama*), to reveal his majestic or glorious form. Kṛṣṇa responds to this request by giving Arjuna a divine eye with which he can see Kṛṣṇa as the creator and destroyer of the universe: a cosmic form of innumerable shapes and colours, containing the entire universe, all gods and all creatures, within it.[44]

The *Gītā* expounds the idea that there are various paths (*mārga*) to liberation, an idea which has been developed in modern Hinduism. The path of action (*karma-yoga*), which, as we have seen, is detachment from the fruits of action or ritual action, is emphasized as a way of reconciling worldly commitment with liberation, an idea which is clearly important to the *Gītā*. Yet above action is the path of devotion (*bhakti-yoga*) as a way of salvation. Indeed, even women and low castes can achieve liberation in this way,[45] a statement in stark contrast to the orthodox brahmanical idea that only the twice-born have access to liberation through renunciation (i.e. through the *āśrama* system). Through devotion, one attains the state of *brahman* and enters the Lord through his grace (*prasāda*). The idea even appears here, for the first time in Hinduism, that a human being, namely Arjuna, is dear (*priya*) to the Lord; there is a bond of love between human and divine.[46]

These paths of action and devotion contrast with the path of knowledge (*jñana-yoga*) mentioned in the text, which refers to knowledge of the absolute (*brahman*) but also refers to the Sāmkhya system of discriminating the various constituents (*tattva*) of the cosmos.[47] The *Bhagavad Gītā* is a rich and open text, as the variety of interpretations placed upon it show. Commentators have put their own emphases on its diverse aspects: the monist philosopher Śaṅkara highlighted knowledge of the absolute (*jñāna*), whereas the Vaiṣṇava Rāmānuja regarded knowledge only as a condition of devotion.

Summary

During the last half of the last millennium BCE devotion (*bhakti*) to a personal Lord (Bhagavān) began to develop in Hindu traditions. This devotionalism is expressed in the 'fifth Veda', the tradition of the Epics and Purāṇas (*Itihāsa Purāṇa*). These texts reflect a brahmanical appropriation of popular traditions on the one hand, and the ascendancy of the ideal of kingship on the other. The theistic traditions centred on Viṣṇu and Śiva particularly begin to develop during this period and we have traced here the rise of Viṣṇu and some of the early traditions which worshipped him or one of his forms. We shall now trace the development of this worship in later traditions, particularly in the south of India.

6 The love of Viṣṇu

So far we have described the Sanskrit narrative traditions which developed in the north and focused on the religions of Viṣṇu reflected in that literature. Although it comes to have pan-Hindu appeal, the *Bhagavad Gītā* originated in the north, as did the cults of Viṣṇu and Kṛṣṇa. However, there is a vast body of devotional literature, both Śaiva and Vaiṣṇava, from the south of India, composed in the Dravidian language of Tamil. While the Sanskrit material is important in understanding the development of theism in India, the Tamil literature had a deep effect upon that development and, in the south, its influence is equal to that of the Sanskrit material. The earliest Tamil literature developed before the onset of Sanskritization and so is originally quite distinct from Sanskrit literature. Sanskritization is the process whereby local or regional forms of culture and religion – local deities, rituals, literary genres – become identified with the 'great tradition' of Sanskrit literature and culture: namely the culture and religion of orthodox, Aryan, Brahmans, which accepts the Veda as revelation and, generally, adheres to *varṇāśrama-dharma*. Tamil began to be cultivated as a literary language around the third–fourth centuries BCE and a descriptive grammar of the early literary Tamil language, the *Tolkāppiyam*, was composed around 100 BCE by a Jain monk in southern Kerala, who seems to have been conversant with Sanskrit grammatical thinking.[1] From the first century BCE to the first, and perhaps through to the sixth century CE, a tradition of bardic poetry developed which was gathered into a number of anthologies collectively known as the *Caṇkam* literature.[2] Once established, Hindu Tamil culture thrived under the rule of the Chola dynasty from the ninth to the thirteenth centuries CE and the Kaveri basin became as important in the development of Hinduism as the Ganges basin in the north.

The process of Sanskritization only began to significantly influence the south after the first few centuries CE and Tamil deities and forms of worship became adapted to northern Sanskrit forms. Yet, nevertheless, a thriving Tamil culture flourished and Tamilnadu became the central region for the development of Hinduism after the Muslim Mughals established their empire in the north. Enormous temple complexes, unsurpassed by any in the north, grew up at Cidambaram, Śriraṇgam, Madurai and Tanjavur. These became bastions of classical, orthodox Hindu doctrines and practices associated with brahmanical worship of the deities and with the cult of the deified king. In the process of Sanskritization, indigenous Tamil deities became identified and absorbed into Aryan, vedic deities. The Tamil deities Mudvalan and Tirumāl became identified with Viṣṇu and Śiva, Koṭṛavai the goddess of war with Durgā, and the important deity Murukaṉ, with Śiva's son, Skanda, the god of war.

Tamil poetry and culture

Before the influence of Sanskritic or brahmanical culture, Tamil culture was itself very rich and any influences or cultural forms from the north were adapted and shaped by indigenous Tamil ways. With regard to devotional religion, there are two important factors which allowed its development in Tamil culture, namely Tamil poetry and the Tamil deity Murukaṉ.

The earliest body of the Caṅkam literature comprises two main groups, the 'Eight Anthologies' and the 'Ten Songs'. These anthologies of bardic poetry have two central concerns: love and war. The class of love poetry is called *akam* ('inside' or 'internal'), while the class of war or heroic poetry is called *puṟam* ('outside' or 'external'). The class of love poetry is particularly significant for it classifies the inner emotions of love (*uri*) into five groups which correspond to five types of external landscape and their symbolic representations; correspondences which are furthermore identified with types of flower. These are love-making, which corresponds to a mountainous landscape, with the mountain flower that blooms every twelve years, symbolized by millet fields and waterfalls; waiting anxiously for the beloved, which corresponds to the seashore, symbolized by sharks and fishermen; separation, which corresponds to an arid landscape, with a desert flower, symbolized by vultures, starving elephants and robbers;

patiently waiting for a wife, which corresponds to a pastoral landscape, with the jasmine flower, symbolized by a bull, cowherd or the rainy season; and anger at a lover's infidelity, real or imagined, which corresponds to an agricultural, river-valley landscape, symbolized by a stork or heron.

The significance of this poetry is that we see within Tamil culture a strong tradition of emotional expression through verse and a pattern of stylized or culturally classified emotional states associated with love. This allows for the wholehearted adoption of *bhakti* and sets the scene for the poetry of emotional devotion so characteristic of Tamil religious literature, and for the development of an emotional *bhakti* which was to significantly influence northern Hindu culture. The Caṅkam poetry reflects an elite culture which propagated an ideology of a very this-worldly nature, depicting the ideal man living a married life, fighting, hunting and making love: a far cry from the ascetic ideal of the northern renouncer tradition. A lower level of society, which the Caṅkam literature hardly mentions, would comprise manual labourers, iron- and goldsmiths, carpenters, potters and farmers.[3]

Within this culture there was little idea of transcendence, as had been developed, for example, in the Upaniṣads. Rather, there is a concept of the divine or supernatural (*kaṭavuḻ*) which can be manifested in possession states. A god mentioned in the Caṅkam anthologies is Murukaṉ, a deity who is young, handsome and heroic, and who accepted blood sacrifice. He is a god of both war and of love. His cult may have been served by priestesses and the texts indicate a possession cult in which young women became possessed by the god and danced 'in a frenzy' (*verī ayartal*).[4] Murukaṉ later became identified with Śiva's son Skanda, the god of war, and absorbed into the Hindu pantheon. Yet his presence here shows, firstly, that this religion was far from the ascetic ideals of renunciation and world-transcendence propagated in the Upaniṣads and also by the renouncer traditions of Jainism and Buddhism, and, secondly, that the 'folk religion' which he seems to represent was important and had official, courtly sanction. Hardy makes the point that the cult of Murukaṉ was not unlike folk religion in the north, and represented a 'very archaic and universally Indian form of popular religion of non-Aryan origin'.[5] Indeed, Parpola has argued that Murukaṉ was a deity of the Indus valley civilization whose name is preserved in the Indus valley language.[6]

The possession cult of Murukaṉ and a developed bardic tradition of love-poetry allowed for the easy absorption of a *bhakti* ideology from the north and a transformation of it into a particularly Tamil form. Kṛṣṇa and the stories of Vṛndāvana begin to move south and infiltrate into the Caṅkam literature from as early as the third century CE. Kṛṣṇa becomes Māyō<u>n</u> and his mythical landscape of Mathura becomes translated into a Tamil landscape. The narrative traditions and cult of Kṛṣṇa become firmly rooted in the south, linking into patterns of culture already established. By the seventh century CE *bhakti*, as an intense, emotional love for a personal Lord, for both Viṣṇu/Kṛṣṇa and Śiva, embodied in a temple icon and expressed in narrative traditions, had developed in the south. This intense devotion was expressed in the poetry of the Vaiṣṇava Āḻvārs and the Śaiva Nāyaṉārs, and was to influence later *bhakti* traditions both in the north and the south. Their songs are still recited in Tamil homes and in temples on public occasions such as weddings.

Bhakti traditions often reject institutionalized forms of religion, such as formal temple worship, yoga and theology, in favour of an immediate experience of the divine. Devotional forms of religion, particularly those which developed in the south during the early medieval period, tend to stress the devotee's emotional outpouring for his or her deity and the sense of losing the limited, self-referential ego in an experience of self-transcending love. This kind of devotional religion which emphasizes personal experience is often centred around a charismatic founder who is deified by the later tradition. The *bhakti* traditions which developed in the south, both Vaiṣṇava and Śaiva, illustrate these general tendencies.

The Āḻvārs and the Tamil Veda

The Āḻvārs, 'those immersed in god', are poet–saints, revered in Vaiṣṇava communities, who, between the sixth and ninth centuries, wandered from temple to temple in south India singing the praises of Viṣṇu. They helped to establish pilgrimage sites (particularly at the famous temple at Śriraṅgam), to convert many people of all castes to the worship of Viṣṇu, and to help stem the growth of Buddhism and Jainism in the south. Tradition maintains that there were twelve Āḻvārs,[7] the most famous of whom is Nammāḻvār and one of whom, Āṇṭāḷ, was a woman.[8] The Āḻvārs came from the whole social spectrum of Tamil society. Nammāḻvār was from a low-caste farming family (*veḷḷāla*), while his disciple, Maturakavi, was a Brahman. Āṇṭāḷ was the daughter of a Brahman priest of the temple of Śrīvillipputtur, himself one of the Āḻvārs. She came to be regarded as an incarnation of Viṣṇu's wife Śrī, and legend has it that she was absorbed into

Viṣṇu's icon in the famous Vaiṣṇava temple of Śriraṅgam. The other Āḻvārs were similarly regarded as incarnations of Viṣṇu or his deified regalia, the mace, conch, discus, *kauṣṭubha* jewel, and ammonite stone (*śālagrāma*). The songs of the Āḻvārs were collected in the tenth century by Nāthamuni, a theologian and a founding father of the Śrī Vaiṣṇava community, in a collection known as the 'Four Thousand Divine Compositions' (*Nālāyira Divyaprabandham* or *Prabandham* for short). This collection proved to be very influential as a scriptural basis for the Śrī Vaiṣṇavas. It attracted a number of significant commentaries and had impact beyond the south in Bengali Vaiṣṇavism. Within this collection the most famous and influential text is the *Tiruvāymoli* of Nammāḻvār (*c.* 880–930), which contains 1,000 verses of songs to Viṣṇu – referred to by his Tamil name Māyōn ('the Dark One') – as both King and Lover, thereby reflecting the old Tamil poetic genres of *akam* and *puṟam*.

The *Tiruvāymoli* ('the ten decads') is regarded as equal to the Veda among Vaiṣṇavas and is called the 'Tamil Veda'. Indeed the Tamil tradition of the Śrī Vaiṣṇavas is known as the 'Dual Vedanta' (*ubhaya vedānta*) because it reveres both the Sanskrit tradition from the Veda and the Tamil tradition of the Āḻvārs. The Tamil Veda contains songs of emotional power, expressing the poet's devotion to Viṣṇu in many of the forms in which he is installed in the temples of Tamilnadu. These 'poems' were intended to be sung and so are more akin to bardic compositions than to the more formal Sanskrit poetry (*kāvya*) of the court. In these poems Nammāḻvār conveys the idea of Viṣṇu's transcendence and formlessness and yet the Lord is also manifested in the form of icons in particular temples. The weeping, dancing and singing of the devotee, possessed by the god, is characteristic of emotional devotionalism, the devotion of longing (*viraha bhakti*), so characteristic of the Āḻvārs and later devotees of Kṛṣṇa-Gopāla. This is a religion of longing, ecstasy and service to a personal Lord who is beyond the cosmos and yet present in the world in specific locations in the sacred geography of Tamilnadu. He is installed in temples and devotion to him must be seen in the context of temple worship (*pūjā*) to these specific forms. Indeed the forms of the Āḻvārs themselves came to be treated as icons or manifestations of the Lord.

Later Vaiṣṇava traditions

The poetry and ecstatic *bhakti* of the Āḻvārs influenced later traditions and was adopted by devotees in different regions and at various temples throughout the land. The *Bhāgavata Purāṇa*, composed in Sanskrit in the south, was influenced by Tamil devotionalism, as was Sanskrit devotional poetry and northern forms of Vaiṣṇavism, particularly in Bengal. Devotionalism, especially in the south, emphasized the expression of emotions, rather than their control through yoga, and emphasized the body as a sacred locus of the Lord in the world, in contrast to the gnostic vision of the body and senses as the prison of the soul, expounded by some systems such as Sāṃkhya. The *bhakti* tradition placed emphasis on the body, the emotions and the embodied forms of the Lord which could be seen and worshipped, rather than on the idea of the soul's world-transcendence, cognition, and the abstract, transpersonal *brahman*. Some of the most fervent *bhakti* poetry was in Tamil, but there were also more philosophical texts in Sanskrit such as the *Bhakti Sūtra* of Śāndilya (eighth century CE). Yet *bhakti* always retained an emotional dimension and placed emphasis on affective experience rather than cognitive understanding. The Nārada *Bhakti Sūtra* (possibly twelfth century) says that Kṛṣṇa should be worshipped in varying degrees of emotional attachment: from perception of the Lord's majestic glory to experiencing the various emotions associated with the roles of Kṛṣṇa's slave, his companion, his parent and finally his wife.[9]

The early medieval period saw the rise of regional kingdoms and the popularization of brahmanical ritual and mythology which sometimes came to be fused with regional and local traditions, and expressed in vernacular languages. A number of traditions developed in Vaiṣṇavism during the medieval period. Many of these traditions are associated with a particular individual saint as their founder, though most of the earlier ones, as Fuller has observed, probably evolved gradually over a long period. Claiming descent from a particular saint is, however, important in order to establish a pupillary succession and so validate the tradition's authenticity. These orders also needed to locate themselves in a wider social context and needed the support of the laity and, particularly, the patronage of the king.[10]

Within Vaiṣṇavism, four traditions or *sampradāyas* are highlighted, based respectively on the teachings of Rāmānuja (*c.* 1017–1137), the famous Śrī Vaiṣṇava theologian; Madhva (thirteenth century), the dualist theologian; Vallabha (1479–1531), the 'pure non-dualist'; and Nimbārka (twelfth century) who emphasizes total surrender to the guru. The historical reality of the development of Vaiṣṇavism is, however, more complex than this. The most important order in the south, directly influenced by the Āḻvārs, was that of the Śrī Vaiṣṇavas. This in turn influenced devotion to Kṛṣṇa in Bengal, or Gauḍīya Vaiṣṇavism, and the cult of Viṭhobā or Viṭṭhala in Maharashtra, as well as the orders, just mentioned, founded by the Vaiṣṇava theologians and saints, Madhva, Nimbārka and Vallabha.

The term 'sect', 'order' or 'tradition' is a rough equivalent of the Sanskrit term *sampradāya*, which refers to a tradition focused on a deity, often regional in character, into which a disciple is initiated by a guru. Furthermore, each guru is seen to be within a line of gurus, a *santāna* or *paramparā*, originating with the founding father or possibly the deity. The idea of pupillary succession is extremely important in all forms of Hinduism as this authenticates the tradition and teachings; disputes over succession, which have sometimes been vehement, can be of deep religious concern, particularly in traditions which see the guru as the embodiment of the divine, possessing the power to bestow the Lord's grace on his devotees. With initiation (*dīkṣā*) into the *sampradāya* the disciple undertakes to abide by the values of the tradition and community, he or she receives a new name and a mantra particularly sacred to that tradition. A *sampradāya* might demand celibacy and comprise only world-renouncers, or it might have a much wider social base, accepting householders of both genders and, possibly, all castes including Untouchables.

These *sampradāyas* developed within the wider mainstream of brahmanical worship based on the Smṛti texts, especially the Purāṇas. Smārta worship (based on *smṛti*) was itself pervaded by forms and ideas derived from non-vedic revelation, the Tantras, but incorporated these forms in a respectable, vedic, way. Indeed the Vaiṣṇava *sampradāyas* generally located themselves within the context of Smārta worship, particularly the Śrī Vaiṣṇava and Gauḍīya Vaiṣṇava traditions which are squarely in the vedic, puranic tradition, yet which nevertheless have absorbed many elements from the non-vedic Tantras.

A number of devotional attitudes to the personal absolute developed, often associated with different *sampradāyas*. The relationship between the disciple and the Lord could be one of servant to master, of parent to child, friend to friend, or lover to beloved. The Bengali Vaiṣṇavas, for example, regarded the attitude of the lover to the beloved as the highest expression of devotion, while the sect of Tukārām viewed the devotional relationship as one of servant to master. However, what is significant here is that the relationship between the devotee and the Lord is modelled on human relationships and that the Lord can be perceived and approached in a variety of ways: the love of God takes many forms.

While it is important to remember that there is a strong element of personal seeking and devotion within *bhakti* traditions, the forms that this devotion will take have been moulded by the devotee's place within the social hierarchy, that is by caste and gender. Even though at an ideological level most *bhakti* traditions have maintained that caste and gender are immaterial to devotion and final salvation, nevertheless some are more tolerant of non-discrimination on the grounds of caste and gender than others. The Śrī Vaiṣṇavas, for example, while not excluding lower castes and women, restrict lower-caste access to their temple at Śriraṅgam, while other sects such as the Raidāsis are themselves low-caste. The most important Vaiṣṇava orders and cults are:

- the Śrī Vaiṣṇavas located in Tamilnadu whose centre is the temple at Śriraṅgam, for whom the theology of Rāmānuja is particularly important.
- the Gauḍīya or Bengali Vaiṣṇavas located mainly in Bengal, Orissa and Vṛndāvana. They revere the teachings of the Bengali saint, Caitanya, and focus their devotion on Kṛṣṇa and Rādhā.
- the cult of Viṭhoba in Maharashtra, particularly in the pilgrimage centre of Pandharpur. Their teachings are derived from the saints (*sant*) Jñāneśvara, Nāmdev, Janābai etc.
- the cult of Rāma located mainly in the north-east at Ayodhya and Janakpur and associated with an annual festival of Rāmlīlā in which the *Rāmāyaṇa* is performed. The ascetic Rāmānandī order is devoted to Rāma and Śītā.
- the northern Sant tradition; while not being strictly Vaiṣṇava, worshipping a transcendent Lord beyond qualities, this tradition nevertheless derives much of its teachings and names of God from Vaiṣṇavism. Especially venerated are Kabīr and Nānak, the founder of Sikhism.

THE ŚRĪ VAIṢṆAVA TRADITION

The Śrī Vaiṣṇava tradition, which developed in Tamilnadu, inherited a dual vision of the universe: on the one hand, the northern Sanskrit tradition of the Pāñcarātra and puranic worship of Viṣṇu, with its emphasis on the Lord as the transcendent cause and sustaining power of the cosmos, and, on the other, the southern Tamil tradition of longing devotion to a personal Lord installed within specific temple icons. The Śrī Vaiṣṇavas therefore revered sacred scriptures in Sanskrit, both the Vedas and the Pāñcarātra Āgamas or Saṃhitās, and the Tamil songs of the Āḻvārs. The Śrī Vaiṣṇavas also revered a line of teachers (*ācārya*) who functioned as theologians and interpreters of the tradition and as hierarchs of the order. The first of these *ācāryas*, and the founder of the Śrī Vaiṣṇavas, was Nāthamuni (tenth century CE) who collected the songs of the Āḻvārs in his *Prabandham*. While his emotional and aesthetic inspiration came from the Tamil poet–saints, Nāthamuni's main intellectual inheritance was the Sanskrit philosophical tradition, particularly the Vedānta, and the theologies of the *Bhagavad Gītā*, the *Viṣṇu Purāṇa* and the Pāñcarātra Āgamas. He is attributed with founding the Śrī Vaiṣṇava tradition and legitimated the tradition by establishing a lineage with the Tamil Āḻvārs. Nāthamuni is said to have gone on pilgrimage to Vṛndāvana in the north, the Vaiṣṇava religious centre and mythological home of Kṛṣṇa, where he received a vision of Viṣṇu in the form Maṉṉaṉār, the icon in his local temple in Tamilnadu. In the vision the god told him to return to his home town. He did so and became an administrator, firstly in the temple of Maṉṉaṉār and later in the Viṣṇu temple at Śriraṅgam which became the centre of the Śrī Vaiṣṇava community. Nāthamuni's grandson, Yāmuna, became the next Śrī Vaiṣṇava *ācārya*, noted for his defence of the Pāñcaratra Āgamas as having revelatory status and of the Pāñcaratra ritual as being equal to orthodox brahmanical rites.[11]

The most famous Śrī Vaiṣṇava leader, whose influence was to extend throughout Hinduism, was Rāmānuja (*c.* 1017–1137). He did not directly meet Yāmuna, but became the recognized leader of the community, developing a Vaiṣṇava theology and interpretation of the Vedānta tradition in the light of his theism, which became known as 'qualified non-dualism' (*viśiṣṭādvaita*; see p. 243). Rāmānuja wrote in Sanskrit, but he was influenced by the *bhakti* poetry of the Āḻvārs. His favoured disciple, Piḷḷāṉ, wrote a commentary on Nammāḻvār's *Tiruvāymoli* in a language which was a mixture of Sanskrit and Tamil, *manipravāla*, thereby elevating the status of the Tamil text, the first text in a Dravidian language to have commentary written on it. Piḷḷāṉ, who was a Śūdra, implies here that caste is not an impediment to salvation.[12]

Salvation or liberation for the Śrī Vaiṣṇavas was conceived as transcending the cycle of reincarnation (*saṃsāra*) and karma and going to Viṣṇu's heaven (*vaikuṇṭha*) at death, where the soul is united with the Lord in a loving relationship, while yet maintaining its distinction. This state is achieved through attachment to the Lord and detachment from the world, or, more specifically, through the religious practice (*upāsana*) of devotion and service (*seva*) to the Lord in one of his incarnations in temple icons (*arcāvatāra*). There is also a path of total surrender (*prapatti*) in which the devotee gives himself up to the Lord who saves him through an act of unmerited divine grace (*śaranāgati*). In the former there is some emphasis on effort and human agency, in the latter the emphasis is entirely on the grace and agency of the Lord.

About 200 years after Rāmānuja's death, the Śrī Vaiṣṇava community had split into sub-sects called the 'northern culture' (*vaṭakalai*) and the 'southern culture' (*tenkalai*). The *vaṭakalai* emphasized the Sanskrit scriptures and salvation through traditional *bhakti-yoga*, that is devotion to the temple icon, while the *teṅkalai* emphasized the Tamil scriptures and surrender to the Lord by his grace. These two theologies became known as the 'monkey' and 'cat' schools respectively. In the 'monkey' school, salvation is achieved by both effort and grace; the devotee clings to God through his effort, while the Lord saves him, as a baby monkey clings to its mother as she moves through the trees. The 'cat' school, on the other hand, emphasized the grace of the Lord, claiming that the devotee is saved only through grace, as a mother cat picks up her young and carries them without any effort on their part. This distinction is brought out in two understandings of a passage in the *Bhagavad Gītā* (18.66), the famous *carama-śloka*, which reads 'Abandoning all laws seek shelter in me alone. I will save you from all sins. Do not fear.' The *teṅkalai* understood this passage to mean that there were two distinct paths, traditional *bhakti-yoga* and the esoteric, superior, path of surrender (*prapatti*). On the other hand, the *vaṭakalai* theologian, Vedāntadeśika (1269–1307), maintained that the verse referred to two groups of people, those who are twice-born and liberated through the performance of ritual devotion and those of lower castes who cannot perform ritual devotion in the temples, and so are liberated through surrender.[13]

The Śrī Vaiṣṇava community, consisting of Brahmans and non-Brahmans, existed within the wider social context of Brahmans who adhered to the puranic worship of Viṣṇu and other deities, namely the Smārtas, and non-Brahman castes who worshipped and became possessed by local village deities. The Śrī Vaiṣṇavas encompass high-caste levels of

Sanskrit learning and theological tradition, while at the same time having a wide popular appeal even amongst lower castes. Yet while the devotionalism of the Āḻvārs had been ecstatic, the devotion of the Śrī Vaiṣṇavas was controlled, occurring in the context of formal temple ritual. This ecstatic dimension in *bhakti* traditions did not, however, die out with the Āḻvārs but developed in northern Vaiṣṇavism, particularly in Bengal.

GAUḌĪYA VAIṢṆAVISM

Devotional traditions focused on Kṛṣṇa the Cowherd developed in northern India, and found articulation in Sanskrit devotional and poetic literature as well as in more popular devotional movements, particularly around Vṛndāvana and in Bengal. The form of Vaiṣṇavism which grew in Bengal (Gauḍīya) developed a theology which laid great emphasis on devotion and the love relationship between the devotee and Kṛṣṇa. Although in Śaivism a direct correspondence between the religious and the aesthetic had been perceived, the Gauḍīya Vaiṣṇava tradition developed a theology in which the categories of aesthetic experience, described in classical poetry (*kāvya*), came to be applied to devotional religious experience. By the early medieval period, there was a thriving tradition of courtly love poetry in Sanskrit, a poetry which was ornate and baroque, expressing prescribed emotions in a particular form. In the court of the Bengali King Lakṣmaṇasena (*c.* 1179–1209), Jayadeva, a poet under his patronage, composed a famous poem, the *Gītagovinda*, about the love of Kṛṣṇa and Rādhā his mistress.[14] Jayadeva is a high-class poet in the classical *kāvya* tradition, who used the formal conventions of *kāvya* – the prescribed vocabulary, the ornamental language and the stock metaphors – to express the love of Rādhā for Kṛṣṇa and, by implication, of the devotee for Kṛṣṇa. As with courtly poetry generally, the theme of the poem is the union, separation and reunion of the lovers. While they meet secretly in the forest for their love-play, the lovers yet know that with the dawn they must be separated, a fact which causes great longing (*viraha*) until their next meeting. This tradition of poetry focused on the love of Kṛṣṇa and Rādhā continued, particularly with the Bengali poetry of Caṇḍīdāsa and the Mathili verses of Vidyāpati (fourteenth/fifteenth century).[15] Their poetry, written from the point of view of Rādhā, expressed her deep emotional longing for Kṛṣṇa, as the devotee longs for the Lord. Caṇḍīdāsa beautifully expresses the essential longing, characteristic of *bhakti*, when he describes Rādhā hearing the sound of Kṛṣṇa's flute. He writes:

Let us not talk of that fatal flute.
It calls a woman away from her home
and drags her by the hair to that Shyam [i.e. Krsna].
A devoted wife forgets her spouse
To be drawn like a deer, thirsty and lost.
Even the wisest ascetics lose their minds
And the plants and trees delight in its sound.
What then can a helpless, innocent girl do?[16]

However, the figure who did most to promote Kṛṣṇa *bhakti* was Kṛṣṇacaitanya or simply Caitanya (1486–1533), who is regarded as an incarnation of Kṛṣṇa and Rādhā in one body. He generated a tradition which continues to this day, and in the West is manifested as the Hare Kṛṣṇa movement. Caitanya was brought up in a Vaiṣṇava Brahman family where he had a conventional Sanskrit education. In 1508 he went to Gaya to perform a memorial rite for his deceased father. There he had a conversion experience induced by a south Indian renouncer who initiated him into the worship of Kṛṣṇa. He returned to his home town of Navadvīpa (Nabadwip) in Bengal where he began to worship Kṛṣṇa with a group of devotees by singing or chanting his praises. He began to experience ecstatic or possessed states of consciousness. In 1510 Caitanya took formal vows of renunciation and moved to the pilgrimage town of Puri in Orissa where Kṛṣṇa is worshipped as Lord Jagannātha in the famous temple. Each year, during his annual festival, the Lord Jagannātha is paraded out of the temple in a huge processional carriage. Caitanya and his followers would accompany the carriage, dancing and singing the Lord's praise. Caitanya spent the remainder of his life at Puri, worshipping Rādhā and Kṛṣṇa, and frequently going into ecstatic states.[17]

Although Caitanya was not the founder of an order in a formal sense, by writing a commentary on the *Brahma Sūtra*, he nevertheless firmly established Gauḍīya Vaiṣṇavism and determined its style and flavour. The central focus of Gauḍīya Vaiṣṇava devotion is the love between Rādhā and Kṛṣṇa, a love which is strongly erotic, though with an eroticism which is regarded as transcendent and not worldly. The eroticism of Gauḍīya devotion is perhaps not dissimilar to the 'bride-mysticism' (*brautmystik*) of Christian mystical theology. Indeed, liberation for the Gauḍīya Vaiṣṇavas is the constant, ecstatic experience of the divine love-play (*līlā*) between Rādhā and Kṛṣṇa in a spiritual or perfected body. This erotic love and attraction between Rādhā and Kṛṣṇa is 'pure love' (*prema*) as opposed to an impure worldly love pervaded by selfish desire (*kāma*).[18] Kṛṣṇa is the supreme Lord (not simply an *avatāra* of Viṣnu) who creates, maintains and destroys the cosmos over and over again. Rādhā is Kṛṣṇa's 'refreshing power' through which the cosmos is manifested, and although they are united, they are yet distinct. Indeed the relationship between the Lord as the 'holder of power' (*śaktimat*) and Rādhā as his power (*śakti*), and between the devotee and the Lord, is characterized as 'inconceivable difference-in-identity' (*acintya-bhedābheda*).

This relationship is manifested in the world in the love between Rādhā and Kṛṣṇa, and an erotic devotional theology was developed by six of Caitanya's disciples, known as the Gosvāmins, focused on this relationship. This theology may have been influenced by a tantric Vaiṣṇava sect, the Sahajiyas, who maintained that ritual sexual union could overcome duality and reflect the divine union of Kṛṣṇa and Rādhā, a tradition which developed into the low-caste, antinomian and ecstatic Bauls.[19] The Gauḍīya Vaiṣṇava tradition, however, rejects these practices as a misunderstanding of a profound spirituality. The works of the Gosvāmins are, indeed, highly orthodox in the sense that they accept the authority of the Veda, but they include within the category of revelation the Purāṇas, especially the *Bhāgavata Purāṇa*.

Although much of the *Bhāgavata Purāṇa* contains reference to Kṛṣṇa's love-play with the *gopīs*, it does not mention by name Rādhā who only appears with the *Gītagovinda* and in later literature and visual art. In Vaiṣṇava mythology, she is an older married woman and the love between her and Kṛṣṇa is conventionally adulterous. Rādhā leaves a shadow of herself by her husband's side and goes out at night, pulled by the sound of Kṛṣṇa's flute, to meet him. This is theologically important and relates to a distinction in Sanskrit poetics between love-in-union (*svakīyā*, 'one's own woman') associated with marriage, and love-in-separation (*parakīyā*, 'another's woman') associated with adulterous love. The former is characterized by lust (*kāma*) and union, the latter by pure love (*prema*) and longing (*viraha*). In loving Kṛṣṇa, Rādhā disobeys wifely duty (*strīdharma*) (see p. 65), for the love of God transcends social obligation. The love between Rādhā and Kṛṣṇa is love-in-separation characterized by longing – as the soul's longing for the Lord is the highest human spirituality.

Rūpagosvāmin wrote two important texts in Sanskrit on Kṛṣṇa devotion, the *Ujjvala-nīlamaṇi* ('The Splendid Blue Jewel') and the *Bhakti-rasāmṛta-sindhu* ('The Ocean of the Immortal Nectar of Devotion'[20]).

Here aesthetic categories which had been developed in Sanskrit poetics were applied to different kinds of devotional emotion and experience. According to Sanskrit poetics, emotion (*bhāva*) can be transformed into aesthetic experience (*rasa*): for example, grief can be transformed into the experience of tragedy, humour into comedy, and sexual desire into the experience of the erotic. Similarly, sexual desire can be transformed into erotic or 'sweet' love (*śrṅgāra-* or *madhūra-bhakti*) for Kṛṣṇa: the sublimation of human sexual love into divine, or transcendent, erotic love. This passionate all-consuming love for Kṛṣṇa is called, by Rūpagosvāmin, *rāgānuga-bhakti*, in contrast to devotion in which the devotee follows rules and injunctions (*vidhi*) laid down in scripture, called *vaidhi-bhakti*. In *rāgānuga-bhakti* Kṛṣṇa can be as close and intimate with the devotee as a lover, whereas in *vaidhi-bhakti* Kṛṣṇa is perceived as a powerful and majestic king. Both paths lead to salvation, though passionate devotion is higher than the more formal approach and leads directly to Kṛṣṇa.

The main practices of the Gauḍiya Vaiṣṇavas to achieve their soteriological goals were the ritual practices of repeating the names of Kṛṣṇa (*nāma japa*), singing hymns (*kīrtana*), worship of temple icons or the *tulasī* plant sacred to Viṣṇu, and, on the path of *rāgānuga-bhakti*, visualizing Kṛṣṇa's acts, particularly the love-play of Kṛṣṇa and the *gopīs* (*līlā smaraṇa*). After initiation the Kṛṣṇa devotee would perform worship in the morning, afternoon and evening. This would involve repetition of Kṛṣṇa's names, such as the famous Hare Kṛṣṇa mantra – *hare kṛṣṇa, hare kṛṣṇa, kṛṣṇa kṛṣṇa, hare hare, hare rāma, hare rāma, rāma rāma, hare hare* – followed by libations for the ancestors and making offerings.[21] The name of the deity embodies his essence, so by repeating it the devotee is invoking his presence. At death the devotee will serve Kṛṣṇa in a perfected spiritual body (*siddha-deha*) in one of the Lord's spiritual abodes.[22]

OTHER KṚṢṆA SECTS

Other Vaiṣṇava *sampradāyas* similarly maintained an element of erotic mysticism. Vallabha (1479–1531) founded a tradition centred on the worship of Kṛṣṇa the Cowherd after receiving a vision of Kṛṣṇa. He wrote commentaries on the *Brahma Sūtra* and *Bhāgavata Purāṇa* and constructed a theology which is a fusion of monistic and devotional ideas, calling his way the 'path of grace' (*puṣṭimārga*) and his doctrine 'pure non-dualism' (*śuddhādvaita*). Vallabha identifies Kṛṣṇa with the absolute (*brahman*) and maintains that the world is not illusory (*māyā*) but is real and is identified with Kṛṣṇa. Liberation occurs, with Kṛṣṇa's grace, through following a path comprising a series of stages until the devotee, as in Gauḍīya Vaiṣṇavism, becomes part of his play (*līlā*), though unlike Gauḍīya Vaiṣṇavism the Puṣṭi Mārga is non-renunciatory, comprising only householders. While maintaining an erotic dimension, the main focus of Puṣṭi Mārga devotion is on Kṛṣṇa as a child and the devotee as the parent. The Puṣṭi Mārga is particularly large in western India, its main temple being at Nathdvara in Rajasthan.[23] An important order developed from the Puṣṭi Mārga in the nineteenth century, the Swaminarayan movement, whose followers take refuge in the sect's founder Swaminarayan, rather than in Kṛṣṇa.[24]

Several other orders focus their attention on the erotic pastimes of Kṛṣṇa. The Rādhāvallābhis founded by Harivaṃśa (1585) concentrate their worship on Rādhā, while an offshoot, the male sect of the Sākhī Bhāvas, who still exist, dress in women's clothing and adopt female mannerisms in order to emulate the *gopīs*. Lastly, the Viṣṇusvāmis should be mentioned, founded in the twelfth century, famous for a Sanskrit text by one of their devotees, Bilvamaṅgala: the *Kṛṣṇakārnāmṛta* ('The Nectar of the Acts of Kṛṣṇa').[25]

THE CULT OF VIṬHOBĀ

Vaiṣṇava devotionalism spread northwards and local deities, associated with the great Hindu gods, became the focus of devotional movements. In Maharashtra, situated by the eastern seaboard within the northern Sanskritic cultural sphere yet strongly influenced by the Dravidian, were a number of Vaiṣṇava devotional movements which can broadly be described as Sant traditions. The term *sant* means 'good man' and refers to saints from all castes who lived between the thirteenth and seventeenth centuries. They taught a path to liberation through devotion to the Lord's name (*nām*), devotion to one's guru, and the devotional meetings or *satsaṅg* ('the community in truth'). The Vaiṣṇava Sants taught devotion to the Lord as a personal being installed in temples, with qualities (*saguṇa*), though another Sant tradition based in the Punjab, from which Sikhism developed, taught devotion to an abstract Lord beyond qualities (*nirguṇa*).

In Maharashtra, within the general Sant category, several devotional traditions were established. The Mahānubhāva Sampradāya, founded by Chakradhār Swami in the thirteenth century, worshipped only Kṛṣṇa, while the most important sect, the Vārkarī Panth ('The Pilgrims' path'), was centred on the worship of Viṭhobā whose main temple, the focus of an important pilgrimage, is at Pandharpur in southern Maharashtra. A devotional literature in Marathi, a Sanskritic language, developed in the writings of a number of Marathi saints, notably Jñāneśvara (thirteenth century), Nāmdev (*c.* 1270–1350), Tukārām (*c.* 1568–1650), Janābai, Eknāth (*c.* 1533–99) and Rāmdas (1608–81), all except Rāmdas belonging to the Vārkarī tradition.[26] By the seventeenth century the Vārkarīs were the most important sect in Maharashtra and the famous King Śivaji, the scourge of the Mughal Aurangzeb, is said to have met Tukārām and been initiated by Rāmdas.

Jñāneśvara is sometimes considered to be the founder of the Vārkarī Panth, though worship of Viṭhobā predates him. He wrote a Marathi commentary on the *Bhagavad Gītā*, the *Jñāneśvari*,[27] which shows influences of – apart from Vaiṣṇava *bhakti* – Advaita Vedānta and the Nāths (see p. 98). His text extols devotion to the Lord and to his guru who, says Jñāneśvara, rescued him from the ocean of worldly existence. For Jñāneśvara liberation is merging with the Lord, though the individual devotee can never comprehend his immensity. Nāmdev is not only revered as a saint in Maharashtra but in the Punjab as well, and some of his verses have found their way into the sacred scripture of the Sikhs, the *Ādi Granth*. Tukārām is perhaps the most revered saint in Maharashtra, who stressed the love of the Lord as the path to liberation and the necessity of the dualism between the devotee and the Lord in order for love to develop. As with many other Sants, Tukārām advocated singing the Lord's praise and a meditational devotionalism in which one attains liberation by sitting in meditation and repeating the Lord's name (*nām*) – a teaching which is common to the Sant traditions of the north as well. In contrast to Gauḍīya Vaiṣṇavism, erotic imagery is not used by the Maharashtrian Sants and the pure devotion (*prema-bhakti*) which they advocate represents the Lord as a loving parent rather than a lover.

While for highly orthoprax Smārta Hindus, low castes and women are excluded from spiritual liberation and forms of worship, for the Maharashtran Sants caste and gender are not obstacles. Although Jñāneśvara was a Brahman, many other Maharashtran Sants were low-caste: Nāmdev was a tailor and Tukārām was a Śūdra. There were also a number of women saints in the Vārkarī tradition, though generally the images of women in the poetry of Eknāth and Tukārām are negative, presenting woman as the temptress and distractor from the male's path of detachment from the world. Notable women Sants are Jñāneśvara 's sister Muktabai, who was an initiate of Nāth Yoga, and Janabai, the maid-servant of Nāmdev, whose verses to Viṭhobā sometimes address him as a woman, Viṭhabai.

That Janabai could address Viṭhobā as a woman demonstrates the ambiguity of the god. While he is generally male, he is sometimes female and referred to as a mother. While he is generally associated with Viṣṇu or Kṛṣṇa, he is sometimes associated with Śiva, thereby blurring the distinction between Vaiṣṇava and Śaiva. Indeed the cult of Viṭhobā goes beyond sectarian divisions and the two pilgrimages each year to his temple at Pandharpur attract a wide cross-section of the community. Up to 6,000 people are attracted to the more important of the pilgrimages during *aśādha* (June–July), though caste divisions during the pilgrimage are not entirely eradicated.[28]

THE SANT TRADITION

While the Vaiṣṇava Sant tradition developed in Maharashtra, focused on devotion to a *saguṇa* form of Viṣṇu or Kṛṣṇa, further north, and especially in the Punjab, another Ṣant tradition developed which advocated devotion to a *nirguṇa* Lord as the ineffable absolute without shape or form, the source and support of the cosmos, by whose grace beings are liberated from the cycle of birth and death. This northern Sant tradition drew on Vaiṣṇava *bhakti*, Sufism and Nāth Yoga, whose terminologies can be found within Sant literature, but rejected external ritual, emphasizing, rather, the personal experience of a transcendent Lord, beyond form. Like the Maharashtrian Sants, these northern Sants composed devotional songs in vernacular languages, namely forms of Hindi and Punjabi. Among the most famous Sants are Kabīr, Nānak, Mīrabai, Raidās and Dādu. Many of these were low-caste, such as Raidās who was an untouchable leather-worker (*chamār*)[29] and Kabīr who was a weaver.[30] However, not all were of low status: Nānak was a 'warrior' (*khatri*) and Mīrabai a princess. Some of the Sants spawned traditions which continue to the present, most notable, of course, being Sikhism from Guru Nānak, but there are also Raidāsis, Dādūpanthis and Kabīrpanthis.

The teachings of the Sants are preserved in collections of poetry in their respective languages and in the sacred scripture of the Sikhs, the *Ādi Granth*. The songs of these Sants would have circulated around north

India during the sixteenth century, being sung at various temples by wandering bards, as would probably have happened in the south with the songs of the Āḻvārs and Nāyaṉārs. The most popular and influential of the Sants was Kabīr. Kabīr (1398–1448) was born into a weaver family in Benares who had converted to Islam one or two generations prior to his birth. Tradition maintains that his guru was the Vaiṣṇava Rāmānanda, who was in the Rāmānuja lineage, though if Rāmānanda was born in 1299, as one text suggests, it is highly unlikely that Kabīr, born almost 100 years later, could have met him. He was influenced by Nāmdev and by the poetry of the Śaiva woman saint, Lallā (fourteenth century). Kabīr's poetry is quite distinctive. One of its striking features is his use of stark images in 'upside-down language' (*ultavāṃsī*), such as 'the cow is sucking at the calf's teat', used to shock his audience out of complacency and to convey the idea that the Lord is ineffable and beyond everyday logic. He is critical of caste, maintaining that it is irrelevant to liberation, and highly critical of Hindu and Muslim religious practices and doctrines current at his time. He writes: 'The Hindu says Ram is the beloved, the Turk says Rahim. Then they kill each other.'[31]

While there are, of course, individual differences between the northern Sants, there are common themes in their teachings. The soul is trapped in the world governed by Death or Time (*kāl*) and illusion (*māyā*), and must return to the Lord through the meditative devotion of repeating his name (*nām simran*) and by the grace of the guru. Through this repetition the soul will perceive the light of God, hear the divine 'unstruck sound' (*anāhata śabda*) of the Lord, and rise up through the hierarchical cosmos, back to its true abode (*sach-khand*). The names for the Lord used by the Sants are generally Vaiṣṇava, such as Rām, Mādhav, Kṛṣṇa and Hari, though sometimes the more Śaiva names of Nātha or Umāpati might be used and even the term Allah is sometimes referred to.

THE CULT OF RĀMA

While the term Rām is used by the Sants to refer to the transcendent Lord, in the Rāma cults the term refers to the Lord as he was incarnated in King Rāma, the hero of the *Rāmāyaṇa*, king of Ayodhya. Devotion to Rāma, as well as his monkey commander Hanumān, became widespread in northern India during the medieval period. Centres of Rāma worship are found in Janakpur, the legendary birthplace of Sītā, and Ayodhya in Andra Pradesh, Rāma's legendary birthplace and capital of his kingdom. Indeed the cult of Rāma continues to have serious consequences in contemporary India as the demolition in 1992 of the Babji Masjid in Ayodhya demonstrates. One sect of Rāma worship predominates in Ayodhya, the Rāmānandī order, who are also found in Nepal near the Bihar border.[32]

The Rāmānandis, whose main centre is at Ayodhya, were founded by Rāmānanda (fifteenth century?), with possible connections with the Śrī Vaiṣṇava tradition. Their literature is expressed in the medium of Hindi, though no writing of Rāmānanda himself is preserved. According to the tradition, he advocated devotion to Rāma and Sītā, a devotion which, in contrast to Gauḍīya Vaiṣṇavism, is devoid of eroticism. In this style of *bhakti* the devotee's attitude is as a servant to the master, rather than as a lover to the beloved, hence Hanumān is hailed as the exemplum of devotional service to his master Rāma. While there are no writings of Rāmānanda himself, the theology of the sect is based on the writings of Tulsidās (1532–1623) who composed the *Rāmacaritmānasa* ('The Sacred Lake of Rama's Deeds'[33]), a version of a version of Vālmīki's *Rāmāyaṇa*, composed in Hindi rather than the sacred language of Sanskrit. The Brahmans of Varanasi, where the text was composed, are said to have been shocked by the composition of such a text in a vernacular language. It was tested by being placed in the Śiva temple for one night, with the Vedas and Purāṇas placed on top of it. In the morning, Tulsidās' text was on top of them all, whereby its authority was legitimized.[34] In this text and other compositions by Tulsidās, Rāma is the supreme Lord and other deities, while being eulogized, are subordinated to him.

The Rāmānandī order is predominantly ascetic and renunciatory. In the past, all castes, including Untouchables, were initiated into it and at initiation all previous caste duties were abandoned and service to Rāma instituted in their place. In contemporary practice, however, caste restrictions are imposed in Rāmānandī temples and only Brahmans can be priests. Originally both sexes were initiated, though now there are few nuns remaining in the order.

The most popular festival associated with Rāma is Rāmlīlā which occurs throughout north India, particularly at Ramnagar near Varanasi. During this festival Tulsidās' *Ramacaritmānasa* is recited by priests of the Maharāja of Varanasi, along with the recitation of dramatic dialogues. The story of Rāma and Sītā is enacted from his birth, through the major events of his life – his marriage, banishment, war against Rāvaṇa – to his triumphant return and the establishing of Rāma's kingdom.[35]

Summary

In this survey of the Vaiṣṇava and associated traditions we can see a process in which an exuberant and emotional form of devotionalism, originating in the south, becomes associated with a more sober tradition of respectful devotion, originating in the north. The patterns of *bhakti* that we see here – such as the association of local or regional deities with the deities of the great Sanskritic tradition, and the establishing of orders by saints – are also followed by devotional movements within Śaivism. Although Śaivism has tended more towards the ideals of yoga and detached asceticism rather than towards emotional devotionalism, there have nevertheless been strong devotional tendencies within it, particularly in the south. To the development of this similarly vast tradition we now turn.

7 Śaiva and tantric religion

Within the developing Hindu traditions we can see the process of Brahmanization or Sanskritization, whereby the great brahmanical tradition of vedic social values, vedic ritual forms and Sanskrit learning absorbs local popular traditions of ritual and ideology. We have seen this, for example, in the cult of Viṭhobā who becomes identified with Viṣṇu and of Murukaṉ who becomes identified with Skanda. Regional traditions expressed in vernacular languages, local deities, local mythologies, ritual forms and possession cults become universalized through Sanskritization. The poetry and emotional devotion of the Āḻvārs becomes a pan-south-Asian phenomenon (i.e. the tradition becomes universalized) when their poetry is absorbed within the brahmanical ideology of the Śrī Vaiṣṇavas (i.e. it becomes Sanskritized). Theology is thus built up from a level of regional ritual and possession cults and in turn influences those cults. Regional ritual and possession form the basis or substratum of brahmanical theology.

A second important process can also be identified, namely the transformations of the ascetic ideal: on the one hand its assimilation into the higher-caste householder's ideology, as in the *Bhagavad Gītā*, on the other its assimilation into the low-caste possession cults of the cremation ground. Between these extremes we have the highly revered, orthodox renouncers such as the Daśanāmis. These manifestations of the ascetic ideal may be linked to the historical question regarding the vedic or non-vedic origins of renunciation, which we have discussed. Yet, whatever its origins, there have been, and still are, ambivalent attitudes towards renouncers amongst householders.[1] At the one extreme is the highly revered, orthodox renouncer, the ideal of many high-caste male householders, yet at the other extreme there is the feared unorthodox ascetic, openly courting pollution and living in the cremation ground. This ambivalent attitude is clearly demonstrated in the religions of Śiva who is himself a god of paradox: both the ideal householder and the ideal ascetic.

Śaivism refers to the traditions which follow the teachings of Śiva (*śivaśāsana*) and which focus on the deity Śiva, or sometimes his consort and power, Śakti. Processes occur in Śaivism which are also found in Vaiṣṇavism: the absorption by brahmanical orthopraxy of non-vedic ritual forms and ideas and the identification of local deities with pan-Hindu ones. In this chapter we will trace the rise of Śiva and the traditions centred on his worship. Like Vaiṣṇavism, Śaivism has absorbed within it a variety of ritual practices and theologies, though it has tended more towards asceticism or the ascetic ideal, even in its householder forms, than has Vaiṣṇavism. Indeed, the genius of Śaivism, or its inspiration, is to be found in the renouncer traditions, in particular the renouncer traditions of the cremation ground. The Śaiva ideals of asceticism contrast with those of Vaiṣṇavism which is strongly associated with the householder, with life in the world and with the ideology of kingship. In other words, Vaiṣṇavism has tended to be more vedic and orthoprax than Śaivism.

The picture is, of course, more complex than this and Śaivism did have royal patronage, but generally ascetic, and sometimes ecstatic, tendencies predominated. While one needs to be cautious of generalizations, it might be argued that Ruth Benedict's distinction, derived from Nietzsche, between Apollonian cultures in which order, control and law are important and Dionysian cultures which revere the 'ecstasy of the dance', can be applied to Vaiṣṇavism and Śaivism at an ideological level.[2] Although there are undoubtedly ecstatic and antinomian dimensions in devotion to Kṛṣṇa, the ideologies of Vaiṣṇavism have tended towards vedic orthopraxy and the maintaining of vedic values. Śaivism, while also having some orthoprax tendencies, unreservedly accepted the non-vedic revelation of the Tantras and draws its inspiration from the polluting cremation-ground asceticism. Some of the ecstatic tendencies of Śaivism are embodied in the mythology of the deity Śiva himself.

The myth of Dakṣa

An important myth in the corpus of Śaiva narratives is the myth of Dakṣa. This story is told in the *Mahābhārata* and there are a number of variants in the Purāṇas. Dakṣa, the son of Brahmā (in the Veda his mother is Aditi), is the father of Satī. Satī becomes the wife of Śiva who is attracted to her because of the power of her austerities as well as her beauty, but, during the wedding, tension builds up between Dakṣa and his unconventional son-in-law. Śiva and Satī retire to Mount Kailāsa and Dakṣa prepares a horse sacrifice to which he invites all the gods except Śiva. While Śiva is not bothered by the snub, Satī is distraught at the insult and goes in anger to her father's sacrifice where she is rebuffed by Dakṣa. In her rage she commits suicide by burning herself through her yogic power. Upon hearing the news of his wife's death, Śiva is enraged and attacks Dakṣa's sacrifice in the terrifying form of Vīrabhadra with his hordes of demonic beings. All is destroyed and Dakṣa is killed, beheaded by Śiva, thereby himself becoming the sacrificial victim. Śiva then resuscitates the sacrifice as well as Dakṣa, in some versions with a goat's head, and the sacrifice proceeds smoothly with Śiva included.[3] In some, possibly later, versions, Śiva finds the body of Satī and, in a state of grief and frenzy, picks up her corpse and dances wildly with it across the universe (see p. 192 for what happens next).

While this myth is multi-levelled and can be understood in a variety of ways, perhaps an obvious reading is that Śiva was originally excluded from the vedic sacrifice; that he is a deity perhaps originally from outside the vedic panthеon, but who came to be accepted as one of the gods. Indeed, in destroying the sacrifice with fire, Śiva is paradoxically fulfilling it and so ensuring that the sacrifice is his. We can, in fact, see in this myth an analogue for the development of Śaivism. As Śiva is outside the vedic fold, so are the traditions associated with him, and as Śiva makes his presence known so forcefully and is, of necessity, absorbed within the vedic pantheon, so Śaiva traditions are incorporated into vedic ideology and practice.

The image of Śiva

Śiva is a god of ambiguity and paradox. He has been described by Wendy Doniger O'Flaherty as the 'erotic ascetic', the ithyphallic and promiscuous god, who is also the celibate yogin, practising austerities in the Himalayas. He is the three-eyed god who has burned Desire with his third eye, who dances in the cremation ground and yet who seduces the sages' wives in the pine forest. He is the wild matted-haired ascetic, yet he is also the ideal family man and householder with a wife, Pārvatī, and their two sons Gaṇeśa and Skanda. He contains all opposites within him and is even described as half male and half female (*ardhanarīśvara*).[4] Śiva is sometimes described as the god of destruction, part of the 'Hindu trinity' with Brahmā as creator and Viṣṇu as sustainer, but for his devotees he is the supreme Lord who creates, maintains and destroys the cosmos. He conceals his true nature from humanity, yet, at the same time, can reveal his nature as an act of grace. While there is a very strong sense of Śiva's transcendence in Śaivism, he is nevertheless represented or installed in a number of forms in temples and shrines, which are also represented in mythology. He is especially worshipped and iconographically depicted in the following forms:

- as the Lord of Yoga meditating on Mount Kailāsa or Kailash in the Himalayas. He is iconographically portrayed as covered in ashes, with a third eye with which he burned Desire (Kāma), with his matted locks in a chignon, a crescent moon in his hair, the Ganges pouring from his locks, garlanded by a snake and sacred *rudrākṣa* beads, seated upon a tiger skin and holding a trident.
- as the family man with his wife, the goddess Pārvatī, and their two sons, Skanda and the elephant-headed Gaṇeśa, with the sacred bull Nandi, standing nearby.
- as Śiva Naṭarāja, the Lord of the Dance, who, in his awe-inspiring dance which expresses his boundless energy, creates, maintains and destroys the cosmos. He is four-armed, dancing upon the dwarf of ignorance (Apasmāra) within a circle of flames.
- in his form as the Śiva *liṅga* or 'icon' found in most Hindu temples.[5] The liṅga represents a phallus within a vulva, symbolic of the union of Śiva with his dynamic energy or *śakti.*

Early worship of Rudra-Śiva

Apart from some speculation over an Indus valley seal as a representation of Śiva (see p. 29), the earliest references to the god are found in the *Ṛg Veda* where three hymns are addressed to him as Rudra, 'the roarer'. Rudra is brown, with a black belly and red back, clothed in a skin. He is ferocious and destructive, the Lord of the storm gods, the Maruts, who attacks 'like a ferocious wild beast', yet he is also the benevolent healer and cooler of disease. These hymns, *Ṛg Veda* 2.33, 1.43 and 1.114, praise Rudra and ask him to leave their communities alone, not to take their children and grandchildren, not to kill their horses and cattle, and, having been

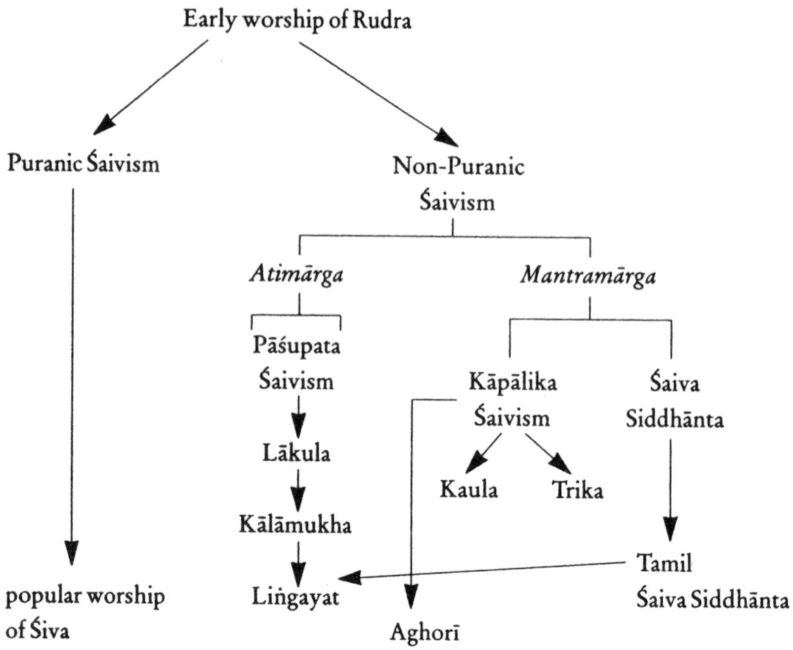

Figure 6 The development of the Śaiva traditions

praised, to go away and strike down someone else instead! In the *Taittirīya Saṃhitā* of the black Yajur Veda and in the *Vājasaneyi Saṃhitā* of the white,[6] is a hymn to the 'hundred names of Rudra' (*śatarudriya*) which further develops the ambiguous nature of the god, speaking of his auspicious form in contrast to his malignant form. He is the god of wild, haunted places, who lives apart from human communities who are terrified by his feral habitations. Yet, as in the *Ṛg Veda*, he is also the healer, the Lord of medicinal herbs, and Paśupati, the Lord of cattle. This hymn is an early example of enumerating the divine names of a deity in order to make contact with him/her. By the first few centuries CE, the recitation of the *Śatarudriya* is claimed, in the *Jābala Upaniṣad*, for instance, to lead to immortality,[7] and the *Śatarudriya* is often referred to in the *Śiva Purāṇa*. The hymn is still recited in Śaiva temples today.[8]

Rudra is a peripheral deity in the vedic pantheon and the descriptions of him as living away from the Aryan communities may indicate that his origins are non-vedic, yet, nevertheless, the fact that he is included in these hymns shows that he is still, however peripherally, part of the vedic pantheon. By the fifth or fourth centuries BCE, however, Rudra-Śiva has risen to a more prominent position and in the *Śvetāśvatara Upaniṣad* has become identified with the supreme absolute, the efficient and material cause of the cosmos.

The Śvetāśvatara Upaniṣad

The *Śvetāśvatara Upaniṣad*, the teachings of the sage with the white mule (*śvetāśvatara*), was composed around the fifth or fourth centuries BCE, chronologically after the *Bṛhadāraṇyaka* and *Chāndogya Upaniṣads*, but before the *Bhagavad Gītā*. This text is very important for understanding the development of Hindu religious thought, for it marks a transition between the simpler monism of the earlier Upaniṣads and the theism of the later Śaiva and Vaiṣṇava traditions. The text begins by asking a series of questions about the origin of the universe and the origin of humanity: what is the cause of all this? Who rules over our various conditions of pleasure and pain? The text then attempts to answer these queries by proposing a theology which elevates Rudra to the status of supreme being, the Lord (Īśa) who is transcendent yet also has cosmological functions, as does Śiva in later traditions. For the *Śvetāśvatara*:

- the Lord is the cause of the cosmos.
- the Lord is a 'magician' (*māyin*) who produces the world through his power (*śakti*) and sustains it.
- the Lord is transcendent, dwelling beyond the cosmos, yet also immanent, dwelling in the hearts of all beings.

There are parallels here with the slightly later Vaiṣṇava theologies of the *Mahānārāyaṇa Upaniṣad* and the *Bhagavad Gītā*, and like those texts there seems to be some distinction between the Lord and the individual soul and, although the term *bhedābheda* is not used, the *Śvetāśvatara* presents a difference-in-identity theology. The soul, which is without gender, journeys from body to body according to its karma until liberated through the efforts of yoga and by the grace (*prasāda*) of the Lord with whom it is united. Indeed the term *bhakti* in the context of one having highest devotion for God and for one's guru as God, occurs here for the first time.[9] However, as this is the last stanza of the text it is probably a later interpolation, for, while the seeds of *bhakti* are here, they have not yet developed.

The formation of Śaivism

While Rudra-Śiva is eulogized in the *Ṛg Veda* and identified with a theistic absolute in the *Śvetāśvatara Upaniṣad*, there are other early references to Śiva and Śaiva worship. In the grammarian Patañjali's 'Great Commentary' (*Mahābhāṣya*) on Pāṇini's famous Sanskrit grammar (second century BCE), he describes a devotee of Śiva, a *Śiva-bhāgavata*, as clad in animal skins and carrying an iron lance as the symbol of his god, perhaps a precursor of Śiva's trident. Coins of Greek, Śāka and Parthian kings who ruled north India (200 BCE – 100 CE) have been found bearing a bull, a symbol of Śiva, and there are references to early Śaiva ascetics in the *Mahābhārata*.[10] However, it is with the Purāṇas that we see Śaivism develop as a major strand of Hindu religiosity.

PURANIC ŚAIVISM

During the Gupta dynasty (*c.* 320–500 CE) puranic religion developed and expanded, and the stories of the Purāṇas spread rapidly, eventually throughout the subcontinent, through the singers or reciters, and indeed composers, of the narratives. This expansion was accompanied by the development of brahmanical forms of worship, the Smārta or *paurāṇika*, based on those texts. With the decline of the Guptas, while this Smārta worship is well established, there occurs an increase of esoteric cults, many of which, or elements of which, become absorbed into brahmanical forms of worship.

The Śaiva Purānas, the most important of which are the *Liṅga*, and the *Śiva Purāṇas*, contain the usual puranic subjects of genealogies, the duties of different castes, Dharma Śāstra material and astrology, as well as exclusively Śaiva elements such as the installing of *liṅgas* in temples, descriptions of the various forms of Śiva, and the nature of Śiva, whose body is the cosmos, as transcendent and immanent. Apart from material on the formal worship of Śiva, Purāṇas such as the *Liṅga* also contain information on asceticism and yoga, particularly the yoga of the Pāśupatas, the earliest Śaiva sect of which we know. The Purāṇas classify Śaivas into four groups, namely the Pāśupata, Lākulīśa, Śaiva and Kāpālika, while Rāmānuja in his commentary on the *Brahma-Sūtra* lists the Śaivas, Pāśupatas, Kāpālins and Kālāmukhas.[11] All these groups are generally outside the vedic or puranic system. Indeed all the Purāṇas were composed within the sphere of vedic or Smārta orthodoxy and texts such as the *Kūrma-Purāṇa* condemn the

Pāśupata system,[12] favouring instead the authority of the *Śatarudriya* and a late Upaniṣad containing Śaiva material, the *Atharvaśiras Upaniṣad*. Although the Purāṇas are pervaded by non-orthodox Śaiva material, they nevertheless distance themselves from these non-orthodox or tantric systems which posed a threat to vedic purity and *dharma*.

A Brahman householder who worshipped Śiva by performing a purāṇic *pūjā*, making offerings by using vedic mantras to orthodox forms of Śiva, was not an initiate into a specific Śaiva sect, but worshipped Śiva within the general context of vedic domestic rites and Smārta adherence to *varṇāśrama-dharma*. In his commentary on the *Brahma Sūtra* (the same verse as commented on by Rāmānuja) Śaṅkara refers to Maheśvaras who worship Śiva, probably meaning those who follow the *paurāṇika* form of worship. As Alexis Sanderson has described, such a brahmanical Śaiva within the Smārta domain, a Maheśvara, can be contrasted with an initiate, technically known as a Śaiva, who has undergone an initiation (*dīkṣā*) and who follows the teachings of Śiva (*śivaśāsana*) contained in Śaiva scriptures (*śāstra*).[13] While the Śaiva initiate hoped for liberation (*mokṣa*), the Śaiva householder or Maheśvara would at death be taken to Śiva's heaven (*Śiva-loka*) at the top of the world egg (where *vaikuṇṭha* would be for the purāṇic Vaiṣṇava).

The Śaiva initiates (as opposed to the lay, *paurāṇika* devotees) can be further classified within a more general distinction, again clearly explicated by Alexis Sanderson, between on the one hand the 'Outer Path' (*atimārga*) and on the other the 'Path of Mantras' (*mantramārga*).[14] These are two main branches described in Śaiva texts, the Āgamas or Tantras. The former, open to ascetics only, is a path exclusively for the purpose of salvation from *saṃsāra*, while the latter, open to ascetics and householders, is a path which leads to eventual salvation, but also to the attainment of supernatural or magical powers (*siddhi*) and pleasure (*bhoga*) in higher worlds along the way. The path of the *atimārga* might also be rendered as the 'higher path' – the path which has transcended the orthodox system of four stages of life (*āśrama*), going even higher than the orthodox stage of renunciation according to the Atimārgins.

PĀŚUPATA ŚAIVISM

Within the higher path (*atimārga*) two important orders existed, the Pāśupata and a sub-branch, the Lākula, part of which was the Kālāmukha order. The Pāśupatas are the oldest Śaiva sect, probably from the second century CE, referred to in the *Nārāṇiya* section of the *Mahābhārata*,[15] though no ancient texts belonging to them have survived. The only Pāśupata scripture which we have is the comparatively late, though pre-tenth-century, *Paśupata Sūtra* with a commentary by Kauṇḍinya.[16] According to tradition, this text is the revelation of Rudra who became the possibly historical sage, Lakulīśa, by entering and reanimating the corpse of a Brahman in a cremation ground. This form is also regarded as the last of Śiva's incarnations (*avatāra*) mentioned in the *Kūrma Purāṇa*.[17] In this form he gave out the teachings contained in the *Pāśupata Sūtra*.

The Pāśupata ascetic had to be a Brahman male, who had undergone the high-caste initiation ceremony. Although he could become a Pāśupata from any stage of life, his high-caste status was still important in his religious practice in so far as he should not speak with low castes nor with women. Indeed one passage of Kauṇḍinya's commentary on the *Pāśupata Sūtra*[18] speaks in misogynistic terms of women as the temptresses of the ascetic, who creates madness in him, and whose sexuality cannot be controlled by scripture. The Pāśupata ascetic had to be a Brahman and had to be celibate (*brahmacārya*), though he was nevertheless disapproved of and rebuked by some vedic, Smārta texts such as the *Kūrma-Purāṇa*.[19] The Pāśupatas seem to have been very much on the edges of orthodox householder society, going beyond the four stages (*āśrama*) to a fifth, 'perfected stage' (*siddha āśrama*) and spurning vedic householder injunctions on purity and family life. Yet, unlike many other Śaiva groups, the Pāśupata never completely abandoned or explicitly rejected vedic values, wishing to see his tradition as in some sense the culmination and fulfilment of vedic life rather than its rejection. Liberation from karma and rebirth occurred at death: a liberation which was conceptualized as acquiring the qualities of omniscience and omnipotence. Although ultimately this liberation was through the grace of Rudra, some effort on the part of the Pāśupata was needed. This took the form of a vow or observance (*vrata*) which involved a spiritual practice (*sādhana*) in three developmental stages.

The first involved the ascetic living by a Śaiva temple, covering himself in ashes while avoiding bathing in water, and worshipping the deity through dancing and singing, meditation on five mantras sacred to Śiva, laughter and temple circumambulation. The second stage was to leave the temple, remove external signs of his cultic affiliation, and behave in public places in anti-social ways such as acting as if deranged, making lewd gestures to young women, snoring loudly while not being asleep, and even acting as if crippled. This behaviour was to invite the abuse of passers-by in order that their merit or good karma would be transferred to the ascetic, while his bad karma would be transferred to those who had abused him. The third and final stage was to withdraw to a remote place, such as a cave or deserted house, in order to meditate upon the five sacred mantras and on the syllable *oṃ*. When this meditation could be achieved effortlessly, he finally withdrew to a cremation ground where he lived from whatever he could find and ultimately died gaining union with Rudra (*rudrasāyujyam*).[20]

SUB-DIVISIONS OF THE PĀŚUPATAS

There were various sub-divisions among the Pāśupatas, the most important of which was the Lākula. These were ascetics who accepted the doctrines of the *Pāśupata Sūtra*, though they were more extreme in their ascetic practices and rejection or transcendence of vedic injunctions than the other Pāśupatas. Sanderson quotes one surviving manuscript of the sect which describes them as wandering, carrying a skull-topped staff (*khaṭvāṅga*), with a skull begging bowl, a garland of human bone, and covered in ashes, with matted hair or shaven head in imitation of their Lord Rudra.[21] Here the ascetic takes his imitation of Rudra to the extreme, as one who has taken the 'great vow' (*mahāvrata*) required of someone for killing a Brahman. The Dharma Śāstras state that one who has killed a Brahman should perform penance by living outside vedic society, in a hut in a forest, carrying the skull of the person slain like a flag, for a twelve-year period, in order to expiate the crime.[22]

This idea is further reinforced by a myth told in a number of variants in the Purāṇas. The essential story is that the god Brahmā feels passion for his daughter and attempts to sleep with her. As a consequence, Śiva, in the form of the terrible Bhairava, cuts off Brahmā's fifth head with his thumb nail. The head does not leave Bhairava's hand, so he wanders around various pilgrimage sites (*tīrtha*) until he reaches Varanasi where the skull falls at the Kapālamocana ('freeing the skull') tīrtha; Śiva is then freed from the sin of Brahmanicide. As the wanderer with the Brahman's (i.e. Brahmā's) skull, Śiva is also known as the beggar Bhikṣāyatana and the skull-bearer Kāpālin. There are a number of versions of this myth,[23] but the main point here is that the narrative serves to reinforce the identification of the Lākula ascetic with the skull-carrying form of Śiva.

Part of the Lākula order were the Kālāmukhas who flourished from the ninth to thirteenth centuries and about whom we gain information mainly from south Indian epigraphic evidence. They were prevalent in Karnataka where they were superseded by the Liṅgayat sect in the thirteenth century. The Kālāmukhas had their own temples and, in spite of strongly heterodox elements in their practices, such as worshipping Rudra in a pot filled with alchohol and covering themselves in the ashes of corpses rather than cow-dung, they regarded themselves as being within the vedic fold.

In contrast to the higher path (*atimārga*) which was thought to lead straight to liberation, the path of mantras (*mantramārga*) leads to liberation via the acquisition of magical powers and experiencing pleasure in higher worlds for initiates. Within this general category are a number of traditions and ritual systems which, Sanderson has shown, can be divided into two broad categories, the Śaiva Siddhānta and non-Siddhānta systems which incorporate a number of other groups and texts.[24] All of these traditions within the path of mantras revered as authoritative revelation a vast body of texts known as the Āgamas and Tantras, texts which were regarded as heterodox by the strictly orthodox vedic tradition. Even so, many of these texts came to infiltrate orthodoxy and came to be revered as authoritative even within Smārta circles. The traditions of the path of mantras are known as the 'tantric traditions', for their revelation comprises the Śaiva tantric texts. Before going on to examine the traditions of the *mantramārga*, we need first to make some general points about the tantric revelation, the Āgamas and Tantras.

The tantric revelation

The Tantras cannot be dated before 600 CE at the very earliest, most were probably composed from the eighth century onwards and by the tenth century a vast body of Sanskrit texts had developed, generally called 'Tantra', though the term 'Agama' is also used and 'Saṃhitā' for Vaiṣṇava texts of the Pāñcarātra (see p. 122). There is a large corpus of Buddhist Tantras which form the textual basis of the Vajrayāna which, though little remains in Sanskrit, are preserved in Tibetan translations. The religious culture of the Tantras is essentially Hindu and the Buddhist tantric material can be shown to have been derived from Śaiva sources.[25] There is a substantial body of Jain Tantras and there was a corpus of Tantras to the Sun (Sūrya) in the Saura tradition, none of which have survived. The tantric texts are regarded as revelation, superior to the Veda, by the traditions which revere them: the Śaiva Tantras are thought to have been revealed by

Śiva, the Vaiṣṇava Tantras by Viṣṇu and the Śākta Tantras by the Goddess, and transmitted to the human world via a series of intermediate sages. While being rejected by vedic orthodoxy, the followers of the Tantras, the *Tāntrikas*, included the orthodox system within their own as a lower level of attainment and understanding. Revelation was, in some sense, progressive, the Tāntrikas placing their own systems at the top of a hierarchy. Tantric Śaiva groups would regard their revelations as the esoteric culmination of Vedic orthodoxy, while Buddhist Vajrayānists would similarly regard their Tantras as the culmination of Mahāyana Buddhism.

The main geographical areas for the early medieval explosion of tantric religion were Kashmir and Nepal, areas in which important manuscripts have been preserved. Bengal and Assam were also important and the Tantras penetrated to the far south. Indeed, the tantric orders and practices of which the texts speak were probably pan-Indian by the tenth or eleventh centuries. Many Tantras have been translated into Tamil and are used as the basis for liturgies in south Indian temples. Tantrism has been so pervasive that all of Hinduism after the eleventh century, perhaps with the exception of the vedic Śrauta tradition, is influenced by it. All forms of Śaiva, Vaiṣṇava and Smārta religion, even those forms which wanted to distance themselves from Tantrism, absorbed elements derived from the Tantras.

The Tantras generally take the form of a dialogue between Śiva and the Goddess (Devī, Pārvatī, Umā). The Goddess, as the disciple, asks the questions and Śiva, as the master, answers. In the Vaiṣṇava Tantras (i.e. Pāñcarātra Saṃhitās) the dialogue is between the Lord (Bhagavān) and the Goddess Śrī or Lakṣmī. In some Tantras focused on the Goddess – those of the Śākta tradition – it is Śiva who does the asking and the Goddess who replies. This narrative structure reflects the importance and centrality of the guru in Tantrism. As the Goddess receives wisdom from Śiva, or in some cases vice versa, so the disciple receives wisdom from his or her master. The meanings of the Tantras are often obscure and it must be remembered that they were compiled within the context of a living, oral tradition and teachings given by the guru. The Tantras often regard themselves as secret, to be revealed by the guru only with the appropriate initiation which wipes away the power of past actions.[26]

While the Tantras are notorious for their erotic and antinomian elements – ritual sex and the consumption of alcohol and meat offered to ferocious deities – most of their contents are of a more sober nature and they contain material on a wide range of topics. Although they are primarily ritual texts, the Tantras also explain the formation of *mantras*, hierarchical cosmologies, initiations, the evolution of sound from subtle to gross levels, yoga, doctrine, appropriate behaviour and temple architecture. Traditionally the Tantras should cover four topics or stand on four 'feet' or 'supports' (*pāda*), namely doctrine (*vidyā*- or *jñāna-pāda*), ritual (*kriyā-pāda*), yoga (*yoga-pāda*) and discipline or correct behaviour (*cārya-pāda*), though only exceptionally do the texts follow this scheme.[27] While there is divergence over doctrine and each tantric system regards itself as superior to the others, there are nevertheless common elements, particularly in respect of spiritual practice (*sādhana*) and ritual: practice cuts across doctrinal distinctions.[28] The most common features contained in the Tantras are the following, though some of these are not unique to the Tantras and not all Tantras contain all these elements:

- the Tantras are concerned with practice or *sādhana*, which involves initiation (*dīkṣā*), ritual and yoga.
- there is a common ritual structure in the Tantras, though variation with regard to deities and mantras. This structure can be summarized as the purification of the body through its symbolic destruction; the creation of a divine body/self through mantra; internal worship or visualization; followed by external worship or *pūjā*. This process involves the use of hand gestures (*mudrā*), mantra repetition and the construction of sacred diagrams (*yantra*, *maṇḍala*).
- the Tantras present elaborate hierarchical cosmologies which absorb the cosmic hierarchies of earlier traditions. For example the highest world of the Śaiva Siddhānta is transcended by further worlds within Kashmir Śaiva traditions.
- the body is divine and contains the cosmic hierarchy within it, and the cosmic polarity of the male deity and his consort, the female energy. The male deity is often Śiva and his Śakti is the Goddess Kuṇḍalinī. Their union within the body is the symbolic expression of liberation.
- the Tantras are concerned with the attaining of magical powers (*siddhi*) and the experience of bliss in higher worlds (*bhoga*) as part of the practitioner's spiritual journey, which is also conceptualized, and experienced, as a journey of the Kuṇḍalinī through the body.
- the Tantras are concerned with possession (*āveśa*) and exorcism.

Although these are common features, the tantric orders tended to be sectarian, regarding their own revelations as going beyond those of other traditions. The Tantras thereby recapitulate a general feature of Hindu traditions: they incorporate previous religious forms and texts within them at a lower level.

The social basis of the Tantras

There is very little known about the social status of the *Tāntrikas*. The Tantras seem to have originated among ascetic groups living in cremation grounds, who were probably not of brahmanical origin, but who were above low-caste groups. Such cremation-ground asceticism goes back a long way in Indian religion and the Pālī canon of Theravāda Buddhism bears witness to it.[29] These ascetics are beyond the pale of vedic orthodoxy: the ascetic ideal is here expressed at a lower social level. By the early medieval period, groups of ecstatic ascetics would imitate their terrible deities such as Bhairava and the goddess Kālī, whom they would appease with non-vegetarian offerings, alcohol and sexual substances. Controlled possession would have been a feature of their practice, in which the practitioner would invite the deity to possess him (*āveśa mām*, 'enter me') but would attempt to control the deity and so gain power. Texts such as the *Netra Tantra* bear witness to cults of possession and exorcism.[30] These ascetic groups would have been supported by low castes who lived by the cremation grounds.

The ideologies of these groups began to influence not only popular religion, but also brahmanical circles, as we see in eleventh-century Kashmir. Here the popular cult of the deity Svacchanda-Bhairava, a form of Śiva, is influenced by tantric asceticism, but more significantly so are the higher social levels of the Brahmans and the court. Indeed the learned Brahman elite, of whom the Śaiva theologian Abhinavagupta was a part, began to transform extreme tantric ideology into a more respectable religion of the higher castes. Tantric influence was a real social concern and its infiltration into courtly circles in Kashmir was caricatured by dramatists such as Kṣemendra.[31] However, after the twelfth century, Tantrism rapidly declined in northern and central India, largely due to Muslim onslaughts and the establishing of the Delhi Sultanate (1206–1526). Kashmir was plundered by Mahmud of Ghazni in 1014, though remained free from Muslim domination until the twelfth century. In the south, beyond the region of Muslim domination, Tantrism has survived and been absorbed into the social matrix. The Tantras are used as temple texts and are quite respectable in Tamilnadu and Kerala where 'Tantris' are high-caste

Nambudri Brahmans who install icons in temples; a long way from Tantrism's cremation-ground origins.

The path of mantras

Although the outer or higher path (*atimārga*) does have the *Pāśupata Sūtra*, it may be the case that it did not have its own distinctive revelation, relying, rather, on the scriptures of other traditions while regarding itself as transcending all scriptures.[32] The revelation of the path of mantras (*mantramārga*), on the other hand, comprises all the Śaiva Tantras; a vast body of texts belonging to a number of groups. The most important distinction with the path of mantras is between the tradition known as the Śaiva Siddhānta on the one hand, and non-Siddhānta groups, or the teachings of Bhairava (*Bhairava-śāstra*), on the other. These are themselves subdivided into a number of traditions. There are twenty-eight Tantras of the Śaiva Siddhānta (divided into ten *Śiva Āgamas* and eighteen *Rudra Āgamas*) and numerous Bhairava Tantras.[33] It is to the Śaiva Siddhānta that we turn first.

THE ŚAIVA SIDDHĀNTA

The Śaiva Siddhānta provides the basic ritual and doctrinal system of the Path of Mantras, which is presupposed by all the non-Siddhānta traditions. While the Śaiva Siddhānta is the most important, normative form of Śaivism in south India, using Tamil scriptures, it originally developed in the north, particularly in Kashmir. In Tamilnadu the tradition comes to incorporate an emotional devotion (*bhakti*) expressed in the hymns of the Tamil saints, as did the parallel Śri Vaiṣṇava tradition. Originally it was not concerned with *bhakti* but with ritual. The Śaiva Siddhānta is a 'dualist' system, maintaining that there is an eternal distinction between the Lord and the soul, in contrast to the monistic 'Kashmir' Śaivism which viewed the Lord and the soul as one. Monistic Śaivism replaced the Śaiva Siddhānta in Kashmir, which then established itself after the eleventh or twelfth century in the south. There were a number of eminent Śaiva Siddhānta theologians who wrote commentaries on tantric texts and composed independent works on ritual and theology, the most significant amongst them being Sadyojoti (eighth century) in Kashmir, and Bhojadeva (eleventh century) and Aghoraśiva (twelfth century) in the south.

According to Śaiva Siddhānta theology there are three distinct categories of existence: the Lord (*pati*), souls (*paśu*), and the mental and material universe which binds them (*paśa*). The Lord, in an aspect called Sadāśiva, performs five actions: the emission of the cosmos, its maintenance, its re-absorption, the concealing of himself, and the revealing of himself through grace. He is wholly transcendent and distinct from the eternal substance of *māyā*, from which the material and mental universe is generated. The Lord is the efficient cause of the cosmos, creating it via a regent, the Lord Ananta, who activates *māyā*, the material cause and substance of which the universe is a transformation. Having been manifested, the cosmos eventually dissolves back again into *māyā* in an endless process of emanation and re-absorption. Bound souls are beings with consciousness who are entangled in the unconscious material universe, by impurity (*mala*), by action and its consequences (*karma*), by *māyā*, and by the Lord's power of will. The soul is eventually liberated from this entanglement by ritual action and by Śiva's grace. The three ontological categories can be summarized as follows:

Pati ('Lord')	Śiva, efficient cause of the cosmos. As Sadāśiva, he performs the five acts of emission, maintenance, re-absorption, concealment and bestowing grace.
paśu ('Soul', lit. 'beast')	The individual soul, distinct from Śiva, bound in the cosmos because of impurity, action, the material substratum (*māyā*) and Śiva's will.
paśa ('bond')	The universe which comprises all mental and material phenomena. The universe, comprising many different worlds, is manifested from *māyā*, its material substratum.

The soteriological goal of the Śaiva Siddhānta, as of most other Indian religions, is liberation from the cycle of reincarnation, conceived as becoming equal to Śiva. Liberation is thought to occur for the initiated Śaiva Siddhāntin at death, which means that he becomes omniscient and omnipotent, like Śiva, but ontologically distinct from him. The soul could never become one with Śiva, but could become a Śiva. To achieve this end the practitioner (*sādhaka*) undergoes initiation by a consecrated teacher (*ācārya*) and undertakes a process of daily and occasional rituals which gradually remove impurity from the soul. There are two initiations which he must undertake, the lesser initiation into the shared scriptures and rituals of the cult (the *samaya-dīkṣā*) and the liberating initiation (*nirvāṇa-dīkṣā*) which ensures the soul's final release. For the Śaiva Siddhānta, the soul's freedom could only be attained by ritual after initiation, because the soul's bondage is ultimately caused by impurity (*mala*) which is a substance. A substance cannot be removed by thought or cognition, but only through action: thought cannot affect the world, but action can. The logic of this effort-oriented doctrine is, however, counterbalanced by a doctrine of grace, in that liberation is not a mechanical process, but is finally attained only due to the power of the Lord.

While this path of ritual is open to all classes, it is not open to women, who are categorized as ineligible for the common initiation, along with children, the old, the mad and the disabled. Women can participate in the worship of Śiva but only vicariously through their husbands who perform the Śaiva liturgies. However, a woman can rise up to Śiva's abode through the merit of her husband's practice.

The dualist Āgamas and Tantras contain details of the domestic and temple worship necessary for salvation. These texts are still used today in the south, and there are ritual manuals (*paddhati*) composed summarizing the procedures, such as that by Somaśambhu (twelfth century) describing a ritual structure, the basics of which are found in all tantric traditions.[34] Essentially Śiva is treated as an honoured guest, and after a process of purification is invited or brought down into the icon or *liṅga* before which the devotee worships and offers his services to the god. Śiva then leaves the *liṅga* concluding the daily ritual. One of the essential practices within this and all tantric ritual is the divinization of the worshipper, for according to the Tantras only a god can worship a god: 'having become Śiva one should worship Śiva'.[35] This practice of identification with the deity could be seen as the ritual expression of a monistic metaphysics, in which the soul and the absolute are ultimately one. This would certainly be true of many tantric systems, but not so with the Śaiva Siddhānta. Rather it means that the practitioner (*sādhaka*) becomes equal to Śiva while remaining ontologically distinct.

KĀPĀLIKA ŚAIVISM

The Śaiva Siddhānta forms the basic ritual and theological system of the Path of Mantras. The other main branch within this division comprises the non-Siddhānta systems. The classification of Tantras and groups within this category is highly complex. These Tantras, distinct from the twenty-eight Āgamas of Śaiva Siddhānta, are called the Bhairava Tantras. This category includes a number of sub-divisions, but they are all characterized by an emphasis on the worship of ferocious forms of Śiva, such as the god Bhairava, and the ferocious Goddess Kālī.[36] The practitioners who composed these texts and who practised asceticism in the cremation ground where they originated, were called Kāpālikas, the 'skull-men', so called because, like the Lākula ascetic of the higher path, they carried a skull-topped staff (*khaṭvāṅga*) and carried a cranium begging bowl; that is, they had undertaken the 'great vow' (*mahāvrata*), the penance for Brahmanicide.

The Kāpālika ascetic was quite the opposite of the respectable Smārta Brahman householder or even Śaiva Siddhāntin. Yet his doctrines and practices were developed on the basis of Śaiva Siddhānta ideology which he radically reinterpreted. The Kāpālika ascetic lived in the cremation grounds, imitating his fierce deities and appeasing these deities with offerings of blood, meat, alcohol and sexual fluids from ritual intercourse unconstrained by caste restrictions. These were highly polluting activities for an orthodox Brahman and even the sight of such an ascetic would pollute him. While meat and wine were common enough among the lower castes, they were impure for a Brahman. An orthodox Brahman would make only pure, vegetarian offerings to his gods and sexual activity would be constrained by the code of *varṇāśrama-dharma*, and excluded from the world of *pūjā*. In place of vegetarian food the Kāpālika offered meat, in place of milk the Kāpālika offered wine. The goal of the Kāpālika was power (*siddhi*) which he thought he could achieve through breaking social taboos, appeasing his deities with offerings which would be anathema to the vedic practitioner, and harnessing the power of his deities through controlled possession.

Within the Bhairava Tantras, there is further division into texts belonging to the 'Seat of Mantras' (*mantrapīṭha*) and those belonging to the 'Seat of Vidyās' (*vidyāpīṭha*). Within the Seat of Mantras were texts belonging to the cult of Śiva in the form of Svacchanda, such as the *Svacchandabhairava-Tantra*, very popular in the Kashmir valley, while the Seat of Vidyās contained texts belonging to extreme cults of the Goddess, the power (*śakti*) of Śiva, the most important of which are the Kaula or Kula, a name which comes to refer to a number of groups as well as a general orientation towards tantric worship of female deities. Kāpālika asceticism has all but died out in India, with the exception of the Aghorīs particularly in Varanasi, who preserve the Kāpālika ethos, eating from skulls, meditating in the cremation grounds, using bodily products to appease their god and, in theory if not practice, performing a corpse-eating ritual.[37]

THE KAULA TRADITION

The Kaula or Kula tradition developed within the context of the Kāpālika cremation-ground asceticism. The term *kula*, meaning 'family', refers to the families of goddesses (*yoginī*) who are the retinues of a number of tantric deities and their consorts. The Kaula divides itself into four transmissions named after the directions, though it is unclear precisely how this self-classification relates to the sociohistorical reality of these groups. The eastern transmission in this model worships Śiva and Śakti as Kuleśvara and Kuleśvarī, surrounded by their retinue of goddesses. The Trika of Kashmir Śaivism develops from this transmission. The northern transmission worships the terrible Goddess Guhyakālī and forms the basis of the Krama system which worships a series of ferocious deities in a sequence (*krama*). The western transmission focuses on the hunch-backed crone Kubjikā and the southern transmission worships the beautiful, erotic, Kāmeśvarī or Tripurasundarī. This forms the basis of the Śrī Vidyā tradition in the south (see pp. 187–9).[38]

Although the development of these tantric groups and their texts is complex, a clear picture emerges of mild cults on the one hand, particularly Śaiva Siddhānta, worshipping Śiva as Sadāśiva, and extreme, Goddess-oriented cults on the other, who worshipped ferocious deities (particularly the goddesses) who demand appeasement with blood, alcohol and erotic offerings. The Śaiva Siddhānta, as the normative system, established itself as a householder's religion, which it remains in the south to this day. The ideology and some of the practices of the extreme Kaula cults were adapted to be palatable to a wider audience. This development has come to be known as 'Kashmir' Śaivism.

KASHMIR ŚAIVISM

Kashmir Śaivism refers to the development of the eastern Kaula transmission known as the Trika ('Threefold') into a householder religion akin to the Śaiva Siddhānta. Unlike the Śaiva Siddhānta, however, the Trika was monistic, maintaining a theology of the identity of the Lord, the individual soul and the universe or bond. These are not separate ontologies but essentially a single reality whose nature is consciousness (*saṃvit*, *cit*). The cosmos is an emanation or vibration of consciousness and individual beings are but manifestations of the absolute 'Great Śiva' (Maheśvara or Parameśvara) whose nature is pure consciousness. The soteriological goal of the Trika initiate is to merge his individual consciousness back into a higher, universal consciousness, manifested at a cult level in the forms of Śiva and also the Goddess Kālī. While the Trika originated as a cremation-ground cult, the monistic ideology and practice came to influence and appeal to Brahman householders who appropriated Trika teachings, absorbing them more into the mainstream of Hindu traditions and articulating a theology distinct from the Śaiva dualists.

Alongside the tantric revelation, a sage called Vasugupta (*c.* 875–925) had a dream in which Śiva told him to go to the Mahādeva mountain in Kashmir. On this mountain he is said to have found verses inscribed upon a rock, the *Śiva Sūtras*, which outline the teaching of Śaiva monism: a text which forms one of the key sources of the tradition. Apart from this divine revelation, there were authors who gave theological articulation to monistic Śaiva texts of human authorship, particularly Somānanda (*c.* 900–50), who first gave theological articulation to monistic Śaivism in his 'Vision of Śiva' (*Śivadṛṣṭi*), and his disciple Utpaladeva (*c.* 925–75), who was the grand-teacher of the greatest Śaiva theologian Abhinavagupta (*c.* 975–1025). While the ritual system or basis of Kashmir Śaivism is the Trika, its theological articulation in the works of these authors is called the 'Recognition' school (Pratyabhijñā). The aim of life is to recognize one's identity with the absolute consciousness of Śiva who, however, becomes Kālī at the Trika's esoteric heart.

Trika practice (*sādhana*), described in Abhinavagupta's compendium the 'Light on the Tantra' (*Tantrāloka*), involved a daily, time-consuming ritual which followed the pattern of Śaiva Siddhānta, as well as forms of yogic practice called the 'methods' (*upāya*) which included the practice of Kuṇḍalinī yoga (see p. 99). The initiate would purify his body through its symbolic destruction, re-create it with the imposition of mantras (*nyāsa*), perform mental or inner worship which involved the visualization of the symbol of Śiva's trident pervading the body, and finally perform an external worship with an external symbolic diagram (*maṇḍala*). The visualized trident is significant for Trika theology in that each prong represents one of three goddesses, from which the name 'Trika' is derived, namely Parā ('the Supreme'), Parāparā ('the Supreme-Non-Supreme') and Aparā (the Non-Supreme). These in turn represent manifestations of pure consciousness expressed as the goddess Kālasaṃkarṣinī. At a deeper layer of Trika liturgy, for the spiritually elect, lies the 'secret ritual' (the *kulayāga*) which involves offering the Goddess meat and alcohol, and ritual sex between the practitioner and his female partner. This ritual act recapitulates the union (*yāmala*) of Śiva and his energy, Śākti, and the aesthetic pleasure (*rasa*) arising from this ritualized sexual congress recapitulates the joy (*ānanda*) and wonder (*camatkāra*) of pure consciousness.[39]

The Trika theologians, particularly Abhinavagupta and his disciple Kṣemarāja (*c.* 1000–50), successfully defeated the dualist interpretation of scripture in Kashmir. The dualist doctrine, however, while vanishing from Kashmir, took root in the south where it fused with Tamil devotionalism. Though probably never popular among lower strata of society, Trika ideology was very influential at a courtly level and many of its ideas and practices were absorbed into orthodox Smārta Brahmanism. With the subjugation of Kashmir by the Muslims in the eleventh century, Kashmir Śaivism all but died out, leaving only an echo of the tradition in modern times.[40] With the Śaiva Siddhānta the story is different, for with its move to the south away from direct Muslim rule, it established thriving temple cultures, sometimes with royal patronage, which still survive today.

THE SOUTHERN ŚAIVA SIDDHĀNTA

As Śaiva Siddhānta faded in Kashmir it developed in Tamilnadu. The theology of the tradition maintained the three categories of the Lord, the soul and the bond, and the liturgy maintained the pattern of the dualist Āgamas. However, the significant feature which profoundly affected the tradition in the south was that it merged with the Tamil Śaiva cult expressed in the Tamil *bhakti* poetry of the sixty-three Tamil Śaiva saints, the Nāyaṉārs, the Śaiva equivalent of the Āḻvārs. The Śaiva Siddhānta absorbed *bhakti* and became a Tamil religion, pervaded by Tamil cultural values and forms, as occurred to Vaiṣṇavism in the south. The cultural context of the Tamil love of poetry, love of the land, and love of life generally, expressed in the early Caṅkam literature of the classical Tamil age prior to the third century CE, transformed the Śaiva Siddhānta into a Tamil, devotional religion. The Śaiva Siddhānta remains strong in Tamilnadu today, and a group of 'original Śaiva' priests, the Ādiśaivas, from five Brahman families, are still qualified to perform worship in Śaiva Siddhānta temples.

As with Vaiṣṇava *bhakti*, Śaiva *bhakti* stresses the loss of the limited self and ephemeral worldly interests, in favour of an emotional, outpouring love for an eternal transcendent Lord. *Bhakti* tends to reject caste and gender restrictions as having any consequence for salvation; all that is needed is love and the grace of the Lord. The devotional traditions of Śaiva Siddhānta and the Liṅgayaṭs (see pp. 171–2) have expressed, though not exclusively, the needs of non-brahmanical social groups. Yet devotionalism within these traditions has in turn been absorbed into more formal structures which the founders of *bhakti* movements may have originally been against.

In the vision of *bhakti* presented in the Tamil sources, what is foremost is the direct relationship between the devotee and the Lord. There is almost a sense of anti-structure in these hymns and a reversal of received social norms: in Māṇikkavācakar's *Tiruvācakam* ('Sacred Verses'), for example, we read of devotees as being 'mad' (*piccu*, *uṉmatta*) with the love of God and straying from accepted social and personal behaviour. Yet, perhaps ironically, *bhakti* and the hymns of the Tamil saints became part of the Śaiva canon and an integral part of structured temple worship, which had the blessing of the Chola kings. Hindu orthodoxy, that is the Brahmans with royal support, did not generally actively repress movements which could be seen as antithetical to orthodox interests, but rather encompassed them within their ideological structures. Indeed, devotion to a temple deity might be seen as an analogue of the subject's devotion to the king, though, unlike a subject's devotion, there is always the possibility that *bhakti* could be wild, uncontrolled and ecstatic.

The texts revered by the southern Śaiva Siddhānta are the Vedas; the twenty-eight dualist Āgamas which form the ritual basis of the tradition; the twelve books of the Tamil Śaiva canon called the *Tirumurai*, which contains the poetry of the Nāyaṉārs; and the Śaiva Siddhānta Śāstras. The *Tirumurai* contains a vast body of material whose dates span a 600-year period from about the sixth to the twelfth centuries. Among the poets whose work appears in the Śaiva canon are Appar, Campantar and Cuntarar (sixth-eighth centuries CE) whose poetry forms the *Tévāram*, a collection compiled and classified on the basis of music in the tenth century by Nampi Antar Nampi. These three poets, along with the later ninth-century saint, Māṇikkavācakar, the author of the *Tiruvācakam*, are regarded as the founding fathers of the Śaiva Siddhānta in the south. These poets praise Śiva and the temples of south India where he lives, forming a network of pilgrimage sites and creating a sacred geography which also became a sacred political geography with the dynasty of the Chola kings (*c.* 870–1280).[41] Under the Cholas, Śaivism enjoyed patronage with the great temple at Cidambaram becoming an important political and religious centre.

During the period from 600 CE to the rise of the Cholas, the period during which the Nāyaṉārs were composing their hymns, the Pallavas who ruled northern Tamilnadu and the Pandeyas who ruled the south, developed a strong social structure akin to feudalism – an embedded hierarchy of patronage which would have involved a sophisticated bureaucracy.[42] There was constant political and military conflict between these kingdoms, as well as with the Chalukya kingdom to the north, as they jostled for territory and power. The *bhakti* movement, both Śaiva and Vaiṣṇava, which stressed the equality of devotees, can be seen in part as a reaction against a system which oppressed the lower social strata and imposed heavy tax burdens in order to finance military struggles. While the *bhakti* movement should not be exaggerated as an articulation of a 'class struggle', there is nevertheless a strong sense in which *bhakti* is opposed to rigid structures and rationalized systems: all devotees of Śiva are his slaves (*aṭiyār*) and each has a personal relationship with him outside any institutionalized religion.[43] Writings against caste can also be found amongst the 'adepts' (Tamil *cittar*, Sanskrit *siddha*), Tamil yogis whose ideas are expressed in Tirumular's *Tirumantiram*.

Another important factor which led to the development of *bhakti* was popular reaction against Buddhism and Jainism, both ascetic and renunciatory traditions, which were well established in the south until about 1200 CE. The Jains particularly bore the brunt of the devotees' invective, being accused of knowing no Tamil or Sanskrit (but only Prakrit), and of being filthy and generally anti-social. The doctrines of renunciation and the 'atheism' of these religions had little appeal to Tamil culture in the medieval period and so they died out, devotion becoming the predominant ideology, and *pūjā* to perceptible deities the practice.

Tamil Śaiva Siddhānta is therefore a fusion of a number of elements. There is brahmanical adherence to the Veda, though practically it is neglected in favour of the Āgamas; a strong cult of temple ritual, based on the Āgamas and focused on Śiva's forms located in temples throughout the sacred Tamil land; and an emotional *bhakti* cult based on the hymns of the

Nāyaṉārs. This emotional *bhakti*, while originating in the south with the poetry of the Nāyaṉārs and Āḻvārs, rapidly spread north and the Liṅgayat tradition in neighbouring Karnataka soon became infected by Tamil devotionalism.

TANTRISM IN KERALA

Tantrism also took root in Kerala, the extreme south-west of India, where it has become one of the predominant traditions of the Nambudri Brahmans. In Kerala, as indeed in Tamilnadu, we can see the importance of Tantrism in the general temple culture and the way in which tantric forms of worship are integral to daily ritual practices. Yet, whereas in Tamilnadu tantric traditions are clearly either Śaiva or Vaiṣṇava, in Kerala these distinctions are not maintained and Kerala Tantrism cannot be classified in this way, incorporating in its worship a number of brahmanical Śaiva and Vaiṣṇava deities, such as Śiva, Viṣṇu, Gaṇeśa, and low-caste regional deities, particularly goddesses. The Tantrism of Kerala appears to be far from the cremation-ground traditions of northern Tantrism and has become completely embedded within orthoprax *vaidika* traditions. In Kerala a Tantri is a Nambudri Brahman belonging to one of a group of families ranked in a status hierarchy. The main function of these Tantris is to install icons in temples, while the daily ritual observances are performed by *pūjāris* of different families. There is a, generally low-caste, tradition of ritual magic to cure sickness and ward off misfortune, the *mantravādam*, and a Tantri might well perform the functions of both temple priest and 'magician' (*mantravādin*).

The precise origins of Tantrism in Kerala are unclear, though the tradition may have come from Kashmir. The two key texts used in temple ritual are the *Tantrasamuccaya* by Cenasnambudri (fifteenth century CE) and the *Īśānaśivagurudeva-paddhati* which dates back to the twelfth century.[44] While these texts are used in the temple tantric cults of the respectable householder religion, they still reflect an archaic tantric worldview and reflect the roots of Tantrism in cremation-ground asceticism. Another important regional tradition, a fusion of *bhakti* with Tantrism, which developed in Andhra Pradesh, was that of the Liṅgayats.

THE LIṄGAYATS

The Liṅgayats, 'wearers of the *liṅga*', or Vīraśaivas, 'heroes for Śiva', were founded by Basava (twelfth century CE), though seem to have had some connections with the Kālāmukha order. Unlike the Kālāmukhas, however, they lay emphasis on devotion rather than asceticism and reject temple worship and icon worship, except for a *liṅga* worn around the neck, which is worshipped daily. The Liṅgayat devotee believes that upon death he will go straight to union with Śiva and that there will be no return to the world. The Liṅgayats therefore need no orthoprax funereal rites and bury their dead, as is done with holy men. There is still a large Liṅgayat community in Karnataka.

Basava (*c.* 1106–67) was a Śaiva Brahman at the court of King Bijjaḷa, the king of Kalyāṇa. He was a social and religious reformer, a devotee of Śiva as the 'Lord of the Meeting of Rivers', who expressed his devotion in poetry and founded a new community. Another notable poet among the Liṅgayat community was a younger contemporary of Basava, Mahādévyakka. She became a wandering, naked ascetic and is iconographically depicted clothed only in her hair. In her poetry she writes of her longing for Śiva and she scorns worldly love as impermanent and unsatisfactory:

> I love the Beautiful One
> with no bond nor fear
> no clan no land
> no landmarks
> for his beauty. . .
>
> Take these husbands who die,
> decay, and feed them
> to your kitchen fires![45]

Basava was vehemently against the caste system and ritualistic religion. He began a community at Kalyāṇa which emphasized egalitarianism, including caste-free marriage, and developed an ethos of what Victor Turner has called *communitas* or 'communion'.[46] Indeed, according to Basava's biographer, a wedding occurred between the son of an outcaste and the daughter of a Brahman. This flouting of social convention led to King Bijjala condemning the couples' fathers to death, an act which, rather than repressing the community, caused a riot against the king who was assassinated. This in turn led to repression of the Liṅgayat community, which nevertheless survived. Basava, who was opposed to the community's violence against the king, lived out his days away from the community he founded.[47]

Summary

As with Vaiṣṇavism, Śaivism is a complex and rich tradition, reaching a clear articulation in the post-Gupta period, though its roots stretch back a long way, perhaps as far as the Indus valley civilization. Śaivism has been generally less orthoprax than Vaiṣṇavism, less concerned with locating itself in the tradition stemming from the vedic revelation. It has provided its own revelation in the Śaiva Tantras, and incorporated the vedic revelation within it at a lower level. As with Vaiṣṇavism, there is a wide diversity of religious forms, ranging from the orthoprax Smārta or paurāṇika worship of Śiva, to ecstatic *bhakti*, and to highly esoteric and antinomian forms of worship in its tantric extreme. Within the tantric realm, among the Tantras where the Goddess predominates, it is difficult to distinguish between Śaiva and Śākta orientations. It is this more exclusive Śākta wing of the tantric material and the religion of the Goddess generally to which we now turn.

8 The Goddess and Śākta traditions

The traditions of Śiva and Viṣṇu have dominated Hindu literature and have been the major focus of devotional attention. Yet there is nevertheless a vital Hindu Goddess tradition and many goddesses are worshipped daily throughout south Asia. The innumerable goddesses of local traditions are generally regarded by Hindus as manifestations or aspects of a single Great Goddess or Mahā Devī, whose worship may go back to prehistoric times if sixth- or fifth-millennia terracotta figurines are taken to be Goddess images. Worship of the Hindu Goddess is also important beyond the bounds of Hinduism in contemporary western revivals of Goddess worship.[1]

The Goddess is a contradictory and ambivalent figure in Hinduism. On the one hand she is the source of life, the benevolent mother who is giving and overflowing, yet on the other she is a terrible malevolent force who demands offerings of blood, meat and alcohol to placate her wrath. Wendy O'Flaherty has referred to two distinct categories of Indian goddesses which reflect these two natures: on the one hand are 'goddesses of tooth' who are erotic, ferocious and dangerous, on the other are 'goddesses of breast' who are auspicious, bountiful and fertile.[2] The goddesses of breast are generally role models of Hindu women who embody maternal qualities of generosity and graciousness, subservient to their divine husbands, while the goddesses of tooth are independent, low-ranking and dominate their consorts if they have any. The high-ranking goddesses of breast are sexually controlled within a brahmanical framework, the low-ranking goddesses of tooth are free, as Wendy O'Flaherty observes, to attack men.[3] There are some exceptions to this distinction and some goddesses, such as Tripurasundarī, are both beautiful and independent. Devī, the Great Goddess, embraces both of these images and her cults express this ambivalence.

Devotees of the Goddess are generally called Śāktas: the followers of Śakti, a name for the Goddess denoting the female 'power' or 'energy' of the universe. The Śākta tradition is, however, less clearly defined than Śaivism or Vaiṣṇavism. Indeed it would be greatly misleading to assume that only Śāktas worship the Goddess. Almost all Hindus will revere her in some capacity, particularly at village level where her demands are very immediate as are her boons. Both Vaiṣṇavism and Śaivism have incorporated the Goddess within them as the consorts or energies (*śakti*) of their male deities. Yet, as we have seen, at its tantric heart Śaivism is pervaded by feminized images of divinity and practice. With Śākta texts this feminized religion becomes overt in both puranic and tantric manifestations. The Goddess, on the edges of the brahmanical world, is incorporated into orthoprax, puranic worship and her tantric worship becomes brahmanized in the later medieval tradition of the Śrī Vidyā. Hindu orthopraxy contains the Goddess within a brahmanical structure. However, on the edges of brahmanical authority amongst the lower castes, the tribals, and in the tantric middle ground between the high and low castes, she maintains a wild independence as a symbol of the reversal of brahmanical values.

In this chapter I will first describe images of the Goddess in myth and iconography which developed during the first millennium CE, and which are still important in contemporary Hinduism. We will then go on to trace developments in the history of Goddess worship among the orthoprax Brahmans, among the tantric traditions, and at village level.

The myth of Devī

There are a number of narrative traditions about the Goddess and minor goddesses in the Purāṇas and Tantras. The most important manifestation of Devī is Durgā, the warrior goddess who slays the buffalo demon Mahiṣa. This myth is central to the cult of Devī and provides the inspiration for her main iconographic representation which shows her as Mahiṣamardinī, the slayer of the buffalo demon. The myth is told in a number of variants in the Purāṇas, especially the *Devībhāgavata Purāṇa* and the *Devīmāhātmya*, a part of the *Mārkaṇḍeya Purāṇa*. The latter text, the earliest work glorifying the Goddess, dates from the fifth to seventh centuries CE. This version in the *Devīmāhātmya* is the simplest and the following account is based on that earlier version.

The buffalo demon, Mahiṣāsura or simply Mahiṣa ('buffalo'), had obtained a boon from Brahmā that he could not be killed by any male. With the confidence of his invincibility, he firstly conquers the world and then, wishing to conquer heaven as well, sends an ultimatum to Indra, the king of the gods. Indra scorns Mahiṣa and a terrible battle ensues in which Indra is defeated and flees to Brahmā for shelter, then to Śiva and finally to Viṣṇu. From the bodies and angered faces of the gods, great energy masses emerge which form into the shape of a beautiful woman, who is, of course, Devī. The gods manifest replicas of their weapons and give them to her, requesting her to defeat the demon Mahiṣa. Her lion mount she receives from the mountain god Himavat and her cup of wine from Kubera, the god of wealth in the north. She gives out a terrible laugh and the gods shout 'victory'. Upon hearing the laughter and the shouting of the gods, Mahiṣa is angered and sends his troops to find out what is going on. They return, telling him of the beauty of the Goddess who is unmarried and who possesses all the qualities of love, heroism, laughter, terror and wonder. Through his envoys, Mahiṣa proposes marriage to Devī who refuses him, and he and his councillors are confused by her amorous demeanour yet her warlike talk. The envoys attack the Goddess when they are rebuked by her and are slain. Mahiṣa himself in a handsome human form goes to Devī and again proposes marriage, but she tells him that she has been born to protect the righteous and that he must flee to hell or fight. He attacks the Goddess, assuming the forms of different animals, but Devī drinks wine, pursues Mahiṣa on her lion, and defeats him, kicking him with her foot, piercing his chest with her trident and decapitating him with her discus as he emerges in human form from the buffalo's body. The remaining demons flee to hell and Devī is praised by the gods whom she promises to help whenever necessary.[4]

A number of themes and attitudes are expressed in this myth. The myth directly confronts brahmanical models of womanhood expressed in the Dharma Śāstras where the nature of woman (*strīsvabhāva*) is passive, unwarlike and where a woman's role is defined in terms of male authority on which a woman should always be dependent as daughter, wife, or mother. Mahiṣa cannot be killed by any male, and a woman, so he thinks, could not possibly be strong enough to defeat him. Mahiṣa's initial reaction is to want to marry the beautiful Devī and thereby contain and control her, and he is confused by her attractiveness which contrasts with her warlike speech, for the Goddess embodies the traditional aesthetic qualities (*rasa*) found in Sanskrit poetics of both heroism (*vīrya*) and eroticism (*śṛṅgāra*). When Mahisa does attack, she drinks wine before going into battle, an act indicative of her origins as a Goddess to whom offerings of alcohol and blood were made. She is far more powerful than the gods, for only she can defeat the all-conquering demon.

Images of the Goddess

The name Devī is interchangeable with Durgā, though Devī incorporates a wider conception of deity. A common term for the Goddess is simply 'Mother'. Throughout South Asia the Goddess is referred to as 'Mother': Mata, Mataji or Ma in the Hindi-speaking north, Amma in the Dravidian languages of the south. Like Śiva, the Goddess embodies paradox and ambiguity: she is erotic yet detached: gentle yet heroic; beautiful yet terrible. These aspects are expressed in a variety of different goddesses at local and pan-Indian levels. Indeed, there is a tendency for local goddesses to become identified with the Great Goddess through the process of Sanskritization, and sometimes for local goddesses to become universalized, as with the local goddess Santoṣī Ma who became a pan-Hindu deity due to a film telling her story. For her devotees, the Goddess is the ultimate reality, knowledge of whom liberates from the cycle of birth and death, yet she is also the ensnaring veil of the 'great illusion' (*mahāmāya*) binding all beings. As the power which both enslaves and liberates, she is Śakti, the energy or power of Śiva. The Goddess generates all forms and so is identified with Viṣṇu's second wife, the Earth (Bhū), and with nature or matter (*prakṛti*). Yet she also destroys the cosmos and the human communities who inhabit it with terrible violence. She can be approached and worshipped in many forms, in natural phenomena, or in human forms as a mother, a wife, an old woman, or a young girl. Her main representations are:

- as Durgā, slayer of the buffalo-demon (Mahiṣāsura), seated on or attended by a lion or tiger (when she is called Ambikā). Durgā, the 'difficult to access', has ten arms and weapons, kicks and pierces Mahiṣa with her trident and beheads him, while yet maintaining a calm and detached demeanour.
- as Kālī and other terrible manifestations, such as Cāmuṇḍā. They are emaciated, blood-drinking and violent forms who haunt the

cremation grounds. Kālī is 'black' or 'blue', garlanded with severed heads, girdled with severed arms, with rolling, intoxicated eyes and a lolling tongue. She dances on the corpse of her husband Śiva.

- as consorts or energies (*śakti*) of the gods, particularly Sarasvatī, Pārvatī and Lakṣmī, the consorts of Brahmā, Śiva and Viṣṇu, who are beautiful models of wifely and maternal devotion (though not devoid of righteous anger). In this category we can also include Rādhā, the consort of Kṛṣṇa, and Sītā, the wife of Rāma.
- as groups of generally ferocious female deities, notably the 'seven mothers' (Saptamātṛkās) whose natures are ambiguous, preying on children yet also destroying demons. In esoteric tantric literature they are associated with letters of the Sanskrit alphabet and the Goddess Mātṛkā is the deity of the complete alphabet.
- as local or regional icons in village or family shrines and temples. Local goddesses are often goddesses of smallpox and other pustular diseases, such as Śītala in the north and Māriyamman̲ in the south.
- as 'aniconic' forms such as stones, poles, weapons, magical diagrams (*yantra*) and stylized female genitals (*yoni*).
- as natural phenomena, particularly rivers (such as the rivers Gaṅgā, the sacred Ganges and the Kaveri), lakes, trees and groves.
- as male and female 'mediums' possessed by a goddess, particularly during festivals.

Early worship of the Goddess

Worship of goddesses may be extremely ancient in south Asia. Female figurines of baked clay have been found in the north-west at Mergarh and Sheri Khan Tarakai, dated to the sixth or fifth millennium, and terracotta figurines have been found at Mohenjo-Daro (*c.* 2500–2000 BCE), the major city of the Indus valley civilization. We do not know the purpose of these figures. It is possible that they served a ritual function, perhaps as offerings or talismans, or simply as gifts. Unfortunately the archaeological record is incomplete, though figurines from the north-west region have been dated to the third and fourth centuries BCE which may represent a continuity of tradition from ancient times, after the collapse of the Indus valley cities.

In early vedic religion, goddesses (*devī*) are insignificant in that they play no role in the sacrifice at this early date, though several are mentioned in the *Ṛg Veda*, the earliest textual record we have. Most notable amongst them are Pṛthivī (the Earth), Aditi (the 'unbound'), Uṣas (the dawn), Nirṛti (destruction) and Vāc (speech). Pṛthivī is Mother Earth whose consort is Dyaus, Father Sky. Aditi is a goddess of some significance as the mother of the Ādityas, a group of seven or eight deities including Dakṣa, Śiva's later father-in-law.[5] She provides safety and wealth and is associated with the cow whose milk nourishes humanity. In the Brāhmaṇas she is identified with the Earth, Pṛthivī.[6] Uṣas is a young girl who brings light to the world each morning by going before the Sun (Sūrya). She is bestower of prosperity and long life, yet conversely, because she announces the passing of the days, she also wears away people's lives. Nirṛti is a goddess of destruction; an early representation of destructive female power found in later Hinduism in local and pan-Hindu goddesses such as Kālī. The hymns of the *Ṛg Veda* implore her to go away and ask the gods for protection from her.[7] In the Brāhmaṇas she is described as dark and living in the south, the direction of death.[8] In contrast Vāc (speech) is a creative power who inspires the sages, reveals the meaning of language and is identified with truth. Speech plays an important part in later Hindu philosophy and in yogic and tantric traditions as the power behind words, particularly mantras. Other goddesses are mentioned in early vedic literature, such as the river Sarasvatī, Night, the Forest, and Diti, the mother of the demons, but their role is subordinated to that of the gods.

As the early texts are all the evidence we have regarding vedic religion, we can conclude from this evidence the following points:

- goddesses have a subordinate position in early vedic religion, male deities being predominant.
- there is no evidence of a 'Great Goddess' in the Vedas, an idea for which there is textual evidence only from the medieval period.
- some of the goddesses in the Veda, notably Pṛthivī and Sarasvatī, survived into later Hindu times. Sarasvatī becomes the Goddess of learning and music and wife of Brahmā; Pṛthivī or Bhū (the Earth) becomes the second wife of Viṣṇu.
- the evidence of goddess worship from the archaeological record and from references in the Veda, suggests that worship of goddesses has non-vedic, and probably non-Aryan, origins.

The formation of Goddess worship

Between the composition of the Vedas and the Purāṇas there is little literary evidence of Goddess worship, though there are Jain and Buddhist

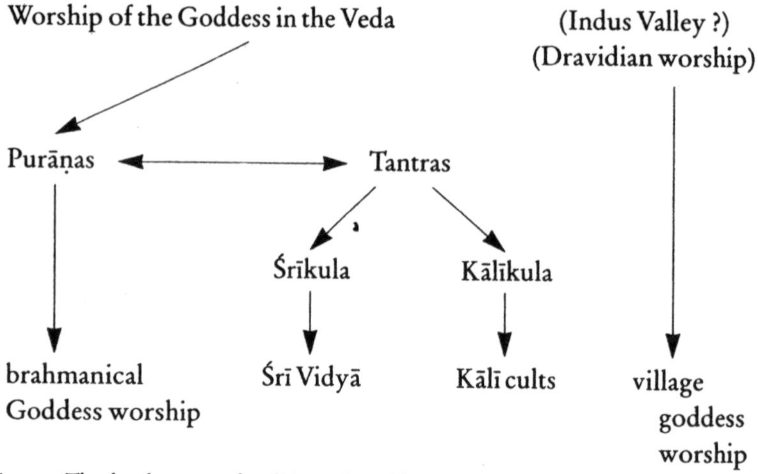

Figure 7 The development of traditions of Goddess worship

sculptures depicting divine female beings, such as on the first-century BCE Buddhist monument (*stūpa*) at Sanchi. A general picture is suggested of low-caste, local goddesses becoming absorbed into, and resisted by, brahmanical tradition. Some of these goddesses were of Dravidian, rather than Aryan, origin. The *Mahābhārata*, composed by Brahmans, presents various images of female destructive power in the form of the seven or eight Mātṛkās, the 'Mothers' and a number of other demonesses. The Mātṛkās are described as dark, living on the periphery of society, and bringing misfortune, particularly upon children who must be protected from their unwanted attentions. The ferocious Kālī is mentioned in the Epic as being generated from the anger of Śiva's consort, the Goddess Umā or Pārvatī, and Durgā is praised in two laudations by Arjuna in order to defeat his enemies.[9] In south India there is evidence of early worship of goddesses. The Virgin Goddess Kanya Kumārī, whose temple is situated at the tip of India, existed in the early centuries of the common era, and the Tamil Caṅkam literature mentions Koṟṟavai, goddess of victory, to whom buffalos were sacrificed and for whom forest warriors, the Maṟvars, were exhorted to ritual suicide.[10] However, it is not until the Purāṇas that we find a more developed Śākta theology and mythology, and the idea of a single, all-embracing 'Great Goddess' (Mahādevī) who encompasses all other deities.

A picture emerges therefore of the gradual incorporation of the Goddess into the brahmanical sphere. This process of assimilation might be seen as the 'upwards' movement of local goddesses; the transformation of probably aniconic entities (that is, deities represented by stones, weapons, poles and natural phenomena) into iconic representations which are eventually assimilated into the brahmanical pantheon as the wives of the gods. The solitary Goddess is herself incorporated into Smārta worship as one of the five deities of the *pañcāyatana pūjā* and universalized in puranic mythology.

THE GODDESS IN THE PURĀṆAS

The earliest work glorifying the Goddess in India is the *Devīmāhātmya* ('The Glory of the Goddess'), part of the *Mārkaṇḍeya Purāṇa*, an early Purāṇa which is dated to between the fifth and seventh centuries CE. This text is extremely popular and is still recited in Durgā temples and throughout India during the Durgā Pūjā, the great autumn festival to the Goddess. The text presents a picture of the ultimate reality as the Goddess, who is also Mahāmāyā, the great illusion. The text demonstrates her salvific power by recounting three myths of how she defeated a number of demons, namely Madhu, and Kaiṭabha, Mahiṣāsura, and Śumbha and Niśumbha. In Vaiṣṇava mythology, Madhu and Kaiṭabha were two demons who attacked Brahmā whilst Viṣṇu slept. Brahmā managed to wake Viṣṇu and he destroyed the demons. This story is retold in the *Devīmāhātmya*, but here the Goddess is made superior to Viṣṇu by being identified with his yogic sleep (*yoganidrā*). Viṣṇu's sleep becomes a manifestation of the Goddess who thereby has him under her spell and is made superior to him. Brahmā implores her to release Viṣṇu from sleep and she does. He then defeats the demons as in the Vaiṣṇava versions of the myth. The account of the defeat of Mahiṣāsura follows and the third myth relates how Kālī sprang from Durgā's forehead, personifying her anger, and defeated the demons Śumbha and Niśumbha.

The later *Devībhāgavata Purāṇa* continues the vision of the *Devimāhātmya* in placing the Goddess as the absolute source of the cosmos. This text is related to the *Bhāgavata Purāṇa*, though, whereas in that text Kṛṣṇa is presented as the highest manifestation of the divine, here it is Devī, who, as it were, retrieves female power (*śakti*) from male authority and makes it her own. The Goddess is not subject to the authority of the gods and, indeed, is superior to them, controlling Viṣṇu through her power of sleep and not wishing to be married to any of them. The Goddess is her own 'master'.[11]

PAN-HINDU GODDESSES

Puranic, Smārta ideology dominated the early medieval period and became pan-Indian. With the Purāṇas the Goddess was assimilated by brahmanical religion and a theology of the Goddess was articulated in puranic narrative traditions. These traditions spread, and archaeological evidence attests to the worship of the Goddess throughout the subcontinent. At Mammalapuram (also known as Mahabalipuram) on the southeast Tamilnadu coast, a seventh-century temple depicts Durgā slaying the buffalo demon and she is also depicted in the cave sculptures at Ellora (sixth–eighth century). The cult of Durgā was therefore very widespread by the early medieval period and the standard myth and icon of her slaying the buffalo demon was well established.

Not only worship of Durgā, but also of Kālī, the personified anger of Durgā, became widespread with the development of puranic Hinduism. Although always on the edges of the controlled, respectable brahmanical world, Kālī nevertheless enjoyed, and still enjoys, great popularity. She is treated with ambivalence by brahmanical orthopraxy, as she dwells on the social periphery, haunting polluting cremation grounds and appealing to untouchable castes and tribals. She has nevertheless attracted brahmanical attention and devotion, particularly in Bengal. Both Ramprasad Sen, a nineteenth-century Bengali poet who wrote devotional verses to her as the 'Mother', and the famous saint Rāmakrishna had visions of her. Kālī demands blood sacrifice and goats are sacrificed to her daily at the famous Kālīghāt temple in Calcutta.

Another popular ferocious Goddess is Cāmuṇḍā who in the *Mārkaṇḍeya Purāṇa* sprang from the furrowed brow of Durgā. In one myth in the *Devīmāhātmya*, the little Mothers (Mātṛkās) manifest from the Goddess, upon which the demon Raktabīja ('Bloody-Seed') appears to challenge them. They attack him, but each drop of blood which falls to the ground gives birth to a replica demon, whose fallen blood in turn gives rise to further demons. The day is saved by Cāmuṇḍā who drinks up the blood of the demon before it touches the ground and so he is eventually defeated.

Other goddesses which have independent cults are less violent than Durgā, Kālī and Cāmuṇḍā. Sarasvatī, the ancient Goddess of the Sarasvatī river in the Veda, is benign. She is identified with the goddess of speech (Vāc) and is, like the muse, the inspirer of poetry, music and learning.

Although she is married to Brahmā, he does not play an important role in her worship and she is iconographically depicted independently of him, seated upon a lotus and playing a musical instrument, the *vīnā*. Many classrooms in Indian schools bear her image upon the wall. Śrī or Lakṣmī, the spouse of Viṣṇu also has an independent cult which had developed by the time of the Purāṇas. She is the goddess of financial reward and good fortune, associated with royal power and iconographically depicted seated upon a lotus and being sprinkled with water by elephants – an act reminiscent of royal consecration. Along with Durgā she is strongly associated with royal power, as can be seen by the Vijayanagara king's ritual identification with the Goddess. Apart from the pan-Hindu goddesses such as these, there are innumerable village or local goddesses, such as the northern and eastern snake goddess Manasā, some without iconographic representation.

Sacrifice and the Goddess

One of the most striking things about the independent Goddess is that she accepts, and demands, blood sacrifice. Sacrifice is part of her cult and central to her mythology in which the slaying of the buffalo demon can be read as the sacrifice of the buffalo. The Goddess drinks wine from a cup as she slays the buffalo demon, which reflects in mythology the idea of her drinking the blood of the sacrificed victim in ritual. Indeed drinking the blood of the victim has been a feature of Goddess worship, particularly in its medieval tantric manifestation. The drinking of blood is an important symbolic element in the mythology of the Goddess; present with the high Hindu deity Durgā, with tantric manifestations of the Goddess, and at local level among the village goddesses. While in the 'purified' brahmanical forms of Hinduism the idea of sacrifice is extracted out of ritual and confined to symbolism or the realms of mythology, in the popular religion of the villages, bloody sacrifice is an integral element in the worship of local goddesses. For example, the Nambudri Brahmans of Kerala would not practise bloody sacrifice as this would be too polluting, yet they make offerings of blood substitute to local or family Goddesses such as Rakteśvarī, the 'Goddess of Blood' (see pp. 210–11).

Non-violence (*ahimsā*) is an important element in Hinduism, particularly among Brahmans and renouncers, yet this ideal contrasts starkly with the eruptive and bloody violence of the goddess. Because the Goddess is all-giving and fecund, she must also be renewed with blood, the power of life, if her bounty is to continue. This renewing blood can be related to the Goddess' menstrual cycles, but is particularly the blood of sacrificial victims which can be seen as substituting for the devotee him or herself. Indeed, if non-violence is an essential element in the Brahman's world in order to maintain ritual purity, then violence might be seen as an essential element in the world of the Kṣatriya. The connection between the Goddess and royal power can be related to sacrifice in so far as one of the ideals of kingship was to wage war upon neighbouring kingdoms. The battlefield thereby can be read as a sacrifice, the killing of the enemies, the killing of sacrificial victims. Indeed the human sacrifice, the sacrifice of the 'great beast' (*mahāpaśu*), is regarded in the Veda as the highest sacrifice, even though human sacrifices may never have actually taken place. There is, then, a correspondence between the king who accepts the 'sacrifice' of both the enemy and his own army, and the Goddess who accepts the sacrifice of animals.

This idea of sacrifice becomes filtered through the layers of Hindu culture in a number of ways. At the level of village goddesses, generally associated with lower castes, the actual sacrifice of animals is commonplace. Amongst Brahman communities the sacrifice of animals and offering of blood will not actually be practised, but will remain present as a symbolic element, while at the level of pan-Hindu mythology, the sacrificial victim becomes a demon. At this level, the ritual practice of sacrifice becomes ethicized: the destruction of the victim becoming the destruction of evil, the destruction of the buffalo becoming the destruction of the buffalo demon, the appeasing of a wrathful deity becoming the stabilizing or rebalancing of the cosmos. The idea of sacrifice to the Goddess is also given esoteric interpretation, as is the idea of vedic sacrifice in the Upaniṣads, by some Tantras in which the sacrifice becomes the sacrifice of the limited, particularized self into the all-pervading Kālī self: the Goddess as absolute, uncontaminated consciousness.

Tantric worship of the Goddess

While the Goddess tradition developing from the Purāṇas was of great importance, an allied tradition of Goddess worship developed from the Tantras. The tantric worship of the Goddess, or Śākta Tantrism, is found in a number of early Tantras of the southern Kaula transmission (see p. 166), composed before the eleventh century. These texts, traditionally counted as sixty-four, can be divided into those whose focus is the benevolent and gentle Goddess, the Tantras of the Śrīkula, the 'family of the Auspicious Goddess', and those whose focus is the ferocious Goddess, the Tantras of the Kālīkula, the 'family of the Black Goddess'. The tradition which developed from the Śrīkula texts came to be known as the Śrī Vidyā, which worshipped the benevolent and beautiful Lalitā Tripurasundarī. The Śrī Vidyā aligned itself with orthoprax brahmanical values, even though some adherents worshipped the Goddess using 'impure substances'. The tradition in the south became aligned with orthodox Vedānta and with the Śaṅkarācārya of Śṛṅgeri and Kanchipuram. The Kālī traditions, in contrast, were less concerned with orthopraxy, and more concerned with the power gained through impurity and going against social and religious norms.

A common feature of tantric ideology is that women represent or manifest the Goddess in a ritual context. As the male worshipper becomes the male deity, especially Śiva, for only a god can worship a god, so his female partner becomes the Goddess. Indeed the Goddess is manifested in all women in varying degrees. A prominent part of tantric practice is the ritual worship of woman or young girl by both male and female devotees. An important ceremony, practised mainly in Bengal and Nepal, is the worship of a young woman (the *kumārī-pūjā*) in which a virgin girl of about twelve is placed upon a 'throne'. The Goddess is installed or brought down into her, as would occur with an icon, and she is worshipped. The ritual deification of the young girl is an important annual festival in Nepal. Yet, while the Goddess is worshipped as a youthful girl, she can also be worshipped in a terrible form as the blood-drinking Kālī or the old and crooked Kubjikā.

THE CULTS OF KĀLĪ

Cults of Kālī or her manifestations are in evidence from among the earliest tantric texts we have, possibly dating to as early as the seventh or eighth centuries. The worship of Kālī is found at the heart of Kashmir Śaivism, traditions whose origins can be found in the cremation-ground cults. While the Śrī Vidyā, according to its self-classification, develops from the southern transmission in the Kaula system, the cults of Kālī are within the northern and eastern transmissions. The *Jayadrathayāmala*, a text of the northern transmission, describes forms of Kālī, which the devotee would visualize, as transcending the male form of Śiva, Bhairava, on whose corpse she stands. Here Kālī is the absolute, identified with light at the heart of pure consciousness from which the universe manifests and to which it returns. The devotee should meditate upon this process of the projection and withdrawal of consciousness, identified with twelve Kālīs, and realize the final, liberating implosion of consciousness into itself, symbolized by the 'thirteenth' Kālī, Kālasaṃkarṣinī.[12] These esoteric traditions, identifying Kālī with states of consciousness, later became concretely expressed in external ritual from the tenth century, focused on the goddess Guhyakālī, visualized as having animal and human heads with eight arms bearing weapons. She is worshipped at an exoteric, popular level in Nepal as Guhyeśvarī and associated with the Goddess Kubjikā (see below).

The texts of the Kālīkula describe macabre rites in the cremation grounds to evoke a goddess and allow the practitioner to achieve salvation through confronting gruesome (*ghora*) experience. In a famous rite, the 'offering to the jackals', jackals are revered as manifestations of Kālī and offerings are made to them at an inauspicious, though powerful, location such as a crossroads, a wood or a cremation ground.[13]

. Another tantric goddess who is the focus of a group of Tantras of the western Kaula transmission is Kubjikā, the 'Crooked One'. This school originated in the western Himalayas, possibly in Kashmir, is known to have existed in Nepal by the twelfth century, and, according to its texts, spread throughout India. The principle text of the school is the 'Tantra of the Teachings of the Crooked Goddess', the *Kubjikāmata Tantra*, which explains the mythology, doctrines and ritual associated with her. Although the text and tradition takes its name from the Goddess worshipped in the form of an old, crooked woman, she is identified with the Supreme Goddess (Parā Devī) and also worshipped in the forms of a girl and a young woman. The school had an esoteric dimension and shows its close links to Kashmir Śaivism by identifying the Goddess with pure consciousness.[14] The Goddess is also associated with the 'coiled' goddess Kuṇḍalinī, the power lying dormant at the base of the body until awakened by yoga to pierce the centres of subtle anatomy and unite with Śiva at the crown of the head. The Kubjikā school is significant because it is in the *Kubjikāmata Tantra* that we first have mention of the classical six centres (*cakra*) of esoteric anatomy which have become pan-Hindu and have been popularized in the West.[15] Earlier Tantras mention varying numbers at various locations. These six centres also became adopted by the Śrī Vidyā tradition.

THE ŚRĪ VIDYĀ TRADITION

The Śrī Vidyā is the cult of Lalitā Tripurasundarī or simply Tripurasundarī ('Beautiful Goddess of the Three Cities'), a tantric form of Śrī/Lakṣmī, who is worshipped in the form of a sacred diagram or *yantra* of nine intersecting triangles, called the *śrīcakra*, and in the form of a fifteen-syllable mantra called the *śrīvidyā*, whence the tradition takes its name. The Tripurasundarī cult can be classified, in its earliest phase, as the latest level of the Mantramārga, the 'Path of Mantra' (see p. 162). The earliest sources of the Śrī Vidyā within this category are two texts, the *Nityāṣodaśikārṇava* ('The Ocean of the Tradition of the Sixteen Nityā Goddesses') which classifies itself in the Mantramārga, and the *Yoginīhṛdaya* ('The Heart of the Yoginī') which are said to form together the *Vāmakeśvara Tantra.*[16] The *Nityāṣodaśikārṇava* is concerned with external rituals and their magical effects, while the *Yoginīhṛdaya* is more esoteric, interpreting the *śrīcakra* as the expansion and contraction of the cosmos. A later text, the *Tantrarāja Tantra* (the 'King of Tantras'), gives a more detailed exposition of these subjects.[17] Apart from these early Tantras, a number of later texts praise the Goddess Tripurasundarī, particularly the extremely popular *Saundaryalaharī* ('The Ocean of Beauty'), the *Lalitāsaharanāma* ('The Thousand Names of Lalita'), and the *Tripura Upaniṣad* ('The Secret of Tripura').[18] The *Saundaryalaharī* and *Lalitāsaharanāma* are traditionally said to have been composed by the Advaita Vedānta philosopher Śaṅkara. Indeed, as Bharati has observed, no indigenous Śrī Vidyā scholar would doubt his authorship of these texts. While in principle it is not impossible that Śaṅkara would compose devotional hymns to the Goddess – this would not be incompatible with the composition of philosophical works in the Indian context[19] – these texts owe more to the non-dualism of Kashmir Śaivism than to Śaṅkara's Vedānta. This can be seen by the Trika ideology which pervades these texts and their terminologies derived from Kashmir Śaivism, such as the idea of the cosmos as the manifestation of sound. Indeed the Kashmiri Trika goddess, Parā, is regarded in some literature of this school to be the inner essence of Tripurasundarī.[20]

However, the Śrī Vidyā which developed in south India became distanced from its Kashmiri tantric roots and the cult of Tripurasundarī was adopted by the southern Vedānta monastic order of the Daśanāmis at Śṛṅgeri and Kanchipuram, traditionally founded by Śaṅkara. The Śrī

Vidyā tradition became popular in the south and the cult of Tripurasundarī penetrated the Śaiva Smārta community as well as the highly orthodox monastic tradition of the Śaṅkarācāryas.

In the theology of the Śrī Vidyā the Goddess is supreme, transcending the cosmos which is yet a manifestation of her. Although visualized and praised in personal terms, the Goddess is also an impersonal force or power. She unfolds the cosmos and contracts it once again in endless cycles of emanation and re-absorption. This process is conceptualized as the manifestation and contraction of the Word, the absolute as primal sound (*śabda*, *nāda*), or the syllable *oṃ*, identified with energy, light and consciousness. Everyday speech is but a gross manifestation of this subtle, all-pervading sound which manifests the cosmos through a series of graded stages from the most subtle, non-material realms, to the gross material world which humans inhabit. This subtle sound is expressed as a 'point' or 'drop' (*bindu*) of energy, prior to extension, which then proceeds to generate the manifold cosmos. The *bindu*, an extremely important term in tantric theology, is associated with the fifteenth phoneme of the Sanskrit alphabet, the nasalized 'dot' (*anusvara*), which symbolizes concentrated, potential energy, ready to burst forth as manifestation. The details of cosmological schemes vary in different texts, but the principles are identical in Śrī Vīdyā texts to those in Kashmir Śaiva Tantras.[21]

This cosmology is symbolized by the cosmogram of the *śrīcakra*, the central icon of the tradition, used as a focus of worship and installed in temples. This diagram or ritual instrument (*yantra*) is both the deity and a representation of the cosmos. The four upward-pointing triangles symbolize the male principle in the universe, namely Śiva, the five downward-pointing triangles represent the female principle, namely Śakti. All these triangles emanate out from the central point or *bindu*. Their interpenetration represents the union of Śiva and the Goddess, which the aspirant or *sādhaka* realizes within his own body through the ritual identification of the *śrīcakra* with his own body.

Integral to the more esoteric practices of the Śrī Vidyā tradition, and closely related to cosmological speculation, is the idea that the material human body is a gross manifestation of a subtle body, which in turn is a manifestation of a supreme or causal body. As the material world is the most solidified coagulation of the subtle worlds, so the body is the most coagulated form of the subtle body, which in turn is a manifestation of a higher form. Salvation or liberation is release from the cycle of birth and death, conceived as a journey which retraces the stages of manifestation back to its source, which is the Goddess. This yogic journey through the cosmos is also conceived as a journey through the body, and the levels of cosmological manifestation are identified with levels along the vertical axis of the body. The Śrī Vidyā yogin will attempt to awaken the dormant power of the Goddess Kuṇḍalinī, who rises up from the 'root centre', at the base of the central channel which pervades the body, to unite with Śiva at the crown of the head, piercing various centres or wheels of energy as she rises (see pp. 98–9). The model used here by the Śrī Vidyā is the standard Haṭha yogic one which went beyond the boundaries of any particular tradition.

Ideas about the universe as a hierarchy of levels and the homology or esoteric correspondences between the body and the cosmos are central to the practice and theology of the Śrī Vidyā, as they are to all other tantric traditions. This is illustrated by the *Tantrarāja Tantra* which describes three aspects or forms (*rūpa*) of Tripurasundarī, the supreme, subtle and gross, which correspond to three ways of worshipping her, with the mind, with speech and with the body. These refer to meditation upon her, or visualization of her form, repeating mantras, and performing external worship by offering flowers, incense and vegetarian offerings. Initiation is, of course, a prerequisite for access to Śrī Vidyā daily and occasional rituals, qualification for which must be determined by a guru, though it is not based on caste as is vedic initiation.

LEFT-HAND TANTRA

Perhaps the most famous controversy which surrounds Tantrism generally, and which is of concern to the Śrī Vidyā in particular, is the ritual use of 'substances' prohibited within Brahmanism. These ritual substances came to be known as the 'five Ms' (*pañcamakāra*) – the initial Sanskrit letter of each being the letter 'M' – or 'five realities' (*pañcatattva*). These are the ritual use of wine (*madya*), fish (*matsya*), meat (*māṃsa*), parched grain (*mudrā*) and sexual union (*maithuna*). The consumption of alcohol, meat and fish is expressly forbidden to Brahmans according to the Laws of Manu,[22] so to ritually use these substances is, for a Brahman, to consciously pollute himself. We have seen that in the Kaula rites of early Śaivism, ferocious female deities were appeased with offerings of blood, alcohol and sexual substances (p. 165). Abhinavagupta speaks about the 'three Ms' of alcohol, meat and copulation, referring to their use as true 'holiness' or 'celibacy' (*brahmacārya*).[23] The five Ms later developed and their use became known as 'left-handed practice' (*vāmācāra*), that is, transgressive practices using impurity, as opposed to the 'right-handed practice' (*dakṣinācāra*), based on purity. The use of parched grain (*mudrā*) is sometimes said to be an aphrodisiac, yet may simply represent the kind of offerings to deities made amongst lower-caste groups.

There is a distinction within the Śrī Vidyā between those who reject the use of the 'five Ms' and those who incorporate them, yet, generally, the Śrī Vidyā tends to distance itself from extreme antinomian tantric groups. Left-handed Tantrism throws up challenging ethical questions for orthoprax Hinduism. The left-hand or Kaula division flouts brahmanical purity laws and conventions in order to gain magical power (*siddhi*), while the right-hand, the 'Conventional' or Samaya division, rejects the literal use of the 'five Ms', or uses symbolic substitutes (*pratinidhi*) instead, such as milk for wine, sesamum for meat or fish, and offerings of flowers for sex. The use of the 'five Ms' in the Śrī Vidyā has been controversial. Lakṣmīdhara (sixteenth century) was a theologian of the 'conventional way' (*samayācāra*) who vehemently rejected the non-vedic and impure practice of the 'five Ms'. Others, however, such as Bhāskararāya (1728–50), were happy to advocate the secret use of prohibited substances.[24] Indeed, it is quite usual for the tantric Brahman householder to maintain brahmanical social values alongside a tantric soteriology which involves the use of otherwise prohibited substances. There is an oft-quoted saying that the tantric Brahman should be secretly a Kaula (i.e. a left-hand tantric practitioner), externally a Śaiva, while remaining vedic in his social practice.[25]

Sex in a ritual setting and the transformation of desire for a spiritual purpose is an ancient practice in Indian religion, stretching back at least to the time of the Buddha,[26] and mystical union with the absolute has been compared, in the *Bṛhadāraṇyaka Upaniṣad* to the joy of sexual union.[27] Sexual union (*maithuna*) becomes important in Tantrism as both symbol and event. The earlier tantric literature seems to emphasize sexual rites as offerings to the deity, whereas later texts indicate that semen should be held back in order to facilitate a yogic transformation to a higher state of awareness. Śākta Tantras even classify people according to three natures or dispositions (*bhāva*) – of being an animal (*paśu*), a hero (*vīra*) or divine (*divya*) – though the classification is not found in Śaiva texts. Only heroes and 'the divine' should perform erotic worship, for those of animal nature are driven by desire which would lead to their destruction.[28] Indeed, whether sexual congress is performed, as in left-handed ritual, or is substituted, as in right-handed ritual, erotic worship taps into a rich and powerful symbolism. The actual or represented union of the tantric practitioners symbolizes the union of Śiva and Śakti, of the male and female polarity in the cosmos, and their joy reflects the joy (*ānanda*) of that ultimate condition. There are also strings of symbolic associations in the Tantras between Śiva, white semen, the moon, passivity and consciousness, on the one hand, and Śakti, red blood, the sun, activity and nature (*prakṛti*), on the other.

Because women are filled with *śakti* in tantric ideology, they are considered to be more powerful than men, yet this power is generally not reflected in social realities where women have remained subordinate.[29] Tantric texts were written by men – usually Brahmans – primarily, though not exclusively, for men. They reflect the concerns of the male practitioner rather than his female partner, regarded as his 'messenger' or door to the divine realm, though some texts make it clear that the ensuing liberation is for both partners. Yet women have a higher ideological status in Tantrism than in strictly orthoprax Brahmanism, even though this might not be reflected in social institutions. The women in these rites were generally from lower-caste groups such as washers, and while these women's social realities were much more restricted than those of their male consorts, the tantric model of the strong, intelligent and beautiful woman contrasts with the brahmanical model of passivity and docile dependence.[30] There were also female tantric renouncers who were greatly revered and who dwelled at sites sacred to the Goddess (*pīṭha*), where tantric yogis would hope to meet them and obtain magical powers through their acquaintance.[31]

Apart from the transgressive Kaula wing of the Śrī Vidyā, other tantric groups which adopted the five Ms arose during the later medieval period. Of particular note is the Vaiṣṇava tradition of the Sahajiyas, which developed from the tantric Buddhist Sahajiyas, adopting a Vaiṣṇava theology.[32] For them, man and woman are physical representations of Kṛṣṇa and Rādhā, and, through erotic ritual, higher states of consciousness, or *samādhi*, can be achieved. The Bauls of Bengal have inherited the Sahajiya ideology and erotic ritual continues to be used by them.[33]

Many of the elements of brahmanical tantric worship are derived from low-caste propitiation of ferocious deities with alcohol and blood offerings, and from the cremation-ground asceticism of the Kāpālikas. Yet these become transformed in the context of the Brahman householder, such as the Śrī Vidyā devotee, into a soteriology in which the tantric Brahman maintains his social status while following the tantric path. While maintaining social status, the tantric Brahman can pursue his soteriological quest for power and liberation, through transcending his social inhibition in a controlled ritual context. It is one thing to perform erotic worship with a low-caste woman in a ritual setting, but quite another to interact with her outside that context. The theological split within the Śrī Vidyā, between the Samayācāra/right-hand path and the Kaula/left-hand path, highlights a tension between the dominant ideology of Brahmanism and an ideology infiltrated by ideas and practices from cremation-ground asceticism and from lower castes, yet which, for the Śrī Vidyā, is controlled by or contained within brahmanical structures and ideology.

THE ŚĀKTA PĪṬHAS

There are various important locations of Goddess worship in both north and south India, such as the temple to the Virgin Goddess, Kanya Kumārī, at Cape Comorin, the Mīnākṣī temple at Madurai, and the Kālī temple in Calcutta. The Goddess is not only located at specific sites but is identified with the Earth and the landscape, so in one sense the whole of 'India' is the Goddess, to the 'four corners' of which a pilgrim can journey and receive great blessing. Yet tantric literature refers specifically to 'seats' (*pīṭha*) of the Goddess which are distinct from these other pilgrimage centres. The locations of these 'seats' are given justification in the myth of Śiva's first wife Satī.

I have already recounted the myth of Dakṣa's sacrifice: how Śiva's father-in-law Dakṣa had not invited him to the sacrifice, how his daughter Satī was so upset that she burned herself to death in the fire of her own yoga, and how Śiva destroyed the sacrifice in the ferocious form of Vīrabhadra (see pp. 149–50). Later versions of the myth, in the *Devībhāgavata Purāṇa* and the *Kālika Purāṇa*, continue the story. Śiva is so upset at the death of his wife that he picks up her corpse in the cremation ground and dances with it on his shoulders in a distraught state. The other gods become worried, fearing the destruction of the universe due to this dance of death, so Viṣṇu hacks at the body of Satī, cutting it away piece by piece, until Śiva returns to a more composed state.[34]

While this is a myth behind the immolation of widows upon their husbands' funeral pyres (*satī*, 'suttee'), it is also an explanation of the *pīṭhas*, which are located where the different parts of Satī's body fell. In the Tantras and Purāṇas there are four principal sites listed, though other texts list more, and the *Kubjikāmata Tantra* says that all women's homes should be worshipped as *pīṭhas*.[35] The standard four 'Great Seats' (*mahāpīṭha*) are at Jalandhāra (possibly Jullundur in the Punjab), Oddiyana or Uddayana (the Swat valley in the far north-west), Purnagiri (of unknown location) and Kāmarupa in Assam. At these places the Goddess' tongue, nipples and vulva (*yoni*) are said to have fallen. The most important of these 'seats' as a living place of pilgrimage is Kāmarupa or Kāmagiri in Assam where Satī's *yoni* fell. Here the Goddess is worshipped in the form of a vulva and her menstrual cycles celebrated by adorning the icon with red powder. This form of the *yoni* is not common, but its history as an icon is well attested.

Regional and local traditions

While esoteric forms of Tantrism are of central importance in the history of Hinduism and have had impact on all its manifestations, they are not directly relevant to the majority of Hindus. The majority of Hindus in India live in villages and most devotees of the Goddess at regional and local levels express their devotion through external worship (*pūjā*) of local goddesses and in pilgrimage to places particularly sacred to the Goddess. While the brahmanical ideology of the Great Goddess spread throughout south Asia, there have been innumerable local goddesses, many without iconic representations, worshipped by local villagers usually belonging to lower castes.

VILLAGE GODDESSES

A distinction can be drawn between 'hot' and 'cool' deities. Hot deities are associated with passion, hot diseases such as smallpox which need to be cooled, pollution and lower social layers. Cool deities are associated with detachment, the cooling of passion, purity and higher social levels. The village goddesses, as well as ferocious goddesses such as Kālī, are classified as hot deities in contrast to the cool, mostly male, deities of the Hindu pantheon, such as Viṣṇu and Śiva. Village deities, the *grāmadevatās*, usually fall within the hot classification. They are almost always female, called 'mothers' (*mata*), associated with a particular village or locality and represented by a simple signifier such as a rock, a pile of stones, a stick, a couple of bricks, a thorn bush with pieces of cloth tied to it as offerings, or in the form of a pot.[36] These aniconic hot goddesses not only accept vegetarian offerings but also demand blood sacrifice (*bali*), of chickens, goats and sometimes buffalos, and need to be appeased with offerings of alcohol. In contrast the cool pan-Hindu deities, present in iconic representations, accept only vegetarian offerings. The Great Goddess shares both categories. She can be hot and ferocious, demanding blood and alcohol, yet also cool and benevolent, accepting only vegetarian offerings, as with Tripurasundarī and Lakṣmī.

A particular goddess might of course have two forms, an iconic cool form within a shrine or temple, and an aniconic hot form outside the shrine, perhaps manifested only during certain festivals. For example, the Tamil goddess Māriyammaṉ might have an immovable icon within her temple, yet accept blood offerings only in a second form such as a pot of water, away from the central shrine. The goddess is thus split into high and low forms, as Fuller describes.[37] These offerings reflect caste ranking to a degree, with lower-caste 'priests', perhaps possessed by the goddess, making offerings of meat to the lower form. While it is true that some deities are affiliated to particular castes – for example Lakṣmī, the goddess of wealth, is revered by trading castes – it would be an oversimplification to regard the ranking of deities as simply a reflection of caste society. While certain village goddesses might not be worshipped by Brahmans or, even within the same caste, the goddess of a particular family (*kula mātā*) would not be worshipped by a different family, other deities have appeal across the social spectrum.

Although sometimes barely distinguishable, the ferocious village goddesses have a name and specific location. They tend to be associated with disease, particularly pustular diseases such as smallpox, and accidental death, and need to be appeased, usually with blood and meat. Although they are unpredictable, they are also protectors of a village or locality. These goddesses have no formal links with the pan-Hindu goddesses, though often villagers might identify the local goddess with the pan-Hindu Great Goddess, even though there may be no iconographic or mythological resemblance. Sometimes the village goddess will have a myth about how she came to be in that particular location.

For example, in Kerala the particularly terrible goddess Mūvāḷamkuḻicāmuṇḍī is worshipped in a number of local shrines, the *teyyam* shrines, and along with other deities is celebrated in local, annual, dance-possession festivals. During these festivals the dancer becomes the goddess and relates her myth. A Brahman, who was performing sorcery upon one of these devotees, attempted to capture the goddess with mantras and confine her in a copper vessel with a lid which he then buried in a hole (*kuḷi*) to the depth of three men (*mūvālam*). She burst out of the ground in a terrible form and pursued the Brahman to a temple of Śiva where she agreed to settle down only if she could be installed there beside Śiva, which duly happened. The goddess is therefore worshipped as the consort of Śiva in the Trikanyalapan temple as well as in the *teyyam* shrines. This myth indicates that, although a hot low-caste deity (her *teyyam* dance is performed by the low Malāyan caste of professional sorcerers), she is yet contained within the power of the high-caste pan-Hindu deity Śiva. Her power is contained and kept in place by the male deity, and absorbed into a brahmanical structure.

Among goddesses who have a regional rather than purely village appeal, yet who are not identified with pan-Hindu deities with large temples, are the smallpox goddesses Śītalā, in the north, and Māriyammaṉ, in the south. Although now eradicated, smallpox has been particularly virulent in some parts of India during the hot season and has been regarded as a visitation or 'possession' by the smallpox goddess. Māriyammaṉ has a couple of myths relating her origin. In one she was a Brahman girl who was deceived into marriage by an Untouchable disguised as a Brahman. Upon realizing what had happened she killed herself and was transformed into the goddess Māriyammaṉ who then burned the Untouchable to ashes. The second myth tells of a pure but powerful wife of a holy man, who could perform miracles, but who one day saw two divine beings making love. She felt jealousy and as a consequence lost her powers, whereupon her husband suspected her fidelity and ordered their son to kill her. The son obediently cut off her head. Eventually she is restored to life as Māriyammaṉ, but instead of upon her own body, her head was placed upon an Untouchable's body, which expresses her ambivalent and angry nature as both Brahman and Untouchable.

Śītalā is a hot goddess who is dormant most of the year but who traditionally erupts with terrific violence during the hot season, spreading her 'grace' in the form of epidemics through villages and needing to be placated. Sometimes these diseases are seen to be the work of demons whom the goddess must defeat, at other times they are the work of the goddess herself. Smallpox victims were seen to be possessed by the goddess and were 'cooled' with water and milk, which are in effect offerings to appease her wrath, though the most effective offering to soften her anger is blood sacrifice.

These hot village goddesses and, indeed, the Great Goddess herself, are intimately associated with the cyclic pattern of the year, particularly the cycle of agricultural activity. The Goddess is associated with the earth, and the changing seasons might be regarded as changing modes of the Goddess. In northern and central India the seasons can be divided into three: the hot season (approximately from March to June), the wet season (approximately June to October) and the dry or winter season (the rest of the year particularly December to January). The ritual cycles of the villages are closely associated with the seasonal changes and worship of the Goddess, identified with the earth, is important during these times. In terms of ritual cycles, the hot season is important for village and regional goddesses, whose festivals occur at that time (the hot goddess worshipped during the hot season), as do many marriages, which allow expression to the 'heat' of passion.[38] Apart from local festivals during the hot season, the most important festival for the Goddess as a pan-Hindu deity is the Durgā-pūjā in October, culminating in the day of *dassera*, the tenth day following the commencement of the 'nine night' (*navarātri*) festival.

It is possible to view the village goddesses in terms of distinctions between popular/brahmanic culture, low caste/high caste, regional/pan-Hindu, little tradition/great tradition, and even Dravidian/Aryan. While these distinctions might be useful in understanding the structural oppositions between village goddesses and pan-Hindu deities, the situation is more complex and many regional goddesses participate in both 'low' and 'high' cultural spheres. The goddess Draupadī, for example, as Alf Hiltebeitel's important study has shown, participates in both realms as pan-Hindu goddess – the wife of the Pāṇḍavas in the epic *Mahābhārata* – and as local or regional deity in Tamilnadu.[39]

Summary

Hinduism cannot be understood without the Goddess, for the Goddess pervades it at all levels, from aniconic village deities to high-caste pan-Hindu goddesses, such as Durgā, or the wives of the male gods, such as Lakṣmī. This chapter has presented central ideas, mythology and iconographic representations of the Goddess in brahmanical Hinduism, in tantric Hinduism and in village Hinduism. We have seen that, while there are innumerable goddesses, each one being unique to a particular place, there are essentially two kinds of Goddess representations: a ferocious form such as Kālī, and a gentle benevolent form such as Tripurasundarī or Lakṣmī. While some goddesses are independent – these tend to be the ferocious forms – others are perfect wives to their divine husbands whom they energize. Indeed, without the Goddess a god such as Śiva is a corpse.

9 Hindu ritual

There are many styles of worship within Hindu traditions and vegetarian and non-vegetarian offerings are made to innumerable deities throughout south Asia. Hindu ritual occurs in the home, in the temple, at wayside shrines, at places of pilgrimage such as the confluence of sacred rivers, and in specially constructed pavilions. Rituals occur to mark special occasions, to ask for blessings or to propitiate gods. Ritual patterns constrain life from birth, through childhood, to marriage and finally death. While ritual behaviour can be extremely diverse, it is nevertheless ritual, encoded in manuals and in behaviour patterns passed through the generations from teacher to student and from parent to child, which gives shape and a degree of unity to Hindu traditions. Alongside ritual, and sometimes intimately connected with it, myths, the narrative traditions of India, also serve to give coherence. While narrative traditions provide people with meaning and understanding of who they are and how they came to be as they are, it is ritual action which anchors people in a sense of deeper identity and belonging. While Hindus have questioned the meanings of ritual and interpreted rituals in a variety of ways, ritual has seldom been abandoned within Hindu traditions. Ritual patterns recur over vast geographical areas in south Asia and have been repeated and handed down from ancient times; many ritual elements, and indeed actual rituals, can be traced to very early Hindu texts.

Ritual and Hindu identity

This ritual continuity may at first suggest a stability of Hindu social relations, yet it cannot be reduced to this or explained in these terms. The social and political contexts in which Hindu rituals have existed have been diverse, from Hindu kingdoms to colonial rule; they have been transported overseas to other countries, such as south-east Asia, and even, in the last hundred years or so, to the other continents of Europe, Africa and America. Of the kinds of ritual described in this chapter, all have been performed within Hinduism for significant periods of time, some probably since the second millennium BCE, others having more recent origin in the medieval period. Of course, rituals change, die out, and new rituals arise, but they change at a far slower rate than the societies in which they are performed: for example, rituals associated with kingship still continue in India. Rituals have a persistence which survives great political upheavals, ecological catastrophes and colonial repression.

The question of the degree to which ritual is affected by history or reflects social and political structures is a difficult one. On the one hand, it is clear that some ritual forms originated during specific historical periods and reflect cultural and political elements present during those times. Yet on the other hand, some ritual structures, most notably those of the vedic solemn (*śrauta*) rituals, seem comparatively unaffected by social, political and economic changes. Because ritual has persisted in the face of great political and economic shifts in south Asia, it cannot be contingent upon economic structures: the realm of ritual and the realm of politics and economics must be distinct. This is not to say that they never coincide, they do, but rather that ritual and the politico-economic are distinct levels or realms within Hindu culture. The ritual realm, and therefore the religious, cannot be reduced to the political. Indeed, ritual might be seen as a comparatively stable and invariant event in contradistinction to a changing, and often unstable, political and economic history. In some sense ritual defies history.

Ritual also cuts across theological distinctions. If it is possible to define Hinduism, it is certainly not possible to do so in terms of doctrine and theological beliefs. Ritual is prior to theology, both historically and conceptually, and various theologies in India have been built upon a ritual basis and make sense only in the context of ritual traditions. The Mīmāṃsā, for example, is based upon the interpretation of vedic rites. In the rich variety of Hindu ritual, we find cultural forms which do not demand belief in any particular doctrine, but rather demand action. It is the persistence of ritual in Hinduism, the patterning of action in certain ways, and its understanding by those who perform it, which provides, and expresses, a sense of identity for Hindu communities: an identity which goes beyond social and political changes and provides Hindus with a sense of belonging in the face of sometimes rapid social change.

While ritual behaviour would seem to provide a sense of continuity and belonging, an argument has recently been put forward by Frits Staal that any meanings attributed to ritual are random. Ritual has often been compared to language as a system of communication. However, with specific and detailed reference to vedic solemn rites, Staal has argued that, while ritual is like language in that it has a structure, a syntax, it is unlike language in that it has no meaning, no semantics. Vedic ritual has a structure which has been transferred through the generations from ancient times, but any meanings attributed to it, by the Brāhmaṇa literature for example, are secondary. Because the interpretations of ritual have changed over time, while its structure has remained constant, these meanings must be arbitrary or at least secondary to the most dominant feature of ritual, its structure and invariant transmission.[1]

Staal's argument is important and needs to be carefully considered, not only for the understanding of vedic ritual, but for ritual studies generally. The issue cannot be considered here, but, while it might be the case that the *śrauta* rites have no meaning in a formal sense, it is far less clear that domestic rituals, the *gṛhya* rites, involving birth, marriage and death, are meaningless activities. Indeed, in such rituals human life experiences are of vital significance and arguably such rites of transition express deep-felt human anxieties and attempt to resolve conflicts. In Hinduism rites of passage form an important part of ritual activity and constrain a person's passage through time from birth to death. A Hindu's sense of identity and belonging is given expression particularly through rites of passage, but not only thus – also in pilgrimage. Pilgrimage, particularly in modern times, has become a central feature of Hinduism, which serves to give coherence to its diversity. I shall here give an account of important ritual processes in Hinduism which give it coherence, namely rites of passage, personal and temple worship (*pūjā*), festivals, sacrifice and pilgrimage.

Rites of passage

There are traditionally two sources for Hindu rites of passage: on the one hand the texts of tradition (*smṛti*), specifically the Gṛhya Sūtras and the Dharma Sūtras and Śāstras; on the other, the regional oral traditions whose legitimacy was recognized in the Dharma Sāstras. In the Gṛhya and Dharma literature, rites of passage are classified as 'occasional ritual' (*naimittika-karma*), rites 'occasioned by a special occurrence',[2] in contrast to daily rites (*nitya-karma*) and rites for a desired purpose or object (*kāmya-karma*). Rites of passage are also classified as 'bodily rites' because of their central concern with the body – the imposition of cultural meanings upon the biological body and its transitions from conception to death. Rites of passage are expressive of, and transform, a person's identity, an identity which is personally or psychologically important and which is recognized by the wider community: they are the formal imposition of an identity and its recognition by a social group.

As we have seen, there is a fundamental distinction in Hinduism between worldly life and soteriology, the former being the concern of the householder, the latter being the concern of the renouncer. Rites of passage are within the realm of the householder's life and are not concerned with liberation. The ritual of renunciation and initiation into various sects, rituals which are concerned with liberation, are not included in the classification of rites of passage. While *Manu* does say that the performance of *dharma* which encompasses rites of passage leads to happiness in the next life,[3] this is distinct from liberation which cannot be attained by rites concerned with social transformation.

Rites of passage mould and help construct social identities. Indeed, the Sanskrit term for such rites is *saṃskāra*, 'constructed' or 'put together', implying the putting together of a person as a social actor and even, to some extent, defining ontological status. By undergoing the various *saṃskāras* a Hindu gains access to resources within the tradition which were previously closed to him or her and enters a new realm or state. The anthropologist Victor Turner has made a distinction between 'state' and 'process'.[4] 'State' refers to a relatively fixed social condition, while 'process' refers to an unfixed, liminal, period of transition between states. Rites of passage are therefore transformative processes linking different states. While 'state' is associated with 'structure' and hierarchy, 'process' is associated with 'anti-structure', 'liminality' and equality. Yet it is important to remember that the temporary anti-structure of process serves to reinforce the structure of state. The *saṃskāras* are rites of passage which serve to legitimize social order and to uphold social institutions. They are important not only for who they include, but also, as Pierre Bourdieu has pointed out, for who they exclude and for the ordering of social groups;

for separating those who have undergone the ritual from those who have not and from those who will never undergo it.[5]

The Dharma Śāstras deal only with male rites of passage, but throughout India women have undergone rites of passage based on oral folk traditions.[6] For high-caste or 'twice-born' Hindu males – those belonging to the top three classes of Brahmans, Kṣatriyas and Vaiśyas – the theoretical model of the *āśrama* system, the Hindu stages of life, maintains that there are four stages or states through which a man may pass: the student (*brahmacārya*), the householder (*gṛhastha*), the hermit or forest-dweller (*vānaprastha*) and the renouncer (*saṃnyāsa*) stages. As we have seen, the first two are concerned with worldly life, the third with a life retired from household duties and the fourth with the transcendence of the social world. Most Hindus remain householders and the *saṃskāras* are concerned wholly with life as a social being, that is, with the first two stages or states.

While there are a varying number of *saṃskāras* recorded in different texts, the important point is that they form a ritual sequence or complete system which expresses the Hindu social order, or *dharma*. The undergoing of any of them implies an acceptance of orthoprax brahmanical values and underlines differences in gender roles and castes. The high-caste boy who undergoes vedic initiation is separated from his younger contemporaries, from lower castes and from women, who are not eligible to undergo the rite. Rites of passage are also rites of exclusion and underline the difference between the high-caste boy and others within the community.

The number of *saṃskāras* varies. Forty are recorded in the *Gautama Dharma Śāstra*, though the standard number in the Gṛhya Sūtras is between twelve and eighteen. The *Manu Smṛti* mentions thirteen, though sixteen tends to be the standard number.[7] They can be divided into prenatal rites, birth, childhood and educational rites, then marriage and death rites. The standard sixteen are:

1. garbhadhāna, the rite of the conception of the embryo or the 'infusion of semen' performed at the time of conception.
2. puṃsavana, the rite of 'bringing forth a boy' to ensure the birth of a male child.
3. simantonnayana, the 'parting the hair' rite of the woman during pregnancy.
4. jātkarman, the birth rite.

5 nāmakaraṇa, the naming ceremony on the tenth or twelfth day after birth.

6 niskramana, the child's first outing.

7 annaprasana, the child's first feeding with solid food.

8 chudakaraṇa, the tonsure ceremony during the first or third year.

9 karṇavedha, the ear-piercing ceremony around the age of three to five.

10 vidyārambha, the 'beginning of knowledge' when the child learns the alphabet between the ages of five and seven.

11 upanayana, the rite of initiation and investiture of the sacred thread, occurring from the age of eight up to about twenty-four.

12 vedārambha, the ritual of beginning the study of the Veda.

13 keśānta, the first shaving of the beard.

14 samavartana, the ritual ending of student life.

15 vivaha, marriage.

16 antyeṣṭi, the funeral ritual.

The most important of these are birth, the initiation ceremony (*upanayana*), marriage (*vivaha*) which marks the beginning of the householder's life, and the funeral rites (*antyeṣṭi*) which end it, though in contemporary Hinduism the initiation rite and marriage are often conflated for reasons of convenience and economy.

THE BIRTH RITES

Birth, especially of a boy, is a joyous and auspicious occasion for Hindus, but it is also hedged about with uncertainty and impurity, for all biological processes are considered to be polluting and so necessitate ritual control. During a woman's first pregnancy, after the hair-parting rite, she will go to the home of her parents for the birth and remain there for some time before being re-incorporated back into her marriage home with a new and higher status of mother, particularly higher if the child is male. The birth of a boy, especially the first child, is considered to be more auspicious than that of a girl, though the birth of a girl is not necessarily regarded as inauspicious. With the birth of a son a man has repaid his debt to the ancestors and has enabled his forefathers to attain the world of heaven. Among the Aiyars, the Tamil-speaking Smārta Brahmans, it is said that the birth of a son enables a generation of ancestors to pass over from the intermediate realm into the world of heaven (*svargaloka*).[8]

HIGH-CASTE INITIATION

Between the ages of eight and twenty-four, a high-caste boy will undergo the vedic initiation or *upanayana* ceremony at which he will be given the sacred thread, the symbol of high-caste males. While the ritual texts have strict age limits on initiation – the *Aśvalāyana Gṛhya Sūtra* states that a Brahman boy should be between eight and sixteen, a Kṣatriya between eleven and twenty-two and a Vaiśya between twelve and twenty-four[9] – contemporary Hindu life is less strict and it is common practice to hold the *upanayana* on the day before the young man's wedding. Through the *upanayana* the high-caste boy gains entry to high-caste society, which excludes him from other spheres of social activity. He is separated off from the world of women and the sphere of the mother, and from lower impure castes, thereby legitimizing social structure and gender roles.

The actual ceremony takes about a day, though there are regional variations with regard to the content of the rite. A common pattern might be for the boy's head to be shaved except for the tuft on the crown, for him to be bathed and dressed in a loin-cloth, girdle and antelope-skin over his shoulder. Oblations are offered into the sacred fire, the boy vows celibacy and is invested with the sacred thread, comprising three times three single strands, the symbol of twice-born status, worn over the left shoulder and annually renewed until either death or renunciation. The boy is taught the famous 'root mantra', the *gāyatri*, which he should recite daily thereafter, is given a secret name and is taught how to make oblations into the fire. The ceremony ends with the 'departure for Kasi', the symbolic gesture of leaving to go to the sacred city of Varanasi in order to study the Veda. The boy is persuaded by his maternal uncle, with some mirth, not to go. A feast follows this and gifts are given to the boy. According to the classical model, after initiation the boy would enter the student stage of life and study the Veda with a teacher.

While vedic initiation is for high-caste males, this does not mean, of course, that women are excluded from membership of high-caste communities. Although, according to *Manu*, marriage is a woman's *upanayana*, serving her husband is equivalent to vedic study, and housework equivalent to the fire oblations,[10] there are nevertheless women's rites of passage. Such women's rites are not based upon Sanskrit treatises, but upon oral folk (*laukika*) traditions, and it is important, as Julia Leslie has pointed out, not to see women in south Asia as 'the passive victims of an oppressive ideology but also (perhaps primarily) as the active agents of their own positive constructs'.[11] While this is an important point, the power of the ideological, brahmanical framework or model should not be underestimated.

In her study of Aiyar women, the Smārta Brahmans of Tamilnadu, Duvvury has shown that they can be seen both as active agents and as constrained within brahmanical orthopraxy. She shows that Aiyar women have their own rites of passage, including a rite during a girl's first menstruation akin to the *upanayana* ceremony. This rite involves the girl's being separated and isolated in a darkened room for three days (though not excluded from the company of friends). On the fourth day a ritual bath is taken and a feast held. The girl is brought to the temple by her mother and to visit other households where older women perform ceremonies of offering lights (*arati*) to her. Alternative rites for women have probably always been a part of south Asian religions, but have not been recorded in Sanskrit treatises, being regarded as folk traditions. While these rites give expression to women's aspirations and express a sense of belonging to a community, they must be understood within the context of the broader framework of brahmanical orthopraxy. Duvvury claims that such rites, while expressing women's hopes, must also be seen within a cultural context which defines women 'largely in terms of their functions as mothers and wives'.[12] In the broader brahmanical framework the folk traditions (*laukika*) are subordinated to the dharmic tradition (*śāstra*), vernacular languages subordinated to Sanskrit, human conventions subordinated to universal law (*dharma*) and women subordinated to men.

MARRIAGE

Marriage (*vivaha*) is and has been the expected norm of Hindu societies unless a person becomes a world-renouncer. With the marriage *saṃskāra* a young high-caste man enters fully into the householder's life in which he can pursue the goals of duty (*dharma*), gaining wealth and worldly success (*artha*), and experiencing pleasure, particularly sexual pleasure (*kāma*). For a woman, marriage marks the end of her childhood life with her family and friends and the beginning of a new life with her husband, probably in his village, with a new set of social relationships to negotiate. Marriages are, of course, arranged. In Dravidian south India cross-cousin marriage tends to be practised, in which case the young couple may already know each other, whereas in the north the couple will be strangers. Marriage can therefore be emotionally stressful and a young woman is culturally expected to show signs of sorrow at leaving her old home and way of life. Yet most young women will desire marriage as a necessary transition to complete womanhood and integration into the world of mature women.

Caste compatibility is the most important factor in a Hindu marriage, though other factors of wealth, occupation and astrological compatibility are taken into account. Within caste (*jāti*), marriage is generally endogamous, yet exogamous with regard to kin group (*gotra*), as is specified in *Manu*.[13] Yet the social realities of marriage in south Asia are more complex than *Manu*'s prescriptions, with regional differences with regard to marriage and kinship patterns. For example, a notable exception to caste endogamy has been among the Nambudri Brahmans of Kerala, where the eldest son would marry a Nambudri woman, but the remaining sons would maintain alliances with low-caste Nayar women. Children from these alliances would belong to the Nayar caste and live in their mother's house or the house of their mother and her brother. The Nambudri father would visit the house, bringing his own food and utensils in order to avoid becoming polluted, even from his own family.[14]

For a Hindu, marriage is probably the most important *saṃskāra*. The marriage of daughters involves a family in great expense as it is an occasion for giving gifts to the bridegroom's family and for arranging an elaborate wedding celebration. Indeed, marriage is, according to Dumont, the main cause of debt in rural communities,[15] as this is an opportunity to demonstrate a family's wealth and status. While there are regional variations in marriage ceremonies, a common pattern is for the bride's father to give her to the groom and his father. Oblations are then offered into the fire. The bride's wrist is tied with a thread and she steps three times upon the groom's family grinding-stone, a gesture symbolic of her intended fidelity. The couple then take seven steps around the sacred fire, the essential part of a Hindu wedding, and the groom offers oblations into the fire, a rite which he has learned during his *upanayana*. If the celebrations occur during the evening, the couple might go outside to see the pole-star and the bride will vow to be constant like that star. After the celebrations, which may go on for a couple of days, the bride will return with the groom to his family home where they will begin treading the path of the householder.

FUNERAL RITES

Death, as in most cultures, is inauspicious in Hinduism and fraught with the danger of pollution for the bereaved and the danger of being haunted by a malevolent ghost. The last *saṃskāra*, called the 'last sacrifice' (*antyeṣṭi*) – for indeed, as Parry shows, cremation is akin to sacrifice[16] – controls the pollution of death and re-integrates the family back into normal social life from which they have been separated by death, and allows the spirit of the deceased to travel on its way. These two concerns are pan-Hindu, though funerary practices vary to some extent in different regions. While cremation is the usual way of disposing of bodies, inhumation is practised among low castes and holy men and children are generally buried. A holy man might be buried in a tomb called a *samādhi* or *samādh*, indicative of the belief that, although he has left his body, he has become absorbed into a higher state of consciousness. A renouncer, having undergone his own funeral during his rite of renunciation, and so transcending his social identity, might simply be placed in a river.

A person is cremated on the day of death if possible. The corpse is bathed, anointed with sandalwood paste, shaved if male, wrapped in a cloth and carried to the cremation ground by male relatives who move as quickly as possible chanting the name of God ('Rām'). On the funeral pyre the corpse's feet point south towards the realm of Yama, the god of death, with the head pointing north to the realm of Kubera, the god of wealth. The funeral pyre is lit, theoretically with the domestic fire of the deceased if he is twice-born, and the remains are gathered up between three and ten days after the funeral and buried, placed in a special area of ground or immersed in a river, preferably the holy Ganges. During the days immediately following the funeral, the family are highly polluted and remain polluted until the final rites (*śrāddha*) are performed. These *śrāddha* rites are offerings to the deceased of rice balls (*piṇḍa*) which construct a body for him in the next world, the world of the ghosts (*preta-loka*). These daily offerings continue for ten days, recapitulating the ten lunar months of the embryo's gestation,[17] at which time the ghostly body is complete and, with the rite known as *sapiṇḍikaraṇa*, moves into the realm of the ancestors (*pitṛ-loka*). In south India the offering of *piṇḍas* to the deceased might take place at the confluence of a sacred river and a ritual to determine whether the ghost still lingers involves offering *piṇḍas* to crows. If the crows eat the offerings then the deceased is happy. This marks the end of the life-cycle rituals, the last ritual reflecting the birth rite at life's beginning.

While the official ideology of brahmanical Hinduism is reincarnation and this is the model generally assumed by renouncer traditions, the funeral rites demonstrate another model of the afterlife operating alongside the reincarnation model. Here the dead go to an intermediate realm, the 'world of the ghosts' (*preta-loka*) and, once they have a complete body constructed through the *piṇḍa* offerings, go into the realm of the ancestors or fathers (*pitṛ-loka*). At village level there are often no coherent beliefs about the afterlife. Generally, a person is regarded as a composite being, after whose death the different elements or powers which constituted the person go to different places. For example, in Kerala a common folk belief is that a person has at least two powers (*śakti*) which separate at death: the 'soul' (*jīva*) or 'life principle' (*ayus*) goes off to the Lord or to heaven (*svargam*, even called *mokṣam*, 'liberation'), while the other power, connected with the body, remains on earth as a ghost (*preta*, *piśāca*). This part of the person connected with the earth is sometimes thought to become a crow.[18] While many non-Brahmans do not claim to believe in reincarnation, there is no cognitive dissonance experienced by Hindus who do, yet who nevertheless perform the correct funeral procedures. This indicates the autonomy of the ritual realm, the ritual pattern of the funeral followed by the creation of the deceased's body in the next world going back to the time of the Vedas, before the ideology of reincarnation made its entrance.[19]

Rites of passage are occasional rituals performed at different junctures of a person's life. There are also rituals performed on a daily basis, not only by Brahmans, but by all Hindus. These constitute the daily worship of deities – making offerings to them and in turn receiving blessings from them.

Pūjā

In contrast to animal sacrifice, *pūjā* is the offering of vegetarian food, flowers and incense to a deity. All deities accept these offerings and are the focuses of *pūjā*, though some accept blood-sacrifice (*bali*) as well. *Pūjā*, a Sanskrit word which can be loosely translated as 'worship', is performed in private homes and in public temples throughout Hindu south Asia. Minimally it might involve making a small offering of a coin to the icon of a deity and receiving the deity's blessing in the form of a mark (*tilak*) of sandalwood paste (*candana*) or red turmeric powder (*kunkuma*) on the forehead. In private homes, *pūjā* would be performed before the icon of the deity installed either in a separate room, in the houses of the better-off, or in the purest room in the house, the kitchen. In the temple a *pūjā* might become very elaborate, with sacred verses (*mantra*) being uttered by the temple priest (*pūjāri/pūcāri*) while the icon is bathed and dressed, and a variety of foods are offered, accompanied by the strong smell of incense and the loud ringing of bells and banging of drums. Many people might be present at such *pūjās* to gaze upon the deity – to have its *darśana* – and to receive back the offered food blessed by the god (*prasāda*).

TEMPLE WORSHIP

Pūjā follows a similar pattern and contains the same elements in different temples throughout India. In south Indian temples, *pūjā* generally conforms to accounts given in sacred texts, the Āgamas and Tantras composed during the medieval period, and in ritual manuals (*paddhati*). Temples will adopt the rites and mantras prescribed in a specific text, such as the *Kāmikāgama* used in many temples in Tamilnadu, or the *Tantrasamuccaya* used in most Kerala temples today.

In temples *pūjā* usually comprises a rite of bathing the icon (*abhiṣeka*), during which various substances are rubbed on the deity's 'body', such as sesame seed oil and curd. The deity is then dressed and decorated in new clothes, given a new sacred thread (the symbol of high-caste birth), and adorned with gold, jewels and perfumes, often receiving a dot of red turmeric on the forehead or bridge of the nose. Plates of boiled rice and sweets are offered to the deity (*naivedya*) to the accompaniment of ringing bells. The rice is later consumed by the priests and temple officiants. After the deity's meal, a curtain is drawn back and the devotees can have the 'vision' (*darśana*) of the deity and see the final stage of the ritual, the display of lamps (*dīpārādhana*), during which the priest waves a variety of camphor lamps in a circular motion before the icon. The rite is now approaching its culmination and might be accompanied by loud drumming, pipes and the blowing of conches. A priest will then take a lamp to the devotees who cup their hands over the flames and touch their eyes and faces, bringing the light and warmth of the deity to themselves. The devotees accept turmeric powder or white ash from the priest to mark their foreheads and the *pūjā* is over. Devotees will take away blessed food (*prasāda*) to be eaten later. The circling lamp, bringing the deity's light and warmth to his or her devotees, is known as the *arati* lamp – a term which is used synonymously with *pūjā*. Chris Fuller notes that, in the Minakshi temple at Madurai, the *pūjā* should ideally be preceded by a preparatory ritual and should end with a fire ritual (*homa*), but this is only performed on important occasions.[20] Many temples, such as the famous Jagannāth temple at Puri, would have had *devadāsī* dancers, the temple 'prostitutes' married to the deity, to perform sacred dances before the shrine.

In temples such as the famous temple of Guruvayur on the Kerala coast, which attracts many thousands of pilgrims, five daily *pūjās* are celebrated. These occur at the junctures of the day (dawn, midday, sunset), and two between dawn and midday. The presiding deity of the temple, Guruvayurappan, 'Lord of Guruvayur', is regarded as a manifestation of Kṛṣṇa. The icon is in a standing posture located in the inner sanctum of the temple where the daily rituals are performed. While the day is technically divided into five *pūjās*, in some sense the entire daily ritual cycle can be seen as a single *pūjā*, the deity being awakened, bathed, paraded around the temple, fed, and offered lights, while blessings are received by his devotees in the form of his vision (*darśanam*), food and coloured powders.[21]

The pattern of worship that we see here in the Guruvayur temple – minimally the making of an offering and the receiving of a blessing – is found, with variations, throughout Hinduism. One further example will illustrate this. A day's journey north of Guruvayur is the small town of Payyanur. Here, along with many other families throughout Kerala, a Nambudri Brahman family performs an annual ritual, the pūjā to the family deity Rakteśvarī. Traditionally each Nambudri family group has an ancestral homestead (*illam*) to which family members return on special ritual occasions. In this particular *pūjā*, the family deity, Rakteśvarī, is appeased through receiving offerings and in turn conveys blessing (*anugraham*) on the family.

Preparations for the *pūjā* are begun on the evening before the ritual itself, during which a frame or *maṇḍalam*, made out of split layers of banana tree stalks, is prepared as an altar. On the day of the ritual, which lasts for a couple of hours, the extended family of parents, children, uncles and aunts, gather at the shrine by the family home in the morning. The Goddess is addressed by a respected elder behind the closed door of the shrine's inner sanctum where she lives. The shrine is lit by a number of lamps and he utters mantras, touching parts of the Goddess' body, thereby empowering them (*nyāsa*). The priest then withdraws from the inner shrine, and lamps are lit on the *maṇḍalam* which functions as the locus for the invocation of the deity who receives offerings. These offerings include three bowls of substitute blood (*guruśi*), coloured black and red, which the priest pours over the *maṇḍalam*. The family then circumambulate the shrine. Finally the *arati* lamp is brought around to the family members for them to take the flame and heat of the Goddess. Red powder, previously offered, is given out to make a mark called a *tilak* on the forehead. The ritual over, the family members partake of a feast which includes a dessert item (*payasam*) made from food offered during the *pūjā* and called *prasādam*.

In this *pūjā* we see the basic elements of Hindu ritual: the offerings to the deity, the repetition of sacred formulae, the closing of the doors of the inner shrine, the offering of light and the receiving of the Goddess' grace in the form of fire. This structure is directly paralleled by the rituals at Guruvayur, and is a pattern, with regional variations, which can be located throughout the subcontinent, and indeed in other countries where Hinduism has journeyed. What is interesting about this *pūjā* is that the offerings of coloured water are symbolic representations of blood. Indeed Rakteśvarī means 'Goddess of blood'. So what are literal offerings of blood to the Goddess amongst lower, more impure, social groups, become, with the Nambudris, substitute or symbolic offerings. The use of actual blood to propitiate the Goddess would be polluting for the Nambudri, so he must use substitutes. Indeed, the Nambudris say that, whereas lower-caste groups use substances, the Nambudri uses mantras.

Festivals

The Hindu year, using the lunar calendar, is punctuated by a number of religious festivals (*utsava*), some of which are pan-Indian, others of which are local. During festivals, which are often particular to specific temples, thousands of people line the streets to witness the procession of the temple icon (*mūrti*) on a carriage (*ratha*) pulled through the town by sometimes hundreds of men. There is a famous festival at the Jagannātha temple in Puri, during which an enormous cart and icon is pulled through the processional street (the English word 'juggernaut' comes from this cart). The icon is often accompanied by a procession of decorated elephants, horses and holy men (*sādhu*) often in a carnival atmosphere. To witness the icon is to have the auspicious 'vision' (*darśana*) of the deity and so to receive its blessing. The processed icon is sometimes distinct from the central icon installed in the temple, and used only on festival occasions or when the deity circumambulates the temple. The principal, pan-Hindu festivals are:

- Kṛṣṇa Jayānti. This falls in the month of Śravana (July–August) and celebrates Kṛṣṇa's birthday.
- Rakhi Bandhan. The full moon day of Śravana during which girls tie coloured threads around their brothers' wrists.
- Gaṇeśa Catūrthi. The festival during Bhadrapada (August–September), sacred to elephant-headed Gaṇeśa, Lord of Beginnings and Obstacles.
- Dassera. This is a holiday during Aśvina (September–October) which marks the end of the monsoon. The first nine days are called *navarātri* ('nine nights') at the end of which time the festival to the Goddess, the Durgā-pūjā, occurs, especially in Bengal. The tenth day of the festival also celebrates the victory of Rāma and his monkey army over the demon Rāvaṇa.
- Divālī or Dipāvalī. The festival of light during Aśvina, celebrated throughout the Hindu world with lamps placed in windows and around doors or floated down rivers, and gifts exchanged.
- Śiva Rātri. The festival sacred to Śiva during Marga (November–December), celebrated especially by Śaivas.
- Holi. The spring festival in Phālguṇa (February–March), characterized by often robustious behaviour, during which people drench each other in water and coloured powder.

Other festivals, though not as popular as the above, are nevertheless celebrated by large numbers of people. Of these the Nāga Pañcamī in south India is popular, during which snakes are fed and worshipped, and the spring festival, Vasant, in the north, when women and girls wear bright yellow dresses. More local festivals also occur such as the 'dance-possession' festivals of the *teyyam* deities in Kerala.

Pilgrimage

Pilgrimage is integral to Hinduism and in modern times, with the development of good communication systems across the vast expanse of India, has become very popular. A pilgrimage is a *tīrṭha yatra*, a journey to a holy place, referred to as a 'ford' (*tīrṭha*), a place for 'crossing over', where the divine world touches or meets the human world. The *tīrṭha* is a place where the transcendent comes to earth, where the higher realms meet the lower, the sacred meets the everyday. A *tīrṭha* is therefore a point of mediation between two realms. Pilgrimages are especially auspicious when undertaken during a temple festival, such as the annual procession of the

Lord Jagannātha at Puri. At such places Hindus can rid themselves of 'sin' (*pāpa*) or accumulated karma, fulfil a vow (*vrata*), or simply enjoy the transforming experience of the pilgrimage. During the period of the pilgrimage there is a tendency for caste restrictions to fall away (though perhaps never wholly) and for people to relate to a collective identity characterized by ideals of equality and communion.[22]

There are many pilgrimage centres in India, some are pan-Hindu, such as the city of Varanasi or the temple of Kanya Kumārī at India's southern tip, while others have more local or regional interest, such as the temple of Guruvayur in Kerala mentioned above. Towns and cities sacred to a particular deity – such as Ayodhya, the birthplace and capital of Rāma – or which have arisen at the confluence of sacred rivers – such as Allahabad at the confluence of the Ganges, the Yāmuna and the mythical Sarasvatī – are extremely popular pilgrimage centres. Traditionally there are seven sacred cities which are the object of pilgrimage, Ayodhya, Mathura, Hardwar, Varanasi, Ujjain, Dwarka and Kanchipuram. Sacred rivers are themselves places of pilgrimage, particularly the Ganges, rising in the Himalayas and flowing down to the sea in West Bengal; the Yāmuna, also rising in the Himalayas and joining the Ganges; the Godavari rising in Maharashtra and flowing through Andhra Pradesh; and the Kaveri, flowing from Karnataka through Tamilnadu. Towns located along the banks of these rivers tend to attract pilgrims, particularly the holy cities, along the Ganges, of Varanasi, Allahabad (or Prayaga), Hardwar and, further up the river, Badrinath and Kedarnath. The actual source of the Ganges, a little further than Kedarnath at Gomukha, attracts many pilgrims in spite of its inaccessibility. Other important pilgrimage centres are Mathura (Kṛṣṇa's birthplace), Vṛndavana (Kṛṣṇa's forest home) and, in the south, Kanchipuram. There are also traditionally four sacred abodes (*dhama*) at the four 'compass points' of India: Badrinath in the north, Puri on the east coast, Rameshwaram in the south and Dwarka on the west coast. It is very auspicious to perform the *dhama yatra*, the pilgrimage to all four centres in a clockwise direction, and so, according to some Hindus, attain salvation.

VARANASI

Varanasi or Benares is perhaps the most important and famous city for Hindus, famous for its *ghats*, the steps going down into the Ganges, along which pilgrims bathe and along which bodies are cremated. Indeed to die in Kāśi, another name for this city sacred to Śiva, is to attain liberation (*mokṣa*) upon death. Of all pilgrimage centres, Varanasi is perhaps the most popular. Varanasi is regarded as the centre, not only of India, but of the cosmos. All the gods are gathered there and all pilgrimage places united in the one. Here is a city which is more than just an urban centre; a place which embraces all places, which is a symbol of a Lord who embraces all phenomena. Varanasi is the great cremation ground (*mahāsmaśāna*) which reflects the cremation ground which is the universe.[23]

KUMBHA MELA

Kumbha Melas are festivals, especially sacred to holy men and women, held at Allahabad, Ujjain, Hardwar and Nasik. The most important is held at Allahabad every twelve years, a cycle that is related to the movement of the planet Jupiter. During the festival, pilgrims and renouncers process into the river Ganges to bathe. The naked *nāga sādhus*, covered in ashes and with matted hair, lead the procession, followed by other orders of ascetics, and finally by ordinary householders.[24] These pilgrimages attract huge crowds and during the Allahabad Kumbha Mela in 1989 an estimated 15 million pilgrims came to bathe in the river.

SABARIMALAI

Let us look at one last example from Sabarimalai in the western Ghats of Kerala. Here there is a temple to the god Aiyappan, the son of Śiva and Mohinī, a female form of Viṣṇu. This pilgrimage occurs during Margali (December–January) and traditionally takes forty-one days. The Aiyappan cult is predominantly male, mainly young men, though prepubescent girls and post-menopausal women are allowed to undertake the pilgrimage. The pilgrims wear black – though some wear ochre – and follow a strict regime of abstention from sex, alcohol, and the eating of meat and eggs for the forty-one-day period of the festival. For the duration of the festival, the pilgrim becomes a renouncer, undergoing a symbolic funeral at his initiation by a guru on the eve of the pilgrimage. Upon reaching the temple, the pilgrim smashes a coconut upon one of the eighteen steps of the temple, a symbol of the dissolution of himself into Aiyappan.[25] The pilgrim should undertake the pilgrimage each year, smashing a coconut on each successive step until all eighteen have been covered.

Astrology

There is a deep belief in Hinduism that human life is influenced by the movements of the planets and astrology is of vital importance in determining an auspicious time, even down to the correct hour, to undertake rituals. It is important in determining the times of pilgrimage, festivals, marriage, and in determining marriage partners. The science of astrology (*jyotiṣa*) comprises one of the Vedāṅgas,[26] the texts developing various aspects of vedic knowledge, designed or used at first to determine the correct time for sacrificing. The astrologer (*jyotiṣī*) is a very significant figure in the lives of Hindus who make major decisions guided by his advice. Pilgrims to Varanasi, for example, will consult astrologers seated on the steps leading into the Ganges, and the parents of many children will have their infants' horoscope drawn up shortly after birth. These will be consulted at all important occasions in the child's life to help determine auspicious times for rites of passage.

Private ritual

The kinds of *pūjā* we have so far described occur within the public realm of the temple or family shrine, notwithstanding the element of privacy in the worship of the deity by the priest behind a screen. These rituals are propitiatory and in return the community receives the blessing of the deity in the form of its *darśana*, *prasāda*, and the hope that the deity will protect and guide them. Some Hindus, however, perform rituals for the sake of spiritual salvation, which is conceptualized in a variety of ways. These seekers after wisdom and liberation from the material world of suffering might be initiated into one of the great traditions of Hinduism, such as a Śaiva tradition whose worship is focused on the god Śiva, a Vaiṣṇava tradition whose worship is focused on Viṣṇu or one of his incarnations, or a Śākta tradition whose focus is the Goddess in one of her manifestations. The genre of texts which form the scriptural basis of many of these traditions are the Āgamas and Tantras already discussed.

A devotee within such a tradition, the Śaiva Siddhānta devotee described by Richard Davis for example,[27] would offer private *pūjās* to his chosen deity (*iṣṭa-devatā*), performed alone before the deity's icon each day, while at the same time maintaining a public ritual life, attending the temple and family shrine, and generally fulfilling his household obligations. Such devotees are generally male, though women are not necessarily excluded from initiation into these traditions. The private rituals incumbent upon the initiate for the purposes of spiritual salvation are supererogatory and do not replace his public ritual obligations. Having performed the correct private rituals, the devotee hopes to attain spiritual salvation either during his lifetime or upon death, depending upon which specific tradition he is initiated into.

While internalized ritual has been the practice of the few – the virtuosi dedicated to the task of liberation and/or the gaining of spiritual power – the majority of Hindus only practice regular *pūjās*, in home and temple, of the kind previously described. An ancient and important form of Hindu worship, which has tended to be marginalized in more recent years with the popularization of ideas about non-violence and the pervasiveness of a brahmanical ideology which stresses vegetarianism, is sacrifice. Sacrifice refers to a ritual in which an animal is killed, usually by low-caste groups, and presented as an offering, usually to a blood-demanding goddess. The practice is widespread at village level, though Brahmans would generally not perform sacrifice, unless during a special vedic *śrauta* ritual, because of the death pollution associated with it.

Sacrifice

As we have seen, there are two kinds of offerings made to deities, 'vegetarian' offerings of fruit, vegetables, rice and so on, which all deities accept, and, in contrast, non-vegetarian offerings or the sacrifice of animals (*bali*), which only some hot deities accept. Animal sacrifice has always been an important dimension in the history of Hindu traditions. Though often frowned upon within modern Hinduism, the sacrifice of fowls, goats and sometimes buffalos is an integral part of the worship and appeasement of certain deities, notably the ferocious, violent or hot goddesses such as Māriyamman̲ and Kālī. Indeed sacrifice of buffalos is connected with royal power and the village buffalo sacrifice can be seen to reflect the grand, royal sacrifices to the Goddess during her 'ten day' festival (*dassera*).

While fowls, goats and sheep are frequently offered (mostly fowls) to ferocious male and female deities, buffalo sacrifice only very rarely occurs, due largely to its prohibition by the Indian government since 1947. However, on occasion, buffalo sacrifices to the Goddess do occur during the autumn 'ten day' festival or Durgā Pūjā, which celebrates her victory over the buffalo demon. Because buffalo sacrifices are rare, so are ethnographies describing them. Alf Hiltebeitel cites an early ethnography by Sir Walter Elliot in 1829 and he himself witnessed and recorded a buffalo sacrifice at Gingee in Tamilnadu in 1984. Here the main recipient of the sacrifice is the goddess Kamalakkaṉṉi, 'Lotus Maiden', whose small temple is half-way up a steep incline to the Gingee Royal Fort. She is joined in the sacrifice by two of her seven sisters, Kāḷiyammaṉ and Māriyammaṉ.

The sacrifice occurs at the end of the ten-day festival and involves the co-ordination of the three temples and a committee who organize it, made up mainly of a caste called Vanniyars, who are Śūdras but who claim Kṣatriya origins. During the celebrations, two buffalos are sacrificed to the goddess in the public cult and a number of cocks and male goats are sacrificed in private cults, by individuals or individual families. The actual sacrifice is performed by the Paṟaiyar caste, Untouchables or Harijans. The goddesses Kamalakkaṉṉi and Kāḷiyammaṉ are brought in the form of their emblems, a trident and a pot respectively. They will meet their sister Māriyammaṉ later, but in the meantime they are accompanied by the fierce male deity Vīrappaṉ: one of the Paṟaiyars who is possessed by the god.

The first buffalo is led to a clearing by a tree outside the Royal Fort, sprinkled with water and its head daubed with red and yellow turmeric powder. The buffalo is thrown to its side, its legs tied above the hoof, and it is beheaded by a number of strokes of a large knife. Buffalos have traditionally been beheaded, though Berreman records a buffalo sacrifice in Nepal during which the victim was hacked to death with swords and knives.[28] In Elliot's 1829 record, reported by Hiltebeitel, a leg of the buffalo is cut off and placed in its mouth. Such ritual humiliation of the victim is a common theme in sacrifice in which ambivalent attitudes are displayed towards the victim who, on the one hand, is sacred and so should be treated with reverence, yet, on the other hand, is the victim of massive violence and is sacred only because it is to be killed.[29] At Gingee, the head is first removed from the sacrificial scene and then head and body taken to the Harijan colony. Villagers who have become possessed by the goddess jump upon the bloodstained ground and women smear the buffalo's blood on their foreheads as a *tilak* mark. The representatives of the goddesses and Vīrappaṉ (those bearing their emblems) dance, intoxicated, on the place of the sacrifice, reflecting, suggests Hiltebeitel, the intoxication of the Goddess upon slaying the buffalo demon. A second buffalo sacrifice occurs at a different location en route to the Harijan colony and the body is taken away as before to where the meat will be divided. In the meantime the two goddesses, Kamalakkaṉṉi and Kāḷiyammaṉ, meet their sister Māriyammaṉ, who is carried from her temple in the form of a pot. Here there is joyful celebration, for the sisters have not been together since the previous year's festival.[30]

Only the Goddess or one of her forms accepts buffalo sacrifices. Such sacrifices are a way in which the village or community can contact the Goddess and, furthermore, they reflect the social hierarchy. The sacrifice at one level represents the community itself with the Goddess at the top. This social stratification is reflected in the offerings to the Goddess during the festival. Within the 'private cults' of individual families, vegetarian offerings are offered to the Goddess and consumed as blessed food (*prasāda*) by the Brahmans. Fowls and goats offered to her by meat-eating castes, the Śūdras, are similarly consumed as blessed food, while the untouchable castes consume the buffalo's meat in their village. Its offal and blood are offered to the demonic beings on the village boundary.[31] The buffalo sacrifice reflects the Hindu cosmos with the divine being at the top of the scale, in this case the Goddess who can absorb the impurity of blood-sacrifice; the Brahmans offering and consuming only vegetarian food next; the lower-ranking meat-eating castes below them; with the highly polluting Harijans below them. The demons are classified here even below the Harijans.

Myth and sacrifice

The violence demonstrated towards the buffalo victim reflects the violence of the Goddess towards the buffalo demon, a violence which is, at the same time, a purifying power. Through performing sacrifice, the donor or community is purified: the sacrificial victim becomes a substitute for the donor or community and, as it were, transforms the sins of the community or donor into the blessing of the Goddess. The sacrificial victim is, at a deeper level, a substitute for the human donor or sacrificer, or perhaps the community as a whole. We do possess texts which refer to a human sacrifice in the Indian traditions, but such a practice may never have actually occurred, existing only as an ideal or possibility.[32] This identification of sacrificial victim with sacrificer is reflected in a number of Hindu myths, most notably in the myth, recorded in the *Devīmāhātmya*, of Durgā slaying and decapitating Mahiṣāsura, who is depicted iconographically as both buffalo and human form in one. The other notable myth which suggests this identification is the myth of Dakṣa in which Śiva beheads him. It is clear that Dakṣa, the instigator of the sacrifice, is identified with the sacrificial victim, and, as O'Flaherty observes, through destroying the sacrifice, Śiva, as Vīrabhadra, is in fact completing the sacrifice by killing Dakṣa, who has become the sacrificial victim.[33]

Ritual purity

Central to Hindu rituals is the idea of purity. Anyone undertaking a ritual, or having a ritual performed on their behalf, should be as free from pollution as possible. The natural functions of the body and bodily products (all bodily fluids, hair and nail clippings) are polluting for the Hindu, who needs to purify himself each day in the ritual morning ablution. There are also graver forms of pollution caused by death and grieving, menstruation and birth and during these times a person would be polluted and so excluded from certain activities such as entering a temple. Indeed, traditionally women were excluded from cooking during menstruation to prevent pollution being spread to the rest of the family. In the presence of the divine at a temple or before the household shrine, the Hindu must be in a state of ritual purity, which means that pollution (*mala*) has been eradicated as far as possible. There are limits to which this is possible of course, and certain classes of people might never be able to be rid of the pollution which accrues to their bodies due to their social group; a low-caste person would not be allowed within the household shrine during the Nambudri's *pūjā* to Rakteśvarī. Similarly, only the Brahman priest is allowed into the inner sanctum of the deity in the temple.

The scale of purity and pollution differentiates individuals from each other, men from women and high caste from low caste. Apart from everyday pollution caused through the body and inadvertent contact with polluting substances, there is a deeper level of purity and pollution which is generally regarded as a property of the body, as a bodily substance. The highest caste, the Brahmans, have a pure bodily substance while the lower castes have impure bodily substance, with the Untouchables being the most polluted. Because of their state of constant pollution due to the substance of the bodies they are born with, the Untouchables are often forbidden entry to Hindu temples or shrines which are administered by Brahmans, though such discrimination is now illegal in India. Yet, despite this legislation, low-caste Hindus and foreigners are frequently excluded from temples because of their polluting properties which would anger the deity. The scale of purity and pollution is an organizing principle and constraint which controls the regulation of bodies in social space in Hinduism. Hindu ritual not only expresses worship to a deity (or asks for protection or appeases the deity), it also makes statements about group identity, by stating, implicitly and explicitly, not only who can be included in any particular rite, but also, as we have seen with rites of passage, who is excluded from those rites.[34]

Ritual and possession

An important aspect of public ritual during festivals is possession (*āveśa*) by the deities of the temples which are the focus of celebration. This usually occurs among lower-caste groups and is often integral to the ritual process. As the divine presence occupies and possesses the icon (*mūrti*) in the temple, so the divine can occupy and enter the body of his or her devotee. The possessed person becomes a manifestation of the divine, their body paralleling the deity's icon (*vigraha, mūrti*). Possession in a ritual context by the deity should be regarded as a blessing and auspicious, though, of course, possession by a ghost or demonic presence would be inauspicious and require exorcism by a ritual specialist. A person might become possessed by the deity regularly on the occasion of the festival and might even become a 'priest' or 'priestess' of the god.[35]

Ritual possession occurs most strikingly in festivals, such as those of the *teyyam* deities of Kerala. These lower-caste festivals occur throughout the Malabar region at innumerable shrines which house the *teyyam* deities in the form of icons or swords. During the festival the deity will possess a *teyyam* dancer who is beautifully adorned as the god, elaborately decorated with headdress and face paint (see plates 19 and 20), who dances around the shrine compound, giving *darśanam* to the onlookers. There is an electric atmosphere during these festivals, as the *teyyam* dances accompanied by the intense, rapid drum-beats of his associates. The festival lasts for about two days, with each deity being performed in turn by a dancer specifically designated to perform that particular deity on the occasion of the festival. He begins his dance by an altar, where chickens will be sacrificed and alcohol offered, and a mirror is held up to him. Upon seeing his reflection he becomes possessed by the deity he is enacting. Before the *teyyam* shrine he sings or chants in Malayalam, a series of laudations to the deity, praising the deity first in the third person, then in the second person and finally the first person, indicating that the possession is complete. The *teyyam* dances with swords and shields taken from the shrine, symbolically attacking the high-spirited crowd. The *teyyam* sometimes marches out of the compound through the streets of the town to the local temple, paralleling the processional march of a temple icon, where he demands the attention of the higher-caste officiant inside. The *teyyam* is refused entry, though sometimes there is an exchange of ritual offerings, and returns to the *teyyam* shrine giving *darśanam* to people on the way and entering some houses and so blessing them. This pattern of knocking at the temple door and being refused entry expresses a hierarchical relationship between the high-caste, pan-Hindu, cool deity installed in the temple and the low-caste, local, hot, *teyyam*. Although there is a clear distinction between the high deity and the *teyyam*, the *teyyams*, while never losing their fierce nature, are nevertheless often identified with the high deities. For example, the *teyyam* Viṣṇumūrti, at a shrine in the small town of Nileshwaram, is identified with Narasiṃha, the ferocious incarnation of Viṣṇu.

The example of the *teyyam* illustrates how possession, as Rich Freeman's extensive study has shown, is a socially and culturally defined phenomenon. The possessed ritual dancer acts in a ritually determined way. The important point is that possession is culturally determined and is not primarily about the inner state of consciousness of the performer. Although the performer may improvise to some extent, the ritual songs he performs about the *teyyam* follow a standard pattern. Freeman observes: 'possession in Teyyam is a fundamentally ritual activity, that is, it is characterized by a highly formalized set of behaviours and beliefs which owe little to individual motivations and dispositions'.[36]

Ritual and mantra

One of the most striking features of all Hindu ritual is the repetition of sacred formulae, usually in Sanskrit, which accompany ritual acts. These are *mantras. Mantra* has been notoriously difficult to define, but very broadly refers to sentences, phrases, or words, mostly though not exclusively in Sanskrit, in verse and in prose, which are recited or chanted for ritual and soteriological purposes.[37] In the orthodox vedic tradition they have been used to evoke deities, for protection, and to magically affect the world, and in tantric traditions they are themselves regarded as deities, or as embodying the power or energy (*śakti*) of a deity. Mantras can be uttered audibly and loudly,[38] they can be whispered (a level which is often regarded as higher than the clearly vocalized mantra) and they can be uttered purely mentally, or in silence regarded as the highest level.[39] Of particular importance is the idea that a mantra is given orally by the teacher or guru, the master of mantra-knowledge, to the student; the guru empowers the mantra, gives the words force or energy, in a way which parallels the icon of a deity in a temple being empowered or brought to life.

Mantras are central to the ritual traditions of Hinduism and, indeed, Hindu traditions can sometimes be defined or delineated by the mantras they use: mantras for Viṣṇu or his incarnations will be repeated by Vaiṣṇavas, mantras for Śiva will be repeated by Śaivas and so on. The most famous vedic mantra is the Gayātrī: 'Oṃ bhūr, bhūva, sva,/tat savitur vareṇyam/bhargo devasya dhīmahi/dhiyo yo naḥ pracodayāt', which can be loosely translated as (*Oṃ*, earth, atmosphere, and sky. May we contemplate the desirable radiance of the god Savitṛ; may he impel our thoughts.'[40] This is taught to young Brahmans during their sacred thread ceremony (*upanayana*) and is thereafter uttered every morning at sunrise by orthodox Brahmans.

Mantras often combine 'seed syllables' (*bīja*), sound units based on Sanskrit phonology but which are not meaningful, with meaningful phrases. For example, 'Oṃ namaḥ śivāya huṃ' contains a meaningful element, 'homage to Śiva' (*namaḥ śivāya*), and the *bījas oṃ* and *huṃ* which are semantically empty. The most famous seed mantra is *oṃ*. First appearing in the *Atharva Veda Saṃhitā*, *Oṃ* becomes identified with absolute reality (*brahman*) in the *Taittirīya Upaniṣad*,[41] with the structure of the cosmos in the *Maṇḍukya Upaniṣad*,[42] and finds a place in all of Hindu ritual, from vedic sacrifice to daily *pūjā* in the temple. It is regarded as the most sacred sound in the Veda and, as Dermot Killingly has observed, represents or encapsulates the entire vedic corpus, being accepted as sacred even outside the Hindu fold in Buddhism and Sikhism.[43] While *oṃ* is not semantically meaningful, it is revered as the sound of the absolute which manifests the cosmos, the essence of the Veda.

Summary

From the examples that have been given, we can see that within Hinduism there is a wide range of ritual practices which focus on deities, each distinct to its tradition and region, yet at the same time displaying features which can be found throughout Hinduism from Kerala to the USA. Hindus perform rituals of sacrifice and *pūjā* to propitiate deities and receive blessings, and some Hindus perform private rituals for the purposes of salvation (*mukti*) and to experience the pleasures of higher worlds or heavens (*bhukti*). Ritual provides continuity of tradition through the generations, arguably conveys implicit Hindu values, and sets the parameters for the Hindu's sense of identity.

10 Hindu theology and philosophy

From the earliest times, alongside systems of ritual and soteriologies using yoga and meditation, elaborate and often highly sophisticated doctrinal schemes and metaphysical speculation developed within Hinduism. The term 'philosophy' has often been used to describe these systems. While there are undoubted similarities between traditional Hindu thinking and modern western philosophy, what traditional Hindu thinkers do would only be partially recognized in contemporary departments of philosophy in western universities. Alternatively, while the term 'theology' conveys not only the systematic and transcendent aspects of Hindu thought, but also emphasizes its exegetical nature, some schools are atheistic and not concerned with a 'theos'. Both terms will be used in the following exposition as appropriate. The Sanskrit terms generally translated as 'philosophy' or 'theology' are *darśana*, a system of thought expressed through a tradition of commentaries upon fundamental texts, and *ānvīkṣikī*, analysis or 'investigative science' within the field of vedic knowledge, particularly used with reference to logic (*nyāya*).[1] The term *darśana*, derived from a verb root *dṛś*, 'to see', has the implication of 'view' or even 'vision' of the world and is used not only to refer to orthodox (*āstika*) systems of Hindu belief, systems acknowledging the Veda as revelation, but also to the heterodox (*nāstika*) views of Jainism, Buddhism and Materialism (Lokāyata). The term *darśana* is also used in a quite different sense to refer to the religious act of gazing upon a temple icon or a living saint.

The orthodox *darśanas* have codified their teachings into aphorisms called *sūtras* ('threads') which are often too condensed to be understood without the use of a commentary (*bhāṣya*). These commentaries form the exegetical expression of the tradition and in turn have sub-commentaries and glosses written on them. It is in the commentarial literature that refined debates and technical refutations of rival schools are to be found. These debates have often been sharp and intellectually rigorous and resist some modern Hindu attempts to collapse the real differences between the various *darśanas*, or to see them as complementary aspects of a single system. General features of orthodox Hindu *darśanas* can be summarized as follows. They:

- assume the revelation of the Veda;
- claim to have liberation (*mokṣa*) as their purpose;
- are exegetical in nature, being expressed primarily through commentaries and sub-commentaries on revelation (the Upaniṣads) and on primary texts called Sūtras, which form the scriptural source of philosophical/theological schools;
- assume a transcendent reality beyond the contingencies of the human condition;
- offer systematic explanations and interpretations;
- are concerned with ideas about the structure of the body, the nature of matter and the functioning of consciousness.

These general features can be seen in relation to the central questions and concerns of Hindu thought, particularly ontology or the nature of being, and epistemology, the theory of knowledge. Questions of ontology have been intimately connected with the philosophy or theology of language, particularly the relation between language, consciousness and being, while epistemological questions have been concerned with valid means of cognition and methods of logic and inference. In debating these issues the *darśanas* develop a common terminology, particularly regarding the six means or methods of valid knowledge (*pramāṇa*): namely perception (*pratyakṣa*), inference (*anumāṇa*), verbal authority (*śabda*), analogy (*upamāna*), presumption (*arthāpatti*), and non-apprehension (*abhāva*). The different *darśanas* accepted all or some of these means of knowledge.

While the flowering of Hindu philosophy and theology occurs between the seventh and seventeenth centuries CE, the origins of philosophical speculation go back to the Veda. Following Frauwallner and Halbfass, the history of Indian philosophy can be broken down into the following broad periods:

- presystematic thought in the Vedas, Upaniṣads, Epics and early Buddhist texts;
- the classical systems of speculation in Hinduism, Buddhism and Jainism;
- the theologies of the theistic schools of the Vaiṣṇavas and Śaivas, which become important during the second millennium CE;
- modern Indian philosophy in the nineteenth and twentieth centuries which responds to western philosophy.[2]

Early, presystematic speculation

One of the earliest texts which demonstrates a sense of metaphysical speculation is a hymn in the *Ṛg Veda* which asks a series of questions about the origin of things, particularly about whether in the beginning there was existence (*sat*) or non-existence (*asat*). Although the terms *sat* and *asat* may not have had a technical, philosophical meaning in these early texts, the hymn displays a remarkable sense of wonder and intellectual sophistication in considering a state prior to existence or non-existence and beyond death or immortality. The text concludes with some irony: 'Whence this creation has arisen – perhaps it formed itself, or perhaps it did not – the one who looks down on it, in the highest heaven, only he knows – or perhaps he does not know.'[3] More systematic speculation begins with the Upaniṣads. Of particular note is chapter 6 of the *Chāndogya Upaniṣad* in which the teacher Uddālaka Āruṇi, one of the earliest theologians, instructs his son who has returned home, conceited, after studying the Veda for twelve years. Uddālaka tells him that existence (*sat*) is identified with *brahman* as the foundation of the cosmos and the essence of all beings.[4]

Of particular importance are vedic speculations about the nature of language, which prefigure a theme and school of thought which develops at a later period. The *Ṛg Veda* contains hymns to the power of speech (*vāc*) which is treated as a goddess who makes men wise.[5] Through speech, which is the prime medium of the vedic seers, truth is revealed and the truth of speech is a power. In the Upaniṣads speech is identified with the absolute *brahman* from which appearances, names and their forms, are manifested. The relation between the unmanifest *brahman* and the world of multiplicity is through the cosmic sound of the mantra *aum*.[6] The text says that as all leaves are held together by a stalk, so all sound is held together by *aum*.[7]

Language and Hindu theology

Any understanding of Hindu theology has to begin with language and communication. Revelation is a communication to humanity through the seers, expressed in language, specifically the 'perfected' language of Sanskrit. The injunctions of the Veda are in language, and the theological commentarial traditions are expressed through language. Language, for the vedic Hindu, inspires, clarifies, and reveals truth and meaning and so is the starting point of theological investigation (*brahmajijñasa*). Language is a fundamental concern of Hindu theology and assumes and uses a long tradition of linguistic analysis. This tradition can be traced back to the 'limbs of the Veda' or Vedāṅgas, the auxiliary sciences in which Brahmans would be trained, which ensure the correct transmission of the Veda through time and the correct performance of rituals. Of the six Vedāṅgas (listed on p. 53), grammar (*vyākaraṇa*) and etymology (*nirukta*) are directly concerned with language as an abstract system, while pronunciation (*śīkṣa*) and prosody (*chaṇḍas*) are concerned with its expression. The science of grammar (*vyākaraṇa*) developed into an independent tradition, itself regarded as a *darśana*, and provided the inspiration and analytical precision for schools more directly concerned with theological topics.

THE GRAMMARIANS

A highly sophisticated science of language developed astonishingly early in India, from at least the fifth century BCE, and provided the inspiration for modern linguistics through the study of Sanskrit and the translation into European languages of some of its key texts during the nineteenth century.

The earliest Hindu linguist we have record of, Pāṇini (*c.* fifth century BCE), in his 'Eight Chapters' (*Aṣṭādhyāyī*) produced a descriptive analytical grammar of Sanskrit, covering the analysis of phonemes, suffixes, sentences, the rules of word combination (*sandhi*), and the formation of verbal roots. This work has yet to be surpassed and a deeper understanding of it has only occurred with the development of modern linguistics in the West. Although there is little of direct theological concern in the 4,000 Sūtras of the text, it is the standard reference work against which later language is measured and which is the reference point for later interpretations of the vedic texts. It also provides the basis for the grammatical school which did have theological, as well as more strictly philosophical, concerns.

LANGUAGE, CONSCIOUSNESS AND BEING

With Bhartṛhari (fifth century CE), the leading thinker of the Grammarian school, grammar is transformed in the service of theology. Bhartṛhari sees grammar as being fundamentally concerned with the nature of existence and, ultimately, about the quest for liberation. The analysis of language becomes not merely a task in itself, or a task to ensure the correct transmission of the Veda, but a path or door leading to liberation, a means of release from transmigration: the immortal *brahman* becomes known through the purification of the word which occurs through the study of grammar.[8] The study and use of 'correct' forms of language produce a force of success or fortune which moves the student away from impure (i.e. incorrect) speech tendencies, towards the pure goal of the vision of the absolute. Through language, and specifically through its precise and deep understanding, humans are saved.

This is to elevate language to a very high status indeed. Bhartṛhari identifies absolute reality with purified language and relates the impure world of human transaction to the pure, timeless absolute through the medium of language. Absolute being does not stand outside or beyond language, but its essence is language. Language is the link between being as timeless, unitary, impersonal stasis and being as contingent, time-bound and particularized experience. The term Bhartṛhari uses for the absolute identified with language is the 'sound absolute' or 'word absolute' (*śabdabrahman*), an ontology which cannot be apprehended due to ignorance (*avidyā*). Ignorance clouds our vision of the sound absolute, though this ignorance itself is a manifestation of that absolute, created by the power of time. From a pure, non-sequential, unmanifested state which Bhartṛhari calls 'the seeing' (*paśyantī*), the sound absolute manifests in a subtle mode in which the power of time begins to function, creating space, sequence, and apprehended by humans as thought. This mental level is the 'middle' realm (*madhyamā*), characterized by the powers of time (which is primary) and space. In the final phase of *vaikharī*, the sound absolute is fully extended and the power of time manifests diversity and causal relationships: time is the force which constrains all events in the universe and is expressed in the sequence of ordinary human language.[9] Language, in its manifested modes of mental (*madhyamā*) and gross (*vaikharī*) speech, is driven and differentiated by time, but its source is the timeless, transcendent and purified 'language' as pure being.

This tripartite division of language and existence is furthermore related by Bhartṛhari to the important 'disclosure theory' of meaning (*sphoṭa*). The level of *vaikharī vāc* is the level of the uttered sentence, which is understood in a flash of comprehension or intuition (*pratibhā*): meaning is apprehended as a sudden gestalt. This flash of understanding is the disclosure (*sphoṭa*) of the meaning of the sentence as a complete integral unit. Those ignorant of a particular language break a sentence up into words and phonemes, but for a native speaker understanding occurs in a direct unitary way, as a person perceives a painting as a whole and not as a collection of lines and colours.[10] *Sphoṭa* is the bursting forth of the meaning of a sentence, or book, or poem; a revelation, as it were, from a more subtle level which has its primary ground in the sound absolute. This absolute, knowledge of which is an 'intuition' (*pratibhā*), is the ultimate goal, as well as source, of language.

Theories about language are also theories about consciousness to which it is intimately connected. Various terms for consciousness – *cit*, *citta*, *caitanya*, *saṃvit* – are the focal point of a number of Indian philosophical and theological systems, most notably the consciousness-only (Vijñānavāda) school of Buddhism and the Recognition (Pratyabhijñā) school of Kashmir Śaivism. Yet the question of consciousness is present in all Indian philosophical systems to some degree, particularly its relation to language and its relation to being. Indeed many schools, notably Kashmir Śaivism and Advaita Vedānta, identify purified or absolute consciousness with being. This purified consciousness is sometimes thought to be beyond language, while everyday communicative language, which expresses desire, prevents consciousness from realizing its true ineffable nature. For the Grammarians language is the distinguishing feature of human consciousness which, at its deepest level, is identical with being. While not agreeing with the Grammarians, all schools of Indian thought respond in some way to the Grammarian school, participating in the debate about language, its relation to consciousness and being, and using a shared philosophical terminology.

The one and the many

Apart from a concern with language and its relation to being, Hindu theologies have been interested in the relation of 'the one' to 'the many'. That is, Hindu revelation and yogic experience refer to an absolute reality which is unitary and without second, yet experience of the world tells us that existence is manifold and diverse. What is the relation between this unique one and the diversified many? Some Hindu theologies maintain that the relation is one of identity, the absolute is ultimately identical with the many and difference is merely illusory; some say that the relation is of difference and that the one and the many are quite ontologically distinct; while others maintain that both identity and difference are true of the relation between the one and the many.[11] Hindu theologies arrive at different positions with regard to this fundamental question.

The question of being is related to the epistemological question of causation. Hindu theories of causation can be broadly categorized into two. One theory, the *satkāryavāda* theory, maintains that the effect is pre-existent in the cause, as a pot (the effect) pre-exists in the clay (the material cause) – the other, the *asatkāryavāda* theory, that the effect does not pre-exist in the cause. The *satkāryavāda* theory can itself be divided into a theory which maintained that the effect is a real transformation (*pariṇāma*) of the cause, and a theory which maintains that the effect is not a transformation, but a mere appearance of the cause (*vivarta*) in a certain way, as a man sees silver coins in the sand but discovers that they are shells. That is, the shells are the cause of the effect (the perception of silver) but the effect is not a real transformation of substance. The Buddhists maintain that the effect is not pre-existent in the cause (and ultimately deconstruct the idea of causation), while the Sāṃkhya school holds that effects are real transformations of substance. The Advaita tradition rejects these views; for them there can only be an apparent transformation of substance, there being in reality only the single substance of *brahman*.

The commentarial tradition

The most notable feature of Indian theology and philosophy is that it is expressed primarily through commentaries and sub-commentaries on sacred texts. Although there are some independent philosophical texts – apart from the terse Sūtra literature which stands at the beginning of a commentarial tradition – the traditions are primarily exegetical. Sūtras are short condensed aphorisms which summarize the teachings of a school. Indeed, the aim of writing commentaries is to bring out the meaning of these aphorisms, to reveal what is already there in the earlier text, to illuminate its truth and not to say something new or original (though, of course, the commentaries inevitably do). A commentary (*bhāṣya*) is an explanation – often extensive – of the Sūtras, while there are also shorter explanations or glosses (*vṛtti*) and further explanations of commentaries (*vārttika*). An author might also compose an auto-commentary on verses which he himself has composed. The commentaries reveal a vibrant and living tradition with creative reading and interpretation at its heart; commentaries are, in the words of Francis Clooney, 'not signs of decay or decline of the original genius of a tradition, its reduction to words, mere scholasticism; they are the blossoming and fruition of that original genius'.[12]

These intellectual traditions become codified, by the medieval period, into a standard list of six orthodox systems, the *saddarśanas*, though there are important schools, notably the Jains and Buddhists, outside of this scheme. In his 'Compendium of All Philosophies', the *Sarvadarśanasaṃgraha*, Mādhava (*c.* 1340 CE) does not refer to the term 'six *darśanas*' but discusses the ideas of sixteen philosophical schools, including the important theological schools of monistic, or Kashmir, and dualistic, or Siddhānta, Śaivism. It must be remembered that the system of the six *darśanas* is a codification and an attempt to make coherent, within the sphere of vedic orthodoxy, traditions of rigorous philosophical debate which have marked differences between them, yet which share a common terminology and a common commentarial style. While the authors within some of the schools share many views in common, it should not be taken for granted that all thinkers within a *darśana* share the same opinions. Indeed the school of Vedānta, for example, covers a wide range of divergent views, though by the late medieval period there is a tendency, within Vedānta, to synthesize views and integrate divergent opinions into a hierarchical scheme with Vedānta at the apex. The six orthodox systems are:

- Sāṃkhya, the 'enumeration' school which posited a dualism between matter (*prakṛti*) and the self (*puruṣa*), both of which are real, though ontologically distinct;
- Yoga, the school of Patañjali which assumes the metaphysics of Sāṃkhya;
- Mīmāṃsā, the tradition of vedic exegesis which assumes the reality of the many;
- Vedānta, the tradition which develops from the Upaniṣads and which argues for the reality of the one and, in one of its forms, denies the reality of the many;
- Nyāya, the school of logic;

- Vaiśeṣika, the atomist school, associated with Nyāya, which assumes the reality of the many; the constituents of existence do not arise from a shared source – rather, each phenomenon is distinct and separate.

These are often coupled together into three groups, namely Sāṃkhya-Yoga, Nyāya-Vaiśeṣika, and Mīmāṃsā-Vedānta, for both historical and conceptual reasons: Sāṃkhya is the theoretical substrate of Classical Yoga; Vedānta is a continuation of Mīmāṃsā; and Nyāya, logic, is used in the metaphysical speculations of Vaiśeṣika. I will here describe the Sāṃkhya and Vedānta schools as these are the most important with regard to the wider religious traditions, Nyāya and Vaiśeṣika being schools of a more technical nature, concerned with categories of being, language and logic.

Sāṃkhya

The Sāṃkhya system is the oldest systematic philosophy to have emerged in the Hindu tradition and is enormously influential on later theological schools, especially tantric Śaivism and the Pāñcarātra. Indeed, other schools of Indian thought, such as Nyāya and Vedānta, developed during the early centuries of the common era partly due to polemical reactions to Sāṃkhya philosophy. The term *sāṃkhya*, which means 'enumeration' or 'calculation', has two senses: one a general sense used in renouncer traditions, including Jainism and Buddhism, to denote the enumeration and categorization of elements which comprise the cosmos; the other a more specific sense to refer to the Sāṃkhya philosophical system which developed a tradition of commentaries upon its key texts and is the backdrop to Patañjali's Yoga. These uses are chronological: the earlier, general tendency to categorize the cosmos and human psychology, which might be called Proto-Sāṃkhya, occurs very early in renouncer traditions, from at least the ninth to the third centuries BCE, while the systematic philosophy, Kārikā Sāṃkhya, develops fairly late from about the fourth century CE.[13]

PROTO-SĀṂKHYA

In the general sense of the enumeration of the elements or constituents of the cosmos, Sāṃkhya-like speculations are found in early Jain, Buddhist and Hindu texts. However, rather than seeing Sāṃkhyan speculations arising out of Jain and Buddhist contexts, it is probably more accurate to see the Jain, Buddhist and early brahmanical speculations, including medical speculation, arising out of a common ideological context in which Sāṃkhya-like enumeration of the categories of experience is central.

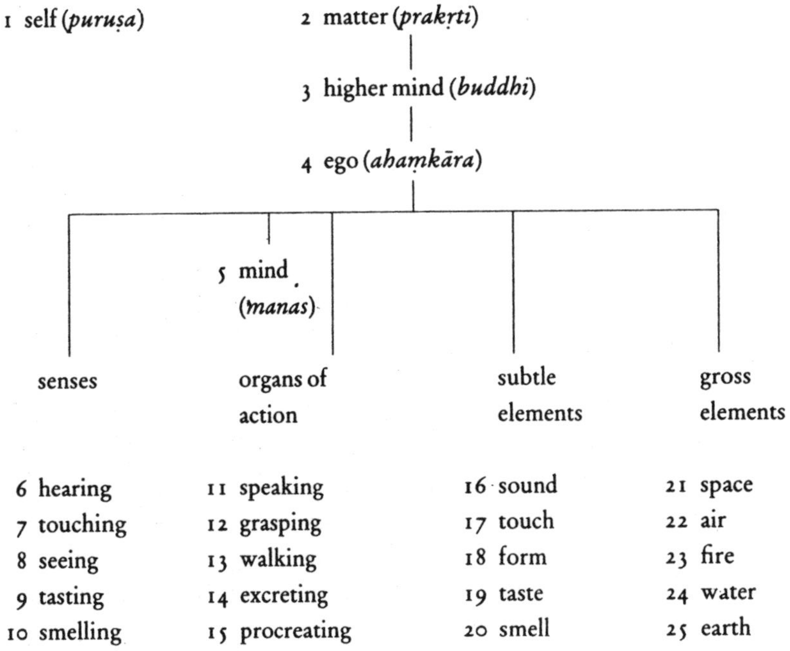

Figure 8 The twenty-five Sāṃkhya *tattvas*

There are striking parallels between the later Sāṃkhya philosophy, medical systems or Ayurveda, and Buddhist systems, particularly the Abhidharma and Yogācāra Buddhism. Indeed, Īśvarakṛṣṇa, an exponent of the philosophical tradition, begins his treatise on Sāṃkhya with the idea of life as suffering (*duḥkha*), a theme very important in Buddhism. Rather than one system borrowing from the other, they may well develop from a common heritage. The earliest enumeration of cosmic principles in the brahmanical tradition comes with the *Chāndogya Upaniṣad* which posits a single (*eka*) being or truth (*sat*) which produces fire, which in turn produces water, which in turn becomes food. The text refers to the sense of self-identity similar to the Sāṃkhyan idea of the ego (*ahaṃkāra*) and also identifies the colours red, white and black with fire, water and earth, reminiscent of the later classification of matter (*prakṛti*) into three qualities (*guṇa*).[14] The enumeration of categories is also found in other Upaniṣads, notably the *Kaṭha* and *Śvetāśvatara Upaniṣads*. Presystematic listings of elements of experience and world are found in the *Mahābhārata*, particularly in the section known as the *Mokṣadharma* and in the *Bhagavad Gītā*. For example, the *Gītā* describes Kṛṣṇa's nature as eightfold, comprising earth, water, fire, wind, ether, mind (*manas*), intellect (*buddhi*) and ego (*ahaṃkāra*),[15] which are categories enumerated in later Sāṃkhya literature.

SĀṂKHYA OF THE SĀṂKHYA-KĀRIKĀS

While these Proto-Sāṃkhya speculations can be located in early texts, a systematic philosophy does not emerge until quite late. The scheme which becomes identified with the philosophical school of Sāṃkhya is articulated by Īśvarakṛṣṇa in his 'Verses on Sāṃkhya', the *Sāṃkhya Kārikās* (350–450 CE), which is a summary of topics taught within an ongoing Sāṃkhya tradition. This text posits a radical dualism between the self or pure consciousness (*puruṣa*) and matter (*prakṛti*), with which it appears to be entangled.[16] Liberation (*kaivalya*) is the discriminative knowledge that pure consciousness is eternally distinct from primordial matter; there is only a proximity between them, the realization of which results in the cessation of suffering and reincarnation.[17] Discrimination allows consciousness to distinguish the self from what is not the self, and so to perceive that the self was never actually bound to matter. This self is transcendent, the silent witness behind the embodied subject of first-person predicates. This empirical self, the self of 'I' statements, is due to the evolution of matter from a primordial state, but is not itself the true subject. Whereas in western philosophical dualism there is distinction made between the mind and the body, in the Sāṃkhya system the dualism is between the self (*puruṣa*) and matter which embraces what in traditional western philosophy has been called 'mind'. The subject of first-person predicates is within the realm of *prakṛti*, the true self is beyond.

Prakṛti, a wider concept than the western category 'matter', which includes the western idea of the 'mind', evolves or transforms from an unmanifested state into a manifested state, through a series of stages or levels in which different categories appear. These categories, or *tattvas* (literally, 'that-ness') comprise the universe of experience. This evolution or transformation (*pariṇāma*) is governed, or kept in balance, by three qualities (*guṇa*), namely the qualities of light (*sattva*), of passion or energy (*rajas*) and of darkness or inertia (*tamas*). These qualities are very important in Hindu thought and later become the basis for a number of associations and classifications. For example the top three classes are associated with the *gunas*, as are categories of food into 'cool' (*sattva*), 'hot' (*rajas*) and 'dulling' (*tamas*). While the self (*puruṣa*) appears to be entangled in matter and appears to transmigrate in a subtle body, it is only the empirical self under the sway of the *guṇas* which does this.

What is interesting about the Sāṃkhya enumeration of the principles of experience into twenty-five categories is that the structure refers both to individual psycho-physiology and to cosmological categories. The evolution of matter is both a cosmic and an individual process; both physiological functions and the constituents of the physical world emerge from the sense of ego. The first transformation from matter is translated as the 'intellect' or 'higher mind' (*buddhi*), also called 'the great one' (*mahat*), and refers to both an individual's psychological functioning and to a higher level in a hierarchical cosmology. From *buddhi* the sense of 'I' or ego (*ahaṃkāra*) develops, from which emerges the mind (*manas*), the five senses and their objects, the five organs of action or motor functioning, five subtle, and five gross elements (see fig. 8).

SĀṂKHYA AND YOGA

Sāṃkhya develops in a context in which renunciation and the practice of yoga are common. Patañjali's yoga system, which was described in chapter 2, adopts the Sāṃkhyan dualistic metaphysics and frames liberation within these boundaries. Īśvarakṛṣṇa's general scheme is assumed by Patañjali, though with some differences. *Buddhi*, ego and mind are subsumed under the general category of 'consciousness' (*citta*) and, whereas Sāṃkhya is concerned with ontology, establishing the existence of the self and enumerating existents in the world, yoga is concerned with the transformation of consciousness and the mapping of various inner states of consciousness. Sāṃkhya is also an atheistic system, whereas the yoga *darśana* admits of the idea of God or the Lord (Īśvara) as a special kind of self (*puruṣa*) which has never been entangled in *prakṛti*, and which can be the focus of meditation. These theistic tendencies are developed in the later tradition and the sixteenth-century theologian Vijñānabhikṣu, while acknowledging that the system does not need it, argues that the idea of a Lord is not irreconcilable with the earlier Sāṃkhya view.

Vijñānabhikṣu represents a tendency to synthesize the views of Sāṃkhya yoga and Vedānta, while also drawing on the wider popular traditions of the Epics and Purāṇas. Through his commentaries he attempts to reconcile the pluralism and atheism of Sāṃkhya with the monism of some forms of Vedānta. The innumerable selves of Sāṃkhya which are ontologically distinct from each other and from matter (*prakṛti*) are nevertheless related to the absolute (*brahman*) and share in its being, as sparks share in the being of fire or a son is related to his father. At liberation these selves rest in their consciousness, purified of entanglement in matter. While acknowledging the independence of souls, matter and absolute, he tries to establish, through the creative reading of texts and commentaries, that *brahman* is transcendent, changeless, pure consciousness, yet is also the efficient and material cause of the universe.[18]

Mīmāṃsā

The Upaniṣads are referred to as the Vedānta, the 'end of the Veda', a term which is also used for the theological tradition developing from them. This immensely rich tradition is so influential that, at a popular level in the West, 'Vedānta' is taken to be Indian philosophy *par excellence*. The Vedānta tradition is, however, divided into two main developments which are both referred to as schools of exegesis or enquiry (*mīmāṃsā*). These are the Pūrva Mīmāṃsā, sometimes simply called Mīmāṃsā, and the Uttara Mīmāṃsā, sometimes simply called Vedānta. While the former is concerned with correct action in accordance with *dharma*, the latter is concerned with correct knowledge (*jñāna*) of *brahman*. It is significant that even the later school is referred to as Mīmāṃsā, a term which emphasizes that we are dealing with an exegetical tradition of commentary and sub-commentary upon sacred texts. For the purposes of clarity, I shall here refer to Pūrva Mīmāṃsā simply as 'Mīmāṃsā' and Uttara Mīmāṃsā as 'Vedānta', but would wish to stress, as Francis Clooney has shown, the exegetical continuity between them.[19]

The Mīmāṃsā traces its origin to the *Pūrva Mīmāṃsā Sūtra* of Jaimini (*c.* 200 BCE) with its commentary, the *Bhāṣya* by Śabara (second–fourth centuries CE), though the origins of Mīmāṃsā must also be sought in the auxiliary sciences (Vedāṅga) particularly the Kalpa Sūtras. Śabara's commentary in turn has sub-commentaries written on it, most notably by Prabhākara and Kumārila Bhaṭṭa (seventh century CE), which represent two distinct interpretations of Mīmāṃsā.[20] Indeed the tradition is split into the Prabhākara and Kumārila branches which differ over the concept of the effects of ritual action (*apūrva*) and the nature of error, though the Kumārila school is the most important representative of the tradition.[21]

The enterprise upon which Jaimini is embarked in his text is stated in the opening verse: 'Now is the investigation into *dharma*' (*athāto dharma-jijñāsa*). *Dharma*, the order of the universe, is revealed in the Veda and the investigation into it shows that the Veda is primarily a series of injunctions (*vidhi*) about ritual action. Ritual action, specifically sacrifice, can be traced to the Veda, and the Mīmāṃsā is rational reflection on its purposes. According to Jaimini, the correct performance of sacrifice produces a transcendent power, called *apūrva*, which produces the result of the sacrifice, particularly the reward of heaven (*svarga*) after death. *Apūrva* is the force postulated which accounts for how the result of a sacrifice can follow its performance, even though there may be a temporal gap between the action and its result. Each part of a ritual, once completed, creates its own *apūrva* which accumulates until the ritual sequence is completed, the results of which will be experienced by the sacrificial patron (*yajamāna*) in heaven. Heaven rather than liberation (*mokṣa*) is the result of sacrifice.

The theory of *apūrva* bears some resemblance to the theory of karma. However, unlike karma, which is a store of action built up over long periods producing results in successive lifetimes, *apūrva* is accumulated only through ritual action during the present lifetime for a post-mortem reward. Indeed there is even a sense in the Mīmāṃsā that ritual action is to be done, not because it produces rewards in heaven, but because it is a vedic injunction (*vidhi*). Sacrifice, according to this view, is action for its own sake, because it is enjoined in vedic revelation, and any future, human reward is secondary. Human desires and purposes are really irrelevant to the performance of vedic ritual; there is what Clooney calls a 'decentering' of the human. It is for this reason that certain classes of people, namely lower castes, women and the deformed, are forbidden from participating in the sacrifice. The ritual performer is not defined by changing personal qualities or knowledge of ritual procedures, since even a Śūdra can acquire this. Rather, the ritual performer is defined by his suitability, according to the Veda, which excludes certain classes; the Śūdra is simply not included within the structures of vedic ritual prescribed by the texts,[22] though this exclusion in itself tells us something about the 'exclusive' nature of vedic brahmanical society.

The early literature of the Mīmāṃsā is interested exclusively in *dharma* and the interpretation of vedic texts, tracing action back to texts and establishing the relevance of texts in ritual. Because of the emphasis on interpretation in order to establish correct meanings, the Mīmāṃsā developed a theory of language which is close to that of the Grammarians. Through the analysis of sentences they try to show how the syntactic unity of a sentence occurs through sentence contiguity, consistency and expectancy of the reader.[23] The Mīmāṃsā concern with language is accompanied by a concern with knowledge. The Mīmāṃsā is realist and pluralist, accepting the reality of the many and rejecting any form of idealism, such as Yogācāra Buddhism, which maintains the primacy of consciousness. The Mīmāṃsā accepts all six means of knowledge (*pramāṇa*) as valid. These methods establish the reality of the objects of knowledge, namely substance (*dravya*), quality (*guṇa*), action (*karma*), and non-existence (*abhāva*), and their sub-categories, which recapitulate those of the Vaiśeṣika school.

Vedānta

The most influential school of theology in India has been the Vedānta, exerting enormous influence on all religious traditions and becoming the central ideology of the Hindu Renaissance in the nineteenth century. It has become the philosophical paradigm of Hinduism *par excellence*. Yet, while there are continuities in Vedānta stretching back to the Upaniṣads, the Vedānta is immensely rich, containing within it a wide variety of theological and philosophical positions. The ambiguity over assigning the terms 'theology' or 'philosophy' to Vedānta stems from its clearly philosophical interests in epistemology, ontology and argument, yet also its exegetical nature which is regarded as a 'theological' enterprise. Contemporary scholarly understandings of Vedānta tend to locate it within a theological system of commentary which stresses the continuities with the earlier tradition of Mīmāṃsā.[24] There are also strong continuities with the Vaiṣṇava tradition and it can be argued that Vedānta is essentially a Vaiṣṇava theological articulation. Indeed even Śaṅkara, who is traditionally regarded as a Śaiva, may have been a Vaiṣṇava, according to some scholars.

As has been noted, the term 'Vedānta' refers to the Upaniṣads and their teachings as well as to the traditions inspired by them, which follow from them. At the head of these traditions are Sūtras, intended for memorization, which summarize the teachings of the Veda and Upaniṣads. While Jaimini's *Pūrva Mīmāṃsā Sūtra* is the foundation text of the Pūra Mīmāṃsā, the source text of the Uttara Mīmāṃsā or Vedānta is Bādarāyaṇa's *Brahma Sūtra*, also called the *Vedānta Sūtra* and *Uttara*

Mīmāṃsā Sūtra. This text was composed around the same time as Jaimini's text (*c.* 200 BCE) and, indeed, the two texts refer to each other's authors. Yet, whereas the *Mīmāṃsā Sūtra* is an investigation into *dharma*, the *Brahma Sūtra* is an investigation into *brahman*. Indeed, it begins in a similar fashion: 'Now is the investigation into the absolute' (*athāto brahma-jijñāsa*). These two texts articulate the two major realms of interest within Hindu traditions, the realm of *dharma*, the concern of the Brahman householder, and the realm of *brahman*, the concern of the renouncer seeking liberation.

A number of schools develop within the Vedānta tradition, whose founders and chief exponents write commentaries on the *Brahma Sūtra*, thereby establishing an independent school (*sampradāya*) of interpretation. Other texts were also the subject of exegetical commentary, most notably the early Upaniṣads and the *Bhagavad Gītā*. This group of texts – the *Brahma Sūtra*, the Upaniṣads and the *Gītā* – forms the 'triple basis' of Vedānta commentarial tradition. The most important Vedānta traditions are Advaita ('Non-Dualist') Vedānta, Viśiṣṭādvaita ('Qualified Non-Dualist') Vedānta and Dvaita ('Dualist') Vedānta.

Advaita Vedānta

Advaita Vedānta is the most famous Indian philosophy and is often, mistakenly, taken to be the only representative of vedantic thought.[25] The term *advaita* means 'Non-Dual' and refers to the tradition's absolute monism which, put simply, maintains the reality of the one over that of the many. The most famous Advaita thinker, and the most famous Indian philosopher ever to have lived, is Śaṅkara or Śaṅkarācārya.

ŚAṄKARA

The dates of Śaṅkara cannot be firmly established but some scholars date him between 788 and 820 CE. He certainly cannot have lived before the middle of the seventh century as he refers to the Mīmāṃsāka theologian Kumārila and the Buddhist Dharmakīrti who can be dated to that century. There are a number of traditional biographies, the *Śaṅkaravijayas*, written by his followers. These texts agree that he was born in Kaladi, a small village in Kerala, which is probably true as there would be no ideological reason for locating his birthplace there; it is not a royal centre or place of religious significance (other than that it is Śaṅkara's birthplace). His father died when he was young and he was brought up by his mother.

As a young Nambudri Brahman boy of about eight, Śaṅkara is said to have vowed to become a renouncer but his mother would not let him. There is a story that one day whilst bathing in a river a crocodile grabbed his leg. He shouted out and his mother came to the river bank. The only hope was to take renunciation there and then, so his mother agreed, upon which the crocodile let him go. He became a renouncer but promised his mother that he would be with her during her last days and perform her funeral rites, which he did. Śaṅkara left home and found a guru, Govinda, by the Narmadā river, whom he eventually left, then travelled north to Varanasi. Here he taught and gathered disciples. He went on a pilgrimage to the source of the Ganges and stayed at Badrinath for four years, where he composed his major works. He returned to Varanasi and continued to teach and debate with other thinkers, including the Mīmāṃsāka Mandanamiśra who converted to Advaita. There is a story that Mandana's wife, Bhāratī, challenged Śaṅkara to a debate about the art of love, about which, being a renouncer, he was woefully ignorant. So Śaṅkara entered into the body of a king for a short period to experience the art of love and returned to defeat Bhāratī in debate. Both she and her husband then became Advaitins. Not only did Śaṅkara compose commentaries, but also established a monastic order, the Daśanāmis, with four centres at Śṛṅgeri, Dwarka, Badrinath and Puri, and Kanchi as a possible fifth. He died aged thirty-two in the Himalayas.

Although many philosophical texts and devotional hymns are attributed to Śaṅkara, scholars are agreed that by 'Śaṅkara' we mean the author of the commentary (*bhaṣya*) on the *Brahma Sūtra*. Apart from this text, three others are positively accepted as being of his authorship: the commentaries on the *Bṛhadāraṇyaka* and *Taittirīya Upaniṣads* and the independent work, the 'Thousand Teachings' (*Upadeśasaharī*).[26] He probably also wrote the commentary on Gauḍapāda's *Kārikā* to the *Māṇḍukya Upaniṣad* and the commentary on the *Bhagavad Gītā*, though there is not universal agreement on this. Gauḍapāda is Śaṅkara's guru's guru whom Śaṅkara calls his supreme teacher (*paramaguru*). Gauḍapāda was influenced by Buddhism and his *Kārikās* are even quoted by the Buddhist philosopher Bhāvaviveka. Generally, however, the Advaita tradition is very opposed to Buddhism and Śaṅkara is vehement in his attack on Buddhist 'heresy' which rejects the Veda. Apart from the theological commentaries, Śaṅkara is attributed by the Advaita and Śrī Vidyā traditions with the authorship of a famous hymn to the Goddess, the

Saundaryalaharī. Śaṅkara's authorship of some of this text is accepted by its translator Norman Brown, and it is certainly possible for a Hindu theologian to have composed both erudite commentaries and a devotional literature, as Bharati has pointed out.[27]

ŚAṄKARA'S THEOLOGY

In his commentaries Śaṅkara develops a theology in which he tries to establish that spiritual ignorance (*avidyā*) or illusion (*māyā*) is caused by the superimposition (*adhyāsa*) of what is not the self onto the self. All knowledge is distorted by superimposition or projection, which prevents us from seeing our true nature as the self's (*ātman*'s) pure subjectivity, ontologically identical with the absolute (*brahman*). In order to realize the truth of the identity of the self with the absolute, a person must develop discrimination. Discrimination allows for a person to distinguish the self from what is not the self, true being from objects, and knowledge (*vidyā*, *jñāna*) from ignorance (*avidyā*). This is the withdrawal or dissolving of projection, as when a man walking on a beach sees silver coins but then discovers that they are shells, or sees a snake in the corner of a house, but then, upon inspection, finds it to be a rope. Śaṅkara opens his commentary on the *Brahma Sūtra* with the following:

> It is a matter of fact that the object and subject, whose respective spheres are the notion of the 'you' and the 'I', and which are opposed to each other as much as darkness and light, cannot be identified, and nor can their respective attributes. Hence it follows that it is wrong to superimpose upon the subject, whose nature is awareness (*cit*) and which has for its sphere the notion of 'I', the object and its attributes whose sphere is the notion of the 'not-I'. And vice-versa [it is wrong to] superimpose the subject and its attributes on the object.[28]

This opening passage sums up a central point of Śaṅkara's thought and gives a flavour of his terse commentarial style. Superimposition of the self on what is not the self, and what is not the self on the self, is the natural propensity of ignorant consciousness. The removal of superimposition is the removal of ignorance and the realization of the self (*ātman*) as the witnessing subject identical with *brahman*. Such knowledge is liberation (*mokṣa*).

Śaṅkara's enterprise is to show how his *advaita* interpretation of sacred scriptures is correct. It is a method of reading the texts and so gaining knowledge of revelation's truth: the process is one of hearing (*śravaṇa*), thinking (*manana*) and reflecting or meditating (*nidhidhyāsana*). While the idea of mystical experience (*anubhava*), which has been stressed in recent times in the West, is important for Śaṅkara as the goal to which revelation leads, he is primarily concerned with the correct interpretation of scripture and the refutation of what he regards as false views. There is no reference in his works to any personal religious experience nor to the experience of the ancient sages. The Veda, of course, is not thought to be of human authorship so personal experience is here irrelevant.[29]

The sacred scriptures can be divided into sections dealing with action (*karmakāṇḍa*) and sections about knowledge (*jñānakāṇḍa*). The Mīmāṃsā maintains that sections about action, that is ritual action, are of primary importance because injunctions to perform *dharma* are the central purpose of the Veda. Śaṅkara, on the other hand, maintains that the knowledge sections are of greater importance, for liberation is the Veda's central message, and only knowledge leads to liberation. No action can discriminate the self from what is not the self, only knowledge can achieve this, as silver is suddenly seen to be shell. This liberating knowledge is referred to in the 'great sayings' (*mahāvākya*) of the Upaniṣads, namely: 'I am the absolute' (*aham brahmāsmi*); 'this self is the absolute' (*ayam ātmā brahma*); 'everything is indeed the absolute' (*sarvam khalu idam brahma*); and 'you are that' (*tattvamasi*). To realize the existential force of these claims is to be liberated and to distinguish between pure being and worldly phenomena. This is not like the heaven of the Mīmāṃsākas, for liberation is not a future state or goal which can be achieved; it can only be woken up to.

Having said this, Śaṅkara does make concessions to the idea of devotion (*bhakti*) to a personal Lord (Īśvara) as a lower level of knowledge. *Brahman*, in its timeless essence as identical with the self, is beyond all predicates and qualities (*nirguṇa*), but in its temporal mode as the Lord it has attributes (*saguṇa*), and so can be approached through devotion as an object of consciousness. To see the absolute as the Lord is to maintain a distinction between self and absolute, which is to retain a vestige of ignorance which must finally be transcended. If reality is one, all distinctions must be illusory.

LATER ADVAITA

After Śaṅkara there are a number of important Advaita theologians who composed texts in the commentarial tradition, working out theological and philosophical problems incipient in earlier Advaita texts, and responding to opponents in other schools. Mandanamiśra, mentioned above, is an older contemporary of Śaṅkara who is a Mīmāṃsā theologian who converted to Advaita. He may or may not be the same as the Advaitin Sureśvara. Vācaspatimiśra (tenth century) wrote commentaries on Advaita texts as well as on other *darśanas*, and Śrī Harśa (*c.* 1150 CE) developed a form of *reductio ad absurdum* argument to show the inherent contradictions in all propositions about the world (particularly Nyāya propositions). Through this method of argument he brings out the undesirable consequences of his opponents' positions. This system of argumentation is essentially the same as that of the Buddhist philosopher Nāgārjuna.[30]

Viśiṣṭādvaita Vedānta

With the development of theism in the great tradition of Vaiṣṇavism, the monistic reading of sacred scripture is resisted. The great theologian and hierarch of the Śrī Vaiṣṇava community, Rāmānuja (see pp. 136–7), composes a commentary, the *Śrī Bhaṣya*, on the *Brahma Sūtra*, and a commentary on the *Gītā*, to refute the monism of Śaṅkara. He also composes a brief independent work, the *Vedānta Saṃgraha.*[31] In these works he argues vehemently against Śaṅkara's monistic reading of sacred scripture, expressing himself forcefully and asserting that the Advaita position is against reason, against the firm understanding of the meaning of language, and goes against the scriptures. The Advaitins, to hold such groundless opinions, must be plagued by the impressions of beginningless sin (*pāpa*)![32] Rāmānuja's interpretation of Vedānta is called 'Qualified Non-Dualism' (*viśiṣṭādvaita*) and articulates a form of Vaiṣṇava theology which came from Rāmānuja's grand-teacher Nāthamuni to his own teacher Yāmuna: a theology which draws upon the wide textual resources of the Epics, Purāṇas and even Pāñcarātra literature.

Like Śaṅkara and the Mīmāṃsākas, Rāmānuja is concerned with exegesis, the careful reading of scripture in order to arrive at an understanding of God and his relation to the plural world. Śaṅkara had maintained that in reading a sacred text there are two levels of truth in operation, one concerned with the higher truth of the unity of *brahman*, the other lower level representing *brahman* as a personal Lord. Rāmānuja rejects this distinction, arguing that all passages of sacred scripture must be taken as equal with each other; it is not methodologically sound to divide up scripture in this way. If we reject this two-levels-of-truth theory with regard to sacred texts, then we see, argues Rāmānuja, that scripture testifies to a supreme soul, the *brahman*, as the essence of the universe and the inner soul of all finite souls, who is yet also a personal being.

Apart from the problem of how to interpret scripture, the main theological concerns of Rāmānuja are the nature of the absolute, or God, and the relations between the absolute, the finite self and the world.[33] With Śaṅkara, Rāmānuja agrees that *brahman* is the one perfect reality which in itself is unchanging. However, he rejects Śaṅkara's idea that the world of manifold experience is illusion (*māyā*) caused through ignorance, and he rejects the idea that the Lord as a personal being is a lower level of truth than the impersonal absolute. Rather, both the one and the many are real; the many being the one's manifold mode of expression. God for Rāmānuja has two aspects or sides. One is the supreme aspect of God in his inner nature or essence (*svarūpa*), the other is his outer nature or accessibility (*saulabhya*). The essence of God has five attributes – of truth (*satya*), knowledge (*jñāna*), infinity, joy and purity – while the accessibility of God is shown in the modes of mercy and love, generosity, affection and parental love. The Lord also has beauty (*saundarya*) in both his essence and in his worldly incarnations, the *avatāras*. Humans come into contact with God's nature through the accessibility of his love – a theology with western parallels in Gregory Palamas' distinction between God's essence and his energy.

The individual self (*jīva*) is distinct from God yet participates in God who is its essence and inner controller (*antaryāmin*) and without whom it would not exist. The relationship between the self and God is one of inseparability, the self is wholly dependent upon God for its being. Both the self and the world participate in God's existence, yet are distinct from, while wholly depending on, him. The relationship between God and the self and the world is expressed in a famous analogy that the universe, comprising conscious selves (*cit*) and unconscious matter (*acit*), is the Lord's body. As the self is related to the body, so the Lord is related to the self and world. The universe of sentient and insentient matter as the body of God is therefore not illusory for Rāmānuja, but expresses his power and is called the realm of glory (*vibhuti*). Through apprehending the glory of the Lord in the world, the devotee can understand the *brahman* to be the supreme Person.[34] A deep understanding of the Lord's nature is the experience of liberation from the beginningless cycle of reincarnation. This is not the removal of ignorance in the Advaita sense of realizing the self's identity with the absolute. Indeed such a notion is nonsensical for Rāmānuja. Ignorance, he says, needs to have a basis or rest on a support. This support cannot be the self, for the idea of the self is the product of ignorance, yet nor can it be *brahman*, for *brahman* is self-luminous consciousness, by definition without ignorance.[35] Rāmānuja here astutely recognizes the Advaita problem concerning the nature of ignorance and to whom it belongs. For Rāmānuja there is real separation of a distinct self from the Lord until such a time as that self is liberated. This liberation is the removal of past karma, not the removal of ignorance. Indeed, even once karma is removed, beings are still individuated by their very natures and not because of extrinsic factors. Some selves are still going through the cycle of reincarnation, some have been liberated, while yet others, such as Viṣṇu's mount, the magnificent bird Garuḍa, were never bound.

The Viśiṣṭādvaita tradition continued after Rāmānuja's death with significant exegetes such as Piḷḷān who wrote a commentary on the Tamil Veda; Vedāntadeśika, the main theologian of the northern school (the Vaṭakalai); and Lokācārya Piḷḷai, the main theologian of the southern school (Teṅkalai). A number of digests have also been composed summarizing the tenets of the Viśiṣṭādvaita theology.

Dvaita Vedānta

Yet another development in the Vedānta exegetical tradition came in the thirteenth century with the south Indian Vaiṣṇava theologian Madhva, who wrote commentaries on a number of Upaniṣads, the *Bhagavad Gītā*, the *Brahma Sūtra*, and the *Bhāgavata Purāṇa*, as well as an independent treatise summarizing the teachings of the *Brahma Sūtra*, the *Aṇuvyākhyāna*.[36] In these writings he establishes a new interpretation of Vedānta, that of dualism (*dvaita*). Madhva was born near the South Kanarese village of Udipi, became a renouncer as a young man, and entered a Vaiṣṇava order of a monastic renouncer tradition, called the Ekānti Vaiṣṇavas, where his guru, Acyuta Prekṣa, was very impressed by Madhva's skill in interpreting the sacred scriptures. Madhva went on a tour of south India with his preceptor and then on a pilgrimage to the source of the Ganges in the north, disputing with Buddhists, Jains and Advaitins along the way. There is even a story that he strongly advised a south Indian king to have thousands of Jain heretics impaled on stakes! Madhva eventually became the hierarch of his monastic community and established a reputation with his commentary on the *Brahma Sūtra*. He established a monastic centre at his birth-place, Udipi, which continues to this day, and installed there a famous icon of Kṛṣṇa.[37]

In complete contrast to the *advaita* of Śaṅkara, Madhva maintains that the correct interpretation of sacred scripture is dualistic: that scripture maintains an eternal distinction between the individual self and the Lord. Whereas the Advaita tradition emphasizes the non-difference (*abheda*) between the self and the absolute, Madhva insists on their complete distinction. Difference or *bheda* is a cornerstone of his theology and scriptural interpretation. Each thing in the universe is itself and unique and cannot be reduced to something else (an idea which is not dissimilar to Wittgenstein's contention that a thing is what it is and not another thing). Each phenomenon in the universe is uniquely itself, made unique by the power of particularity (*viśeṣa*). While each thing is unique, there are nevertheless five categories of difference (*bheda*): between the Lord and the self (*jīvātman*); between innumerable selves; between the Lord and matter (*prakṛti*); between the self and matter; and between phenomena within matter. Yet while there are these distinctions and phenomena exist independently of each other, nothing can exist outside of the Lord's will. As the body depends upon the self, so all beings and matter depend upon the Lord who is their support.

The Lord in his essence is unknowable, yet he pervades the self as its inner witness and pervades matter as the inner controller. There is a graded hierarchy of selves which exist at different levels of the hierarchical cosmos, the purer selves being higher than the impure. These selves are distinguished into three broad categories: those who are liberated such as gods and sages; those not yet liberated, though capable of liberation; and those incapable of liberation, including selves which are eternally transmigrant, the damned in hell, and various classes of demons. Liberation is the self's enjoyment of its innate being, consciousness and bliss (*saccidānanda*), which is a participation in the bliss of the Lord, attained through devotion (*bhakti*) to an icon and the Lord's grace.[38]

Śaiva theology

Although Śaṅkara is reputed to have been a Śaiva, the Vedānta tradition is a discourse broadly within the parameters of Vaiṣṇavism. A Śaiva understanding of Vedānta does develop in the thirteenth century with the teachings of Śrī Kaṇṭha's Śivādvaita, but, apart from this, Śaiva theology develops outside Vedānta, drawing not so much on vedic resources as on its own Śaiva revelation in the Tantras and Āgamas. It is significant that Śaiva theologies are excluded from the orthodox (*astika*) list of six *darśanas*, showing that from a strictly vedic perspective they are on the edges of orthodoxy. Yet they are included in Mādhava's *Sarvadarśana Saṃgraha*, showing that they are still within the sphere of orthodox discourse and disputation. While all Śaiva traditions have a theology, even if only implicit, the two most significant developments for the history of Indian theology are the dualistic and monistic schools of Śaivism: the Śaiva Ṣiddhānta and Kashmir Śaivism or the Recognition school (Pratyabhijñā).[39]

The developments of the Saiva traditions have been outlined (chapter 7); it remains here to summarize the essential points of Śaiva theology. As we have seen, there is a dualistic Śaiva Siddhānta which developed in the north and then in the south where it incorporated Tamil *bhakti*, and a monistic school known as Kashmir Śaivism, though this tradition also existed in the south. The dualists maintain that the Lord (*pati*) is distinct from the soul (*paśu*) and world (*paśa*), whereas the monists proclaim self, world and Lord to be essentially one reality: consciousness purified of content. The ontological status of the self became the central focus of theological debate – dualists such as Sadyojoti (eighth century CE), Bhojadeva (eleventh century) and Aghoraśiva (twelfth century) arguing, in their commentaries on tantric texts such as the *Mṛgendrāgama* and in independent treatises (most notably Sadyojoti's *Naranareśvaraprakāśa* and Bhojadeva's *Tattvaprakāśa*), that the self is distinct from Śiva, but is ultimately equal with him (*Śivatulya*). The theologians of the monistic school, called the Recognition school or Pratyabhijñā – most notably Somānanda (*c.* 900–50), Utpala (*c.* 925–75), Abhinavagupta (*c.* 975–1025) and Kṣemarāja (*c.* 1000–50) – argued that the self, characterized by consciousness, is identical with Śiva who is the being whose consciousness is total.

With the Pratyabhijñā tradition, two conceptually distinct metaphysical positions are maintained simultaneously. On the one hand is a pure monism which holds that the one, defined as pure consciousness, is real and the many is false. In this view there can be no distinctions in ultimate reality and so no impurity: the self has to wake up to the realization of its identity with pure consciousness. Kṣemarāja says that, because of the ontological identity of consciousness and its object, there is nothing which is impure (*aśuci*). On the other hand the Pratyabhijñā maintains a cosmological doctrine of emanation, that the cosmos emanates from the one. Another way of saying this is that consciousness manifests itself through its vibration (*spanda*) as subjects and objects of knowledge in a hierarchical sequence: the purer forms being at the 'top' of the hierarchy, the forms polluted by the impurities of action (*karma-mala*), illusion (*māyīya-mala*) and egoity or individuality (*āṇava-mala*) being at the bottom.[40] The Pratyabhijñā, particularly the work of Abhinavagupta, also develops a theological aesthetics in which different aesthetic emotions (*rasa*) are seen as akin to religious emotions and the ultimate aesthetic experience of tranquillity (*śāntarasa*) is identified with the religious or mystical experience of union with Śiva.[41]

Modern developments

While the flowering of Hindu theology – the period during which the most influential theologians flourished – is over, issues within traditional Hindu theology and philosophy have continued to be debated into the modern period. Commentaries and independent treatises within the *darśanas*, upon sacred scriptures and their commentaries, continue to be composed. The Sāṃkhya, Advaita, Grammarian and Nyāya traditions are not simply the subjects of scholarly study, but are living intellectual traditions, outside the secular university system.

Although Hindu theology and philosophy continues in a fairly traditional way, since colonialism the Hindu systems have been exposed to outside influences, and dialogue between western and Indian philosophy has occurred. This dialogue has mainly confined itself to the English-speaking, and 'English-educated', Indian world, which has responded to Orientalism and attempted to show the equality (or even superiority) of Indian thought to western. Since the nineteenth century and the revitalizing work of Swami Vivekānanda, the intellectual climate within Indian university departments of philosophy has been that of Advaita Vedānta, and there has been keen interest in western metaphysics which can be assimilated to Advaita. Although European phenomenology and existentialism have had a strong influence on the work of twentieth-century Indian philosophers such as K. C. Bhattacharya and J. L. Mehta, respectively, analytical philosophy, as taught in British and American universities, has also had an important impact.[42] One of India's most erudite scholars to engage with western and Indian philosophy is the one-time president of India, Sarvapalli Radhakrishnan. In his numerous books, such as *Eastern Religions and Western Thought* – a grand survey of western and Indian ideas – he seeks to reconcile western rationalism with Hinduism, presenting Hinduism as an essentially rationalistic and humanistic religious experience.[43] This approach ignores the Hindu traditions of region and village – the pragmatic Hinduism of everyday ritual – or relegates such religious expressions to an 'irrational' past. However, the emphasizing of Hinduism as a rational discourse which is also in touch with the 'spirit' has been highly relevant and important in forming contemporary Hindu identity. It is to the formation of this contemporary sense of identity and some of its nationalistic expressions that we turn next.

Summary

In this survey of Hindu theological and philosophical traditions we have seen how wide-ranging they are. Although Advaita Vedānta has become extremely popular as the philosophy of Hinduism *par excellence*, there is nevertheless a variety of irreducible metaphysical positions and a long history of rigorous philosophical debate. The rigorous nature of philosophical argument – within the given parameters of revelation, the rhetoric of liberation, and assumptions about the nature of knowledge – has not been part of the West's recent perception of Hinduism. This has been partly due to the romantic construction of India as 'mystical', and partly due to the erosion of these traditions in the pre-colonial and colonial periods. There is no single orthodox Hindu view with regard to theology, but Hindu theological/philosophical traditions have shared a common terminology and concern about common issues. Two areas which have been important in Indian metaphysics have been highlighted. The first concerns language, the nature of revelation, and the relation between language and being, and the second concerns ontology, the relation of the one to the many. The concern with language has stemmed partly from Sanskrit, the language of the gods (*devavāṇī*), being perceived as sacred. The concern with ontology has stemmed from reconciling the plurality of experience with the 'one' absolute revealed by revelation and experienced in yoga. These issues are still alive in Hindu philosophical debate, though now widened to incorporate traditional concerns of western philosophy.

11 Hinduism and the modern world

The decline of the Mughal empire by 1720 left a power struggle in India, which resulted in British supremacy following Clive's defeat of the Nawab of Bengal at the battle of Plasey in 1757. By the middle of the nineteenth century British power was at its height. Hindu traditions, which in the eighteenth century had been introverted and unresponsive to external events and ideas, began to respond to the British, and particularly Christian, presence. Hindu reform movements developed which attempted to restore the perceived greatness of Hinduiṣm's ancient past, to adopt rationalist elements from within Christianity, and to pay particular attention to social and ethical concerns. These Hindu reforms, instigated by a number of significant figures, particularly Rām Mohan Roy, are referred to as the 'Hindu Renaissance: a religious and political movement which is closely related to a burgeoning Indian nationalism. This nationalism eventually resulted in the ousting of the British and the establishing of India as a secular state in 1948, and has found expression more recently in Hindu nationalist movements and political parties.

Hinduism as a global religion with a distinct identity has arisen since the nineteenth century, due in large part to the reformers. The Hinduism which they have promoted is the kind which is best known in the West, largely due to its use of English as a medium of communication, its adoption of Christian elements and its outward-looking perspective. Even though Hindu revivalism is strongly informed by a brahmanical culture, it is least representative of Hindu traditions which have been passed through the generations from pre-colonial days, whose language is not English, but Sanskrit and the Indian vernaculars. These traditions include the brahmanical systems of theology and Sanskrit learning and popular or regional ritual and narrative systems, centred around local and regional temples. While Hindu revivalism is of vital importance in the development of Hinduism as a world religion, the influence of these traditions of Sanskrit learning and popular ritual upon it has been minimal; the Hindu renaissance has had a tendency to play down the differences between theological traditions and to relegate ritual to a 'popular' level, below the ethical spirituality of the Upaniṣads and the *Gītā*.

The Hindu Renaissance is characterized by the following features:

- an emphasis on reason to establish the truth of the Veda;
- the rejection of icon worship, regarded as idolatry;
- the rejection of caste (or some elements of it), child-marriage and the practice of widow-burning (*satī*);
- the construction of Hinduism as an ethical spirituality, equal, or superior, to Christianity and Islam.

Many of the Hindu reformers wrote in English and attracted the interest of the English-speaking world. Other reformers, such as Nārāyaṇa Guru in Kerala, who fought for the rights of the untouchable caste of Tikkas, communicated in Malayalam and so had a restricted audience. The most significant figure in this awakening of a new Hindu awareness at the beginning of the nineteenth century was Rām Mohan Roy, sometimes called the father of modern India.

Rām Mohan Roy

Rām Mohan Roy (1772–1833) came from a traditional Bengali Brahman family – his father was a Bengali Vaiṣṇava, his mother a Śākta – and he was educated at the Muslim University at Patna, where he studied Arabic and Persian philosophical literature. This Muslim, and particularly Sufi, influence engendered in Roy a strong dislike of image worship. He also studied Sanskrit in Varanasi, as well as English, and even studied Hebrew and Greek with a view to translating the Bible into Bengali. After his extensive education, he entered the employment of the East India Company in Calcutta. The growth of the British empire in India would not have been possible without the East India Company, which developed vast trading networks, centred in Bengal, and set up educational establishments for training young Indian men to work for the administration under British rule. It is in the context of these establishments that the seeds of a later nationalism and Hindu revivalism are found. Roy developed his ideas while employed by the East India Company, but left the company in 1814, having become wealthy, to devote himself full-time to religious and social reform. To further his ideas he founded a society, the Brahmo Samāj, dedicated to the reform of Hinduism. He died in Bristol after contracting an illness whilst on a visit to Britain.[1]

The essential belief of Roy is that God is a transcendent, immutable being who is the creator of the cosmos, but who cannot be known in his essence which is ineffable. All religions agree about this and differ only in inessentials; Roy therefore advocates a tolerant position – often associated with Hinduism as a whole – which maintains that all religions are essentially one. This God can be known through reason and the observation of the natural world or cosmos, the effect of God. God, for Roy, is a God of nature worshipped through reason. The main philosophical influences on Roy come from both East and West: from the Upaniṣads and the theology of Śaṅkara, from Islamic, especially Sufi, theology, and from Unitarianism and Deism. Indeed the ethical religion arrived at through reason which Roy advocates is strongly reminiscent of the eighteenth-century English Deists: God and his moral laws can be known through reason and the observation of nature. Roy's central vision is to restore and purify Hinduism by returning to the teachings of the Upaniṣads and the *Brahma Sūtra*, which he sees as embodying a timeless wisdom, opposed to 'idol worship' and the ethical degeneracy into which he thinks Hinduism had fallen. In order to improve the political as well as moral standing of Hindus, it is necessary, thinks Roy, for them to give up icon worship, the proliferation of ritual systems, and to abandon immoral practices such as child-marriage and widow-burning (*satī*). Roy vehemently condemned this practice in which the widow would often be tied down on the pyre, whether she had voluntarily agreed or not. This he had witnessed as a youth when a sister-in-law was subjected to being burned alive in this way – an incident which left a deep impression on the young man. In a number of letters and petitions presented to the House of Commons in London, he advocated the banning of *satī*, or 'suttee' as the British called it, a practice which was made illegal by the British government in 1829, partly due to Roy's pressure.

Reason and ethics are central concepts for Roy. Because of reason, the doctrine of karma and reincarnation should be rejected, but also because of reason the theology surrounding Jesus, such as the doctrine of atonement and the trinity, should also be rejected as irrational. Reason, rather than revelation, leads to the discovery of universal ethical codes, whereas dogmas lead to irrationality and unethical behaviour. The adoption of a purified, rational and ethical religion – the essential qualities of Hinduism according to Roy – would be the transformation of Indian society.

The Brahmo Samāj

In order to promote his ideas of restoring Hinduism to the rational, ethical religion it once was (as he perceived it), Roy founded a movement in 1828 called the Brahmo Samāj.[2] This movement or society was modelled on Christian reform movements and met regularly for religious services. During these services passages would be read from the Upanisads, sermons delivered and hymns sung, some of which were composed by Roy himself. The Brahmo Samāj held regular meetings in Calcutta and the Trust Deed of the Brahmo Samāj, signed by Roy and seven associates, states the purposes of a building set aside for worship as being to provide 'a place of public meeting of all sorts and descriptions of people without distinction as shall behave and conduct themselves in an orderly and sober religious and devout manner for the worship and adoration of the Eternal Unsearchable and Immutable Being who is the Author and Preserver of the Universe'.[3]

After his death, the two leaders of the society who continued Roy's message of social reform were Debendranath Tagore (1817–1905), the father of the famous poet Rabindranath Tagore, and Keshab Chandra Sen (1838–84). Tagore, like Roy, was against the all-pervasive tantric and puranic forms of ritual and image worship, which he saw as idolatry. Only the impersonal absolute of the Upaniṣads should be the focus of religious devotion. Sen, his younger, aggressively enthusiastic contemporary, profoundly influenced by Christianity, generally agreed. However, because of Sen a split occurred in the movement. The young enthusiast Sen, and his followers, abandoned the wearing of the sacred thread, arguing for social equality even between Brahman and Śūdra. This was too much for the more conservative members of the society who followed Tagore in retaining it. The majority sided with Sen, but further splits in the movement weakened the power of its influence.

While the Brahmo Samāj appealed to lower-class Brahmans and the emerging, urban middle classes of merchants and traders, it had little appeal at a popular, village level where ritual and devotion to deity icons is the main focus of religion. Indeed, Roy, a highly educated intellectual, did not really understand the deep devotion to deities of the rural poor. Nor did the ideas of the Brahmo Samāj have much appeal to highly orthoprax Brahmans whose main concern is the maintenance of ritual purity. Nevertheless, with the Brahmo Samāj, we have the beginnings of a sense of a Hindu national identity, albeit of a highly 'deistic' and abstract kind, which is developed much further and more aggressively by another society, the Ārya Samāj, founded by Dayānanda Sarasvatī.

Dayānanda Sarasvatī and the Ārya Samāj

Dayānanda Sarasvatī (1824–83) was born in Gujarat to a Śaiva Brahman family. At ten he was initiated by his father into a cult of the Śiva *liṅga*. However, Dayānanda lost his faith in the Śaiva religion of image worship during an all-night vigil. Seated with his father in a Śāiva temple during the festival of *Navarātri*, he saw mice climbing over the temple icon, eating the food which had been offered to the deity and so defiling it. If the icon were a powerful deity, reasoned Dayānanda, it surely would not allow such sacrilege. His father's explanations about the nature of symbolism, that the icon in the temple, once consecrated, is a representation and embodiment of a higher power, did not allay Dayānanda's scepticism and he became a renouncer to seek the truth of Hinduism beyond 'superstition' – also thereby avoiding the marriage arrangements being made by his parents. He wandered as an itinerant holy man, having taken the personal name Dayānanda and the name of the renunciate order Sarasvatī, on a personal religious quest to find truth. At Mathura he met an old blind guru, Virjānanda Sarasvatī, who predicted that he would restore Hinduism to its vedic glory. Dayānanda then abandoned his quest for personal liberation and became a reformer and preacher, intent upon the transformation of Hinduism. He argued that the Veda is revelation and that Hindu 'superstitions' should be abandoned along with reverence for other scriptures such as the Epics and Purāṇas. He did, however, accept the teachings of the Dharma Śāstras, such as the 'Laws of Manu', which reveal the formless and omnipresent God which Dayānanda believed in. In 1875 he founded a society in Bombay, the Ārya Samāj (the 'Noble' or 'Aryan' Society), to promote his Hindu reformation.

Like Roy who influenced him, Dayānanda advocated a return to a purer form of vedic religion whose focus is an eternal, omnipotent, impersonal God. He wanted to return to the eternal law or *sanātana dharma*, which Hindus had moved away from by worshipping icons and incarnations, by going on pilgrimages, and by revering the stories and doctrines of the Epics and Purāṇas. All these things are not found in the four Vedas, Dayānanda maintained. The other scriptures are later accretions which detract from the purity of the vedic message. His metaphysics were basic, more in line with Viśiṣṭādvaita teachings than with Advaita teachings: that liberation (*mokṣa*) is not a merging of the soul into God, but a freedom from suffering in which the soul retains its distinct identity. However, more significant than his metaphysics are his social teachings about caste, education, language and the reformation of Hinduism into an aggressive, political force against Christianity and Islam. It was the reforming aspects of the Ārya Samāj, and its counter-offensive against attacks on Hinduism by Christianity, which attracted the merchant classes who made up its membership, as well as overseas Hindus in South Africa and Fiji.

Dayānanda does not condemn the caste system but reinterprets it to mean that class (*varṇa*) refers to individual differences in character, qualifications and accomplishments. Were class to be determined by personal proclivity and merit, then, he reasoned, the higher classes would maintain high standards for fear of their children becoming lower-class, and lower classes would exert themselves to join the classes above them.[4] Dayānanda advocated radical social reforms, including marriage from choice rather than by arrangement and the eradication of child-marriage which would reduce the number of widows and so alleviate a large social problem. He also advocated the temporary legal alliance of widows and widowers, called a *niyoga* marriage, for companionship as well as the rearing of children. Education, he maintained, should be available to both sexes, for through education, particularly education in grammar, *dharma*, medicine and trades, Hindus would learn to be responsible, good Hindus. Dayānanda even claimed that all modern scientific discoveries are previewed in the Veda, a claim which is still maintained by many Hindus today.

The Ārya Samāj founded schools, the *gurukulas*, still in existence throughout India, which promulgated the cause of Hindu unity and vedic or Aryan culture. The teaching of Sanskrit, the symbol of India's great past, is significant in this programme, as well as the teaching of Hindi which Dayānanda advocated as the national language. There is a strong link between language and national identity and in promoting Sanskrit and Hindi the Ārya Samāj promoted a certain view of India which, while elevating Dayānanda's vision of Hinduism, occluded other elements and forces within Indian society, particularly Islam, Christianity, and Dravidian, notably Tamil, Hindu religions. Indeed, the Ārya Samāj has not been open to pluralist understandings of Hinduism, advocating, rather, an aggressive Hindu nationalism, based on a 'return' to the ancient Vedas and being critical of the tradition which has developed since then. While adopting many modern elements, the society has, in a way, rejected history in order to return to a perceived past of Hindu purity.

Highly successful in the Punjab, the Ārya Samāj reconverted to Hinduism many low-caste converts to Islam and Christianity, in a ceremony known as the 'purification' (*śuddhi*), which transformed Untouchables into twice-born Hindus. With its success in the Punjab, Dayānanda moved the society's headquarters to Lahore, now in Pakistan, and after his death the movement split into a conservative branch and a progressive branch who wanted a 'progressive education' and the abandonment of brahmanical dietary restrictions. The Ārya Samāj has been a powerful voice in the development of Hindu nationalist politics, but intolerant of other faiths and views. While the influence of the Ārya Samāj can be seen in contemporary Indian politics and cultural life, another force within Hinduism, of tolerance and accommodation, is also found, stemming in the modern world from the Bengali saint Rāmakrishna and his devoted disciple and interpreter, Vivekānanda.

Rāmakrishna and Vivekānanda

Paramahamsa Rāmakrishna (1836–86) was a Hindu mystic who declared the unity of all religions. He was born to a Vaiṣṇava Brahman family in Bengal and became a priest of the Kālī temple at Dakṣineśvar, a few miles north of Calcutta. He became ecstatically devoted to Kālī, the Mother, and displayed great longing for her, weeping and pleading with her to reveal herself to him. People began to think that he was mad and his family married him off in the hope that a family life would eventually calm him down. He was married in his home village to a five-year-old girl, and returned to Calcutta where she would join him once she had grown up. Back at the temple, Rāmakrishna's love and devotion to Kālī increased and he eventually lost outward sensations and perceived an inner vision of the Goddess. These visions became more frequent and his trance-like states grew longer in duration until it became impossible for him to carry out the daily services and priestly functions at the temple. His nephew was appointed to carry on as functioning priest and Rāmakrishna was left to his devotions. At the age of seventeen, his wife walked the thirty miles to Dakṣineśvar to be with her husband. By that time he had become transformed through his religious practices and could not be a husband in a conventional sense. Rāmakrishna worshipped his wife as a manifestation of the Mother and she served him in the temple until his death.

Before his wife joined him, two significant teachers came to Rāmakrishna. The first was a learned Brahman woman, Bhairavī, a tantric initiate who taught Rāmakrishna to control energies within his body and to control passion. The second was a naked, wandering sādhu, Totapuri, who taught Rāmakrishna how to meditate and how to realize union with the absolute in the state of *nirvikalpa samādhi*, a high state of concentration in which there is no awareness of subject–object distinction.

After this experience of unity, he next realized the Vaiṣṇava ideal of love for God through devotion to Kṛṣṇa, as Rādhā is devoted, and experienced a vision of Kṛṣṇa. He had visions of other deities, including Jesus Christ, and practised the paths of other religions, including Christianity and Islam. Having practised and, according to Rāmakrishna, realized the goals of these religions, he concluded that all religions are true. All religions are different paths to the One, the eternal undivided being which is absolute knowledge and bliss. Different religions cannot express the totality of this One, but each manifests an aspect of it. Both Kālī and *brahman* are different aspects of the same reality.[5]

During his lifetime Rāmakrishna attracted a number of middle-class intellectual Hindus who would come to hear and be with the saint in Dakṣineśvar. Among them was a young man, Narendranath ('Naren') Datta, a member of the Brahmo Samāj, strongly influenced by western science and rationalism. He had a profound religious experience with Rāmakrishna when the master put his feet upon Naren's chest and he fell into a deep trance. He abandoned his career in law to become a devoted disciple of Rāmakrishna and eventually became a world-renouncer, taking on the name Vivekānanda.

Swami Vivekānanda (1863–1902) is a figure of great importance in the development of a modern Hindu self-understanding and in formulating the West's view of Hinduism. As a renouncer he wandered the length and breadth of India, meditating for a time on a rock off Cape Comorin at the tip of India, where a temple now stands. Here he achieved the state of *samādhi* which Rāmakrishna had attained, and resolved to bring his vision of Hinduism to the world. His philosophy is the vedantic idea that the divine, the absolute, exists within all beings regardless of social status. Human beings can achieve union with this innate divinity (as Rāmakrishna had done) and seeing the divine as the essence of others will promote love and social harmony. Vivekānanda went to the World Parliament of Religions held at Chicago in 1893 where he made an immense impact and is now, perhaps, the most remembered figure at that occasion. Here he preached a doctrine of the unity of all religions and tolerance: that there should be recognition of diversity and that there is value in diversity, furthermore, that India did not need missionaries to convert its people to Christianity, nor churches, but material support to stop starvation. Vivekānanda is partly to blame for the commonly held belief that the East is spiritual while the West is materialistic. He was convinced of the spiritual superiority of the East, while acknowledging the material, technological and scientific superiority of the West. This dichotomy has tended to reinforce the image of India as the West's 'other'; the reality being more complex as both cultures contain strong 'spiritual' and 'material' features.

Vivekānanda stayed in the West to promote his ideas and founded the Vedānta Society in New York in 1895. Indeed, Vivekānanda might be seen as the first effective proponent of Hinduism as a world religion. Upon returning to India in 1895 he founded the Rāmakrishna Mission, a monastic order which differs from traditional Hindu orders in promoting education and social reform, and in helping the sick. The mission lays great importance on this aspect of its work which it regards as *karma yoga*, the yoga of action or good works, and there are colleges, high schools and hospitals run by the Rāmakrishna Mission throughout India. The order disseminates Vivekānanda's vision of Hindu modernism as Neo-Vedānta: that there is an essential unity to Hinduism underlying the diversity of its many forms. Whereas Christianity accepts only itself as the truth, claimed Vivekānanda, Hinduism is pluralistic and accepts all religions as aspects of the one truth. This message had great popularity among India's emergent, English-educated, middle classes, along with Vivekānanda's stress on Hinduism as a 'scientific' religion, something of which Indians should be proud rather than apologetic. While this view of Hinduism tends to override the differences within Hindu traditions (let alone between world religions), and has been criticized as leading to a kind of woolly thinking very different from the intellectual thoroughness of the theological traditions,[6] it nevertheless provides a strong ideology to link into Indian nationalism on the one hand, and the construction of Hinduism as a world religion on the other. Vivekānanda might be regarded as the first to clearly articulate the idea of Hinduism as a world religion, taking its place alongside Christianity, Islam, Judaism and Buddhism.[7] The vision of Hinduism promoted by Vivekānanda is one generally accepted by most English-speaking middle-class Hindus today. Vivekānanda's Neo-Vedānta and his ideas of social change feed into the ideas of another reformer who was to change the face of Indian politics and public life, Mohandās Karmachand Gandhi.

Gandhi

Gandhi (1869–1948) was born in Gujarat into a family of the Bania (a merchant) caste who were devout Vaiṣṇavas. His religious context was therefore *bhakti* with Islamic as well as Jain influence. Gandhi studied law in London where he communicated with Tolstoy and met with Theosophy, a European movement which sought spiritual wisdom in the East. Indeed, it was with a couple of Theosophists that Gandhi read Edwin Arnold's translation of the *Bhagavad Gītā* which deeply affected him. He also advocated vegetarianism and supported the British Vegetarian Society. He returned to Bombay to practise law, but in 1893 took a job defending a Muslim merchant in Durban, South Africa. There is a famous story of how Gandhi, who was travelling in a first-class compartment of a train with a first-class ticket, was forcibly ejected due to South Africa's apartheid policies at the time. This experience left a deep impression on him and reinforced his commitment to freeing people from oppression however he could. He founded the Natal Indian Congress to try to alleviate the conditions of Indians in the Natal state.

After twenty-one years in South Africa, working out his political philosophy of non-violence and passive resistance to realize social change, he returned to India in 1915 where he joined the nationalist movement and worked for Indian independence through peaceful means. He founded a hermitage, the Satyagraha Ashram, just outside of Ahmedabad, where he occupied a spartan cell. Here his community promoted cottage industries such as spinning. He organized passive resistance to the British, including a march to the sea against the Salt Tax where Gandhi and his followers symbolically picked up grains of salt from the shore. This action flouted the Salt Law and, along with a further protest at the Dharasana Salt Works, resulted in thousands of arrests, including that of Gandhi himself.

Gandhi's fundamental idea is that Truth (*satya*), God, who is the supreme being (*sat*), and self (*ātman*) are one in essence. The ideal and pursuit of Truth are central themes in Gandhi's writing and in his political and social work. Indeed, he subtitled his autobiography *The Story of My Experiments with Truth*.[8] Because all are united in an essential oneness, there should be harmony and non-violence (*ahiṃsā*) between people. Non-violence is the central idea for which Gandhi is remembered, and which he applied to great effect in political situations, though curiously it is an ideal which is not found in his favourite text, the *Bhagavad Gītā*. Non-violence is a manifestation of the Truth, or God, and so his method of passive resistance, applied so effectively against the British, Gandhi called 'holding fast to the truth' or *satyāgraha*.

Satyāgraha became a word used by Gandhi to denote his movement for Indian nationhood, a force, he said, 'born of Truth and Love or Non-violence'.[9] *Satyāgraha* would lead to the welfare of all (*sarvodaya*). It is the practical expression of a higher reality: a moral code and a self-discipline which requires the control of the senses, especially the control of sexuality; the control of anger and violence; and a dedication to the cause of justice and truth. Gandhi's followers were even called *satyāgrahis*, followers of *satyāgraha*, and he expected high standards from them including sexual renunciation. Chastity or *brahmacārya* was of central importance for Gandhi as a way to realize God and also to control the burgeoning population.

The welfare of all included the emancipation of the Untouchables, whom Gandhi called Harijans, the 'children of God'. Relegated to performing low-status work which would pollute the high castes, they had little political or economic power. The plight of the Untouchables could, thought Gandhi, only be alleviated by non-violence and holding fast to the truth. Their manumission by the high castes would not only be a freeing of the Untouchables from economic and social oppression, but would effect a transformation of the whole society. All Indians would benefit. Gandhi's abhorrence of untouchability was not an abhorrence of a society structured according to divisions determined by occupation, which Gandhi saw as the original, classical *varṇāśrama-dharma* of orthodox brahmanical Hinduism. Yet he wanted this structure to be transformed and the blight of untouchability eradicated. Partly due to Gandhi's influence, in post-independence India the idea of untouchability has been officially abolished and it is an offence to disadvantage a person in education or profession because of untouchability. Yet in practice the institution remains stubbornly intransigent, though there is a strong movement to alleviate the social conditions and raise the status of 'the children of God', who reject Gandhi's title as rather patronizing, preferring to be called 'Dalits', the 'Oppressed'. This movement has made some progress in raising the awareness of these groups and giving them a cohesive identity, even discovering a history of 'Dalit literature' and, in the form of a political party, the BSP, successfully battling in some states against the conservative Hindu political party, the BJP.

The Indian nationalist struggle, in which Gandhi became the leading voice in the Congress Party, resulted in Indian independence and the British withdrawal from India in 1947. To Gandhi's great distress, the partitioning of the Punjab to create Pakistan was accompanied by massacres of Hindus by Muslims and Muslims by Hindus. Sikhs too were victims of the slaughter. Gandhi tried to calm the situation by addressing groups of people and urging Hindus to respect Muslims. It was due to this tolerant attitude that he attracted the anger of militant nationalist Hindus, and Nathuram Godse, a member of the militant organization, the RSS, assassinated Gandhi at a Delhi prayer meeting in 1948. Yet Gandhi's legacy has lived on in India and he is widely revered as a saint.

With Gandhi we see one way in which Hinduism and modern nationalism mix together. Gandhi's Hinduism is a religion of strong ethical commitment to social justice and truth which he identifies with God. His non-violence is informed by the non-violence of Jainism and the renouncer tradition and also by Christian passivism. He is influenced by the renouncer ideals of renunciation, particularly celibacy which in the Hindu view bestows great spiritual power. Yet Gandhi displays little interest in ritual or Hindu mythology except in so far as they have bearing on ethical issues he was concerned about. Indeed, Gandhi fought for the rights of Untouchables to enter Hindu temples. Gandhi's is an ethical Hinduism, one in which ritual and deities are subordinated to a vision of tolerance, peace and truth. In Gandhi's thought, and in the Hindu revivalism of the last two centuries generally, there is little concern for the aesthetic and sensual aspects of Hindu culture – Gandhi has even been referred to as a puritan[10] – but it is the Renaissance Hinduism, of which Gandhi is a part, which has found articulate expression in the modern world.

Hindu political nationalism

The man who assassinated Gandhi was a member of an extreme nationalist organization, the RSS. In contrast to the committed secularism of the Congress Party, in the face of the religious and cultural pluralism of India, a number of right-wing Hindu nationalist groups have developed, wishing to promote India as a Hindu, rather than a secular, state. This Hindu nationalism must be seen in the context of an India which has been subjected throughout history to foreign invasion and, at the present time, the 'invasion' of western ideas and material goods. There is a certain nostalgia for India's great past and a desire for the order and the clear traditional values of the *varṇāśrama-dharma.* There is a construction of a Hindu identity, which is very modern in being closely associated with the idea of the nation-state, and which projects this identity into the past. This identity is constructed in apposition to the foreign 'other', particularly Indian Muslims and, to a lesser extent, Christians, and in opposition to modernization and a western secularist ideology. These nationalist tendencies and movements have given moral sanction to violence in the perceived struggle for Hindu rights.

The Ārya Samāj was an advocate of a nationalism informed by the idea of Hindu *dharma* and more extreme nationalist groups have emerged from this. In 1909 the first vice-chancellor of Benares Hindu University, Pandit Mohan Malaviya, who was a member of the Ārya Samāj, founded the Hindū Mahā-Sabhā, a right-wing Hindu political party who set themselves against the Congress Party and the Muslim League in the days before independence, though the party has failed to make much of a mark in the post-independence years. The party's most vociferous leader was Vinayak Damodar Savarkar who made a distinction between 'Hindu Dharma', the religion of the various traditions, and 'Hindutva', the socio-political force to unite all Hindus against foreign influences. The idea of 'Hindutva' ('Hinduness' or 'Hindudom') has also been taken up by more recent Hindu political groups. The Hindū Mahā-Sabhā promotes the idea of India as 'Hindustan' and the rights of Hindus to legislate and govern themselves in accordance with Hindu ideology.[11]

THE RSS

One of the members of the Hindū Mahā-Sabhā, K. V. Hedgewar (1890–1940), founded, in 1925, the highly influential Rāṣṭriya Svayam-

Sevak Saṅgh or RSS, an organization which continues to this day.[12] This is not a political party as such, but a powerful cultural organization to promote the interests of Hindus against those of Muslims, Christians and Communists. By remaining as a cultural organization and not as a political party, the RSS has wielded considerable influence upon India's political and cultural life, sponsoring Hindu institutions such as temples and schools. RSS members dress in black and can be seen training in military fashion throughout India in the early mornings. A related organization, the Viśva Hindu Pariṣad (VHP) founded in 1964, has similar aims to the RSS and draws on the same sources of support. These organizations have had particular appeal to lower-middle-class male youths, providing them with a strong sense of identity and an outlet for their nationalist aspirations. One of the RSS aims has been to provide a context in which Hindus can be nationalized and nationalists Hinduized.[13]

The fact that the RSS is not a political party means that its members are free to join other political parties and influence them from within. Indeed there have been divisions in the Congress Party between liberal secularists and Hindu traditionalists, some of whom have been RSS members. The organization was banned for about a year by Nehru, but this was lifted and the organization continues unabated. Much of the communal violence in India's recent history has been carried out by RSS members and the RSS has been extremely influential in awakening Hindu political aspirations and the idea of a Hindu nation.

THE BJP

The most important Hindu nationalist political party is the BJP. This is a development of the Jana Saṅgh, a party founded in 1951 by Shyama Prasad Mookerjee, to give voice to Hindu nationalism and to oppose the Congress Party. During the 1950s and 1960s the Jana Saṅgh tried to replace Congress as the main party in the Hindi-speaking north, stressing policies such as the introduction of Hindi as the national language, a ban on the slaughter of cows, and the recognition of the state of Israel: policies which are implicitly anti-Muslim. The party failed, however, in its efforts to replace the Congress Party. The Jana Saṅgh joined a coalition of other anti-Congress groups to form the Janata Party – formally dissolving the Jana Saṅgh – which defeated Mrs Gandhi and the Congress Party in the election of 1977, having been suppressed by her government during the emergency regime (1975–7). However, internal squabbles prevented effective government and Mrs Gandhi was returned to office in 1980. After this defeat the Janata Party fragmented and in April 1980 the Bharatiya Janata Party or BJP was formed.[14] The BJP is a Hindu nationalist party which wishes to uphold the rights of Hindus and establish in India a Hindu value system, as opposed to the secularist values derived from the West and supported by the Congress Party. The BJP has attracted wide support, particularly from India's educated classes both in the north and south, and, while maintaining the values of *varṇāśrama-dharma*, has campaigned on a platform of standing up for all Hindus and correcting social injustices. While communal violence is often associated with the BJP, it should be remembered that not all BJP members and supporters approve of violence as a tool to gain political ends.

REGIONAL NATIONALISMS

While the RSS and the BJP have pan-Hindu appeal, there are other Hindu nationalist groups particular to a region. Among these, the Shiv Sena ('the army of Śiva') movement founded in 1966 in Bombay by Bal Thakkeray is especially important. The Shiv Sena's intention is to protect the rights of Maharastrian Hindus and to rid Maharashtra of 'foreign influences', by which it means Muslims and, to a lesser extent, Christians. The movement is responsible for communal rioting against Muslims in Bombay, following the demolition of the mosque Babri Masjid in Ayodhya in 1992. Indeed the Muslim community's property has been looted and burned, and many lives have been taken, by the Shiv Sena.[15] There have been reactions by the Muslim and Christian communities to the Shiv Sena with the formation of Muslim and Christian Senas, though these have been ineffective in protecting the communities they are said to represent.

THE PROBLEM OF COMMUNALISM

The most significant act of communal violence to have occurred in the recent history of India took place in 1992. In 1991 the BJP attracted attention by going on a 'pilgrimage' through India to collect bricks to build a temple to Rāma at Ayodhya. On 6 December 1992, the Babri Masjid, a mosque erected in Ayodhya in 1528 by Babur, was demolished by an estimated 100,000 volunteers or *kar sevaks*, assembled there at the call of the RSS, VHP and BJP, though the parliamentary leader of the BJP, L. K. Advani, commented that the mosque's destruction was 'unfortunate'.[16] One of the motives behind the destruction was the belief that Rāma, the incarnation of Viṣṇu, had been born on the exact spot where the mosque stood. The demolition was accompanied by the looting and destruction of Muslim homes, the destruction of other mosques, and the brutal rape and murder of Muslims in Ayodhya. Communal riots in other parts of India followed the Ayodhya incident, as well as reactive Muslim violence against Hindus in other countries such as Bangladesh. The rationale behind the highly organized campaign of violence at Ayodhya has been that, in the past, Muslim rulers destroyed Hindu temples, thereby damaging Hindu pride, so the destruction of the Babri Masjid is justified.[17]

There are no clear explanations of Hindu communal violence. No doubt deeply rooted historical antagonisms are part of the cause; the sense of a religious identity with clearly demarcated boundaries, and the idea of 'collective effervescence' put forward by the sociologist Emile Durkheim are probably contributory factors as well.[18] Communal violence, associated with literal or fundamentalist understandings of a religious narrative, are an all-too-common feature of the modern world and not confined to India. The problem of communalism is not solely an Indian one, but is particularly poignant in the contemporary Indian context. The belligerent nature of conservative Hindu movements such as the Shiv Sena is in complete contrast to Gandhi's voice of tolerance and non-violence, but the factious voices of these groups are not easily appeased.

Global Hinduism

In contrast to the narrow nationalism of groups such as the RSS, there are also tendencies within Hinduism towards universalization or globalization. Global Hinduism is the kind of Hinduism which has wide appeal and which is becoming a world religion alongside Christianity, Islam and Buddhism, both for the Hindu diaspora communities and for Westerners seeking their sense of belonging in non-western cultures and religions. This kind of Hinduism lays emphasis on what it regards as universal spiritual values such as social justice, peace and the spiritual transformation of humanity. Global Hinduism is the kind of religion given expression by Vivekānanda and Gandhi, which has a sense of India as its point of reference, but which has transcended national boundaries. This kind of religion maintains that Hinduism contains the oldest revelation available to humanity, the Veda; believes in a transcendent God without attributes who is nevertheless manifested in the innumerable forms of the Hindu gods and holy persons; believes in reincarnation; overrides differences between traditions; and tends to avoid the issue of caste or reinterprets it, along the lines of Gandhi, so that caste is simply a way of organizing society according to profession. The philosophy here is predominantly the Neo-Vedānta of Swami Vivekānanda, though other voices, the theistic Hare Kṛṣṇa movement and even Śaiva Siddhānta, have contributed to it. This kind of global Hinduism appeals to more educated, English-speaking, urban Hindus, many of whom live outside India.

THE HINDU DIASPORA

While Hinduism is intimately linked to the sacred land of India, its cultural influence spread in the medieval period to south-east Asia and beyond as far as Java and Bali. Kings of south-east Asia modelled themselves on Hindu kings, Sanskrit was a sacred language and Brahmans performed rituals in courts.

From the last century, Hinduism has spread to other parts of the world through a process of migration. This more recent Hindu diaspora, due to the British exporting labour for plantations and other work such as building railways, has placed Hindus in all continents: in South and East Africa, the Pacific islands, South America, the West Indies, North America, Europe and Australia.

Indian immigration into the USA increased dramatically after 1965 when quotas limiting immigration were removed from the Immigration Act. These Hindu communities have continued to practise their religious faith and to convert old churches and schools into temples or build new temples by subscription in more affluent communities. In Britain, Hinduism has developed with the arrival of East African Hindus in 1965 and communities which have arisen as a consequence of direct immigration from India, particularly Gujarat. Of the 300,000 Hindus in Britain today, 70% are Gujarati by ethnicity, 15% Punjabi, and 15% from the rest of India.[19] The Hindu communities in Britain are not homogenous. The Gujarati and Punjabi Hindus, for example, as Kim Knott has observed, 'speak different languages, eat different kinds of foods, and dress differently'.[20] These Hindu communities worship predominantly in their homes, but also in temples to various deities including Kṛṣṇa, Rāma, Durgā and Gaṇeśa, especially during festivals.

The Hinduism of the diaspora has moved away from the strict *varṇāśrama-dharma* system towards the kind of universalism propounded by the Hindu reformers such as Vivekānanda and Gandhi. The

Indian cultural centre, the Bharatiya Vidya Bhavan in London, is an example of a centre dedicated to the dissemination of Indian culture, inspired by the universalist Hindu ideals of Gandhi. Yet there are nevertheless some nationalist tendencies within diaspora communities, and attitudes to caste show little sign of being eroded – something which is demonstrated by the rarity of inter-caste marriages.[21]

THE WOMEN'S MOVEMENT

Global Hinduism, inspired by the teachings of the Hindu reformers, is developing. In this Global Hinduism women's voices are beginning to be heard. The Indian women's movement has been influenced by that of the West and its reactions to Hinduism follow the western feminist reactions to Christianity: some believe it to be inherently patriarchal, while others believe that patriarchy can be separated from the spiritual values of the religion. In traditional Hinduism, as we have seen, women's nature was thought to be different to that of men, being passive, nurturing and giving. In the contemporary Indian women's movement, expressed, for example, in the magazine *Manushi*, there is an attitude that women and men are equal and that statements about 'women's nature' and duty subordinate and oppress women.[22] It is within Global Hinduism that attitudes to women can be more easily changed than within the classical model of *varṇāśrama-dharma*.

THE 'PIZZA-EFFECT'

Global Hinduism has developed during the present century partly due to re-enculturation: what Agehananda Bharati, somewhat playfully, has called the 'pizza-effect'. The original pizza was a hot baked bread which was exported to America from Italy, embellished, and returned to Italy where it became a national dish. Similarly, elements of Hindu culture, such as yoga, *bhakti*, gurus, some Hindu teachings, dance and music, have been exported to the West, due largely to the Hindu Renaissance, where they have gained great popularity and then gained popularity among urban Hindus in India as a consequence.[23] The globalization of Hinduism has been due initially to Swami Vivekānanda's work, his founding of Vedānta societies and the Rāmakrishna Mission, and to the work of his disciples and other Hindus strongly influenced by his message of universalism and tolerance. However, many other teachers have followed in his wake, bringing to the West teachings which have become an important cultural force in western societies, and which in turn have become an important cultural force in India, their place of origin.

Hinduism in the West

The interaction between Hinduism and western culture arose due to western contacts with India and the colonial process. Vasco da Gama opened a seaway to India in around 1500 and the spice trade developed as well as the settling on the western seaboard of Catholic missionaries, who were the first to be genuinely interested in Hindu traditions, if only for the purposes of conversion. The missionaries learned the languages of the people they wished to convert. Of particular note was Roberto de Nobili (1577–1656) who tried to understand the Hindu worldview, trying to find in Hindu scriptures a 'non-idolatrous sense of God', in order to convert India to Christianity. In the eighteenth century French missionaries collaborated with Hindu pandits on textual research, and a French Jesuit, J. F. Pons, produced a Sanskrit grammar in Latin in around 1733. This was the beginning of Indology and the 'scientific' interest of the West in India.

Towards the end of the eighteenth century British 'Orientalists', centred in Bengal, began the systematic study of Sanskrit and Sanskrit literature. Among these , Sir William Jones (1746–94), C. Wilkins (1749–1836) and Thomas Colebrooke (1765–1837) were the pioneers whose work led to the establishment of the discipline of Indology, which concentrated on the philological study of Sanskrit texts. The discipline developed through the nineteenth century, the philosopher Friedrich Schlegel becoming the first professor of Sanskrit at Bonn in 1818. H. H. Wilson became the first Boden Professor of Sanskrit at Oxford (professor from 1832 to 1860), followed by Monier Monier-Williams (professor from 1860 to 1888) whose Sanskrit dictionary is still widely used, though based on the massive German scholarship of the seven-volume Sanskrit dictionary by R. Roth and Otto Bothlingk.[24] Freidrich Max Müller was a Sanskritist and pioneer of the comparative study of religion, editing the Sacred Books of the East series. In the United States, Indology was developed by a number of scholars at New York, Yale and Harvard. Of particular note are C. R. Lanman (1850–1941), whose Sanskrit reader is still used in universities,[25] William Dwight Whitney (1827–94), and Maurice Bloomfield (1885–1928), uncle of the famous linguist Leonard Bloomfield.[26] Some Christian theologians during the nineteenth century also took Hinduism seriously and the beginnings of interfaith dialogue can be seen here. One of the earliest of these was Rowland Williams of Lampeter who presented a sympathetic view of Hindu doctrines, though inevitably regarding Christianity as superior.[27] However, notwithstanding advances made by Indologists in the understanding of Sanskrit, Indian religions and Indian history, Indology has come under recent criticism for its colonial inheritance and its claims to 'objective' knowledge of texts; knowledge always being set within cultural presuppositions and boundaries.[28]

As well as to the missionaries and Indologists, Hindu ideas, especially what they regarded as pantheism, were of interest to western philosophers in the German Romantic tradition such as J. G. Herder (1744–1803), Friedrich Schlegel (1772–1829), and Hegel (1770–1831). Hegel was among the first to take Hindu theology seriously and incorporated Hindu thought into his grand philosophical scheme, though inevitably relegating it to a lower level than western philosophy. Schelling (1775–1854), Hegel's younger colleague, regarded Vedānta as an 'exalted idealism'[29] and enthusiasm for Indian thought was taken up by Arthur Schopenhauer (1788–1860) who regarded India as a land of ancient wisdom. Schopenhauer's philosophical heir, Friedrich Nietzsche (1844–1900), also admired Hindu ideas and referred to the 'Laws of Manu' as a text far superior to the New Testament.[30] These thinkers are not concerned with accurate readings of Hindu texts and philosophy, but are interested in using Hindu thought to back up or contribute to their own. The legacy of this tradition is also found in the novels of Hermann Hesse (1877–1962) and the psychologist Carl Gustav Jung (1875–1961) who constructed India as humanity's spiritual home and the location where symbols are most manifested from the collective unconscious.[31]

Not only did Hindu ideas, notably Vedānta, have some impact in the German intellectual world, but also in America with the New England Transcendentalists, Ralph Waldo Emerson (1803–82) and Henry David Thoreau (1817–62). Their interest influenced the Unitarian Association who aligned themselves with the Brahmo Samāj. Indeed, the first Hindu to speak about Hinduism in the West, even before Vivekānanda, did so at the invitation of the Unitarian Association; Protap Chunder Mozoomdar in 1883 delivered a lecture to a group in the home of Emerson's widow.[32]

Hindu gurus in the West

Since the end of the nineteenth century, Westerners, regarding themselves as seekers after truth reacting against the 'organized religion' of their homelands, went to India in search of spiritual truth and often found it there in the form of various gurus. Apart from the teachers of the Hindu Renaissance, the most important western movement responsible for the transmission of Hinduism to the West is Theosophy.

The Theosophical Society had been founded in 1875 in New York by a Russian psychic, Madame Blavatsky, and Colonel Alcott (1832–1907), to promote and explore esoteric knowledge. In 1877 the society moved to India, where its headquarters remain at Madras and where it maintains a good library and continues to publish texts and monographs on Hinduism and Theosophy. The Theosophical Society influenced western intellectuals such as the poet W. B. Yeats and the novelists Aldous Huxley and Christopher Isherwood, and many Hindu ideas entered the West via Theosophy. Upon the death of Madame Blavatsky, Annie Besant (1847–1933) took over the society's leadership and trained a young boy to become a world spiritual leader. Jiddu Krishnamurti (1895–1986) was educated in England by Annie Besant and in 1925 she declared him to be the Messiah and founded the Order of the Star in the East to promote this idea. Krishnamurti unequivocally rejected this role and went on to teach a doctrine of pure awareness, ultimately derived from Advaita Vedānta, called 'objectless awareness'. Krishnamurti has a large following in the West and had dialogues with modern nuclear physicists, such as David Bohm, interested in his ideas and the interface between science and eastern religions.[33] Apparent conceptual affiliations between contemporary science and some 'eastern' doctrines have attracted wide interest in recent years (which has served to reinforce constructions of 'the East' as 'mystical').[34]

Among Hindu teachers to attract a wide western following is Aurobindo Ghose (1872–1950). As a young man Aurobindo was involved with the Indian independence movement and jailed for terrorist activities as a result. While in prison he had a religious experience, achieving a state of *samādhi* through yoga. Upon release, he went to Pondicherry where he started an ashram and lived a life of study and contemplation for forty years, developing a philosophical system inspired by Vedānta, but integrating elements from Yoga, Tantra and the theory of evolution: the spiritual path is a path towards higher forms of awareness and an integration of matter with spirit. He called his system 'integral Yoga'.[35] Aurobindo's writing on his system is voluminous. Significantly he wrote in English and addressed an English-speaking audience from both India and the West.

His legacy lives on in the town Auroville, near Pondicherry, founded by him and his companion, a French woman known as the 'Mother' who took over spiritual leadership of the community after his death.

Of the same generation as Aurobindo, but with a much lower profile, was the Tamil mystic Ramana Maharshi (1879–1950) who lived and taught at Tiruvannamali. His teachings, which are pure Advaita, and simple lifestyle attracted many Westerners whom he taught to ask the question 'Who am I?' Through meditating upon this, a person's various roles and personae are thought to be stripped away to reveal the truth of the self as pure consciousness.[36] The teachings of Ramana have inspired many other gurus such as the low-caste Bombay cigarette- (*bīḍī*-) maker Nisarga Datta Maharaj, who, having experienced a state of non-dual consciousness, proceeded to teach. These teachings have had wide influence in the West and have produced 'western' gurus such as Jean Klein and Andrew Cohen who continue to attract large crowds of – mainly – western devotees.

Two other contemporaries of Aurobindo and Ramana Maharshi to attract western interest have been Paramahamsa Yogānanda (1890–1952) who founded the Self-Realization Fellowship, and Sawan Singh, the master of the Radhasoami Satsang at Beas. Yogānanda was a renouncer who achieved states of *samādhi* and wrote a fascinating autobiography of his spiritual journey and the founding in California of the Self-Realization Fellowship.[37] The Punjabi mystic of the Sant tradition, Sawan Singh (master from 1903 to 1948), also attracted a western audience, though his teachings were very different: rather than 'self-realization', he taught 'God-realization' through the practice of the yoga of inner sound (see pp. 100–1). Dr Julian Johnson, a Protestant preacher, took Sawan Singh as his spiritual master and was instrumental in the development of the Radhasoami Satsang in the West.[38]

During the 1960s many Hindu – as well as Buddhist and Chinese – ideas and practices came to the West and had a large impact upon the counterculture then developing. Dominant figures in popular culture – pop stars such as the Beatles and poets such as Alan Ginsberg – promoted Hindu ideas and gurus. During this period, after the lifting of immigration restrictions in the USA in 1965, there was a flow of Indian gurus to the West, such as Maharishi Mahesh Yogi, the founder of the Transcendental Meditation (TM) movement; the then teenage guru Maharaji, who founded the Divine Light Mission (since renamed Elan Vital);

Bhaktivedānta Prabhupada, who brought the Hare Kṛṣṇa movement to the West in 1965; Swami Muktānanda who founded Siddha Yoga; and Bhagavan Shree Rajneesh, who radically reinterpreted the traditional Hindu understanding of renunciation, calling his followers Sannyāsis, and who fused eastern meditation with western psychotherapies. Other teachers who have had an influence on the West have remained in India, such as Ānandamāyī, regarded as a living deity and identified with the Goddess Durgā; Satya Sai Baba, who commands a large following in India and abroad, famous for his magical powers of producing images and sacred ash from his fingertips; and Swami Śivānanda from Rishikesh, who taught the Neo-Vedānta formulated by Vivekānanda. Some of Śivānanda's disciples, such as Swami Chinmayānanda, have started centres throughout the world and have taught further swamis to carry on their Neo-Vedānta teachings.

This great influx of Hindu teachers and ideas to the West during the 1960s and 1970s has contributed to Global Hinduism. These teachings are not homogenous and there are great differences between the various teachers; for example, Bhaktivedānta Prabhupada's teachings focusing on the theistic deity Kṛṣṇa are very different from the monistic teachings of TM's Maharishi. Many of these teachers who set up movements have since died and passed on their spiritual authority to others, very often Westerners. Upon the demise of Prabhupada, eleven western gurus were chosen to succeed as spiritual heads of the Hare Kṛṣṇa movement, but many problems followed upon their appointment and the movement has since veered away from investing absolute authority in a few, fallible, human teachers. Swami Muktānanda appointed an Indian woman, Cidvilāsānanda, as his successor and she now heads the massive organization of Siddha Yoga, based mainly in Gorakhpur, India, and in South Fallsburg, USA. Muktānanda's guru, Swami Nityānanda, in the early 1960s, initiated a New York art dealer, Rudi, whose successor, after Rudi's death in a plane accident, is an American, Swami Cetanānanda, founder of the Nityānanda Institute. Some western gurus derive their teachings from Hinduism, but proclaim themselves to be self-realized and in some sense outside any original Hindu tradition – for example, Da Avabhāsa Kalki (alias Da Free John), Lee Lozowick and Jean Klein, who emphasize the direct experience of a non-dual reality through surrender to the master.[39]

Many of these gurus have been adopted by urban Hindus in India through the 'pizza effect' previously outlined. Centres of the Hare Kṛṣṇa movement – Bhaktivedānta Manor near Watford, England, for example – have been adopted by Hindu communities living outside India as their own. It will be increasingly difficult, or desirable, to separate out the more recent manifestations of Hinduism in the teachings of the gurus who have come to the West from more traditional understandings of the diaspora communities. Indeed the new religious movements loosely referred to as 'New Age', many of whose ideas are derived from Hinduism via Theosophy, may also contribute to Global Hinduism in the future.

Summary

There would seem to be two forces at work within Hinduism in the modern world: on the one hand a trend towards a universalization which contributes to contemporary global culture and processes, yet on the other a trend towards exclusive, local or national identity formations. Both of these trends have emerged during the last two centuries. Hinduism as a global religion, expressed in the ideas of the Hindu Renaissance, has developed since the nineteenth century as a reaction to colonialism and Christianity. This kind of Hinduism has been inclusive and has firmly established itself on the world stage, reformulating 'Hinduism' and discovering its ancient origins. Through the work of Rām Mohan Roy and later of Vivekānanda and his followers, Hinduism has become a world religion which has had a deep impact both on India and on the West at all cultural levels, from the scholarly study of texts in Indology departments in universities, to devotion to popular gurus. Yet in contrast to these universalizing tendencies, there has also developed a Hindu political nationalism which connects Hinduism, or Hindu Dharma, with the nation-state of India. This political nationalism has inspired friction between the Hindu, Muslim and Christian communities in India and evoked some terrible violence. Hinduism has, as have all religions, been a cause of bloodshed and intolerence. Yet Hinduism also contains within it profound resources for peace and reconciliation – forces which demand expression, and which may contribute to finding solutions to the global problems which face the human community in the coming century.

Notes

Introduction

1 Sachau, *Alberuni's India*, vol. 1 (London: Trubner and Co., 1888), pp. 22–3.

1 Points of departure

1 The March 1991 census of India estimated the population to be 843,930,861.

2 See Klostermaier, *A Survey of Hinduism* (Albany: SUNY Press, 1994).

3 Knott and Toon, *Muslims, Sikhs and Hindus in the UK: Problems in the Estimation of Religious Statistics*, Religious Research Paper 6 (Theology and Religious Studies Department, University of Leeds, 1982).

4 R. Thapar, *Interpreting Early India* (Delhi: Oxford University Press, 1993), p. 77.

5 C. Smith, *The Meaning and End of Religion* (San Francisco: Harper and Row, 1962), p. 207; Frykenberg, 'The Emergence of Modern "Hinduism"', in Sontheimer and Kulke (eds.), *Hinduism Reconsidered* (Delhi: Manohar, 1991), pp. 30–1.

6 O'Connell, 'The Word "Hindu" in Gaudiiya Vaiṣṇava Texts', *Journal of the American Oriental Society*, 93.3 (1973), pp. 340–4.

7 Quoted in B. K. Smith, 'Exorcising the Transcendent: Strategies for Redefining Hinduism and Religion', *History of Religions* (Aug. 1987), p. 36.

8 Lakoff, *Women, Fire and Dangerous Things: What Categories Reveal About the Mind* (Chicago and London: University of Chicago Press, 1987).

9 Ibid. p. 12.

10 Piatigorsky, 'Some Phenomenological Observations on the Study of

Indian Religion', in Burghardt and Cantille (eds.), *Indian Religion* (London: Curzon, 1985), pp. 208–24.

11 J. Z. Smith, *Imagining Religion, From Babylon to Jonestown* (University of Chicago Press, 1982), p. xi.

12 Smart, 'The Formation Rather than the Origin of a Tradition', *DISKUS: A Disembodied Journal of Religious Studies*, 1. (1993), p. 1.

13 W. C. Smith, *The Meaning and End of Religion*, p. 65; see also H. von Stietencron, 'Hinduism: On the Proper Use of A Deceptive Term', in Sontheimer and Kulke, *Hinduism Reconsidered*, pp. 11–27; also Halbfass, *Tradition and Reflection* (Albany: SUNY Press, 1991), pp. 1–22. For an interesting, brief survey of the idea of 'Hinduism' and the development of recent scholarship about it, see Hardy, 'Hinduism', in King (ed.), *Turning Points in Religious Studies* (Edinburgh: T. and T. Clark, 1990), pp. 145–55.

14 Inden, *Imagining India* (Oxford and Cambridge: Blackwells, 1990).

15 Durkheim, *The Elementary Forms of the Religious Life* (London: Allen and Unwin, 1964), p. 37.

16 Berger, *The Sacred Canopy, Elements of a Sociological Theory of Religion* (New York: Anchor Books, 1990), p. 26. I am also influenced here by Clifford Geertz' definition of religion as that which 'tunes human actions to an envisaged cosmic order and projects images of cosmic order on to the plane of human experience': Geertz, *The Interpretation of Cultures* (London: Fontana, 1993), p. 90.

17 Otto, *The Idea of the Holy*, 2nd edn (Oxford, London and New York: Oxford University Press, 1982).

18 For a discussion of this distinction see Smart, *Reasons and Faiths* (London: Routledge and Kegan Paul, 1958) and more recently his *The World's Religions* (Cambridge University Press, 1989), pp. 13–14.

19 For example, the important work by Dirks, *The Hollow Crown* (Ann Arbor: University of Michigan Press, 1993), pp. 106–7.

20 J. Z. Smith, *Imagining Religion*, p. 55. I have used the term 'icon' in preference to 'image' as a translation of the terms *murti* and *vigraha* to indicate the physical manifestation of a deity. My use of the term has been influenced by Charles Pierce's understanding of the icon as 'a sign which refers to the Object that it denotes merely by virtue of characters of its own, and which it possesses just the same, whether any such object actually exists or not' (Peirce, *Collected Papers of Charles Sanders Peirce*, vol. 11 (Cambridge, Mass.: Harvard

University Press, 1932), p. 247). There are also parallels between the Hindu *murti* and the Christian Orthodox 'icon' as a material centre which, according to Vladamir Lossky, contains an energy and divine truth (quoted in Miguel, 'Théologie de l'icone', in Viller, Cavallera and de Guibert (eds.), *Dictionnaire de spiritualité*, vol. VII (Paris: Beauchesme, 1971), p. 1236). On this account a person can be an icon as well as an 'object' of stone or wood.

21 Smart, *The World's Religions*, p. 9.

22 Bourdieu, *Outline* (Cambridge University Press, 1991), pp. 1–2.

23 See ibid. pp. 3–9. Also Fauré, *The Rhetoric of Immediacy: A Cultural Critique of Chan/Zen Buddhism* (Princeton University Press, 1991), p. 304.

24 See Piatigorsky, 'Some Phenomenological Observations on the Study of Indian Religion'.

25 The terms 'secondary' and 'indirect revelation' referring to this literature of human authorship, are used by Alexis Sanderson. See Sanderson, 'Śaivism and the Tantric Traditions', in Sutherland, Houlden, Clarke and Hardy (eds.), *The World's Religions* (London: Routledge, 1988), p. 662.

26 Brian Smith has defined Hinduism as 'the religion of those humans who create, perpetuate, and transform traditions with legitimizing reference to the authority of the Veda'. B. K. Smith, 'Exorcising the Transcendent', p. 40.

27 Halbfass, *Tradition and Reflection*, pp. 1–22.

28 Zaehner relates *dharma* to the Sanskrit root *dhṛ* which means 'to hold, have or maintain'. He defines *dharma* as 'the "form" of things as they are and the power that keeps them as they are and not otherwise'. Zaehner, *Hinduism* (Oxford University Press, 1966), p. 2.

29 Staal, *Rules Without Meaning, Ritual, Mantras and the Human Sciences* (New York: Peter Lang, 1989), p. 389.

30 Gombrich, *Theravāda Buddhism* (London and New York: Routledge and Kegan Paul, 1988), pp. 25–7.

31 L. Dumont, 'World Renunciation in Indian Religions', in his *Homo Hierarchicus* (Chicago and London: University of Chicago Press, 1980), pp. 267–86.

32 See L. Dumont, *Homo Hierarchicus*; Milner, *Status and Sacredness, A general Theory of Status Relations and an Analysis of Indian Culture* (New York and Oxford: Oxford University Press, 1994); Carman and

Marglin (eds.), *Purity and Auspiciousness in Indian Society* (Leiden: Brill, 1985).

33 Fuller, *The Camphor Flame* (Princeton University Press, 1992), p. 3.

34 Ibid. p. 4.

35 See Fauré, *The Rhetoric of Immediacy*, pp. 13–14.

36 Von Stietencron, 'Hinduism: On the Proper Use of a Deceptive Term', in Sontheimer and Kulke, *Hinduism Reconsidered*, pp. 11–27.

37 See Staal, 'Sanskrit and Sanskritization', *Journal of Asian Studies*, 23.3 (1963), pp. 261–75.

38 For a discussion of these levels see Fauré, *The Rhetoric of Immediacy*, pp. 80–7.

39 Biardeau (ed.), *Autour de la Déesse hindoue* (Paris: Editions de l'Ecole des Hautes Etudes en Sciences Sociales, 1981), pp. 9–16. See also Hiltebeitel's important work on the Draupadi cult in Tamilnadu: Hiltebeitel, *The Cult of Draupadī*, vol. I: *Mythologies from Gingee to Kuruksetra* (Chicago and London: University of Chicago Press, 1988); vol. II: *On Hindu Ritual and the Goddess* (Chicago and London: University of Chicago Press, 1991).

40 See Appadurai, Korom and Miles (eds.), *Gender, Genre and Power in South Asian Expressive Traditions* (Philadelphia: University of Pennsylvania Press, 1991).

41 Guha, 'The Prose of Counter-Insurgency', in Dirks, Eley and Ortner (eds.), *Culture, Power, History: A Reader in Contemporary Social Theory* (Princeton University Press, 1994), p. 337.

42 Inden, *Imagining India*.

43 For a good summary of the structuralist position (Marx, Dumont) versus theories of practice (Bourdieu, Giddens), and how these relate to the caste system, see Milner, *Status and Sacredness*.

44 See the Indian feminist journal *Manushi: Women Bhakta Poets*, 50, 51, 52 (Jan.–June 1989).

45 See Bechert, 'The Date of the Buddha Reconsidered', *Indologica Taurinensia*, 10 (1982), pp. 29–36.

46 Gombrich, *Theravāḍa Buddhism*, p. 6.

47 Thapar, *Interpreting Early India*, pp. 136–73.

48 Kalhaṇa, *Rājataraṅgiṇī*. Dutt (trs.), *Kings of Kashmira: Being a Translation of the Sanskrita Work Rājataraṅgiṇī of Kalhaṇa Pandita*, 3 vols. (1879; Delhi: MLBD, reprint 1990).

2 Ancient origins

1 Writing on the idea of the 'trace' in relation to 'origin' the French philosopher Derrida writes: 'the trace is not only the disappearance of origin, it means . . . that the origin did not even disappear, that it was never constituted except reciprocally by a non-origin, the trace, which thus becomes the origin of the origin'; Derrida, *Of Grammatology* (Baltimore: Johns Hopkins University Press, 1976), p. 61.

2 Wheeler, *The Indus Civilization; The Cambridge History of India Supplementary Volume* (Cambridge University Press, 1953); Dales and Kenoyer, *Excavations at Mohenjo Daro, Pakistan*, Museum Monograph (Philadelphia: University of Pennsylvania Press, 1993).

3 Parpola, *Deciphering the Indus Script* (Cambridge University Press, 1994), p. 8.

4 Jarrige and Santoni, 'The Antecedents of Civilization in the Indus Valley', *Scientific American*, 243.8 (1980), pp. 102–10. See Allchin and Allchin, *The Rise of Civilization in India and Pakistan* (Cambridge University Press, 1982), pp. 105–7.

5 Allchin and Allchin, *The Rise of Civilization in India and Pakistan*, pp. 166–225. Parpola, *Deciphering the Indus Script*, pp. 9–12.

6 Asko Parpola and Russian scholars have argued that the script is Dravidian. See Parpola, *Deciphering the Indus Script*. Subash Kak in a number of papers has argued that the Indus script is of an Indo-European language and that the script bears some close resemblances to the Brahmi script, the precursor of *devanagari* in which Sanskrit is commonly written. See his 'On the Decipherment of the Indus Script – A preliminary Study of its Connections with Brahmi', *The Indian Journal of History of Science*, 22.1 (1987), pp. 51–62.

7 Renfrew, *Archaeology and Language; The Puzzle of Indo-European Origins* (London: Jonathan Cape, 1987), p. 185.

8 Allchin and Allchin, *The Rise of Civilization in India and Pakistan*, p. 183.

9 Marshall, *Mohenjo-Daro and the Indus Civilization*, 3 vols. (London: University of Oxford Press, 1931), vol. 1, p. 52. See also Allchin and Allchin, *The Rise of Civilization in India and Pakistan*, pp. 213–315. On the seals see Fairservis, *The Roots of Ancient India* (University of Chicago Press, 1975), pp. 274–7. For a discussion of the proto-Śiva see Hiltebeitel 'The Indus Valley "proto-Siva", Re-examination through Reflection on the Goddess, the Buffalo, and the Symbolism

of the *vāhanas*', *Anthropos*, 73.5–6 (1978), pp. 767–79; Srinivasan, 'Unhinging Siva from the Indus Civilization', *Journal of the Royal Asiatic Society of Great Britain and Ireland*, 1 (1984), pp. 77–89.

10 Parpola, *Deciphering the Indus Script*, pp. 248–50.

11 Ibid. pp. 256–71.

12 For a discussion of this motif see ibid. pp. 246–8.

13 Wheeler, *The Indus Civilization*, p. 92.

14 Poliakov, *The Aryan Myth* (New York: Basic Books, 1974).

15 Shaffer, 'Indo-Aryan Invasions: Myth or Reality?', in Lukacs (ed.), *The People of South Asia: The Biological Anthropology of India, Pakistan and Nepal* (New York and London: Plenum Press, 1984), pp. 77–90.

16 Inden, *Imagining India*, p. 89.

17 Tripathi, *The Painted Grey Ware: An Iron Age Culture of Northern India* (Delhi: Concept Publishing Co., 1976).

18 Shaffer, 'Bronze Age Iron from Afghanistan: Its Implications for South Asian Proto-history', in Kennedy and Possehl (eds.), *Studies in the Archeology and Paleoanthropology of South Asia* (New Delhi: Oxford and IBH Publishers, 1983), pp. 65–102.

19 Shaffer, 'Indo-Aryan Invasions: Myth or Reality?', p. 88.

20 Parpola, *Deciphering the Indus Script*, pp. 152–3.

21 Renfrew, *Archaeology and Language*, p. 192.

22 Parpola, *Deciphering the Indus Script*, pp. 142–59. For the horse argument specifically see pp. 155–9.

23 Emeneau and Burrow, *Dravidian Borrowings from Indo-Aryan* (Berkeley: University of California Press, 1962).

24 Parpola, *Deciphering the Indus Script*, pp. 167–8.

25 *Ait.Ar.* 5.5.3.

26 The standard German translation of the *Ṛg Veda Saṃhitā* is by Geldner, *Der Rigveda: Aus dem Sanskrit ins Deutsche übersetzt und mit einem laufenden Kommentar versehen*, 3 vols., Harvard Oriental Series, 33, 34, 35 (Cambridge, Mass.: Harvard University Press, 1951). English translations are by Müller and Oldenberg, *Vedic Hymns*. 2 vols., SBE 32, 46 (Delhi: MLBD, reprint 1973) and there is an accessible translation of some hymns by O'Flaherty: *The Rig Veda*.

27 See Kak, 'On the Chronology of Ancient India', *Indian Journal of History of Science*, 22.3 (1987), pp. 222–34. See also Frawley, *Gods*,

Sages and Kings: Vedic Secrets of Ancient Civilization (Salt Lake City: Passages Press, 1991).

28 Müller, *The Six Systems of Indian Philosophy* (London: Longmans, Green and Co., 1899), pp. 44–7.

29 Staal, *Rules without Meaning*, p. 37.

30 *Ait.Ar.* 3.1.1.

31 Coburn, '"Scripture" in India: Towards a Typology of the Word in Hindu Life', in Levering (ed.), *Rethinking Scripture; Essays from a Comparative Perspective* (Albany: SUNY Press, 1989), p. 112.

32 This older group comprises fourteen texts, namely the *Bṛhadāraṇyaka*, *Chāndogya*, *Aitareya*, *Taittirīya*, *Kauṣītaki*, *Kena*, *Īśa*, *Kaṭha*, *Śvetāśvatara*, *Praśna*, *Muṇḍaka*, *Mahānārāyaṇa*, *Māṇḍukya* and *Maitrī*. Of these the oldest group are from the *Bṛhadāraṇyaka* to the *Kauṣītaki*.

33 Jamison, *Ravenous Hyenas and the wounded Sun* (Ithaca and London: Cornell University Press, 1991), p. 17.

34 *RV* 2.1.1.3.

35 *Ap. S.S.* See Heesterman, *The Broken World of Sacrifice: Essays in Ancient Indian Ritual* (Chicago and London: University of Chicago Press, 1993), p. 10.

36 Staal, *Rules Without Meaning*, p. 68. Also Staal (ed.), *AGNI. The Vedic Ritual of the Fire Altar*, 2 vols. (Berkeley: University of California Press).

37 Staal, *AGNI*. For a concise summary of the *soma* sequence see Staal, *Rules without Meaning*, pp. 81–3.

38 Wasson, *Soma, the Divine Mushroom of Immortality*. Ethno-Mycological Studies 1 (New York: Harcourt, Brace and World, 1968).

39 Parpola, *Deciphering the Indus Script*, p. 149.

40 Staal, *Exploring Mysticism* (Harmondsworth: Penguin, 1975), pp. 187–93.

41 For an account of the horse sacrifice see P. E. Dumont, *L'Aśvamedha: description du sacrifice solennel du cheval dans le culte vedique d'aprés les textes du Yajurveda blanc*, Paris: Geuthner 1927.

42 *RV* 1.162; *Sat.Br.* 13.2.8; 13.5.2.

43 The horse sacrifice and symbolic copulation with the horse seems to have been a common Indo-European theme with parallels as far away as Ireland. See O'Flaherty, *Women, Androgynes and Other Mythical*

Beasts (London and Chicago: University of Chicago Press, 1980), p. 168.

44 René Girard, *Violence and the Sacred* (Baltimore and London: The Johns Hopkins University Press, 1977).

45 See Bourdieu, *Language and Symbolic Power* (Cambridge: Polity Press, 1991), pp. 117–26.

46 *BAU* 3.9.1–2.

47 Müller, *The Six Systemṣ of Indian Philosophy*, p. 47.

48 *Sat.Br.* 5.1.1.1–2.

49 *RV* 4.5.

50 *RV* 9.74.

51 *RV* 10.51.

52 *RV* 4.26.

53 *RV* 1.32.

54 For an account of the Ādityas see Brereton, *The Rgvedic Adityas* (New Haven: American Oriental Series 63, 1981).

55 *RV* 7.89.

56 *RV* 10.129.

57 *RV* 10.129, in O'Flaherty's translation *The Rig Veda*, p. 25.

58 Bhaṭṭa-Bhāskara on the *Taittirīya-Saṃhitā* 1.5.1 quoted by Gonda, *Mantra Interpretation in the Śatapatha Brāhmaṇa* (Leiden: Brill, 1988), p. 1.

59 Durkheim, *The Elementary Forms of the Religious Life* (London: Allen and Unwin, 1962), p. 237.

60 See O'Flaherty, *Women, Androgynes and Other Mythical Beasts*, p. 21.

61 Eliade, 'Cosmical Homology and Yoga', *Journal of the Indian Society of Oriental Arts*, 5 (1937), pp. 188–203.

62 *RV* 10.90.

63 See Lincoln, *Myth, Cosmos and Society: Indo-European Themes of Creation and Destruction* (Cambridge, Mass.: Harvard University Press, 1986), pp. 141–4.

64 Dumézil, 'Métiers et classes fonctionnelles chez divers peuples Indo-Européens', *Annales (Économies, Sociétés, Civilisations 13e année)*, 4 (Oct.–Dec. 1958), pp. 716–24.

65 E. Aguilar i Matas, *Rg-vedic Society* (Leiden: Brill, 1991), pp. 11–12.

3 *Dharma*

1 Witzel, 'On Localization of the Vedic Texts and Schools', in Pollet (ed.), *India and the Ancient World*, Orientalia Lovaniensia Analecta 25 (Department Oriéntalistik, Leuven University: 1987), pp. 194–200.

2 Coward, Lipner and Young (eds.), *Hindu Ethics* (Albany: SUNY Press, 1991), p. 2; Zaehner, *Hinduism*, pp. 102–24.

3 Heesterman, *The Inner Conflict of Traditions: Essays in Indian Ritual, Kingship and Society* (University of Chicago Press, 1985), p. 3.

4 *MS* 1.1.2.

5 *Gautama Dharma Sūtra* 1.1–2.

6 *Manu* 6.7 and 6.12.

7 *Baud.SS.* 1.23. See Staal, *Rules Without Meaning*, pp. 355–9.

8 Staal, *Rules Without Meaning*, pp. 364–5.

9 Lingat, *The Classical Law of India* (Berkeley: University of California Press, 1973), pp. 73–4.

10 M. Derrett, 'Appendix by the translator', in Lingat, *The Classical Law of India*, p. 273.

11 *Gaut.Dh.* 28.49–51; *Manu* 12.112.

12 Doniger, *The Laws of Manu*, p. xlvi.

13 *Manu* 1.85; 1.110.

14 *Manu* 10.97.

15 B. K. Smith, *Classifying the Universe: The Ancient Indian* Varna *System and the Origins of Caste* (New York and Oxford: Oxford University Press, 1994).

16 *Vis.Smrt.* 2.4–14.

17 E. V. Daniel, *Fluid Signs: Being a Person the Tamil Way* (Berkeley: University of California Press, 1984), pp. 235–6.

18 Marriott, 'Hindu Transactions: Diversity without Dualism', in B. Kapferer (ed.), *Transaction and Meaning: Directions in the Anthropology of Exchange and Symbolic Behaviour* (Philadelphia: Institute for the Study of Human Issues, 1976), pp. 109–42.

19 Halbfass, *Tradition and Reflection*, p. 350.

20 *Manu* 10.24; 3.15.

21 *Ibid.* 3.17; 11.68; 8.371–2.

22 *Ibid.* 10.16.

23 *Ibid.* 5.85.

24 *Ibid.* 10.51.

25 Giles, *The Travels of Fa-hsien (399–414 AD), or Record of the Buddhist Kingdoms* (Cambridge University Press, 1923), p. 21.

26 L. Dumont, *Homo Hierarchicus*, p. 54.

27 Olivelle, *The* Āśrama *System: The History and Hermeneutics of a Religious Tradition* (New York, Oxford: Oxford University Press, 1993), pp. 7, 24–8.

28 Ibid. pp. 19–20.

29 Ibid. pp. 80–1.

30 *Ath.V.* 11.5.

31 Gonda, *Change and Continuity in Indian Religion* (1965 New Delhi: Munshiram Manoharlal, reprint 1985), p. 285.

32 *Ibid.* 3.1–2.

33 *Ibid.* 6.8. Doniger's translation, *The Laws of Manu*, p. 117.

34 *Manu* 6.13; 6.23–4.

35 *Ibid.* 3.77–8; 12.86.

36 Ibid. 1.88.

37 Ibid. 6.43–4; 57.

38 L. Dumont, 'World Renunciation in Indian Religions', in *Homo Hierarchicus*, pp. 267–86.

39 *Manu* 3.60.

40 Biardeau, *Hinduism. The Anthropology of a Civilization* (New Delhi: Oxford University Press, 1989), p. 50.

41 *Manu* 5.147–8.

42 Ibid. 5.165–6.

43 Leslie, 'Suttee or Satī: Victim or Victor?', in Leslie (ed.), *Roles and Rituals for Hindu Women* (London: Pinter Publishers, 1991), pp. 175–91. See also Hawley (ed.), *Satī, the Blessing and the Curse: The Burning of Wives in India* (New York, Oxford: Oxford University Press, 1994).

44 Leslie, *The Perfect Wife: The Orthodox Hindu Woman According to the Strīdharmapaddhati of Tryambakayajvan*, Oxford University South Asian Series (Delhi: Oxford University Press, 1989), pp. 305–16.

45 Fuller, *The Camphor Flame*, pp. 106–27. Also Dirks, *The Hollow Crown*.

46 *RV* 1.32.15. O'Flaherty's translation, *The Rig Veda*, p. 151.

47 *RV* 10.173; *Ath. V.* 6.87–8.

48 Gupta and Gombrich, 'Kings, Power and the Goddess', *South Asia Research*, 6.2 (1986), pp. 123–38.

49 *Manu* 7.5–7. Doniger's translation, *The Laws of Manu*, p. 128.

50 Inden, *Imagining India*, p. 228.

51 Stein, *Peasant, State and Society in Medieval South India* (Delhi: Oxford University Press, 1980), pp. 22, 264.

52 Inden, 'Kings and Omens', in Carman and Marglin (eds.), *Purity and Auspiciousness in Indian Society* (Leiden: Brill, 1985), p. 38.

53 Kantorowicz, *The King's Two Bodies* (Princeton University Press, 1957).

54 *Ath. V.* 3.4.2.

55 *Manu* 7.35.

56 Ibid. 7.12–24.

57 L. Dumont, *Homo Hierarchicus*, pp. 97–108.

58 Heesterman, *The Inner Conflict of Tradition*, p. 7.

59 Ibid. p. 9.

60 See Inden's review of Heesterman's *The Inner Conflict of Tradition*: Inden, 'Tradition Against Itself', *American Ethnologist*, 13.4 (1986), pp. 762–75.

61 Dirks, *The Hollow Crown*, p. 249.

4 Yoga and renunciation

1 *YS* 2.15.

2 Bronkhorst, *The Two Traditions of Meditation in Ancient India* (Delhi: MLBD, 1993), pp. 68–111.

3 Masefield, *Divine Revelation in Pali Buddhism* (London: Allen & Unwin, 1986), p. 160.

4 The hymn reads:

> Long-hair holds fire, holds the drug, holds sky and earth. Long-hair reveals everything, so that everyone can see the sun. Long-hair declares the light.
>
> These ascetics, swathed in wind, put dirty red rags on. When gods enter them, they ride with the rush of the wind.
>
> 'Crazy with asceticism, we have mounted the wind. Our bodies are all you mere mortals can see.'

> He sails through the air, looking down on all shapes below. The ascetic is friend to this god and that god, devoted to what is well done.
>
> The stallion of the wind, friend of gales, lashed on by gods – the ascetic lives in the two seas, on the east and on the west.
>
> He moves with the motion of heavenly girls and youths, of wild beasts. Long-hair, reading their minds, is their sweet, their most exciting friend.
>
> The wind has churned it up; Kunaṃnamā prepared it for him. Long-hair drinks from the cup, sharing the drug with Rudra.
>
> O'Flaherty, *The Rig Veda*, pp. 137–8.

If Kunaṃnamā is a hunch-backed goddess, we have here perhaps a precursor of the 'crooked' tantric goddess Kubjikā.

5 Staal, *Exploring Mysticism*, pp. 185–7.

6 Werner, 'Yoga and the Ṛg Veda: An Interpretation of the Kesin Hymn', *Religious Studies*, 13 (1976), pp. 289–93.

7 *RV* 1.114.

8 Heesterman, *The Broken World of Sacrifice*, pp. 178–9. On the Vrātyas generally see Eliade, *Yoga: Immortality and Freedom* (Princeton University Press, 1973), pp. 103–4; Feuerstein, *Yoga, The Technology of Ecstasy* (Wellingborough: Crucible, 1989), pp. 111–14; Hauer, *Der Vrātya*, vol 1: *Die Vrātya als nichtbrahmanische Kultgenossenschaften arischer Herkunft* (Stuttgart: Kohlhammer Verlag, 1927); Heesterman, 'Vrātya and Sacrifice', *Indo-Iranian Journal*, 6 (1962), pp. 1–37.

9 Eliade, *Yoga*, p. 103.

10 Gombrich, *Theravāda Buddhism*, pp. 57–8.

11 Wheatley, *The Pivot of the Four Quarters* (Chicago: Aldine Publishing Co., 1971), p. 8. See also Eck 'The City as Sacred Centre', in B. Smith and H. B. Reynolds (eds.), *The City as Sacred Centre: Essays on Six Asian Contexts* (Leiden, New York and Cologne: Brill, 1987).

12 Gombrich, *Theravāda Buddhism*, pp. 51–8; Olivelle, *The Saṃnyāsa Upaniṣads*, pp. 30–3.

13 B. S. Turner, *Religion and Social Theory* (London: SAGE Publications, 1991), p. 163.

14 Gokhale, 'The Early Buddhist Elite', *Journal of Indian History*, 42.2 (1965), pp. 391–402.

15 Gombrich, *Theravāda Buddhism*, pp. 58–9.

16 *Sutta Nipata* 3.9.

17 For the Ājīvikas see Basham, *History and Doctrines of the Ājīvikas* (Delhi: MLBD, 1981). For the Jains, see Dundas, *The Jains* (London: Routledge and Kegan Paul, 1992). For the materialists, see Chattopadhyaya, *Lokāyata* (New Delhi: People's Publishing House, 1959).

18 Thapar, *Interpreting Early India*, p. 63.

19 Bronkhorst, *The Two Traditions of Meditation*, pp. 45–53.

20 *BAU* 6.5.1–4.

21 Ibid. 1.1.1–2.

22 *Ch.U.* 1.1.9–10. Translation by Radhakrishnan, *The Principal Upaniṣads*, pp. 331–3.

23 Staal, *Rules Without Meaning*, pp. 117–20.

24 *Sat.Br.* 10.2.5.11.

25 *BAU* 4.1.1–7.

26 *Ch.U.* 6.13.1–3.

27 Ibid. 1.12.1–5.

28 *Tait.Up.* 3.6.1 and 3.8.1. Translation by Radhakrishnan, *The Principal Upaniṣads*, pp. 557, 149, 150.

29 *RV* 10.16.

30 For a discussion of this debate and papers presenting various viewpoints, see O'Flaherty (ed.), *Karma and Rebirth in Classical Indian Traditions* (Berkeley and Los Angeles: University of California Press, 1980). Also Boyer, 'Etude sur l'origine de la doctrine du samsara', *Journal Asiatique*, 2 (1901), 451–99.

31 *BAU* 3.2.13.

32 Ibid. 4.4.3.

33 *Svet.U.* 5.7.

34 Heesterman, *The Inner Conflict of Tradition*, p. 40.

35 Ibid. p. 34.

36 *Manu* 2.87–100; 6.42–9.

37 Biardeau, *Hinduism, the Anthropology of a Civilization*, p. 159. See also Biardeau and Malamoud, *Le Sacrifice dans l'Inde ancienne* (Paris: Presses Universitaires de France, 1976).

38 L. Dumont, *Homo Hierarchicus*, p. 272.

39 Inden, *Imagining India*, p. 203.

40 Olivelle, *Saṃnyāsa Upaniṣads*, p. 21.

41 *BAU* 4.5.1–2, in Radhakrishnan, *The Principal Upaniṣads*, p. 281.

42 Gombrich, *Theravāda Buddhism*, p. 107.

43 *Vis.Smrt.* 96.12.

44 *Nar.U.* in Olivelle, *Saṃnyāsa Upanisads*, pp. 191–2.

45 Olivelle, *Saṃnyāsa Upaniṣads*, p. 94.

46 For a brief though clear account see Hartsuiker, *Sādhus, the Holy Men of India* (London: Thames and Hudson, 1993), pp. 31–5.

47 *BAU* 4.4.23.

48 *Kat.U.* 2.3.10–11.

49 *Ibid.* 1.3.3–9.

50 *Svet.U.* 2.8–14.

51 *Mait.U.* 2.7–3.1–2; 6.18.

52 *YS* 1.2.

53 Svātmarāma, *The Haṭhayogapradīpikā* (Madras: The Adyar Library Research Centre, 1972).

54 See Silburn, *Kuṇḍalinī, the Energy from the Depths* (Albany: SUNY Press, 1988).

55 *Tait.U.* 1.6.1.

56 *Hat.Yog.* 3.32–8.

57 *Ibid.* 3.42.

58 Ibid. 4.65–102.

59 Juergensmeyer, *Radhasoami Reality, The Logic of a Modern Faith* (Princeton University Press, 1991), 90–1.

60 *YS* 3.16–49.

61 *YS bhāṣya* 1.45.

5 Narrative traditions and early Vaiṣṇavism

1 *Mahābhārata, Critical Edition with Pratika Index*, 28 vols. (Poona: Bhandarkar Oriental Research Institute, 1923–72). An English translation of this edition was initiated by Van Buitenen, of which three volumes have appeared. Van Buitenen, *The Mahābhārata.*

2 *Mbh.* 3.52–79.

3 Ibid. 1.68–72.

4 Van Buitenen, *The Bhagavadgītā*, p. 3.

5 There are several editions and translations of the *Rāmāyaṇa* in India. A recent translation based on the Vālmīki text is under the general editorship of Robert P. Goldman: Goldman (ed.), *The Rāmāyaṇa of Vālmīki: An Epic of Ancient India*, vol. I: *Balakāṇḍa* (Princeton University Press, 1984); Pollock, vol. II: *Ayodhyākāṇḍa* (Princeton University Press, 1986); Pollock, vol. III: *Araṇyakāṇḍa* (Princeton University Press, 1991).

6 P. Richman (ed.), *Many Rāmāyaṇas* (Delhi: Oxford University Press, 1991).

7 Ananda Ashram in New York State, for example, stage regular productions of the *Rāmāyaṇa*.

8 Scheckner, *The Future of Ritual* (London and New York: Routledge, 1993), pp. 131–83.

9 Whalling, *The Rise of the Religious Significance of Rama* (Delhi: MLBD, 1980).

10 Hardy, *Viraha Bhakti* (Delhi: Oxford University Press, 1983), p. 86. Also Hacker, *Prahlāda, Werden und Wandlungen einer Idealgestalt*, Akademie der Wissenschaften und der Literatur in Mainz, Abhandlungen der Geistes- und Sozialwissenschaftlichen Klasse 13 (Wiesbaden: Franz Steiner Verlag, 1960). Also Bailey, 'On the Object of Study in Purāṇic Research; Three Recent Books on the Purāṇas', *Review of the Asian Studies Association of Australia*, 10.3 (1987), pp. 106–14.

11 *Vis.Pur.* 1.30–2.

12 See Hardy, *The Religious Culture of India: Power, Love and Wisdom* (Cambridge University Press, 1994), p. 29.

13 *Vis.Pur.* 2.214; *Manu* 1.37–40. For an account of Indian cosmologies see Gombrich, 'Ancient Indian Cosmology', in Blacker and Loewe (eds.), *Ancient Cosmologies* (London: George Allen and Unwin, 1975), pp. 110–42.

14 *Vis.Pur.* 3; 4.21–4.

15 *RV* 91.22.16–21.

16 Ibid. 1.154.

17 *Vay.Pur.* 2.36.74–86.

18 *Bh.G.* 4.7. Translation by van Buitenen, *The Bhagavadgītā*, p. 87.

19 *Mat.Pur.* 1.11–34; 2.1–19 (from the *Sat.Br.* 1.8.1.1–6).

20 *Vis.Pur.* 1.4.3–11, 25–9, 45–9.

21 Hardy, *The Religious Culture of India*, pp. 299–301.

22 *Vis.Pur.* 1.4.17; 1.19.80; 5.9.28.

23 Hardy, *Viraha Bhakti*, pp. 17–18 and *passim*.

24 *Ast.* 4.3.98.

25 *Mahaniddesa*, vol. 1, ed. de la Vallée Poussin (London: Pali Text Society, 1916) 89, 92.

26 *Bh.G.* 10.37.

27 *Mahbhas.* 4.3.98.

28 See Hardy, *Viraha Bhakti*, pp. 18–19.

29 *Ch.U.* 3.117.6.

30 *Bh.G.* 11.21, 24, 31.

31 *Sat.Br.* 12.3.4; 13.6.1.

32 *Manu* 1.10.

33 *Mbh.* 12.341.

34 *Mahnar.U.* 201–69.

35 Tawney (trs.), *Somadeva's Kathā Saritsāgara, or Ocean of Streams of Story*, ed. Penzer, 10 vols. (1924–8; Delhi: MLBD, reprint 1968), 54.19, 21–3.

36 *Sat.Br.* 13.6.1.

37 *Mbh.* 12.337, 63–4.

38 See Schrader, *Introduction to the Pāñcarātra and the Ahirbudhnya Saṃhitā*, (Madras: Adyar Library and Research Centre, reprint 1973), pp. 23–4.

39 See Neeval, *Yāmuna's Vedānta and Pāñcarātra: Integrating the Classical with the Popular* (Montana: Scholar's Press, 1977).

40 *Jay.Sam.* 4.8.

41 *Bh.G.* 2.21–2. Translation by van Buitenen, *The Bhagavadgītā*, pp. 75–7.

42 *Bh.G.* 2.31–3.

43 Ibid. 4.9–23.

44 Ibid. 11.5–49.

45 Ibid. 9.33.

46 Ibid. 18.54–5, 65.

47 Ibid. 3.3; 13.5–19.

6 The love of Viṣṇu

1 Zvelebil, *The Smile of Murugan* (Leiden: Brill, 1973), pp. 131–54.

2 Ibid. p. 4; Hardy, *Viraha Bhakti*, pp. 124–31.

3 Kailasapathy, *Tamil Heroic Poetry* (Oxford University Press, 1968), pp. 258–64.

4 Ibid. pp. 63–4.

5 Hardy, *Viraha Bhakti*, p. 141.

6 Parpola, *Deciphering the Indus Script*, pp. 225–32.

7 The twelve are: Poykai, Pūtam, Péy, Tiruppāṉ, Tirumaḻicai, Toṇṭaraṭippoṭi, Kulacékaraṉ, Periyāḻvār, Āṇṭāḷ, Tirumaṅkai, Nammāḻvār and Maturakavi.

8 See Meenakshi, 'Andal: She Who Rules', *Manushi, Tenth Anniversary Issue: Women Bhakta Poets*, 50–2 (Delhi: Manushi Trust, 1989), pp. 34–8.

9 Tyagisananda, *Aphorisms on the Gospel of Divine Love or the Nārada Bhakti Sūtras* (Madras: Ramakrishna Math, 1972), pp. 82–3.

10 Fuller, *The Camphor Flame*, p. 165.

11 Neeval, *Yāmuna's Vedānta and Pāñcarātra*, ch. 1.

12 For an account of Nammāḻvār and the place of his text in the Śrī Vaiṣṇava tradition, see Carman and Narayanan, *The Tamil Veda* (Chicago and London: University of Chicago Press, 1989).

13 Mumme, 'Haunted by Śaṅkara's Ghost: The Śrīvaiṣṇava Interpretation of Bhagavad Gītā 18.66', in Timm (ed.), *Texts in Context: Traditional Hermeneutics in South Asia* (Albany: SUNY Press, 1992), pp. 69–84.

14 Stoler-Miller, *Love Song of the Dark Lord* (New York: Columbia University Press, 1977).

15 For some good translations of these poets see Bhattacharya, *Love Songs of Chandidās* (London; Allen and Unwin, 1967); Bhattacharya, *Love Songs of Vidyāpati* (London: Allen and Unwin, 1963); Dimock & Levertov, *In Praise of Krishna: Songs from the Bengali* (New York: Anchor Books, 1967).

16 Bhattacharya, *Love Songs of Chandidās*, p. 107.

17 Majumdar, *Caitanya: His Life and Doctrine* (Bombay: Bharatiya Vidya Bhavan, 1969).

18 Siegel, *Sacred and Profane Dimensions of Love in Indian Traditions as Exemplified in The Gītagovinda of Jayadeva* (Oxford University Press, 1978), pp. 137–77.

19 For an account of the Sahajiyas and the Bauls, see Dasgupta, *Obscure Religious Cults* (Calcutta: Mukhopadhyay, 1969); Dimock, *The Place of the Hidden Moon* (Chicago University Press, 1966).

20 Bon Maharaj (trs.), *The Bhakti-rasamrta-sindhu* vol. 1 (Vrindaban: Institute of Oriental Philosophy, 1965).

21 See Joshi, *Le rituel de la dévotion kṛṣṇaite* (Pondicherry: Institut Français d'Indologie, 1959), pp. 32–3.

22 Haberman, *Acting as a Way of Salvation: A Study of Rāgānuga Bhakti* (New York and Oxford: Oxford University Press, 1988), pp. 87–93.

23 Barz, *The Bhakti Sect of Vallabhācarya* (Faridabad: Thompson Press, 1976).

24 Williams, *The New Face of Hinduism, the Swaminarayan Religion* (Cambridge University Press, 1984).

25 Wilson (trs.), *The Love of Krishna: The Krsnakarnamrta of Lilasuka Bilvamangala* (Leiden: Brill, 1973).

26 See Deleury, *The Cult of Vitoba* (Poona: Deccan College Postgraduate and Research Institute, 1960); Ranade, *Mysticism in India: The Poet–Saints of Maharashtra* (Albany: SUNY Press, reprint 1983).

27 Tulpe (trs.), *Jnaneshwar's Gita: A Rendering of the Jnaneshwari* (Albany: SUNY Press, 1989).

28 For an excellent personal account of the pilgrimage see Karve, 'On the Road: A Maharashtrian Pilgrimage', in Zelliott & Bernsten (eds.), *Essays on Religion in Maharashtra* (Albany: SUNY Press, 1988). Also Fuller, *The Camphor Flame*, pp. 210–14.

29 For an account of Raidās, see Callewaert & Friedlander, *The Life and Works of Raidas* (Delhi: Manohar, 1992).

30 Vaudeville, *Kabir*, vol. 1 (Oxford: Clarendon Press, 1974).

31 Hess & Singh, *The Bijak of Kabir* (San Francisco: North Point Press, 1983), p. 42.

32 Van der Veer, *Gods on Earth: The Management of Religious Experience and Identity in a North Indian Pilgrimage Centre* (London: Athlone, 1988). Fuller, *The Camphor Flame*, pp. 163–9.

33 Hill, *The Holy Lake of the Acts of Rama, an English translation of Tulsi Das's Ramacaritmanasa* (Calcutta: Oxford University Press, 1952).

34 Lamb, 'Personalizing *Ramayan*: Ramnamis and Their Use of the *Ramacaritmanas*', in Richman, *Many Rāmāyaṇas*, p. 237.

35 Scheckner, *The Future of Ritual*, pp. 131–83.

7 Śaiva and tantric religion

1 See Madan, *Non-renunciation* (Delhi: Oxford University Press, 1987), pp. 17–47.

2 Benedict, *Patterns of Culture* (1934; London: RKP, reprint 1971), pp. 56–8.

3 *Śiva-Purāna*, trs. A Board of Scholars (Delhi: AITM, 1970) 2.16–43.

4 O'Flaherty, *Asceticism and Eroticism in the Mythology of Śiva* (Oxford University Press, 1973). Reissued as *Siva, the Erotic Ascetic* (New York: Oxford University Press, 1981).

5 The *liṅga* is often described as an 'aniconic' representation, meaning that it is not a human representation. The *liṅga* can therefore be described as an 'aniconic icon' in the sense of 'icon' as a 'spiritualization' of a physical form.

6 *Tait.Sam.* 4.5.1; *Vaj.Sam.* 16.1–66.

7 *Jab.U.* 3.66.

8 See Gonda, 'The *Śatarudriya*', in Nagatomi, Matilal and Masson (eds.), *Sanskrit and Indian Studies: Essays in Honour of Daniel H. H. Ingalls* (Dordrecht: Reidel, 1979), pp. 75–91.

9 *Svet.U.* 6.23.

10 Bhandarkar, *Vaiṣṇavism, Śaivism and Minor Religious Systems* (1913; New Delhi: Asian Educational Services, reprint 1983), p. 165.

11 *Sribha.* 2.2.37.

12 *Kur.Pur.* 1.14.30; 1.20.69.

13 Sanderson, 'Śaivism and the Tantric Traditions'; A. Sanderson, 'Purity and Power Among the Brahmans of Kashmir', in Carrithers, Collins and Lukes (eds.), *The Category of the Person: Anthropology, Philosophy, History* (Cambridge University Press, 1985), pp. 190–8.

14 Sanderson, 'Śaivism and the Tantric Traditions,' pp. 664–90.

15 *Mbh. śantiparvan* 349.64.

16 Chakraborti, *Pāśupata-sūtram with Pañcārtha-bhāṣya of Kauṇḍinya.*

17 *Kur.Pur.* 1.51.10.

18 *Pas.Su.* 1.9.

19 *Kur.Pur.* 1.14.30; 1.20.69.

20 *Pas.Su.* 4.1–24.

21 Sanderson, 'Śaivism and the Tantric Traditions', pp. 665–6.

22 *Manu* 11.73.

23 O'Flaherty, *Siva, the Erotic Ascetic*, pp. 123–27. Kramrisch, *The Presence of Śiva* (Princeton University Press, 1981), pp. 259–65.

24 Sanderson, 'Śaivism and the Tantric Traditions', pp. 667–9.

25 Snellgrove, *Indo-Tibetan Buddhism: Indian Buddhists and Their Tibetan Successors* (London: Serindia Publications, 1987), pp. 152–60.

26 On the obscure terminological symbolism or 'intentional language' (*sandhabhāṣa*) of the Tantras see Bharati, *The Tantric Tradition* (London: Rider, 1970), pp. 164–84.

27 One text which does is the *Mṛgendrāgama*. See Brunner-Lachaux, *Mṛgendrāgama: section des rites et section du comportement* (Pondicherry: Institut Français d'Indologie, 1985).

28 Bharati, *The Tantric Tradition*, p. 27: 'tantric *sadhana* follows a single pattern, Vajrayāna Buddhist and Hindu tantric *sādhana* is indistinguishable, in spite of the immense disparity between the two philosophies'.

29 Norman, *The Elder's Verses*, vol. II (London: Luzac, 1971), p. 123.

30 Brunner, 'Un Tantra du nord: le Netra Tantra', *Bulletin de l'École française d'Extrême-Orient*, 61 (1974), pp. 125–96.

31 Sanderson, 'Purity and Power', pp. 190–216; Dyczkowski, *The Doctrine of Vibration* (Albany: SUNY Press, 1987), pp. 14–17.

32 Dyczkowski, *The Canon of the Śaivāgama and the Kubjikātantras of the Western Kaula Tradition* (Albany: SUNY Press, 1988), pp. 31–2.

33 Sanderson, 'Saivism and the Tantric Traditions', p. 668.

34 Brunner-Lachaux, *Somaśambhupaddhati*, 3 vols. (Pondicherry: Institut Français d'Indologie, 1963, 1968, 1977). See also Davis, *Ritual in an Oscillating Universe: Worshipping Śiva in Medieval India* (Princeton University Press, 1991).

35 *Sp.Nir.* p. 50.

36 Sanderson, 'Śaivism and the Tantric Traditions', p. 668.

37 Parry, 'The Aghori Ascetics of Benares', in Burghardt and Cantille (eds.), *Indian Religion* (London: Curzon, 1985), pp. 51–78; Parry, 'Sacrificial Death and the Necrophagus Ascetic', in Parry and Bloch (eds), *Death and the Regeneration of Life* (Cambridge University

Press, 1982); Parry, *Death in Banaras* (Cambridge University Press, 1994), pp. 251–71.

38 See Padoux, *Le Coeur de la Yogini. Yoginīhṛdaya avec le commentaire Dīpika d'Amṛtānanda* (Paris: Diffusion de Boccard, 1994), pp. 8–10.

39 For both forms of Trika ritual see Sanderson, 'Śaivism and the Tantric Traditions', pp. 672–74; Sanderson, 'Mandala and the Āgamic Identity of the Trika of Kashmir', in Padoux (ed.), *Mantras et diagrammes rituels dans l'Hindouisme* (Paris: CNRS, 1986), pp. 169–207; Flood, *Body and Cosmology in Kashmir Śaivism* (San Francisco: Mellen Research University Press, 1993), pp. 269–301.

40 Madan, 'The ideology of the Householder among the Kashmiri Pandits', in Madan (ed.), *Way of Life, King, Householder, Renouncer* (Delhi: Vikas Publishing House, 1982), pp. 223–49. For a modern exponent of the Pratyabhijñā, see Lakshman Jee, *Kashmir Śaivism: The Secret Supreme* (Albany: Universal Śaiva Trust, 1988).

41 Peterson, *Poems to Śiva, The Hymns of the Tamil Saints* (Princeton University Press, 1989), pp. 13–14.

42 Feudalism as a model for understanding south Asia has, however, been questioned. See Stein, *Peasant, State and Society in Medieval South India*.

43 Zvelebil, *The Smile of Murugan*, pp. 185–95.

44 For an account of Kerala Tantrism see Unni, 'Introduction', in Ganapati Sastri (ed.), *Tantra Samuccaya of Nārāyaṇa* (Delhi: Nag Publishers, 1990), pp. 1–75.

45 Ramanujan, *Speaking of Śiva* (Harmondsworth: Penguin, 1973), p. 134.

46 Turner, *The Ritual Process* (Harmondsworth: Penguin, 1974), pp. 80–154.

47 Ramanujan, *Speaking of Śiva*, pp. 61–5.

8 The Goddess and Śākta traditions

1 Gross, 'Hindu Female Deities as a Resource for the Contemporary Rediscovery of the Goddess', *Journal of the American Academy of Religion*, 46.3 (1978), pp. 269–92.

2 O'Flaherty, *Women, Androgynes and Other Mythical Beasts*, p. 91. For a very good general account of the Goddess and goddesses, see Kinsley, *Hindu Goddesses: Visions of the Feminine in the Hindu Religious Tradition* (Berkeley and Los Angeles: University of

California Press, 1986). See also N. N. Bhattacharyya, *History of the Śākta Religion* (Delhi: Munshiram Manoharlal, 1974); Payne, *The Śāktas* (Calcutta: YMCA Publishing House, 1933).

3 O'Flaherty, *Women, Androgynes and Other Mythical Beasts*, p. 91.

4 Vijnanananda (trs.), *The Śrimad Devi Bhāgavatam*, Sacred Books of the Hindus 26 (New Delhi: Oriental Books, reprint 1977). See C. M. Brown, *The Triumph of the Goddess: Canonical Models and Theological Visions of the Devi-Bhāgavata Purāṇa* (Albany: SUNY Press, 1990), for a comparison of the myth in other Purāṇas.

5 *RV* 1.113.19; 2.27.1; 7.60.5; 8.47.9.

6 *Sat.Br.* 2.2.1.19; 3.2.3.6.

7 *RV* 10.59.

8 *Sat.Br.* 5.2.3.3.

9 Kinsley, *Hindu Goddesses*, pp. 107–9; 152–5.

10 Hiltebeitel, *The Cult of Draupadī*, vol. 1 (University of Chicago Press, 1988), p. 318.

11 *Dbh.Pur.* v.23.60. See C. M. Brown, *The Triumph of the Goddess*, p. 119.

12 Sanderson, 'Śaivism and the Tantric Traditions', pp. 674–8.

13 Goudriaan and Gupta, *Hindu Tantric and Śākta Literature* (Wiesbaden: Otto Harrassowitz, 1981), pp. 79–80.

14 Dyczkowski, *The Canon of the Śaivāgama*, pp. 87–92.

15 Sanderson, 'Śaivism and the Tantric Traditions', p. 687.

16 Ibid. p. 689; Goudriaan and Gupta, *Hindu Tantric and Śākta Literature*, pp. 59–64.

17 Goudriaan and Gupta, *Hindu Tantric and Śākta Literature*, pp. 64–8. This text was made comparatively famous by an early British exponent and scholar of Tantrism, Arthur Avalon (alias Sir John Woodroffe), who published it in his Tantrik Texts series (no. 8, Madras: Ganesh & Co., 1918).

18 Sastri and Srinivasa Ayyangar (trs.), *Saundaryalaharī of Śrī Śaṃkara-Bhagavatpāda* (Madras: Theosophical Publishing House, 1977); Shastri, *The Lalitāsaharanāma with the Saubhāgyabhāskarabhāṣya of Bhāskararāya* (Bombay: Nirnaya Sagar, 1935). Also see Brooks, *The Secret of the Three Cities: An Introduction to Śākta Hinduism* (Chicago and London: University of Chicago Press, 1990).

19 See Bharati, *Hindu Views and Ways and the Hindu–Muslim Interface* (Santa Barbara: Ross Erickson, 1982), pp. 23–40.

20 Sanderson, 'The Visualization of the Deities of the Trika', in Padoux (ed.), *L'Image Divine: culte et méditation dans l'Hindouisme* (Paris: Centre National de la Recherche Scientifique, 1990), pp. 80–2.

21 Padoux, *Vāc, the Concept of the Word in Selected Hindu Tantras* (Albany: SUNY Press, 1990), pp. 105–24.

22 O'Flaherty, *The Laws of Manu* (Harmondsworth: Penguin, 1991) 10.88.

23 *TA* 29.97–8.

24 Brooks, *The Secret of the Three Cities*, p. 28.

25 Sanderson, 'Purity and Power', pp. 190–8.

26 Eliade, *Yoga*, p. 258.

27 *BAU* 4.3.21: 'As a man embraced by his beloved knows neither the outer nor the inner, so a man embraced by the essence of wisdom knows neither the outer nor the inner.' (My translation.)

28 See Bharati, *The Tantric Tradition*, pp. 236–40.

29 This picture of the socially subordinate role of women has been recently challenged with regard to Buddhist Tantra. See Shaw, *Passionate Enlightenment: Women in Tantric Buddhism* (Princeton University Press, 1994).

30 Sanderson, 'Purity and Power', p. 202; Gupta, 'Women in the Śaiva/Śākta Ethos', in Leslie, *Roles and Rituals for Hindu Women*, pp. 193–210.

31 *Kau.* 16.7–10.

32 Dasgupta, *Obscure Religious Cults*; Dimock, *The Place of the Hidden Moon*.

33 Das, 'Problematic Aspects of the Sexual Rituals of the Bauls of Bengal', *Journal of the American Oriental Society*, 112.3 (1992), pp. 388–432.

34 O'Flaherty, *Hindu Myths* (Harmondsworth: Penguin, 1975), pp. 250–1.

35 *KBT*, p. 24.

36 Pocock, *Body, Mind and Wealth: A Study of Belief and Practice in an Indian Village* (Oxford: Blackwell, 1973), p. 42; Eliade, *Yoga*, pp. 349–50.

37 Fuller, *The Camphor Flame*, pp. 91–2.

38 Babb, *The Divine Hierarchy* (New York: Columbia University Press, 1975), p. 128.

39 Hiltebeitel, *The Cult of Draupadī*.

9 Hindu ritual

1 Staal, *Rules Without Meaning*.

2 *Ap.Gr.S.* 1.1.11.

3 *Manu* 2.9.

4 Turner, *The Forest of Symbols* (Ithaca and London: Cornell University Press, 1970), p. 93.

5 For this reason Pierre Bourdieu has referred to rites of passage as 'rites of institution'. Bourdieu, *Language and Symbolic Power*, pp. 117–26.

6 See Duvvury, *Play, Symbolism and Ritual: A Study of Tamil Brahman Women's Rites of Passage* (New York: Peter Lang, 1991).

7 *Manu* 2.16; 26; 29. Pandey, *Hindu Saṃskāras* (Delhi: MLBD, 1969).

8 Duvvury, *Play, Symbolism and Ritual*, p. 182.

9 *As.Gr.S.* 1.19.1–7; *Manu* 2.36.

10 *Manu* 2.67.

11 Leslie, *Roles and Rituals for Hindu Women*, p. 1.

12 Duvvury, *Play, Symbolism and Ritual*, p. 229.

13 *Manu* 3.4–5.

14 L. Dumont, *Homo Hierarchicus*, p. 119.

15 Ibid. p. 110.

16 Parry, *Death in Banaras*, pp. 151–90.

17 Knipe, 'Sapiṇḍikaraṇa: The Hindu Rite of Entry into Heaven', in Reynolds and Waugh (eds.), *Religious Encounters with Death* (University Park: Pennsylvania State University Press, 1977), pp. 111–24.

18 See Freeman, *Purity and Violence: Sacred Power in the Teyyam Worship of Malabar*, Ph.D. dissertation (Philadelphia: University of Pennsylvania, 1991), pp. 113–14.

19 See O'Flaherty, *Karma and Rebirth in Classical Indian Traditions*, pp. xviii–xx, 3–37.

20 Fuller, *The Camphor Flame*, pp. 64–6.

21 See Vaidyanathan, *Śrī Krishna: The Lord of Guruvayur* (Bombay: Bharatiya Vidya Bhavan, 1992).

22 See V. Turner, *The Ritual Process: Structure and Anti-structure* (Harmondsworth: Penguin, 1969), pp. 80–154.

23 See Eck, *Banaras: City of Light* (London: Routledge and Kegan Paul, 1984).

24 For a first-hand account of the Kumbha Mela in 1959 see Bharati, *The Ochre Robe* (Santa Barbara: Ross Erikson, 1980), pp. 228–31.

25 Daniel, *Fluid Signs*, pp. 245–78.

26 Pingree, *Jyotiḥśāstra. Astral and Mathematical Literature*, A History of Indian Literature 4 (Weisbaden: Otto Harrassowitz, 1981).

27 Davis, *Ritual in an Oscillating Universe*, pp. 101–9.

28 Berreman, *Hindus of the Himalayas: Ethnography and Change*, 2nd edn (Berkeley, Los Angeles, London: University of California Press, 1972), pp. 378–9.

29 Girard, *Violence and the Sacred*, p. 1.

30 Hiltebeitel, 'On the Handling of the Meat, and Related Matters, in Two South Indian Buffalo Sacrifices', *L'Uomo*, 9.1/2 (1985), pp. 171–99.

31 Hiltebeitel, 'On the Handling of the Meat, and Related Matters', p. 191.

32 Lincoln, *Myth, Cosmos and Society: Indo-European Themes of Creation and Destruction* (Cambridge, Mass: Harvard University Press, 1986), p. 186.

33 O'Flaherty, *Other People's Myths: The Cave of Echoes*, (New York: Macmillan, 1988), p. 99.

34 Bourdieu, *Language and Symbolic Power*, pp. 117–26.

35 See Obeyesekere, *Medusa's Hair* (Chicago and London: University of Chicago Press, 1984) for an account of possession as both cultural formation and an expression of personal biography.

36 Freeman, 'Performing Possession: Ritual and Consciousness in the Teyyam Complex', in Bruckner, Lutze and Malik (eds.), *Flags of Flame; Studies in South Asian Folk Culture* (New Delhi, Manohar Publishers, 1993), p. 116.

37 See Alper (ed.), *Understanding Mantras* (Albany: SUNY Press, 1989), pp. 3–5.

38 *Ap.S.S.* 24.1.8–15.

39 *Manu* 2.85.

40 *RV* 3.62.10.

41 *Tait.Up.* 1.8.

42 *Māṇḍūkya Upaniṣad* 1 in Radhakrishnan, *The Principal Upanisads*, pp. 693–705.

43 Killingly, 'Om: the sacred syllable in the Veda', in Lipner (ed.), *A Net Cast Wide: Investigations into Indian Thought In Memory of David Friedman* (Newcastle upon Tyne: Grevatt and Grevatt, 1987), p. 14.

10 Hindu theology and philosophy

1 Halbfass, *India and Europe, An Essay in Understanding* (Albany: SUNY Press, 1988), pp. 263–86.

2 Ibid. p. 35.

3 *RV* 10.129. Translation by O'Flaherty, *The Rig Veda*, pp. 25–6.

4 *Ch.U.* 6.2.1–2. Translation by Radhakrishnan, *The Principal Upaniṣads*, pp. 447–9.

5 *RV* 10.125.

6 *Ch.U.* 2.23.3; 6.1.3. See Coward and Raja, *The Philosophy of the Grammarians*, Encyclopaedia of Indian Philosophies (Princeton University Press, 1990), pp. 101–5.

7 *Ch.U.* 2.23.3.

8 *Vakpad.* 1.131.

9 Coward and Raja, *The Philosophy of the Grammarians*, pp. 40–1.

10 Ibid. pp. 10–11. See also Coward, *The Sphoṭa Theory of Language* (Delhi: MLBD, 1986); Raja, *Indian Theories of Meaning* (Madras: Adyar Library and Research Centre, 1963), pp. 95–148.

11 On these three positions see Pereira, *Hindu Theology: Themes, Texts and Structures* (Delhi: MLBD, reprint 1991), pp. 37–40.

12 Clooney, *Theology After Vedānta: An Experiment in Comparative Theology* (Delhi: Sri Satguru Publications, 1993), p. 21.

13 See Larson and Bhattacharya, *Sāṃkhya; A Dualist Tradition in Indian Philosophy* (Delhi: MLBD, 1987), pp. 3–41.

14 *Ch.U.* 7.25; 6.2–4.

15 *Bh.G.* 7.4.

16 *Sam.Kar.* 20–1.

17 Ibid. 62–4.

18 Rukmani, *Yogavārttika of Vijñānabhikṣu*, vol. 1 (Delhi: Munshiram Manoharlal, 1981), pp. 9–12.

19 See Clooney, *Theology After Vedānta*, pp. 23–30.

20 Jha, *Pūrva Mīmāṃsā in Its Sources* (Banaras Hindu University Press, 1942). There are English translations by Jha of Kumārila Bhaṭṭa's *Ślokavārtika* (Calcutta: Asiatic Society, 1907) and Kumārila's *Tantravārtika*, 2 vols. (Delhi: MLBD, reprint 1983).

21 Halbfass, *Tradition and Reflection*, p. 32.

22 Clooney, *Thinking Ritually; Rediscovering the Pūrva Mīmāṃsā of Jaimini* (Vienna: De Nobili Research Library, 1990), p. 192.

23 Raja, *Indian Theories of Meaning*, pp. 151–73.

24 See Clooney, 'Binding the Text, Vedanta as Philosophy and Commentary', in Rimm (ed.), *Texts in Context, Traditional Hermeneutics in South Asia* (Albany: SUNY Press, 1992), pp. 47–68; Halbfass, *Human Reason and Vedic Revelation in the Philosophy of Śaṅkara*, Studien zur Indologie und Iranistik 9, (Reinbeck: Verlag für Orientalistische Fachpublikation, 1983); Murty, *Revelation and Reason in Advaita Vedānta* (Delhi: MLBD, 1974).

25 Potter, *Advaita Vedānta Up to Śaṃkara and his Pupils*, Encyclopaedia of Indian Philosophies 3 (Delhi: MLBD, 1981), p. 6.

26 Ibid. p. 116. For translations into English of the *Brahma Sūtra Bhaṣya*, see Thibaut, *Vedānta Sūtras*, SBE 34, 38 (Delhi: AVF Books, 1987); Gambirananda, *Brahmasūtrabhaṣya* (Calcutta: Advaita Ashrama, 1965).

27 Bharati, *Hindu Views and Ways and the Hindu–Muslim Interface*, pp. 23–40. N. Brown, *The Saundaryālaharī or Flood of Beauty* (Cambridge, Mass: Harvard University Press, 1958).

28 *BSB* 1.1 in Thibaut, *Vedānta Sūtras*, p. 3 (with some amendment of the translation).

29 See Halbfass, *Tradition and Reflection*, p. 302.

30 Granoff, *Philosophy and Argument in Late Vedānta* (Boston and London: Reidel, 1978). See Dasgupta, *History of Indian Philosophy*, vol. II (1922; Delhi: MLBD, 1988) for a history of the later Advaitins.

31 Thibaut, *The Vedānta Sūtras with Commentary by Rāmānuja*, SBE 48 (Delhi: MLBD, reprint 1976); Van Buitenen, *Rāmānuja on the Bhagavadgītā: A Condensed Rendering of his Gītabhāṣya with Copious Notes and an Introduction* (Delhi: MLBD, 1974); Van

Buitenen, *Rāmānuja's Vedāntasaṃgraha* (Poona: Deccan College Postgraduate and Research Institute, 1956).

32 Thibaut, *The Vedānta Sūtras with Commentary by Rāmānuja*, p. 436.

33 For Rāmānuja's theology see Carman, *The Theology of Rāmānuja: An Essay in Interreligious Understanding* (New Haven and London: Yale University Press, 1974).

34 See Hunt Overzee, *The Body Divine, The Symbol of the Body in the Work of Teilhard de Chardin and Rāmānuja* (Cambridge University Press, 1992).

35 See Dasgupta, *History of Indian Philosophy*, vol. II, pp. 175–9.

36 The *Aṇuvyākhyāna* is translated into French by Siauve, *La voie vers la connaissance de Dieu selon l'Aṇuvyākhyāna de Madhva* (Pondicherry: Institut Français d'Indologie, 1957). The *Gītā* commentary is translated into English by Rau, *The Bhagavad Gītā and Commentaries According to Śrī Madwacharya's Bhāṣyas* (Madras: Minerva Press, 1906).

37 Rau, *The Bhagavad Gītā and Commentaries*, pp. vii–xviii.

38 For a thorough account of Madhva's teaching see Dasgupta, *A History of Indian Philosophy*, vol. IV, pp. 101–203.

39 For Śaiva Siddhānta theology see Dunuwila, *Śaiva Siddhānta Theology* (Delhi: MLBD, 1985); Dasgupta, *A History of Indian Philosophy*, vol. V; Dhavamony *Love of God according to Śaiva Siddhānta* (Oxford: Clarendon Press, 1971). For Kashmir Śaiva theology see Dyczkowski, *The Doctrine of Vibration*, and *The Stanzas on Vibration* (Albany: SUNY Press, 1992).

40 See Flood, *Body and Cosmology in Kashmir Śaivism*, pp. 55–74.

41 See Masson and Patwardhan, *Śāntarasa and Abhinavagupta's Philosophy of Aesthetics* (Poona: Deccan College 1969); Gnoli, *The Aesthetic Experience According to Abhinavagupta*, Serie Orientale Roma 9 (Rome: Is MEO, 1956).

42 See, for example, Chatterjee (ed.), *Contemporary Indian Philosophy* (London: George Allen and Unwin, 1974).

43 Radhakrishnan, *Eastern Religions And Western Thought* (Oxford University Press, 1939), pp. 20–1.

11 Hinduism and the modern world

1 For an account of Roy and his work see Crawford, *Ram Mohan Roy: Social, Political and Religious Reform in Nineteenth Century India*

(New York: Paragon House, 1987); Killingly, *Rammohun Roy in Hindu and Christian Tradition: The Teape Lectures 1990*. Newcastle upon Tyne: Grevatt and Grevatt, 1993.

2 Kopf, *The Brahmo Samāj and the Shaping of the Modern Indian Mind* (Princeton University Press, 1978).

3 Collet, *The Life and Letters of Raja Rammohan Roy* (Calcutta: Sadharan Brahmo Samaj, 1962), p. 471.

4 Richards (ed.), *A Sourcebook of Modern Hinduism* (London and Dublin: Curzon Press, 1985), p. 56.

5 For an account of Rāmakrishna's life see Müller, *Rāmakrishna, His Life and Sayings* (London: Longmans, Green and Co., 1900); Nikhilananda, *The Gospel of Sri Rāmakrishna* (New York: Rāmakrishna-Vivekānanda Center, 1980); and Hixon, *Great Swan* (Boston: Shambala, 1993). For an interesting, if somewhat reductionistic, psychological analysis of Rāmakrishna, see Sil, *Rāmakrishna Paramahamsa, A Psychological Profile* (Leiden: Brill, 1991).

6 See Bharati, 'The Hindu Renaissance and its Apologetic Pattern', *Journal of Asian Studies*, 29.2 (1970), pp. 267–87; also Bharati, *The Ochre Robe*, p. 116.

7 See Sharpe, *Western Images of the Bhagavad Gita* (London: Duckworth, 1985), p. 68.

8 Gandhi, *An Autobiography or The Story of My Experiments with Truth* (Harmondsworth: Penguin, 1982). The standard biography of Gandhi in eight volumes is Tendulkar, *Mahatma: Life and Work of Mohandas Karamchand Gandhi* (Bombay: V. K. Javeri, 1951–4). For a one-volume biography see Fischer, *The Life of Mahatma Gandhi* (Bombay: Bharatya Vidya Bhavon, 1959).

9 Quoted in Richards, *The Philosophy of Gandhi* (London and Dublin: Curzon Press, 1982), p. 48.

10 Bharati, *Hindu Views and Ways and the Hindu–Muslim Interface*, pp. 17–18.

11 On origins of the Mahā Sabhā see Gordon, 'The Hindu Mahasabha and the Indian National Congress, 1915 to 1926', *Modern Asian Studies*, 9.2 (1975), pp. 145–71.

12 See Anderson and Damle, *The Brotherhood in Saffron: The Rashtriya Swayamsevak Sangh and Hindu Revivalism* (Boulder: Westview Press, 1987).

13 Graham, *Hindu Nationalism and Indian Politics* (Cambridge University Press, 1990), p. 18.

14 For an account of the Jana Saṅgh and BJP see ibid.

15 See, for example, the graphic accounts of Shiv Sena violence in *Manushi*, 74–5 (1993), pp. 22–32.

16 *Guardian*, 7 December 1992, p. 22.

17 See *Manushi*, 79 (November–December 1994).

18 Gold, 'Rational Action and Uncontrolled Violence: Explaining Hindu Communalism', *Religion*, 22 (1991), pp. 357–76. Also Gold, 'Organized Hinduism: From Vedic Truth to Hindu Nurture', in Martz and Appleby (eds.), *Fundamentalisms Observed* (University of Chicago Press, 1991), pp. 531–93.

19 Nesbitt and Jackson, 'Sketches of Formal Hindu Nurture', in Hayward (ed.), *World Religions in Education: Religions in Britain*, SHAP Mailing (London: Commission for Racial Equality, 1986), p. 25.

20 Knott, 'Hinduism in Britain', in Hayward (ed.) *World Religions in Education: Religions in Britain*, SHAP Mailing (London: Commission for Racial Equality, 1986), p. 10.

21 For studies of Hindus in diaspora, see, for example, Knott, *Hinduism in Leeds* (University of Leeds Press, 1986); Vertovec, *Hindu Trinidad* (London: Macmillan, 1992).

22 See Kumar, *The History of Doing: An Illustrated Account of Movements for Women's Rights and Feminism in India, 1800–1990* (London: Verso Press, 1994).

23 Bharati, 'The Hindu Renaissance and Its Apologetic Patterns', p. 273.

24 Roth and Bothlingk, *St. Petersburg Wörterbuch* (Delhi: MLBD, reprint 1991).

25 Lanman, *A Sanskrit Reader, Text and Vocabulary and Notes* (Massachussets: Harvard University Press, 1884).

26 See Staal (ed.), *A Reader on the Sanskrit Grammarians* (Cambridge, Mass., and London: M.I.T Press, 1973), pp. 138–272.

27 Williams, *Parameśwara-jnyāna-goshti: A Dialogue of the Knowledge of the Supreme Lord in which are compared the claims of Christianity and Hinduism* (Cambridge: Deighton, Bell and Co., 1856).

28 For an excellent account of western scholarship and India, see Halbfass, *India and Europe*.

29 Ibid. p. 102.

30 Nietzsche, *The Twilight of the Idols and the Anti Christ* (Harmondsworth: Penguin, 1968) pp. 56–9.

31 For an account of the influence of the East on Jung, see Coward, *Jung and Eastern Thought* (Albany: SUNY Press, 1984).

32 Melton, 'The Attitude of Americans Toward Hinduism from 1883 to 1983 with Special Reference to the International Society for Krishna Consciousness' (unpublished paper, 1985); Riepe, *The Philosophy of India and Its Impact on American Thought* (Springfield: Charles C. Thomas, 1970).

33 Jayakar, *J. Krishnamurti: A Biography* (Delhi: Penguin, 1987).

34 See for example Capra, *The Tao of Physics – An Exploration of the Parallels Between Modern Physics and Eastern Mysticism* (London: Flamingo Paperback, 1983).

35 Ghose, *The Life Divine* (Pondicherry: Sri Aurobindo Ashram, 1973); Ghose, *Synthesis of Yoga* (Pondicherry: Sri Aurobindo Ashram, 1971); Ghose, *On Himself, Compiled from Notes and Letters* (Pondicherry: Sri Aurobindo Ashram, 1972).

36 Miller and Miller (eds.), *The Spiritual Teaching of Ramana Maharshi* (Boulder and London: Shambala, 1972), pp. 3–14.

37 Yogānanda, *The Autobiography of a Yogi* (London: Rider and Co., 1950)

38 J. Johnson, *The Path of the Masters: The Science of Surat Shabd Yoga* (Beas: Radha Soami Satsang, 1975). See also Juergensmeyer, *Radhasoami Reality*.

39 The literature put out by these movements and teachers is vast, though there are comparatively few scholarly studies. On Rajneesh see Thompson and Heelas, *The Way of the Heart* (Wellingborough: Aquarian Press, 1986). On Hare Kṛṣṇa see Knott, *My Sweet Lord* (Wellingborough: Aquarian Press, 1986). For Anandamayima see Das Gupta, *The Mother As Revealled to Me* (Banaras: Shree Anandamayi Sangha, 1954). For the Maharishi, see Eban (ed.), *Maharishi the Guru. The Story of Maharishi Mahesh Yogi* (Bombay: Pearl Publications, 1968). Accounts of some of these groups can be found in Barker (ed.), *New Religious Movements: A Perspective for Understanding Society* (New York: Mellen, 1982); Needham, *The New Religions* (New York: Crossroad Press, 1984); Hardy, 'How "Indian" are the new Indian Religions?', *Religion Today. A Journal of Contemporary Religions*, 1.2/3 (Oct.–Dec. 1984), pp. 15–16. On the idea of 'holy madness' in the teaching and life of many western gurus see Feuerstein, *Holy Madness* (New York: Arkana, 1990).

Plate 1 A Śaiva holy man by the Kanyakumarī Temple, Tamilnadu

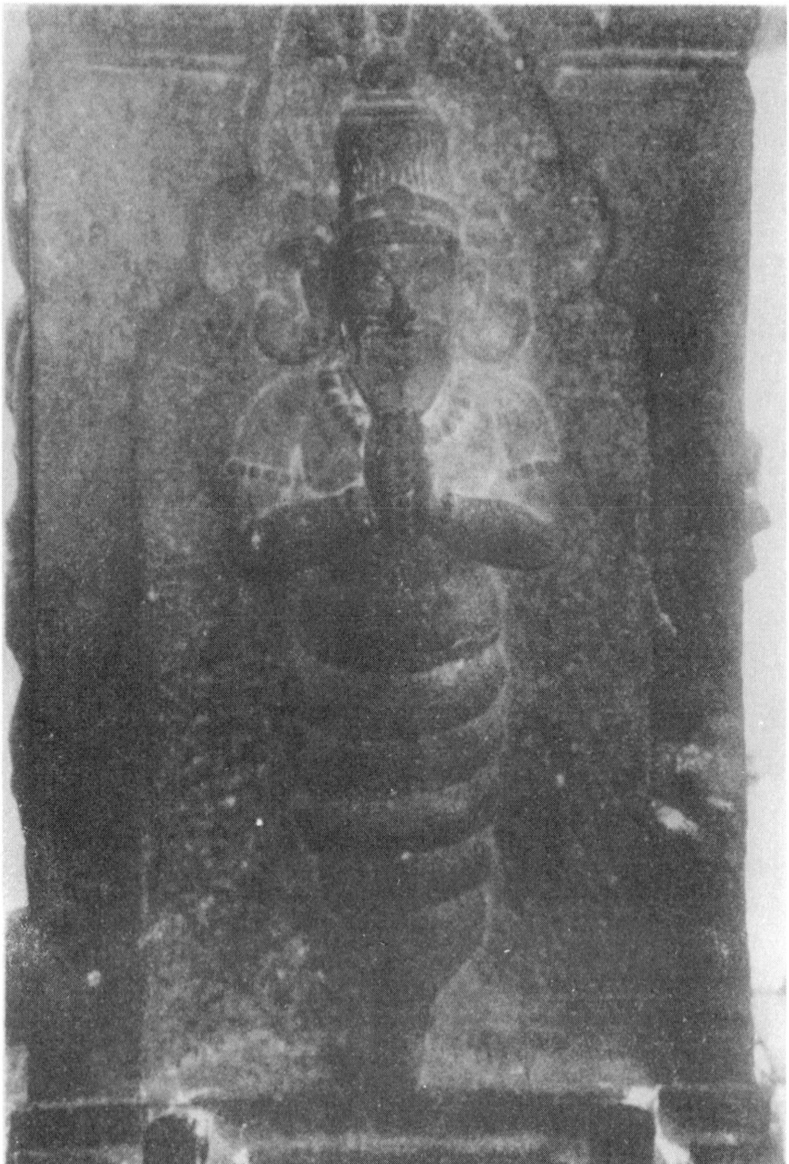

Plate 2 A mythical representation of Patañjali, the Grammarian and possibly the author of the *Yoga Sūtra*, as half man, half serpent. Śiva gave him this boon so that he would not crush insects with his feet. From the Śiva Naṭarāja Temple, Cidambaram, Tamilnadu

Plate 3 Lord Kṛṣṇa. A popular representation

Plate 4 Lord Kṛṣṇa with Rādhā. A popular representation

Plate 5 Lord Śiva the ascetic. A popular representation

Plate 6 Śiva Naṭarāja, the Dancing Śiva. Bronze, *c.* 1100 CE

Plate 7 A Śiva *liṅga* covered in petals, Cidambaram

Plate 8 Lord Gaṇeśa This unusual twelfth- or thirteenth-century representation from Orissa, shows him with five heads, with his Śakti seated upon his knee

Plate 9 The Goddess Durgā slaying the buffalo demon. Siva Naṭarāja Temple, Cidambaram

Plate 10 The ferocious Goddess Cāmuṇḍā seated upon a corpse. Orissa, eighth or ninth century CE

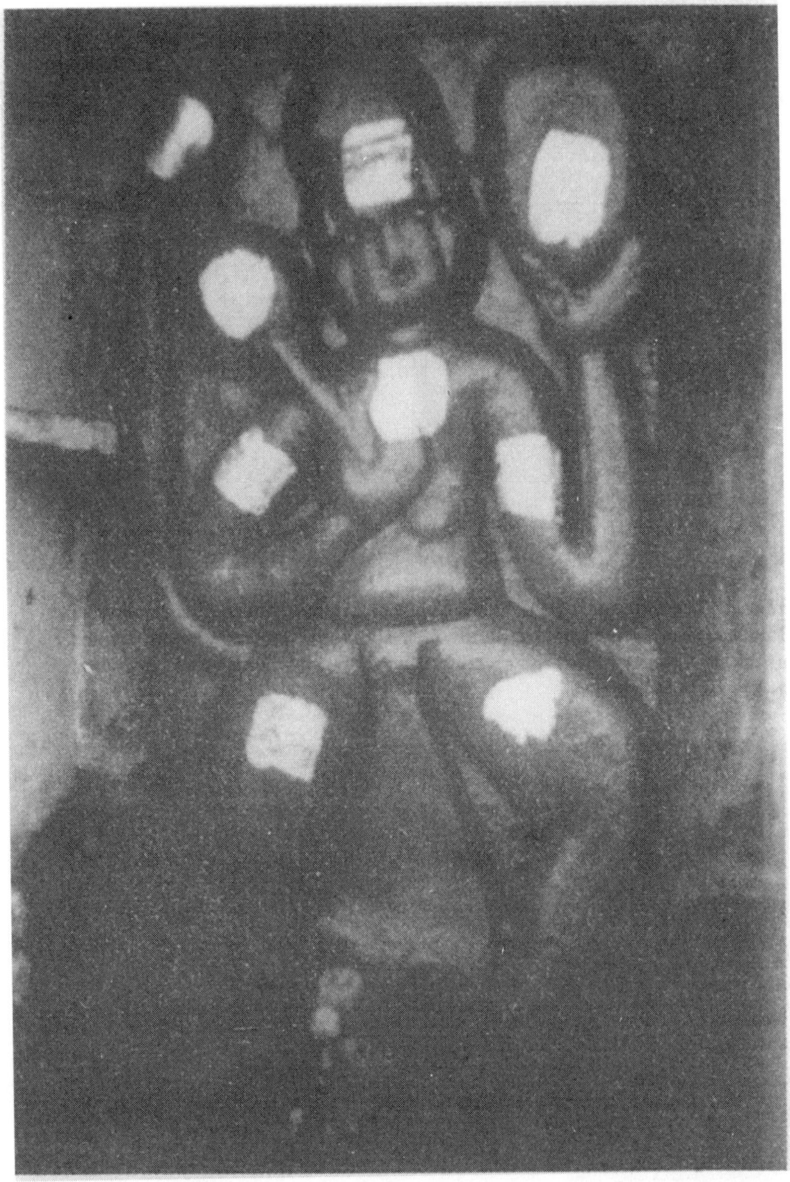

Plate 11 Hanumān, the monkey-god

Plate 12 The Descent of the Goddess Gaṅgā or Arjuna's Penance, Mahabalipuram, Tamilnadu, seventh century CE. In this rock carving we can see an ascetic (Arjuna?) practising austerity (*tapas*) and representations of various divine beings, including Nāgas in the Ganges itself

Plate 13 The Kapaleśvarī Tempıe, Madras

Plate 14 The south gateway (*gopura*) of the Śiva Naṭarāja Temple at Cidambaram

Plate 15 A young girl offering a flower to Lord Kṛṣṇa's footprint

Plate 16 A serpent (*nāga*) shrine, Bhagamandala, Karnataka

Plate 17 Teyyam Shrine housing three teyyam deities, Nileshwaram, Kerala

Plate 18 Teyyam Shrine, housing the two teyyam deities. Kerala

Plate 19 The teyyam Goddess Mūvāḷamkuḻicāmuṇḍī

Plate 20 The teyyam deity Viṣṇumūrti

Bibliography

Allchin, B. and R. Allchin. *The Rise of Civilization in India and Pakistan*. Cambridge University Press, 1982.

Alper, H. (ed.). *Understanding Mantras*. Albany: SUNY Press, 1989.

Alston, A. J. *Śaṅkara on the Absolute*. London: Sheti Sadan, 1980.

—*Śaṅkara on the Soul*. London: Sheti Sadan, 1981.

Amore, R. C., and L. D. Shinn. *Lustful Maidens and Ascetic Kings: Buddhist and Hindu Stories of Life*. New York: Oxford University Press, 1981.

Anderson, W. K., and S. D. Dhamle. *The Brotherhood in Saffron: The Rashtriya Swayamsevak Saṅgh and Hindu Revivalism*. Boulder: Westview Press, 1987.

Appadurai, A., F. J. Korom and M. A. Miles (eds.). *Gender, Genre and Power in South Asian Expressive Traditions*. Philadelphia: University of Pennsylvania Press, 1991.

Aranya, Swami H. *Yoga Philosophy of Patañjali*. Albany: SUNY Press, 1983

Babb, L. *The Divine Hierarchy*. New York: Columbia University Press, 1975.

Bailey, G. M. 'On the Object of Study in Puranic Research; Three Recent Books on the Purāṇas', *Review of the Asian Studies Association of Australia*, 10.3 (1987), pp. 106–14.

Banerjea, A. K. *Philosophy of Gorakhnath*. Gorakhpur: Mahant Dig Vijai Nath Trust, 1962.

Barker, E. (ed.). *New Religious Movements: A Perspective for Understanding Society*. New York: Mellen, 1982.

Bary, W. T. de (ed.). *Sources of the Indian Tradition*. New York: Columbia University Press, 1958.

Barz, R. *The Bhakti Sect of Vallabhācarya*. Faridabad: Thompson Press, 1976.

Basham, A. L. *The Wonder That Was India*. New York: Grove Press, 1959.

—*History and Doctrines of the Ājīvikas*. Delhi: MLBD, 1981.

Beane, C. W. *Myth, Cult and Symbol in Sakta Hinduism: A Study of the Indian Mother Goddess*. Leiden: Brill, 1977.

Bechert, H. 'The Date of the Buddha Reconsidered', *Indologica Taurinensia*, 10 (1982), pp. 29–36.

Benedict, R. *Patterns of Culture*. [1934] London: RKP, reprint 1971.

Berger, P. *The Sacred Canopy, Elements of a Sociological Theory of Religion*. New York: Anchor Books, 1990.

Berreman, G. D. *Hindus of the Himalayas: Ethnography and Change*, 2nd edn. Berkeley, Los Angeles, London: University of California Press, 1972.

Bhandarkar, R. G. *Vaiṣṇavism, Śaivism and Minor Religious Systems*. [1913] New Delhi: Asian Educational Services, reprint 1983.

Bharati, A. *The Tantric Tradition*. London: Rider, 1965.

—'The Hindu Renaissance and its Apologetic Patterns', *Journal of Asian Studies*, 29.2 (1970), pp. 267–87.

—*The Ochre Robe*. Santa Barbara: Ross Erikson, 1980.

—*Hindu Views and Ways and the Hindu–Muslim Interface*. Santa Barbara: Ross Erickson, 1982.

Bhattacharya, D. *Love Songs of Vidyāpati*. London: Allen and Unwin, 1963.

—*Love Songs of Chandidās*. London: Allen and Unwin, 1967.

Bhattacharyya, H. (ed.). *The Cultural Heritage of India*, 4 vols. Calcutta: Ramakrishna Mission, 1953–6.

Bhattacharyya, N. N. *History of the Śākta Religion*. Delhi: Munshiram Manoharlal, 1974.

Biardeau, M. (ed.). *Autour de la Déesse hindoue*. Paris: Editions de l'Ecole des hautes Etudes en Sciences Sociales, 1981.

—*Hinduism, The Anthropology of a Civilization*. New Delhi: Oxford University Press, 1989.

Biardeau, M., and C. Malamoud. *Le sacrifice dans l'Inde ancienne*. Paris: Presses Universitaires de France, 1976.

Blacker, C., and M. Loewe (eds.). *Ancient Cosmologies*. London: George Allen and Unwin, 1975.

Bloomfield, M. *Hymns of the Atharva Veda*, SBE 42. Delhi: MLBD, reprint 1967.

Blurton, T. P. *Hindu Art*. London: British Museum Press, 1992.

Bon Maharaj, T. S. B. H. (trs.). *The Bhakti-radamrta-sindhu*, vol. 1. Vrindaban: Institute of Oriental Philosophy, 1965.

Bourdieu, P. *Outline of a Theory of Practice*. Cambridge University Press, 1991.

—*Language and Symbolic Power*. Cambridge: Polity Press, 1991.

Boyer, A. M. 'Etude sur l'origine de la doctrine du samsara', *Journal Asiatique*, 2 (1901), pp. 451–99.

Brereton, J. P. *The Rgvedic Adityas*, American Oriental Series 63. New Haven: Harvard University Press, 1981.

Brockington, J. *The Sacred Thread*. Edinburgh University Press, 1981.

Bronkhorst, J. *The Two Traditions of Meditation in Ancient India*. Delhi: MLBD, 1993.

Brooks, D. R. *The Secret of the Three Cities: An Introduction to Śākta Hinduism*. Chicago and London: University of Chicago Press, 1990.

Brown, C. M. *The Triumph of the Goddess: The Canonical Models and Theological Visions of the Devi-Bhāgavata Purāṇa*. Albany: SUNY Press, 1990.

Brown, N. *The Saundaryālaharī or Flood of Beauty*. Cambridge, Mass.: Harvard University Press, 1958.

Brunner, H. 'Un Tantra du nord: le Netra Tantra', *Bulletin de l'Ecole Française d'Extréme-Orient*, 61 (1974), pp. 125–96.

Brunner-Lachaux, H. *Somaśambhupaddhati*. 3 vols. Pondicherry: Institut Français d'Indologie, 1963, 1968, 1977.

—*Mṛgendrāgama: section des rites et section du comportement*. Pondicherry: Institut Français d'Indologie, 1985.

Buck, W. *The Mahābhārata Retold*. Berkeley and Los Angeles: University of California Press, 1973.

Buitenen, J. A. B. van. *Rāmānuja's Vedāntasaṃgraha*. Poona: Deccan College Postgraduate and Research Institute, 1956.

—*Rāmānuja on the Bhagavadgītā: A Condensed Rendering of his Gītabhāṣya with Copious Notes and an Introduction*. Delhi: MLBD, 1974.

—*The Mahābhārata*, 3 vols. University of Chicago Press, 1973–8.

—*The Bhagavadgītā in the Mahābhārata*. Chicago and London: University of Chicago Press, 1981.

Burghardt, R., and A. Cantille (eds.). *Indian Religion*. London: Curzon, 1985.

Callewaert, W. M., and P. G. Friedlander. *The Life and Works of Raidas*. Delhi: Manohar, 1992.

Capra, F. *The Tao of Physics – An Exploration of the Parallels Between Modern Physics and Eastern Mysticism*. London: Flamingo Paperback, 1983.

Carman, J. B. *The Theology of Rāmānuja: An Essay in Interreligious Understanding*. New Haven and London: Yale University Press, 1974.

Carman, J. B., and F. A. Marglin (eds.). *Purity and Auspiciousness in Indian Society*. Leiden: Brill, 1985.

Carman, J. B., and V. Narayanan. *The Tamil Veda*. Chicago and London: University of Chicago Press, 1989.

Carrithers, M., S. Collins and S. Lukes (eds.). *The Category of the Person: Anthropology, Philosophy, History*. Cambridge University Press, 1985.

Carstairs, G. M. *The Twice Born*. London: Hogarth Press, 1957.

Chakraborti, H. (trs.). *Pāśupata-Sūtram with Pañcārtha-bhāṣya of Kauṇḍinya*. Calcutta: Academic Publishers, 1970.

Chatterjee, M. (ed.). *Contemporary Indian Philosophy*. London: George Allen and Unwin, 1974.

Chattopadhyaya, D. *Lokāyata*. New Delhi: People's Publishing House, 1959.

Chemparthy, G. *An Indian Rational Theology: Introduction to Udayana's Nyāyakusumañjali*. Vienna: De Nobili Research Library, 1972.

Clooney, F. X. *Thinking Ritually; Rediscovering the Pūrva Mīmāṃsā of Jaimini*. Vienna: De Nobili Research Library, 1990.

—'Binding the Text, Vedanta as Philosophy and Commentary', in Timm, *Texts in Context, Traditional Hermeneutics in South Asia*, pp. 47–68.

—*Theology After Vedānta: An Experiment in Comparative Theology*. Delhi: Sri Satguru Publications, 1993.

Clothey, F. *The Many Faces of Murukan: The History and Meaning of a South Indian God*. The Hague: Mouton, 1978.

Coburn, T. '"Scripture" in India: Towards a Typology of the Word in Hindu Life,' in M. Levering, *Rethinking Scripture; Essays from a Comparative Perspective*, p. 112.

Collet, S. D. *The Life and Letters of Raja Rammohan Roy*. Calcutta: Sadharan Brahmo Samaj, 1962.

Courtright, P. B. *Ganeśa: Lord of Obstacles, Lord of Beginnings*. New York: Oxford University Press, 1962.

Coward, H. G. *Jung and Eastern Thought*. Albany: SUNY Press, 1984.

—*The Sphoṭa Theory of Language*. Delhi: MLBD, 1986.

Coward, H. G., and K. K. Raja. *The Philosophy of the Grammarians*, Encyclopaedia of Indian Philosophies 5. Princeton University Press, 1990.

Coward, H. G., J. J. Lipner and K. K. Young (eds.). *Hindu Ethics*. Albany: SUNY Press, 1991.

Cowell, E. B. *Sarva Darśana Saṃgraha: A Review of the Different Systems of Indian Philosophy*. London: Kegan Paul, 1904.

Crawford, S. C. *Ram Mohan Roy: Social, Political and Religious Reform in Nineteenth Century India*. New York: Paragon House, 1987.

Dales, G., and J. M. Kenoyer. *Excavations at Mohenjo Daro, Pakistan*. Philadelphia: University of Pennsylvania Museum Monograph, 1993.

Dandekar, R. N. *Exercises in Indology*. Delhi: Ajanta Publications, 1981.

Daniel, E. V. *Fluid Signs: Being a Person the Tamil Way*. Berkeley: University of California Press, 1984.

Daniélou, A. *The Gods of India*. New York: Inner Traditions International, 1985.

Das, R. P. 'Problematic Aspects of the Sexual Rituals of the Bauls of Bengal', *Journal of the American Oriental Society*, 112.3 (1992), pp. 388–432.

Das Gupta, C. *The Mother As Revealled to Me*. Banaras: Shree Anandamayi Sangha, 1954.

Dasgupta, S. N. *History of Indian Philosophy*, 5 vols. [1922] Delhi: MLBD, 1988.

—*Obscure Religious Cults*. Calcutta: Mukhopadhyay, 1969.

Davies, J. *Sāṅkhya Kārikā of Īśvara Kṛṣṇa*. Calcutta: Susil Gupta, 1947.

Davis, R. H. *Ritual in an Oscillating Universe: Worshipping Śiva in Medieval India*. Princeton University Press, 1991.

Dehejia, V. *Slaves of the Lord*. Delhi: Munishiram Manoharlal, 1988.

Deleury, G. A. *The Cult of Vitoba*. Poona: Deccan College Postgraduate and Research Institute, 1960.

Derrett, J. D. *Dharmasutras and Juridical Literature*. History of Indian Literatures, fasc. 1. Wiesbaden: Otto Harrassowitz, 1973.

—*Essays in Classical and Modern Hindu Law*, 4 vols. Leiden: Brill, 1976–8.

Derrida, J. *Of Grammatology*. Baltimore: Johns Hopkins University Press, 1976.

Deussen, P. *The Philosophy of the Upanisads*. [1905] New York: Dover Publications, reprint 1966.

Deutsch, E., and J. A. B. van Buitenen. *A Source Book of Advaita Vedānta*. Honolulu: University of Hawaii, 1971.

Dhavamony, M. *Love of God According to Śaiva Siddhānta*. Oxford: Clarendon Press, 1971.

Diehl, C. G. *Instrument and Purpose: Studies on Rites and Rituals in South India*. Lund: C. W. K. Gleerup, 1956.

Dimock, E. *The Place of the Hidden Moon*. University of Chicago Press, 1966.

Dimock, E., and D. Levertov. *In Praise of Krishna: Songs from the Bengali*. New York: Anchor Books, 1967.

Dirks, N. B. *The Hollow Crown*. Ann Arbor: University of Michigan Press, 1993.

Dirks, N. B., G. Eley and S. B. Ortner (eds.). *Culture, Power, History: A Reader in Contemporary Social Theory*. Princeton University Press, 1994.

Doniger, W. (trs.). *The Laws of Manu*. Harmondsworth: Penguin, 1991.

Dowson, J. A. *A Classical Dictionary of Hindu Mythology and Religion, Geography, History and Literature*. London: Routledge and Kegan Paul, 1961.

Dumézil, G. 'Métiers et classes fonctionnelles chez divers peuples Indo-Européens', *Annales, Economies, Sociétés, Civilisations* (13e année), 4 (Oct.–Dec. 1958), pp. 716–24.

Dumont, L. *Homo Hierarchicus: The Caste System and its Implications*. Chicago and London: University of Chicago Press, 1980.

Dumont, P. E. *L'Aśvamedha: description du sacrifice solennel du cheval dans le culte vedique d'après les textes du Yajurveda blanc*. Paris: Geuthner 1927.

Dundas, P. *The Jains*. London: Routledge and Kegan Paul, 1992.

Dunuwila, R. A. *Śaiva Siddhānta Theology*. Delhi: MLBD, 1985.

Durkheim, E. *The Elementary Forms of the Religious Life*. London: Allen and Unwin, 1964.

Dutt, J. C. (trs.). *Kings of Kashmira: Being a Translation of the Sanskrita Work Rājataraṅgiṇī of Kalhaṇa Pandita*, 3 vols. [1879.] Delhi: MLBD, reprint 1990.

Duvvury, V. K. *Play, Symbolism and Ritual: A Study of Tamil Brahman Women's Rites of Passage*. New York: Peter Lang, 1991.

Dyczkowski, M. S. G. *The Doctrine of Vibration*. Albany: SUNY Press, 1987.

—*The Canon of the Śaivāgama and the Kubjikā Tantras of the Western Kaula Tradition*. Albany: SUNY Press, 1988.

—*The Stanzas on Vibration*. Albany: SUNY Press, 1992.

Eban, M. (ed.). *Maharishi the Guru. The Story of Maharishi Mahesh Yogi*. Bombay: Pearl Publications, 1968.

Eck, D. *Banaras: City of Light*. London: Routledge and Kegan Paul, 1984.

Eggeling, J. *The Śatapatha-Brahmana*, 5 vols. SBE 12, 26, 41, 43, 44. Delhi: MLBD, reprint 1978–82.

Eliade, M. 'Cosmical Homology and Yoga', *Journal of the Indian Society of Oriental Arts*, 5 (1937), pp. 188–203.

—*Yoga: Immortality and Freedom*. Princeton University Press, 1973.

Emeneau, M. B., and T. Burrow. *Dravidian Borrowings from Indo-Aryan*. Berkeley: University of California Press, 1962.

Fairservis, W. A. *The Roots of Ancient India*. University of Chicago Press, 1975.

Fauré, B. *The Rhetoric of Immediacy: A Cultural Critique of Chan/Zen Buddhism*. Princeton University Press, 1991.

Feuerstein, G. *Yoga, The Technology of Ecstasy*. Wellingborough: Crucible, 1989.

—*Holy Madness*. New York: Arkana, 1990.

Fischer, L. *The Life of Mahatma Gandhi*. Bombay: Bharatiya Vidya Bhavan, 1959.

Flood, G. D. *Body and Cosmology in Kashmir Śaivism*. San Francisco: Mellen Research University Press, 1993.

—'Ritual, Cosmos and the Divine Body in the Jayākhyasaṃhitā', *Wiener Zeitschrift für die Kunde Sudasiens*, supplement (1993), pp. 167–77.

Frawley, D. *Gods, Sages and Kings: Vedic Secrets of Ancient Civilization*. Salt Lake City: Passages Press, 1991.

Freeman, J. R. *Purity and Violence: Sacred Power in the Teyyam Worship of Malabar*, Ph.D. dissertation. Philadelphia: University of Pennsylvania, 1991.

—'Performing Possession: Ritual and Consciousness in the Teyyam Complex', in H. Bruckner, L. Lutze and A. Malik (eds.), *Flags of Flame; Studies in South Asian Folk Culture*. New Delhi: Manohar Publishers, 1993.

Frykenberg, R. E. 'The Emergence of Modern "Hinduism"', in Sontheimer and Kulke, *Hinduism Reconsidered*, pp. 29–49.

Fuller, C. *Servants of the Goddess: The Priests of a South Indian Temple*. Cambridge University Press, 1984.

—*The Camphor Flame: Popular Hinduism and Society in India*. Princeton University Press, 1992.

Gambirananda, Swami. *Brahmasūtrabhāṣya*. Calcutta: Advaita Ashrama, 1965.

Gandhi, M. K. *An Autobiography or The Story of My Experiments with Truth*. Harmondsworth: Penguin, 1982.

Geertz, C. *The Interpretation of Cultures*. London: Fontana, 1993.

Geldner, K. F. *Der Rigveda: Aus dem Sanskrit ins Deutsche übersetzt und mit einem laufenden Kommentar versehen*, 3 vols. Harvard Oriental Series 33, 34, 35. Cambridge, Mass.: Harvard University Press, 1951.

Ghose, A. *Synthesis of Yoga*. Pondicherry: Sri Aurobindo Ashram, 1971.

—*On Himself, Compiled from Notes and Letters*. Pondicherry: Sri Aurobindo Ashram, 1972.

—*The Life Divine*. Pondicherry: Sri Aurobindo Ashram, 1973.

Ghurye, G. S. *Indian Sadhus*. Bombay: Popular Prakashan, 1964.

Giles, H. A. *The Travels of Fa-hsien (399–414 AD), or Record of the Buddhist Kingdoms*. Cambridge University Press, 1923.

Girard, R. *Violence and the Sacred*. Baltimore and London; Johns Hopkins University Press, 1977.

Gnoli, R. *The Aesthetic Experience According to Abhinavagupta*, Serie Orientale Roma 9. Rome: Is MEO, 1956.

Gokhale, B. G. 'The Early Buddhist Elite', *Journal of Indian History*, 42.2 (1965), pp. 391–402.

Gold, D. 'Organized Hinduism: From Vedic Truth to Hindu Nurture', in M. Martz and S. Appleby (eds.), *Fundamentalisms Observed*. University of Chicago Press, 1991, pp. 531–93.

—'Rational Action and Uncontrolled Violence: Explaining Hindu Communalism', *Religion*, 22 (1991), pp. 357–76.

Goldman, R. P. (gen. ed.). *The Rāmānuja of Vālmīki: An Epic of Ancient India*, vol. I: *Balakāṇḍa*, ed. R. P. Goldman, Princeton University Press, 1984; vol. II: *Ayodhyākāṇḍa*, ed. S. I. Pollock, Princeton University Press, 1986; vol. III: *Aranyakāṇḍa*, ed. S. I. Pollock, Princeton University Press, 1991.

Gombrich, R. F. 'Ancient Indian Cosmology', in Blacker and Loewe, *Ancient Cosmologies*, pp. 110–42.

—*Theravāda Buddhism: A Social History from Ancient Benares to Modern Colombo*. London and New York: Routledge and Kegan Paul, 1988.

Gonda, J. 'The Indian Mantra', *Oriens*, 16 (1963), pp. 244–97.

—*The Vision of the Vedic Seers*. Amsterdam: North Holland Publishing Co., 1963.

—*Change and Continuity in Indian Religion*. [1965] New Delhi: Munshiram Manoharlal, reprint 1985.

—*Ancient Indian Kingship from the Religious Point of View*, Leiden: Brill, 1966.

—*Loka: World and Heaven in the Veda*. Amsterdam: North Holland Publishing Co., 1966.

—*Vedic Literature*, History of Indian Literature 1', fasc. 1. Wiesbaden: Otto Harrassowitz, 1975.

—*The Ritual Sūtras*, History of Indian Literature 1, fasc. 2. Wiesbaden: Otto Harrassowitz, 1977.

—'The *Śatarudriya*', in Nagatomi, Matilal and Masson, *Sanskrit and Indian Studies: Essays in Honour of Daniel H. H. Ingalls*, pp. 75–91.

—*Vedic Ritual, The Non-Solemn Rites*. Leiden: Brill, 1980.

—*Mantra Interpretation in the Śatapatha Brāhmaṇa*. Leiden: Brill, 1988.

Gordon, R. 'The Hindu Maharabha and the Indian National Congress, 1915 to 1926', *Modern Asia Studies*, 9.2 (1975), pp. 145–71.

Goudriaan, T., and S. Gupta. *Hindu Tantric and Śākta Literature*, History of Indian Literature 2, fasc. 2. Wiesbaden: Otto Harrassowitz, 1981.

Graham, B. D. *Hindu Nationalism and Indian Politics*. Cambridge University Press, 1990, p. 18.

Granoff, P. *Philosophy and Argument in Late Vedānta*. Boston and London: Reidel, 1978.

Griffiths, R. T. H. *Texts of the White Yajur Veda*. Banaras: Lazarus, 1957.

Gross, R. 'Hindu Female Deities as a Resource for the Contemporary Rediscovery of the Goddess', *Journal of the American Academy of Religion*, 46.3 (1978), pp. 269–92.

Guha, R. 'The Prose of Counter-Insurgency', in Dirks, Eley and Ortner, *Culture, Power, History: A Reader in Contemporary Social Theory*, pp. 336–71.

Gupta, S. 'Yoga and Antarayāga in Pāñcaratra', in T. Goudriaan (ed.), *Ritual and Speculation in Early Tantrism*. Albany: SUNY Press, 1992, pp. 175–208.

Gupta, S., and R. Gombrich. 'Kings, Power and the Goddess', *South Asia Research*, 6.2 (1986), pp. 123–38.

Gupta, S., D. J. Hoens and T. Goudriaan. *Hindu Tantrism. Handbuch der Orientalistik*. Leiden: Brill, 1979.

Haberman, D. L. *Acting as a Way of Salvation: A Study of Rāgānuga Bhakti*. New York and Oxford: Oxford University Press, 1988.

Hacker, P. *Prahlāda, Werden und Wandlungen einer Ideal-gestalt*. Akademie der Wissenschaften und der Literatur in Mainz, Abhandlungen der Geistes- und Sozialwissenschaftlichen Klasse 13. Wiesbaden: Franz Steiner Verlag, 1960.

Halbfass, W. *Human Reason and Vedic Revelation in the Philosophy of Śaṅkara*. Studien zur Indologie und Iranistik 9. Reinbeck: Verlag für Orientalistische Fachpublikation, 1983.

—*India and Europe, An Essay in Understanding*. Albany: SUNY Press, 1988.

—*Tradition and Reflection: Explorations in Indian Thought*. Albany: SUNY Press, 1991.

—*On Being and What There Is: Classical Vaisesika and the History of Indian Ontology*. Albany: SUNY Press, 1992.

Hardy, F. *Viraha Bhakti*. Delhi: Oxford University Press, 1983.

—'How "Indian" are the New Indian Religions?', *Religion Today. A Journal of Contemporary Religions*, 1.2/3 (Oct.–Dec. 1984), pp. 15–16.

—'Hinduism', in U. King (ed.), *Turning Points in Religious Studies*. Edinburgh: T. and T. Clark, 1990, pp. 145–55.

—*The Religious Culture of India: Power, Love and Wisdom*. Cambridge University Press, 1994.

Hart, G. *The Relationship Between Tamil and Classical Sanskrit Literature*, History of Indian Literature 10, fasc. 2. Wiesbaden: Otto Harrassowitz, 1976.

Hartsuiker, D. *Sādhus, the Holy Men of India*. London: Thames and Hudson, 1993.

Hauer, J. W. *Der Vrātya*, vol I: *Die Vrātya als nicht-brahmanische Kultgenossenschaften arischer Herkunft*. Stuttgart: Kohlhammer Verlag, 1927.

Hawley, J. S. *At Play with Kṛṣṇa: Pilgrimage Dramas from Brindaban*. Princeton University Press, 1981.

—(ed.) *Satī, the Blessing and the Curse: The Burning of Wives in India*. New York and Oxford: Oxford University Press, 1994.

Hawley, J. S., and D. M. Wulff (eds.), *The Divine Consort: Rādhā and the Goddesses of India*. Berkeley: University of California Press, 1982.

Hayward, M. (ed.). *World Religions in Education: Religions in Britain*, SHAP Mailing. London: Commission for Racial Equality, 1986.

Heesterman, J. C. 'Vrātya and Sacrifice', *Indo-Iranian Journal*, 6 (1962), pp. 1–37.

—*The Inner Conflict of Tradition: An Essay in Indian Ritual, Kingship and Society*. University of Chicago Press, 1985.

—*The Broken World of Sacrifice: Essays in Ancient Indian Ritual*. Chicago and London: University of Chicago Press, 1993.

Hess, L., and S. Singh. *The Bijak of Kabir.* San Francisco: North Point Press, 1983.

Hill, W. D. P. *The Holy Lake of the Acts of Rama, an English translation of Tulsi Das's Ramacaṅrtmanasa*. Calcutta: Oxford University Press, 1952.

Hiltebeitel, A. *The Ritual of Battle: Krishna in the Mahābhārata*. Ithaca: Cornell University Press, 1976.

—'The Indus Valley "proto-Siva", Re-examination through Reflection on the Goddess, the Buffalo, and the Symbolism of the *vāhanas*', *Anthropos*, 73.5–6 (1978), pp. 767–79.

—'On the Handling of the Meat, and Related Matters, in Two South Indian Buffalo Sacrifices', *L'Uomo*, 9.1/2 (1985), pp. 171–99.

—*The Cult of Draupadī*, vol. I: *Mythologies from Gingee to Kuruksetra*; vol. II: *On Hindu Ritual and the Goddess*. Chicago and London: Chicago University Press, 1988, 1991.

Hiriyanna, M. *Outlines of Indian Philosophy*. London: George Allen and Unwin, 1958.

Hixon, L. *Great Swan*. Boston: Shambala, 1993.

Hopkins, T. J. *The Hindu Religious Tradition*. Belmont: Dickenson, 1971.

Hulin, M. *Sāṃkhya Literature*, History of Indian Literature 6, fasc. 3. Wiesbaden: Otto Harrassowitz, 1978.

Hume, R. (trs.). *Principal Upaniṣads*. Oxford University Press, 1921.

Hunt Overzee, A. *The Body Divine, The Symbol of the Body in the Work of Teilhard de Chardin and Rāmānuja*. Cambridge University Press, 1992.

Inden, R. 'Hierarchies of Kings in Early Medieval India', in Madan, *Way of Life, King, Householder, Renouncer: Essays in Honour of Louis Dumont*, pp. 99–125.

—'Kings and Omens', in Carman and Marglin, *Purity and Auspiciousness in Indian Society*, pp. 30–40.

—'Tradition Against Itself', *American Ethnologist*, 13.4 (1986), pp. 762–75.

—*Imagining India*. Oxford and Cambridge, Mass.: Blackwells, 1990.

Jackson, R., and D. Killingly. *Approaches to Hinduism*. London: John Murray, 1988.

Jackson, R., and E. Nesbitt. *Hindu Children in Britain*. Stoke on Trent: Trentham Books, 1993.

Jamison, S. W. *Ravenous Hyenas and the Wounded Sun: Myth and Ritual in Ancient India*. New York: Cornell University Press, 1991.

Jarrige, J. F. and M. Santoni. 'The Antecedents of Civilization in the Indus Valley', *Scientific American*, 243.8 (1980), pp. 102–10.

Jayakar, P. *J. Krishnamurti: A Biography*. Delhi: Penguin, 1987.

Jha, G. *Tantravārtika*, 2 vols. [1903.] Delhi: MLBD, reprint 1983.

—*Ślokavārtika*. Calcutta: Asiatic Society, 1907.

—*Jaimini's Mīmaṃsasūtra with Śabara's Commentary and Notes*. 3 vols. Baroda: Gaekwad, 1933–6.

—*Pūrva Mīmāṃsā in Its Sources*. Banaras Hindu University Press, 1942.

Johnson, J. *The Path of the Masters: The Science of Surat Shabd Yoga*. Beas: Radha Soami Satsang, 1975.

Johnson, W. *The Bhagavadgītā*. Oxford University Press, 1994.

Joshi, R. V. *Le rituel de la dévotion kṛṣṇaite*. Pondicherry: Institut Français d'Indologie, 1959.

Juergensmeyer, M. *Radhasoami Reality, The Logic of a Modern Faith*. Princeton University Press, 1991.

Kailasapathy, K. *Tamil Heroic Poetry*. Oxford University Press, 1968.

Kak, S. 'On the Decipherment of the Indus Script – A preliminary Study of its Connections with Brahmi', *Indian Journal of History of Science*, 22.1 (1987), pp. 51–62.

—'On the Chronology of Ancient India', *Indian Journal of History of Science*, 22.3 (1987), pp. 222–34.

Kane, P. V. *History of Dharmaśāstra*, 5 vols. Poona: Bhandarkar Oriental Research Institute, 1930–62.

Kantorowicz, E. H. *The King's Two Bodies.* Princeton University Press, 1957.

Karve, I. 'On the Road: A Maharahshtrian Pilgrimage', in E. Zelliott and M. Bernsten (eds.), *Essays on Religion in Maherashtra.* Albany: SUNY Press, 1988.

Keith, A. B. *A History of Sanskrit Literature.* Oxford University Press, 1920.

—*The Religion and Philosophy of the Veda and Upaniṣads.* Cambridge, Mass.: Harvard University Press, 1925.

Kennedy, K. A. R., and G. L. Possehl (eds.). *Studies in the Archeology and Paleoanthropology of South Asia.* New Delhi: Oxford University Press and IBH Publishers, 1983.

Killingly, D. 'Om: the sacred syllable in the Veda', in J. Lipner (ed.), *A Net Cast Wide: Investigations into Indian Thought In Memory of David Friedman.* Newcastle upon Tyne: Grevatt and Grevatt, 1987, pp. 14–31.

—*Rammohun Roy in Hindu and Christian Tradition: The Teape Lectures 1990.* Newcastle upon Tyne: Grevatt and Grevatt, 1993.

Kinsley, D. *The Sword and the Flute: Kālī and Kṛṣṇa, Dark Visions of the Terrible and the Sublime in Hindu Mythology.* Berkeley: University of California Press, 1975.

—*Hinduism, A Cultural Perspective.* Englewood Cliffs, N.J.: Prentice Hall, 1982.

—*Hindu Goddesses: Visions of the Feminine in the Hindu Religious Tradition.* Berkeley and Los Angeles: University of California Press, 1986.

Klostermaier, K. *A Survey of Hinduism.* Albany: SUNY Press, 1994.

Knipe, D. 'Sapiṇḍikarana: The Hindu Rite of Entry into Heaven', in Reynolds and Waugh, *Religious Encounters with Death*, pp. 111–24.

Knott, K. *Hinduism in Leeds.* University of Leeds Press, 1986.

—*My Sweet Lord*. Wellingborough: Aquarian Press, 1986.

Knott, K. and R. Toon. *Muslims, Sikhs and Hindus in the UK: Problems in the Estimation of Religious Statistics*, Religious Research Paper 6. Theology and Religious Studies Department, University of Leeds, 1982.

Kopf, D. *The Brahmo Samāj and the Shaping of the Modern Indian Mind*. Princeton University Press, 1978.

Kramrisch, S. *The Hindu Temple*, 2 vols. [1946] Delhi: MLBD, reprint 1977.

—*The Presence of Śiva*. Princeton University Press, 1981.

Kulke, H., and D. Rothermund. *A History of India*. London and New York: Routledge, 1990.

Kumar, R. *The History of Doing: An Illustrated Account of Movements for Women's Rights and Feminism in India, 1800–1990*. London, Verso Press, 1994.

Lakoff, G. *Women, Fire and Dangerous Things: What Categories Reveal About the Mind.* Chicago and London: University of Chicago Press, 1987.

Lakshman Jee, Swami. *Kashmir Śaivism: The Secret Supreme*. Albany: Universal Śaiva Trust, 1988.

Lanman, C. *A Sanskrit Reader, Text and Vocabulary and Notes*. Cambridge, Mass.: Harvard University Press, 1884.

Lannoy, R. *The Speaking Tree*. Oxford University Press, 1971.

Larson, G., and R. S. Bhattacharya. *Sāṃkhya: A Dualist Tradition in Indian Philosophy*. Delhi: MLBD, 1987.

Leggett, T. *Śaṅkara on the Yoga Sūtras*, 2 vols. London, Boston, Henly: RKP, 1981, 1983.

Leslie, Julia. *The Perfect Wife: The Orthodox Hindu Woman According to the Strīdharmapaddhati of Tryambakayajvan*. Oxford University South Asian Series. Delhi: Oxford University Press, 1989.

—(eds.). *Roles and Rituals for Hindu Women*. London: Pinter Publishers, 1991.

Levering, M. (ed.). *Rethinking Scripture; Essays from a Comparative Perspective*. Albany: SUNY Press, 1989.

Lincoln, B. *Myth, Cosmos and Society: Indo-European Themes of Creation and Destruction*. Cambridge, Mass.: Harvard University Press, 1986.

Lingat, R. *The Classical Law of India*. Berkeley: University of California Press, 1973.

Lipner, J. *Hindus: Their Religious Beliefs and Practices*. London: Routledge, 1994.

Lorenzen, D. N. *The Kāpālikas and Kālamukhas: Two Lost Śaivite Sects*. [1972.] Delhi: MLBD, reprint 1991.

Lukacs, J. R. (ed.). *The People of South Asia: The Biological Anthropology of India, Pakistan and Nepal*. New York and London: Plenum Press, 1984.

Madan, T. N. *Non-renunciation*. Delhi: Oxford University Press, 1987.

—(ed.). *Way of Life, King, Householder, Renouncer: Essays in Honour of Louis Dumont*. Delhi: Vikas Publishing House, 1982.

Mahābhārata, Critical Edition with Pratika Index. 28 vols. Peona: Bhandarkar Oriental Research Institute, 1923–72.

Mahaniddesa, vol. 1, ed. L. de la Vallée Poussin. London: Pali Text Society, 1916.

Majumdar, A. K. *Caitanya: His Life and Doctrine*. Bombay: Bharatiya Vidya Bhavan, 1969.

Marglin, F. A. *Wives of the God-King: The Rituals of the Devadasis of Puri*. Delhi: Oxford University Press, 1985.

Marriott, M. 'Hindu Transactions: Diversity without Dualism', in B. Kapferer (ed.), *Transaction and Meaning: Directions in the Anthropology of Exchange and Symbolic Behaviour*. Philadelphia: Institute for the Study of Human Issues, 1976, pp. 109–42.

Marshall, J. *Mohenjo-Daro and the Indus Civilization*, 3 vols. London: Oxford University Press, 1931.

Masefield, P. *Divine Revelation in Pali Buddhism* London: Allen & Unwin, 1986.

Masson, J., and M. V. Patwardhan. *Śāntarasa and Abhinavagupta's Philosophy of Aesthetics*. Poona: Deccan College, 1969.

Matas, E. Aguilar i. *Ṛg-vedic Society*. Leiden: Brill, 1991.

Matilal, B. K. *Logic, Language and Reality*. Delhi: Mies, 1985.

—*The Word and the World: India's Contribution to the Study of Language*. Delhi: Oxford University Press, 1990.

Meenakshi, K. 'Andal: She Who Rules', *Manushi, Tenth Anniversary Issue: Women Bhakta Poets* (Delhi: Manushi Trust), 50–2 (Jan.–June 1989), pp. 34–8.

Meister, M. W. (ed.). *Discourses on Śiva*. Philadelphia: University of Pennsylvania Press, 1984.

Melton, J. G. 'The Attitude of Americans Toward Hinduism from 1883 to 1983 with Special Reference to the International Society for Krishna Consciousness', unpublished paper, 1985.

Miguel, P. 'Théologie de l'icone', in M. Viller, F. Cavallera and J. de Gübert (eds), *Dictionnaire de spiritualité*, vol. VII b. Paris: Beauchesme, 1971, pp. 123–69.

Miller, J., and G. Miller (eds.). *The Spiritual Teaching of Ramana Maharshi*. Boulder and London: Shambala, 1972.

Milner, M. Jr. *Status and Sacredness. A General Theory of Status Relations and an Analysis of Indian Culture*. New York and Oxford: Oxford University Press, 1994.

Morinis, E. A. *Pilgrimage in the Hindu Tradition: A Case Study of West Bengal*. New York and New Delhi: Oxford University Press, 1984.

Müller, M. *The Six Systems of Indian Philosophy*. London: Longmans, Green and Co., 1899.

—*Rāmakrishna, His Life and Sayings*. London: Longmans, Green and Co., 1900.

Müller, M., and H. Oldenberg. *Vedic Hymns*, 2 vols. SBE 32, 46. Delhi: MLBD, reprint 1973.

Mumme, P. Y. 'Haunted by Śaṅkara's Ghost: The Śrīvaiṣṇava Interpretation of Bhagavad Gītā 18.66', in Timm, *Texts in Context: Traditional Hermeneutics in South Asia*, pp. 69–84.

Murty, S. *Revelation and Reason in Advaita Vedānta*. Delhi: MLBD, 1974.

Nag, K. and D. Burman. *The English Works of Raja Rammohun Roy*. Calcutta: Sadharan Brahmo Samaj, 1948.

Nagatomi, M., B. K. Matilal and J. M. Masson (eds.). *Sanskrit and Indian Studies: Essays in Honour of Daniel H. H. Ingalls*. Dordrecht: Reidel, 1979.

Needham, J. *The New Religions*. New York: Crossroad Press, 1984.

Neeval, W. G. *Yāmuna's Vedānta and Pāñcarātra: Integrating the Classical with the Popular*. Chicago: Scholar's Press, 1977.

Nietzsche, F. *The Twilight of the Idols and the Anti Christ*. Harmondsworth: Penguin, 1968.

Nikhilananda, Swami. *The Gospel of Sri Rāmakrishna*. New York: Rāmakrishna-Vivekānanda Center, 1980.

Norman, K. R. *The Elder's Verses*, vol. II. London: Luzac, 1971.

Oberhammer, G. *Philosophy of Religion in Hindu Thought*. Delhi: Sri Satguru Publications, 1989.

Obeyesekere, G. *Medusa's Hair*. Chicago and London: University of Chicago Press, 1984.

O'Connell, J. T. 'The Word "Hindu" in Gaudiya Vaiṣṇava Texts', *Journal of the American Oriental Society*, 93.3 (1973), pp. 340–4.

O'Flaherty, W. D. *Hindu Myths*. Harmondsworth: Penguin, 1975.

—*The Origins of Evil in Hindu Mythology*. University of Chicago Press, 1976.

—*Women, Androgynes and Other Mythical Beasts*. Chicago and London: University of Chicago Press, 1980.

—*The Rig Veda*. Harmondsworth: Penguin, 1981.

—*Śiva, the Erotic Ascetic*. New York: Oxford University Press, 1981.

—*Tales of Sex and Violence. Folklore, Sacrifice, and Danger in the Jaiminīya Brāhmaṇa*. University of Chicago Press, 1985.

—*Other People's Myths: The Cave of Echoes*. New York: Macmillan, 1988.

—*The Laws of Manu*. Harmondsworth: Penguin, 1991.

—(ed.). *Karma and Rebirth in Classical Indian Traditions*. Berkeley and Los Angeles: University of California Press, 1980.

O'Flaherty, W. D., and J. D. M. Derrett. *The Concept of Duty in Southeast Asia*. New Delhi: Vikas, 1978.

Olivelle, P. *The Saṃnyāsa Upaniṣads, Hindu Scriptures on Asceticism and Renunciation*. New York and Oxford: Oxford University Press, 1992.

—*The Āśrama System: The History and Hermeneutics of a Religious Tradition*. New York and Oxford: Oxford University Press, 1993.

Otto, R. *The Idea of the Holy*, 2nd edn. Oxford, London and New York: Oxford University Press, 1982.

Padoux, A. *Vāc, The Concept of the Word in Selected Hindu Tantras*. Albany: SUNY Press, 1990.

—*Le Coeur de la Yogini. Yoginīhṛdaya avec le commentaire Dīpika d'Amṛtānanda*. Paris: Diffusion de Boccard, 1994.

—(ed.). *Mantras et diagrammes rituels dans l'hindouisme*. Paris: Centre National de la Recherche Scientifique, 1986.

—*L'Image divine: culte et méditation dans l'hindouisme*. Paris: Centre National de la Recherche Scientifique, 1990.

Pandey, R. *Hindu Saṃskāras: A Socio-Religious Study of the Hindu Sacraments*. Delhi: MLBD, 1969.

Parpola, A. *Deciphering the Indus Script*. Cambridge University Press, 1994.

Parry, J. 'Sacrificial Death and the Necrophagus Ascetic', in J. Parry and M. Bloch (eds.), *Death and the Regeneration of Life*. Cambridge University Press, 1982, pp. 75–102.

—'The Aghori Ascetics of Benares', in Burghardt and Cantille, *Indian Religion*, pp. 51–78.

—*Death in Banaras*. Cambridge University Press, 1994.

Payne, A. *The Śāktas*. Calcutta: YMCA Publishing House, 1933.

Peirce, C. *Collected Papers of Charles Sanders Peirce*, vol. 11. Cambridge, Mass.: Harvard University Press, 1932.

Pereira, J. *Hindu Theology: Themes, Texts and Structures*. [1976.] Delhi: MLBD, reprint 1991.

Peterson, I. *Poems to Śiva, The Hymns of the Tamil Saints*. Princeton University Press, 1989.

Piatigorsky, A. 'Some Phenomenological Observations on the Study of Indian Religion', in Burghardt and Cantille, *Indian Religion*, pp. 208–24.

Pillai, K. R. *The Vākyapādīya*. Varanasi: MLBD, 1971.

Pingree, D. *Jyotiḥśāstra. Astral and Mathematical Literature*, A History of Indian Literature 6, fasc. 4. Weisbaden: Otto Harrassowitz, 1981.

Pintchman, T. *The Rise of the Goddess in the Hindu Tradition*. Albany: SUNY Press, 1994.

Pocock, D. *Body, Mind and Wealth: A Study of Belief and Practice in an Indian Village*. Oxford: Blackwell, 1973.

Poliakov, L. *The Aryan Myth*. New York: Basic Books, 1974.

Potter, K. *Presuppositions of India's Philosophies*. Englewood Cliffs, N.J.: Prentice Hall, 1963.

—*Advaita Vedānta Up to Śaṃkara and his Pupils*, Encyclopaedia of Indian Philosophies 3. Delhi: MLBD, 1981.

Radhakrishnan, S. *Eastern Religions And Western Thought*. Oxford University Press, 1939.

—*The Principal Upaniṣads*. London: Unwin Hyman, 1953.

Raja, K. *Indian Theories of Meaning*. Madras: Adyar Library and Research Centre, 1963.

Ramanujan, A. K. *Speaking of Śiva*. Harmondsworth: Penguin, 1973.

Ranade, R. D. *Mysticism in India: The Poet–Saints of Maharashtra*. Albany: SUNY Press, reprint 1982.

Rangarajan, L. N. *The Ārthashāstra: Edited, Rearranged, Translated and Introduced*. Delhi: Penguin, 1992.

Rao, V. N. R. *Śiva's Warriors: The Basava Purāṇa of Palkuriki Somanātha*. Princeton University Press, 1990.

Rau, S. S. *The Bhagavad Gītā and Commentaries According to Śrī Madwacharya's Bhāṣyas*. Madras: Minerva Press, 1906.

Renfrew, C. *Archaeology and Language: The Puzzle of Indo-European Origins*. London: Jonathan Cape, 1987.

Renou, L. *Etudes védiques et paninéennes*, 17 vols. Paris: Publications de l'Institut de Civilisation Indienne, 1955–69.

Reynolds, F. E., and E. H. Waugh (eds.). *Religious Encounters with Death*. University Park: Pennsylvania State University Press, 1977.

Richards, G. *The Philosophy of Gandhi*. London and Dublin: Curzon Press, 1982.

—(ed.). *A Sourcebook of Modern Hinduism*. London and Dublin: Curzon Press, 1985.

Richman, P. (ed.). *Many Rāmāyaṇas: The Diversity of a Narrative Tradition in South Asia*. Delhi: Oxford University Press, 1991.

Riepe, D. *The Philosophy of India and Its Impact on American Thought*. Springfield: Charles C. Thomas, 1970.

Rocher, L. *The Purāṇas*, History of Indian Literature 2, fasc. 3. Wiesbaden: Otto Harrassowitz, 1986.

Rosen, S. (ed.). *Vaishnavism: Contemporary Scholars Discuss the Gaudiya Tradition*. New York: FOLK Books, 1992.

Roth, R., and O. Bothlingk. *St. Petersburg Wörterbuch*. Delhi: MLBD, reprint 1991.

Rukmani, T. S. *Yogavārttika of Vijñānabhikṣu*, 4 vols. Delhi: Munshiram Manoharlal, 1981.

Sachau, E. C. *Alberuni's India: An Account of the Religion, Philosophy, Literature, Geography, Chronology, Astronomy, Customs, Laws and Astrology of India about AD 1030*, 2 vols. London: Trubner and Co., 1888.

Sanderson, A. 'Purity and Power Among the Brahmans of Kashmir', in Carrithers, Collins and Lukes, *The Category of the Person: Anthropology, Philosophy, History*, pp. 190–216.

—'Mandala and the Āgamic Identity of the Trika of Kashmir', in Padoux, *Mantras et diagrammes rituels dans l'hindouisme*, pp. 169–207.

—'Saivism and the Tantric Traditions', in Sutherland et al., *The World's Religions*, pp. 660–704.

—'The Visualization of the Deities of the Trika', in Padoux, *L'Image divine: culte et méditation dans l'Hindouisme*, pp. 80–2.

Sastri, P. S. S., and T. R. S. Ayyangar (trs.). *Saundaryalaharī of Śrī Śaṃkara-Bhagavatpāda*. Madras: Theosophical Publishing House, 1977.

Scheckner, R. *The Future of Ritual*. London and New York: Routledge, 1993.

Schrader, O. *Introduction to the Pāñcarātra and the Ahirbudhnya Saṃhitā*. [1916.] Madras: Adyar Library and Research Centre, reprint 1973.

Shaffer, J. G. 'Bronze Age Iron from Afghanistan: Its Implications for South Asian Proto-history', in Kennedy and Possehi, *Studies in the Archeology and Paleoanthropology of South Asia*, pp. 65–102.

—'Indo-Aryan Invasions: Cultural Myth or Archaeological Reality?' in *The People of South Asia: The Biological Anthropology of India, Pakistan and Nepal*, pp. 77–90.

Sharpe, E. *Western Images of the Bhagavad Gita*. London: Duckworth, 1985.

Shastri, M. K. *The Lalitāsaharanāma with the Saubhāgya-bhāskarabhāṣya of Bhāskararāya*. Bombay: Nirnaya Sagar, 1935.

Shaw, M. *Passionate Enlightenment: Women in Tantric Buddhism*. Princeton University Press, 1994.

Shulman, D. *Tamil Temple Myths: Sacrifice and Divine Marriage in the South Indian Saiva Tradition*. Princeton University Press, 1980.

Siauve, S. *La voie vers la connaissance de Dieu Selon l'Aṇuvyākhyāna de Madhva*. Pondicherry: Institut Français d'Indologie, 1957.

Siegel, L. *Sacred and Profane Dimensions of Love in Indian Traditions as Exemplified in the Gītagovinda of Jayadeva*. Oxford University Press, 1978.

Sil, N. P. *Rāmakrishna Paramahamsa, A Psychological Profile*. Leiden: Brill, 1991.

Silburn, L. *Kuṇḍalinī, the Energy from the Depths*. Albany: SUNY Press, 1988.

Singer, M. (ed.). *Kṛṣṇa, Myths, Rites and Attitudes*. Honolulu: East–West Centre, 1966.

Śiva-Purāna, trs. A Board of Scholars. Delhi: AITM, 1970.

Smart, N. *Reasons and Faiths*. London: Routledge and Kegan Paul, 1958.

—*Doctrine and Argument in Indian Philosophy*. London; Allen and Unwin, 1964.

—*The World's Religions*. Cambridge University Press, 1989.

—'The Formation Rather than the Origin of a Tradition', *DISKUS: A Disembodied Journal of Religious Studies*, 1. (1993), p. 1.

Smith, B. and H. B. Reynolds (eds.). *The City as a Sacred Centre: Essays on Six Asian Contexts*. Leiden, New York, Cologne: Brill, 1987.

Smith, B. K. 'Exorcising the Transcendent: Strategies for Redefining Hinduism and Religion', *History of Religions* (Aug. 1987), pp. 32–55.

—*Classifying the Universe: The Ancient Indian* Varna *System and the Origins of Caste*. New York and Oxford: Oxford University Press, 1994.

Smith, D. *Ratnākara's Harivijaya, An Introduction to the Sanskrit Court Epic*. Delhi: Oxford University Press, 1985.

Smith, J. Z. *Imagining Religion, From Babylon to Jonestown*. University of Chicago Press, 1982.

Smith, W. C. *The Meaning and End of Religion*. New York: Macmillan, 1962.

Snellgrove, D. *Indo-Tibetan Buddhism: Indian Buddhists and Their Tibetan Successors*. London: Serindia Publications, 1987.

Sontheimer, G. D. *Pastoral Deities in Western India*. Delhi: Oxford University Press, 1993.

Sontheimer, G. D., and H. Kulke (eds.). *Hinduism Reconsidered*. Delhi: Manohar, 1991.

Srinivasan, D. 'Unhinging Śiva from the Indus Civilization', *Journal of the Royal Asiatic Society of Great Britain and Ireland*, 1 (1984), pp. 77–89.

Staal, F. 'Sanskrit and Sanskritization', *Journal of Asian Studies*, 23.3 (1963), pp. 261–75.

—*Exploring Mysticism*. Harmondsworth: Penguin, 1975.

—*Rules Without Meaning, Ritual, Mantras and the Human Sciences*. New York: Peter Lang, 1989.

—(ed.). *A Reader on the Sanskrit Grammarians*. Cambridge, Mass., and London: MIT Press, 1973.

—*AGNI. The Vedic Ritual of the Fire Altar*, 2 vols. Berkeley: University of California Press, 1983.

Stein, B. *Peasant, State and Society in Medieval South India*. Delhi: Oxford University Press, 1980.

Stern, R. W. *Changing India: Bourgeois Revolution on the Subcontinent*. Cambridge University Press, 1993.

Stoler-Miller, B. *Love Song of the Dark Lord*. New York: Columbia University Press, 1977.

Sutherland, S., L. Houlden, P. Clarke and F. Hardy (eds.). *The World's Religions*. London: Routledge, 1988.

Svātmarāma. *The Haṭhayogapradīpikā*. Madras: The Adyar Library Research Centre, 1972.

Tawney, C. H. (trs.). *Somadeva's Kathā Saritsāgara, or Ocean of Streams of Story*, ed. N. M. Penzer, 10 vols. (1924–28) Delhi: MLBD, reprint 1968.

Tendulkar, D. G. *Mahatma: Life and Work of Mohandas Karamchand Gandhi*. Bombay: V. K. Javeri, 1951–4.

Thapar, R. *Interpreting Early India*. Delhi: Oxford University Press, 1993.

Thibaut, G. *Vedānta Sūtras with Commentary by Śaṅkarācārya*, 2 vols., SBE 34, 38. [1903.] Delhi: MLBD, reprint 1987.

—*The Vedānta-sūtras with Commentary by Rāmānuja*, SBE 48. Delhi: MLBD, reprint 1976.

Thompson, J. and P. Heelas. *The Way of the Heart*. Wellingborough: Aquarian Press, 1986.

Timm, J. (ed.). *Texts in Context: Traditional Hermeneutics in South Asia*. Albany: SUNY Press, 1992.

Tripathi, V. *The Painted Grey Ware: An Iron Age Culture of Northern India*. Delhi: Concept Publishing Co., 1976.

Tulpe, S. G. (trs.). *Jnaneshwar's Gita: A Rendering of the Jnaneshwari*. Albany: SUNY Press, 1989.

Turner, B. S. *Religion and Social Theory*. London: SAGE Publications, 1991.

Turner, V. *The Forest of Symbols*. Ithaca and London: Cornell University Press, 1970.

—*The Ritual Process: Structure and Anti-structure*. Harmondsworth: Penguin, 1974.

Tyagisananda, Swami. *Aphorisms on the Gospel of Divine Love or the Nārada Bhakti Sūtras*. Madras: Ramakrishna Math, 1972.

Unni, N. P. 'Introduction', in T. G. Sastri (ed.), *Tantra Samuccaya of Nārāyaṇa*. Delhi: Nag Publishers, 1990, pp. 1–75.

Vaidyanathan, K. R. *Śri Krishna: The Lord of Guruvayur*. Bombay: Bharatiya Vidya Bhavan, 1992.

Van der Veer, P. *Gods on Earth: The Management of Religious Experience and Identity in a North Indian Pilgrimage Centre*. London: Athlone, 1988.

Vaudeville, C. *Kabir*, vol. 1. Oxford: Clarendon Press, 1974.

Vertovec, S. *Hindu Trinidad*. London: Macmillan, 1992.

Vijnanananda, Swami (trs.). *The Śrimad Devi Bhāgavatam*. Sacred Books of the Hindus 26. New Delhi: Oriental Books, reprint 1977.

Wasson, G. *Soma, the Divine Mushroom of Immortality*. Ethno-Mycological Studies 1. New York: Harcourt, Brace and World, 1968.

Weber, M. *The Religions of India*. New York: The Free Press, 1958.

Werner, K. 'Yoga and the Ṛg Veda: An Interpretation of the Kesin Hymn', *Religious Studies*, 13 (1976), pp. 289–93.

—(ed.). *The Yogi and the Mystic*. London: Curzon Press, 1989.

—*Love Divine*. London: Curzon Press, 1993.

Whalling, F. *The Rise of the Religious Significance of Rama*. Delhi: MLBD, 1980.

Wheatley, P. *The Pivot of the Four Quarters*. Chicago: Aldine Publishing Co., 1971.

Wheeler, M. *The Indus Civilization: The Cambridge History of India Supplementary Volume*. Cambridge University Press, 1953.

Williams, R. *Parameśwara-jnyāna-goshti: A Dialogue of the Knowledge of the Supreme Lord in which are compared the claims of Christianity and Hinduism*. Cambridge: Deighton, Bell and Co., 1856.

Williams, R. *The New Face of Hinduism, the Swaminarayan Religion*. Cambridge University Press, 1984.

Wilson, F. (trs.). *The Love of Krishna: The Krsnakarnamrta of Lilasuka Bilvamangala*. Leiden: Brill, 1973.

Witzel, M. 'On Localization of the Vedic Texts and Schools', in G. Pollet (ed.). *India and the Ancient World*, Orientalia Lovaniensia Analecta 25. Department Oriéntalistik, Leuven University, 1987.

Woodroffe, J. *The Serpent Power*. Madras: Ganesh and Co., 1973.

Yocum, G. *Hymns to the Dancing Siva: A Study of Manikkavacakar's Tiruvācakam*. Columbia: South Asia Books, 1982.

Yogānanda, P. *The Autobiography of a Yogi*. London: Rider and Co., 1950.

Zaehner, R. C. *Hinduism*. Oxford University Press, 1966.

Zimmer, H. *Myths and Symbols in Indian Art and Civilization*. New York: Harper Row, 1963.

Zvelebil, K. *The Smile of Murugan*. Leiden: Brill, 1973.

Index

Aśvalayana Gṛhya Sūtra 38, 204
Aśvalayana Śrauta Sūtra 38, 39
Aśvins 47
Atharvaśiras Upaniṣad 155
Atharva Veda Saṃhitā 36, 37, 42, 79, 222
atimārga 155, 158, 162
ātman see also self 85, 86, 95, 241, 260
Aurangzeb 143
auspicious, the 15
auspiciousness 66–7
Australia 5, 266
avatāra 115–17, 118
  of Śiva 156
Avesta 30
  avestan 27
Ayodhya 108, 264, 265
Ayurveda 233

Babji Masjid 264–5
Badrinath 92, 213, 240
Balarāma 116, 117, 120
Bali 114, 116
bandhu 36, 48, 75
Banerjee, R. D. 24
Basava 171, 172
Baudhāyana 38, 54, 55
Bauls 140, 191
Beatles, the 271
Bechert, Heinz 20
belief(s) 6, 7, 12, 199, 258, 264
  about life after death 207–8
Benedict, Ruth 149
Bengali 27
Bengali Vaiṣṇavism 135, 138–41
Berger, Peter 9
Berreman, G. D. 217
Besant, Annie 270
Besnagar inscription 119
Bhagavad Gītā 14, 96, 107, 115, 119, 124–7, 136, 137, 143, 239, 240
  Gandhi influenced by 259
  Madhva's commentary on 245
  Sāṃkhya in 234
  Śaṅkara's commentary on 240
Bhagavān 103, 114, 124
Bhāgavata(s) 119, 123–4
Bhāgavata Purāṇa 110, 120, 133, 140, 181
  Madhva's commentary on 245
Bhagavatī 103, 114
Bhairava 161, 162, 165
bhakti 11, 96, 103, 113, 125, 130, 131, 132, 135, 138, 139, 143, 144, 173
  as rejection of formal religion 131
  ecstatic 132
  in Śaiva Siddhānta 162, 168–71
  in *Śvetāśvatara-Upaniṣad* 153
  poetry 136
  Śaṅkara's view of 242
  Tamil culture and 129; *see also* Bhāgavata(s), Bengali Vaiṣṇavism, Caitanya, Śrī Vaiṣṇavasa
Bhakti Sūtra 133
bhakti-yoga 126, 137
Bhaktivedānta Swami Prabhupada 272
Bhandarkar Oriental Institute 105
Bhāratī 240
Bharati, Agehananda 187, 241, 367
Bharaty Vidya Bhavan 267
Bhārgava family 105, 106
Bhartṛhari 228–9
Bhāskararāya 190
Bhattacharya, K. C. 248
Bhāvaviveka 240
Bhaviṣya Purāṇa 110
Bhikṣāyatana 157
Bhīma 106
bhoga 155
Bhojadeva 162, 247
Bhṛgu 105
bhūr 45, 222
bhuvas 45, 222
Biardeau, Madeleine 18, 65, 88, 89
bīja 222
Bilvamaṅgala 142
bindu 188
birth rites 200, 202, 203
BJP 263–4
Blavatsky, Madame 270
bliss 85
blood offerings 18, 165, 183–4, 208, 216
  substitute blood 210
Bloomfield, L. 268
Boar *avatāra* 116
body 48–9, 57, 65, 77, 188–9
  as chariot 95
  corresponds to cosmos 48
  creation of divine 160
  creation of in next world 207
  identified with *oṃ* 84
  in *bhakti* 133
  in Rāmānuja's theology 244; *see also* esoteric anatomy, Kuṇḍalinī
Boethlink, O. and R. Roth 268
Bohm, David 270
Bourdieu, Pierre 10, 201
Brahmā 110, 115, 150, 157, 176, 179
Brahmā Purāṇa 110
Brahma Sūtra 125, 139, 141, 154–5
  Madhva's commentary on 245
  Rāmānuja's commentary on 243
  Śaṅkara's commentary on 240
brahmacārin 13, 62, 63
brahmacārya; *see also* celibacy 62, 65, 156, 190, 260